Lecture Notes in Computer Science 7722

Commenced Publication in 1973
Founding and Former Series Editors:
Gerhard Goos, Juris Hartmanis, and Jan van Leeuwen

Editorial Board

David Hutchison
Lancaster University, UK
Takeo Kanade
Carnegie Mellon University, Pittsburgh, PA, USA
Josef Kittler
University of Surrey, Guildford, UK
Jon M. Kleinberg
Cornell University, Ithaca, NY, USA
Alfred Kobsa
University of California, Irvine, CA, USA
Friedemann Mattern
ETH Zurich, Switzerland
John C. Mitchell
Stanford University, CA, USA
Moni Naor
Weizmann Institute of Science, Rehovot, Israel
Oscar Nierstrasz
University of Bern, Switzerland
C. Pandu Rangan
Indian Institute of Technology, Madras, India
Bernhard Steffen
TU Dortmund University, Germany
Madhu Sudan
Microsoft Research, Cambridge, MA, USA
Demetri Terzopoulos
University of California, Los Angeles, CA, USA
Doug Tygar
University of California, Berkeley, CA, USA
Gerhard Weikum
Max Planck Institute for Informatics, Saarbruecken, Germany

Bernhard M. Hämmerli   Nils Kalstad Svendsen
Javier Lopez (Eds.)

Critical Information Infrastructures Security

7th International Workshop, CRITIS 2012
Lillehammer, Norway, September 17-18, 2012
Revised Selected Papers

 Springer

Volume Editors

Bernhard M. Hämmerli
Hochschule Luzern - Technik und Architektur, CEO Acris GmbH
Bodenhofstrasse 29, 6005 Luzern, Switzerland
and
Gjøvik University College
Teknologivegen 22, 2815 Gjøvik, Norway
E-mail: bmhaemmerli@acris.ch

Nils Kalstad Svendsen
Gjøvik University College, Faculty of Computer Science and Media Technology
Teknologivegen 22, 2815 Gjøvik, Norway
E-mail: nils.svendsen@hig.no

Javier Lopez
University of Malaga, Department of Computer Science
E.T.S. Ingenieria Informatica
Campus de Teatinos s/n, 29071 Malaga, Spain
E-mail: jlm@lcc.uma.es

ISSN 0302-9743   e-ISSN 1611-3349
ISBN 978-3-642-41484-8   e-ISBN 978-3-642-41485-5
DOI 10.1007/978-3-642-41485-5
Springer Heidelberg New York Dordrecht London

Library of Congress Control Number: 2013951247

CR Subject Classification (1998): K.6.5, K.4, C.2, C.4, E.3, J.1

LNCS Sublibrary: SL 4 – Security and Cryptology

Typesetting: Camera-ready by author, data conversion by Scientific Publishing Services, Chennai, India

Printed on acid-free paper

Springer is part of Springer Science+Business Media (www.springer.com)

Preface

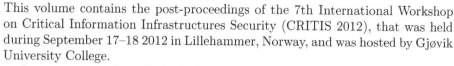

This volume contains the post-proceedings of the 7th International Workshop on Critical Information Infrastructures Security (CRITIS 2012), that was held during September 17–18 2012 in Lillehammer, Norway, and was hosted by Gjøvik University College.

In response to the 2007 call for papers, 67 papers were submitted. Each paper was reviewed by three members of the Program Committee, on the basis of significance, novelty, technical quality, and critical infrastructures relevance of the work reported therein. At the end of the reviewing process, only 23 papers were selected for presentation; hence, acceptance rate was 34%. All those papers are included in these proceedings, though revisions were not checked and the authors bear full responsibility for the content of their papers. Additionally, 10 short papers and 9 industry papers were presented at the event, but those are not included in these proceedings.

CRITIS 2012 was very fortunate to have four exceptional invited speakers: Roar Sundseth, Major General from the Norwegian Cyber Defence; Konstantinos Moulinos, expert in network & information security from ENISA; Alain Desausoi, Chief Security Officer from SWIFT; and, Alfonso Valdes, Managing Director Smart Grid Technologies from University of Illinois. The four of them provided a high added value to the quality of the conference with very significant talks on different and interesting aspects of critical information infrastructures.

Other persons deserve many thanks for their contribution to the success of the conference. Special thanks to Nils Kalstad Svendsen, who as general chair provided an impressive support in the local organization of the workshop. Also thanks to Dimitris Gritzalis, general co-chair, for his highly valuable ideas and suggestions during the organization of the event. Local co-chairs, Asbjørn Lund and Tore Orderløkken greatly contributed to the success of CRITIS 2012, as well as honorary co-chairs Roar Sundseth and Evangelos Ouzounis, and publicity chair Cristina Alcaraz. Without the hard work of these colleagues and the rest of the local organization team, this conference would not have been possible.

CRITIS 2012 thanks the members of the Program Committee who performed an excellent job during the review process, which is the essence of the quality of the event, and last but not least, the authors who submitted papers as well as the participants from all over the world who chose to honor us with their attendance.

August 2013

Bernhard Hämmerli
Nils Kalstad Svendsen
Javier Lopez

Organization

Program Committee Co-chairs

Bernhard M. Hämmerli	University of Applied Sciences Lucerne, GUC Gjøvik and CEO Acris GmbH
Javier Lopez	University of Malaga, Spain

General Co-chairs

Nils Kalstad Svendsen	Gjøvik University College, Norway
Dimitris Gritzalis	Athens University of Economics & Business, Greece

Local Co-chairs

Asbjørn Lund	Oppland County Governor, Norway
Tore Orderløkken	NorSIS, Norway

Publicity Chair

Cristina Alcaraz	University of Malaga, Spain and NIST, USA

Program Committee

Eirik Albrechtsen	SINTEF and Norwegian University of Science and Technology, Norway
Cristina Alcaraz	University Malaga, Spain
Jan Audestad	Gjøvik University College, Norway
Robin Bloomfield	City University London, UK
Sandro Bologna	AIIC, Italy
Stefan Brem	Federal Office for Civil Protection, Switzerland
Matt Broda	Microsoft, UK
Arslan Brömme	Vattenfall, Germany
João Batista Camargo	University of São Paulo, Brazil
Genseric Cantournet	Telecom Italia, Italy
Emiliano Casalicchio	Università di Tor Vergata, Italy
Jorge Cuellar	Siemens, Germany
Peter Daniel	Selex Communication Ltd., UK
Gregorio D'Agostino	ENEA, Italy
Geert Deconinck	K.U. Leuven, Belgium
Giovanna Dondossola	RSE, Italy

Stelios Dritsas   Athens University of Economics & Business,
                                     Greece
Myriam Dunn   ETH Centre for Security Studies, Switzerland
Claudia Eckert   Fraunhofer AISEC, Germany
Igor Nai Fovino   EU Joint Research Centre Ispra, E.C.
Steven Furnell   University of Plymouth, UK
Katrin Franke   Gjøvik University Collage, Norway
Richard Garber   DRDC Centre for Security Science, Canada
Robert Ghanea-Hercock   British Telecom, UK
Adrian Gheorghe   Old Dominion University, USA
Janusz Gorski   Gdansk University of Technology, Poland
Stefanos Gritzalis   University of the Aegean, Greece
Jorge L. Hernandez-Ardieta   INDRA, Spain
Jan Hovden   Norwegian University of Science and
                                     Technology, Norway
Chris Johnson   Glasgow University, UK
Floor Koornneef   Delft University of Technology,
                                     The Netherlands
Panos Kotzanikolaou   University of Piraeus, Greece
Christoph Krauss   Fraunhofer AISEC, Germany
Eric Luiijf   TNO, The Netherlands
Paulo Maciel   Federal University of Pernambuco, Brazil
Fabio Martinelli   CNR, Italy
Marcelo Masera   EU Joint Research Centre Petten,
                                     The Netherlands
Amin Massoud   University of Minnesota, USA
Tom McCutcheon   Defence Science and Technology Laboratory,
                                     UK
Doug Montgomery   U.S. National Institutes of Standards and
                                     Technolog, USA
Igor Nai Fovino   EU Joint Research Centre Ispra, E.C.
Janne Hagen   Proactima, Norway
Eiji Okamoto   University of Tsukuba, Japan
Cirian Osborn   Centre for the Protection of National
                                     Infrastructure, UK
Evangelos Ouzounis   European Network and Information Security
                                     Agency, Greece
Stefano Panzieri   University Roma Tre, Italy
Stefan Pickl   Universität der Bundeswehr München,
                                     Germany
Margrete Raaum   CERT University of Oslo, Norway
Dirk Reinermann   German Information Security Agency,
                                     Germany
Arturo Ribagorda   Universidad Carlos III, Spain
Andrea Rigoni   Global CyberSecurity Center, Italy

Table of Contents

Session 4: SCADA

Session 5: Cyber Issues

Session 6: CI Analysis

Session 7: CIP Sectors

Session 8: CI Assessment

Session 9: Threat Modeling

Approach to Enhance the Efficiency of Security Operation Centers to Heterogeneous IDS Landscapes

Björn-C. Bösch

Carl-von-Ossietzky-University Oldenburg
Faculty II - Department of Computing Science
System Software and Distributed Systems Group
Uhlhornsweg, Building A4
26111 Oldenburg, Germany

Abstract. Critical infrastructures include large scale environments with different platforms and / or platform generations. The maintenance interval of such large scaled, distributed systems to patch vulnerabilities increases with the amount of entities. IDS are necessary to protect the vulnerable system / entity until the patch will be applied to the distributed entity. This paper presents an approach to separate the IDS manager from the rest of an IDS by a standardized IDS parameterization independent of its scope (host based or network based IDS) and vendor. The exchange of the parameterization was integrated via communication modules in three open source IDS to demonstrate the common applicability of the format. An enhanced IDS model of the IETF will be illustrated.

Keywords: IDXP, Intrusion Detection, Standardization, Parameterization, IDS Management.

1 Introduction

As long as interconnected systems exist, automation of attacks increases continuously and attack tools with graphical interfaces are available in a few days after the vulnerability is disclosed [1]. Complexity of attacks increases when at the same time the knowledge to exploit the vulnerability for an attack decreases [2]. As result, the group of potential (and participating) attackers expands.

In recent years, common network techniques e.g. IP find the one's way into industrial systems. Today, communication systems, traffic light systems, shunting switch control systems, intelligent building management systems, telemedicine environments, production lines, point of sale systems, management systems for electrical generating stations, etc. are operated on basis of IP. These environments are critical infrastructures for economy and public life. Over the past few years, these environments became an increased focus of attacks [3], [4] or [5].

B. Hämmerli, N. Kalstad Svendsen, and J. Lopez (Eds.): CRITIS 2012, LNCS 7722, pp. 1–9, 2013.
© Springer-Verlag Berlin Heidelberg 2013

Industrial environments are mostly large scaled meshes of entities. The environmental security of distributed entities could be only particial influenced. Each single entity is potentially vulnerable against environmental attacks and is a potential entry into the mesh for an attacker. The time interval to maintain each single entity will be greater with the sum of additional entities, within fixes could be installed. The entity is vulnerable until it will be effectively patched. Intrusion Detections Systems (IDS) are necessary to protect the distributed entity against malicious actions until it is patched.

Detailed knowledge of application and communication is necessary to protect the distributed entities and their services. In large scaled environments different platforms and / or platform generations interact with each other. Therefore different platforms and entity vendors as well as IDS could be parallel in place. To protect a large number of distributed entities against a high severity exposure vulnerability, all IDS have to be updated and parameterized in a short time window. To operate distributed intrusion detection entities effectively, a standardized communication and parameterization between the entities and a supervising management system is required.

Today, IDS are isolated and coexisting solutions. There is no combination or interaction between IDS. Each IDS provides its individual software maintenance solution with (automated) update communication from the IDS management network through the vendors via the Internet. No supervising coordinating entity operates as software distributor to maintain all IDS entities, vendor and analyzing level independent. To operate IDS in larger distributed critical infrastructures a supervising management system for every different IDS is necessary. Benefits of IDS related works like [6] do not have impact to other IDS within the analyzer mesh.

To start the interaction between IDS the IETF has designed some exchange formats in the last years. The Intrusion Object Description and Exchange Format (IODEF) [7] and Intrusion Detection Message Exchange Format (IDMEF) [8] are standardized exchange formats relating to IDS. The IODEF is focused on standardized data formates for incident information and exchange procedures between Computer Security Incident Response Teams (CSIRT). The integration of different sites and IDS into one reporting tool is focus of IDMEF. IODEF and IDMEF handle the output of IDS. They are designed to process incidents and its information, but they are not designed to maintain and customize IDS. Therefore these formats are unsuitable to customize and administer IDS.

This work is focused on the question: Is it possible to operate a heterogeneous IDS landscape with a standardized format under one IDS manager?

The remaining paper is organized as follows: Section 2 describes the solution approach including enrichments of the IDS model, a brief parameterization format overview and points out the integrations. The results are drawn up and concluded in section 3.

2   Solution Approach

This section illustrates the architectural integration in the IDS model. Subsequent the parameterization format structure and the integrations in three open source IDS are pointed out.

2.1   IDS Model

Current multi-vendor IDS architectures do not interact with each other. They are in independent coexistence. Based on IDMEF it is possible to integrate an additional general monitoring system as notification umbrella. This requires additional budgets for hardware and software as well as recurrent budgets for maintenance and operating costs, including professional training. This work analyses common IDS architectures which IDS entities are possible to share.

Based on the IETF IDS model and its definitions [9], the IDS architecture was analyzed. The entities Analyzer and Sensor are vendor-specific entities. The Manager is the single entity that is able to share with other IDS. Today, the Manager's functionality could be partial shared in a multi-vendor IDS architecture by a notification umbrella system with IDMEF. To share the Manager's functionality of an IDS completely, the communication between an independent Manager and vendor-specific Analyzers has to be standardized.

Today, IDMEF standardizes notifications to a monitoring application. As transport protocol the Intrusion Detection eXchange Protocol (IDXP) [10] is already created on top of the Blocks Extensible Exchange Protocol (BEEP) [11]. The BEEP framework provides already appropriate confidentiality, integrity and authentication for the communication.

IDXP provides already a streamtype option with the values "alert", "heartbeat" or "config". The value "alert" is used by IDMEF. The other two values are still available for new usage. The value "heartbeat" is provided for synchronization of two or more Analyzers, acting as one Analyzer. The IDXP could be used as communication framework, but the heartbeat exchange format is not needed to be standardized in an one vendor heartbeat environment. This work uses IDXP with the streamtype option "config" as communication framework.

The Manager will be separated from the rest of the IDS with a standardized communication between Manager and Analyzer. The communication between Analyzer and Sensor will be still vendor-specific. The communication in the IETF IDS model was evolute. As visualized in fig. 1, the Security Policy will be applied from the Administrator to the Manager and distributed to the addressed Analyzers and forwarded to each single Sensor instead from the Administrator to all IDS entities directly. The Security Process between Operator and Administrator enforces a continuous improvement of the security policy by design (Deming Cycle). Operators and Administrators use the Manager as single point of human interface to run the IDS.

The modifications of the communication in the IDS model effectuate control loops in entity interactions of the IDS. Fig. 1 illustrates that there are two control loops outside and two inside technical IDS entities.

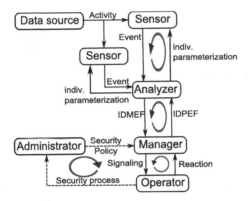

Fig. 1. Control loops with standardized communication within the IDS model

The first control loop is between Analyzer and Operator, where the Manager signalizes the Operator the events and the Operator carries out the reaction to the event by using the Manager. The second control loop outside the IDS starts the Security Process based on the Deming Cycle with Plan-Do-Check-Act-Model (PDCA). The Security Process starts also on the IDS Manager with an event signalization to the Operator (Do). Now, the Operator checks if this was a correct notification and not a false positive (Check). He initiates the Security Process in case of false positives / negatives to the Administrator (Act). The Administrator adjusts the Security Policy on the Manager (Plan). The next control loop was originated by separation of the Manager and Analyzer by the standardized formats IDMEF and IDPEF. Additional analyzing functionality could be integrated in the Manager to adjust other Analyzers automatically. Between Analyzer and Sensor is an additional control loop where the Analyzer applies the Security Policy to the Sensors and gets the events back. These two control loops within the IDS improve interaction between the IDS entities.

2.2 Parameterization Format Overview

IDPEF was created on top of IDXP. The purpose of this format is to parameterize the analyzer to the individual implementation and to maintain the IDS in operations. The parameterization methodology is described in [12] and [13]. Like IDMEF and IODEF, Extensible Markup Language (XML) [14] is also used for IDPEF.

As illustrated in fig. 2, IDPEF is split in three core sections with a root node named "IDPEF-Message". The node section "entity" includes parameter to operate the sensor (e.g. NTP-server, IP-addresses, etc.) and service information like location, field service contact, etc. Updates are scheduled and transferred within the node section "update". This two sections are designed without any restriction or frame condition, but in accordance to the set out requirements [15] for IDPEF.

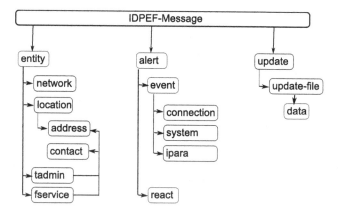

Fig. 2. IDPEF node structure

Parameters of every event and response are defined within the section "alert".
Each IDPEF parameter is mapped bi-unique to the corresponding parameter of
each single IDS. In each single "event" node, common attributes for the event
are defined here. These are displayed name, additional information of the event,
severity, priority, impact and which security value was affected in case of a cause.
An "enable/disable" option is added to the event and every attribute in child
nodes of the "event" node. Within the child nodes individual parameters, system
and connection related attributes are defined. The other child node of alert
are the "react" node. The "react" node includes general parameters like IP-
address, structure of the notification, etc. to set up the notification and responses
communication. The complete XML Schema Definition for IDPEF was defined
in [16].

2.3 Integrations

The attributes of IDPEF [16] are mapped into the open source IDS Snort [17],
Samhain [18], OSSec [19] and Bro [20].

This theoretical approach was implemented first in the the first three IDS,
to test the common applicability of this format - the implementation in Bro
[20] follows. The implementations do not modify IDS executables. Only existing
configuration files are processed and modified.

As human interface an IDPEF web front-end was created that enables IDXP
based communication to one selected Analyzer. Attribute values are modified
over the front-end and send back as IDPEF update to the Analyzer. Additional
software updates including upload of update files and new references are scheduled within the front-end and send as IDPEF update message to the Analyzer.

On site of the Analyzer an individual IDXP / IDPEF communication module
modifies configuration files of operating system respectively IDS software and
schedules updates and their execution. The general structure of the IDXP /
IDPEF communication module is illustrated in fig. 3.

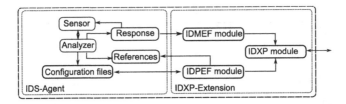

Fig. 3. IDXP-Extension for the IDS analyzer

Fig. 4. Assignment of snort rule to reference and customizing parameters

Each attribute of individual IDS configuration files is assigned as baseline or customizing parameter. Baseline parameters are not transferred into or modified by IDPEF. Customizing parameters are bi-unique mapped to an IDPEF attribute.

Snort's IDPEF communication module maps "preprocessor", "variable", "output" and "config" parameters as well as rules into IDPEF. Dynamic loaded libraries are categorized as baseline parameters.

Customizing parameters are selected and mapped into IDPEF for each Snort rule. As schematically illustrated in fig. 4 the parameters are mixed within the rule. Parameters of the rule head are mapped into IDPEF. The general rule options and post detection rule options are classified as customizing parameters. The payload detection rule options and the non-payload detection rule options are classified as baseline parameters, because they are part of the signatures and are not mapped in IDPEF.

Samhain's configuration file includes customizing sections only. Each section and its parameters are mapped bi-unique into IDPEF. Only the sections "external" and a high percentage of "Misc" were not integrated in this implementation. These sections contain mostly baseline configuration parameters.

OSSec's configuration bases on XML structures. All nodes in the core configuration file (ossec.conf) are mapped in IDPEF. The structure of OSSec rules is split in a grouping rule without alert function and baseline-information in the "match" node. The corresponding sub rules are connected with the "if_sid" or "if_matched_sid" node with the grouping rule node. Additional baseline-information are provided in the nodes "match" and "regex". For the proof-of-concept integration every single rule, including the remaining nodes and attributes, was mapped separately into IDPEF. The grouping rule does not contain any customizing parameter and does not have any impact on the evaluation of the applicability of IDPEF. A more complex solution with a change of the configuration structure of OSSec is able to address the sub rule structure adequate.

3   Conclusion

The integrations demonstrate that Analyzers of different IDS solutions are able to be operated with one common parameterization format. Only one central administration entity is necessary to operate, manage, maintain and administrate a heterogeneous IDS landscape. All analyzers could be parameterized with a smart format. Customizing of IDS attributes are due to a small set of parameters and values. Baseline configuration and references depend on the internal processing and they are not able to be standardized by external modifications only. The analyzing technique influences the quality and performance of detection and is the remaining differentiating feature for IDS. So detection references (i.e. signatures) have to be still vendor-specific.

The configurations of all three IDS mix baseline and customization parameters. A separation of baseline and customizing configuration is helpful to apply IDPEF as common customizing file for IDS.

All connections are initialized from the Manager to Analyzer. All updates (parameter and software) are controlled, downloaded and distributed to each single IDS entity by one central management entity in the test environment. The communication is easier to control, because there is one communication port from the Manager to all IDS entities necessary and the content could be inspected by a security device. All IDS communication is initialized from the supervising Manager to the distributed Analyzers. There is no outgoing connection from an IDS Analyzer necessary.

A wide distributed mesh of entities with IDS functionality could be managed with one supervising Manager. It is not a constraint to operate IDS with vendor-specific Managers or to operate more than one Manager. Critical infrastructure meshes could be enriched with intrusion detection functionality to protect each component of the mesh against temporarily unsolved vulnerabilities. A consistently frond-end with bulk change feature supports security operation centers to update and change parameters for a special kind of IDS or group by selected entity parameters.

An extension for standardized IDXP communication is necessary on site of the Analyzers. This depends on internal processing of the Analyzer's software and the version. These modules are very individual and part of the Analyzer's software. New software releases should be providing this communication functionality by the Analyzer's software itself. In addition to the communication exchange enrichments, sourcing and analyzing entities could be focused more on data sourcing and analyzing.

Specialized systems management manufacturers are able to enrich their products with common IDS management. Competing IDS management products will be providing more comfort, usability and reporting features. Central Managers are able to provide consistency checks for large distributed environments, bulk parameter changes or comfortable update scheduling.

A supervising IDS management enables to control each Analyzer including download and distribution of software individual or by criteria check. No access from the IDS LAN to networks with lower security level (e.g. the Internet) or higher security level like the central systems management network is required. This improves the security level of the administrative IDS network.

On the whole, the Manager is an independent entity of an IDS. It could be separated from the rest of the IDS. Different IDS could be operated with one consistent administration front-end. Intelligent update job execution supports an efficient operation of larger IDS meshes. These findings enable to operate large scaled IDS meshes and make new and independent evolution streams for IDS Analyzers as well as Managers possible. As a consequence each distributed component of large scale critical infrastructure meshes could be protected by an IDS.

References

1. Symantec: Threat Report for July 04 - December 04, vol. VII (2005), vhttp://eval.veritas.com/mktginfo/enterprise/white_papers/ent-whitepaper_symantec_internet_security_threat_report_vii.pdf (last visit May 20, 2007)
2. Baker, M.: Security Basics (March 09, 2006), http://impact.asu.edu/cse494sp09/SecurityBasics.ppt (last visit: March 09, 2012)
3. Broad, W.J., Sanger, D.E.: Iran Reports a Major Setback at a Nuclear Power Plant (February 25, 2011), http://www.nytimes.com/2011/02/26/world/middleeast/26nuke.html?_r=2 (last visit: April 21, 2012)
4. Sternstein, A.: Hackers manipulated railway computers, TSA memo says (January 23, 2012), http://www.nextgov.com/nextgov/ng_20120123_3491.php?oref=topstory (last visit: April 21, 2012)
5. Clayton, M.: Major cyber attack aimed at natural gas pipeline companies (2012), http://www.csmonitor.com/USA/2012/0505/Alert-Major-cyber-attack-aimed-at-natural-gas-pipeline-companies (last visit: May 13, 2012)
6. Xiaoyong, L.: An automatic scheme to construct Snort rules from honeypots data. Journal of Systems Engineering and Electronics 16(2), 466–470 (2005)
7. Danyliw, R., Meijer, J., Demchenko, Y.: The Intrusion Object Description and Exchange Format (IODEF), RfC 5070 (2007), http://www.ietf.org/rfc/rfc5070.txt (last visit April 29, 2012)
8. Debar, H., Curry, D., Feinstein, B.: The Intrusion Detection Message Exchange Format (IDMEF), RfC 4765 (2007), http://www.ietf.org/rfc/rfc4765.txt (last visit September 01, 2007)
9. Wood, M., Erlinger, M.: Intrusion Detection Message Exchange Requirements, RfC 4766 (March 2007), http://www.ietf.org/rfc/rfc4766.txt (last visit September 01, 2007)
10. Feinstein, B., Matthews, G.: The Intrusion Detection Exchange Protocol (IDXP), RfC 4767 (2007), http://www.ietf.org/rfc/rfc4767.txt (last visit September 01, 2007)
11. M. Rose: The Blocks Extensible Exchange Protocol Core, RfC 3080 (March 2001), http://www.ietf.org/rfc/rfc3080.txt (last visit September 01, 2007)
12. Bösch, B.-C.: Intrusion Detection Parameterization Exchange Data Model. In: 35th Jubilee International Convention on Information and Communication Technology, Electronics and Mircoelectronics 2012 (May 2012)

13. Bösch, B.-C.: Standardized Parameterization of Intrusion Detection Systems. International Journal of Advanced Research in Computer Engineering & Technology (IJARCET), 1–5 (May 2012)
14. W3C: Extensible Markup Language (XML) (2011), http://www.w3.org/XML/ (last visit: December 03, 2011)
15. Bösch, B.-C.: Ein einheitliches Austauschformat zum Parametrisieren verschiedener IDS. In: UpTimes of German UNIX User Group Frühjahresfachgespräche 2012, pp. 51–59 (March 2012)
16. Bösch, B.-C.: Intrusion Detection Parameterization Exchange Format (unpublished 2011)
17. SNORT, http://www.sort.org (last visit: December 03, 2011)
18. Samhain: http://la-samhna.de/ (last visit: December 03, 2011)
19. OSSec, http://www.ossec.net (last visit: December 03, 2011)
20. Bro, http://www.bro-ids.org (last visit: December 03, 2011)

Enhancing SIEM Technology
to Protect Critical Infrastructures

Luigi Coppolino[1,2], Salvatore D'Antonio[1], Valerio Formicola[1], and Luigi Romano[1]

[1] University of Naples "Parthenope", Department of Technology, Naples, Italy
{salvatore.dantonio,valerio.formicola,luigi.romano,
luigi.coppolino}@uniparthenope.it
[2] Epsilon S.r.l., Naples, Italy
luigi.coppolino@epsilonline.com

Abstract. Coordinated and targeted cyber-attacks on Critical Infrastructures (CIs) and Supervisory Control And Data Acquisition (SCADA) systems are increasing and becoming more sophisticated. Typically, SCADA has been designed without having security in mind, which is indeed approached by reusing solutions to protect solely Information Technology (IT) based infrastructures, such as the Security Information and Events Management (SIEM) systems. According to the National Institute of Standards and Technology (NIST), these systems are often ineffective for CIs protection. In this paper we analyze limits of current SIEMs and propose a framework developed in the MASSIF Project to enhance services for data treatment. Particularly, the Generic Event Translation (GET) module collects security data from heterogeneous sources, by providing intelligence at the edge of the SIEM; the Resilient Storage (RS), reliably stores data related to relevant security breaches. We illustrate a prototypal deployment for the dam monitoring and control case study.

Keywords: Security Information and Event Management (SIEM), Supervisory Control and Data Acquisition (SCADA), dam.

1   Rationale and Contribution

As a consequence of the technology shift and of new economical and socio-political motivations [1][2], coordinated and targeted cyber-attacks on Critical Infrastructures (CIs) are increasing and becoming more sophisticated [3][4]. Mostly, such infrastructures rely on legacy Supervisory Control And Data Acquisition (SCADA) systems that have been designed without having security in mind - originally they were isolated proprietary systems - and that are managed by people with good skills in the specific application domains, but with very limited knowledge of security [5].

Security of SCADA is traditionally approached by reusing systems designed to protect solely Information Technology (IT) based infrastructures. One of the most effective solutions is represented by Security Information and Events Management (SIEM) systems. Unfortunately, according to the National Institute of Standards and Technology (NIST) [6], they are often ineffective for CIs protection.

B. Hämmerli, N. Kalstad Svendsen, and J. Lopez (Eds.): CRITIS 2012, LNCS 7722, pp. 10–21, 2013.

In this paper we present an enhanced SIEM specifically targeting Critical Infrastructures protection, which is being developed within the context of the European Commission funded project MASSIF [7]. A first contribution of this paper is an analysis of the main limits of current SIEM solutions when applied to protecting CIs. The proposed analysis has been conducted considering the requirements inferred from the four case studies considered in the MASSIF project [8] and from our experiences with a previous project targeting CIs, namely the INSPIRE project [9]. Most of such limits come from the well-known conflicting requirements between performance and security [10][11], and between privacy and security [12]. A second main contribution of the paper is the design and implementation of a framework to overcome the identified limits by enhancing data collection and storage services of a SIEM. The solution is composed of some modules that we name Generic Event Translation (GET) and Resilient Storage (RS). They allow to: i) increase the heterogeneity and number of data sources; ii) move part of the data processing toward the edge of the distributed IT system managing the CI, with a number of advantages for the protection of the CI; iii) provide post-accidental support allowing a precise and reliable reconstruction of the happening of a security breach and forensic evidence of such a circumstance. A final contribution of this paper is the application of the proposed solution to protect a real CI, namely a dam. This use case is one of the four use cases analyzed in the MASSIF project and was selected because it is a very challenging scenario.

In Section 2, the paper discusses the main features of current SIEM technologies and considers the limits of such solutions when applied to protect Critical Infrastructures. Section 3 briefly introduces the MASSIF project, i.e. its key aspects and challenges, and highlights the data service components in the context of the MASSIF framework. Section 4 presents the implementation of such solution and its usage for the dam monitoring and control case study. Section 5 closes the paper with final remarks and an overview of future plans.

2   Limits of Current SIEM Solutions

Security of IT systems is focused on preserving Confidentiality-Integrity-Availability (CIA) properties, whilst, in the CIs, human and environmental safety is emphasized. In order to re-design current SIEMs, MASSIF project has analyzed four real world scenarios and has identified the main limits of current State of the Art (SotA) technology [8] when deployed to protect CIs. In the following we shortly summarize them.

As traditional SIEMs analyze solely IT infrastructure events [13][14][15][16] – events generated by IT devices and applications – they fail in detecting security occurrences which do not produce evidence at infrastructure level. Instead, SIEMs should be able to process events from different system layers and various domains into one more comprehensive view of security-aware processes. This requires that data collectors should be able to integrate legacy and novel information sources in an effective and flexible way, by interpreting multi-layer and multi-domain data formats, typically characterized by heterogeneous syntax and semantics.

SCADA and SIEMs have to be deployed together in the same environment, thus they compete for the same resources, such as connection bandwidth, which are often very limited. This requires that SIEMs for CIs should limit the consumption of shared resources as much as possible.

Complex CIs are often multi-tenant and involve several stakeholders, organizations and domains, and, so, dissemination of private data should be limited. Traditional SIEMs applied to CIs may expose sensitive data to third parties, such as stakeholders of intermediate communication nodes and remote correlation servers. Additionally, correlation may be more effectively operated when the security information is contextualized, detailed data can be retrieved on-demand and analysis can exploit knowledge of the specific application domain. This requires that SIEM for CIs should provide mechanisms to treat and pre-correlate data at the edge of the SIEM architecture, very close to the field devices.

The evolution of current field devices moves toward the generation of huge amounts of data and in performing even more complex operations. This ultimately details the dynamics of physical world events very precisely, which may result in overwhelming the SIEM for CIs with huge amounts of security related patterns and alerts. SIEMs for CIs would require High Volume Performance at the edge of the network, specifically in data treatment components, such as data collectors, data parsers and event correlators.

Considering the attractiveness of CIs and the potential impact of their exposition, security events may be used for forensic purposes. In order to use SIEM reports as forensic proof, digital evidence (e-evidence) properties like Authentication, Admissibility and Best-evidence should be granted [17]. This requires that SIEM storage systems should guarantee: data authenticity, which ensures about event source; fault and intrusion tolerance, which ensures about admissibility and no-hearsay of evidence; privacy, which forbids disclosing of sensitive data to unauthorized parties. Moreover, storage systems of SIEMs should guarantee that forensic events, and only such events, must be kept, while unnecessary details must be deleted or made anonymous ("least persistence principle").

Data channels of distributed systems – and SIEMs - are vulnerable to faults and malicious activities which may impact correct and timely dissemination of events from data sources to central engines and may invalidate SIEM analysis. SIEM for CIs should be able to disseminate events in a reliable manner. Also if this aspect has been considered in the project and addressed in [18], it will not be further discussed.

In the following we will discuss how we have faced such limits in the context of the MASSIF project. Additional requirements and limits can be retrieved at the application level, that is the services offered on top of the SIEM (e.g. predictive security monitoring, attack modeling and simulation, event-driven inference engines, decision support and reaction/countermeasure systems, advanced visualization systems, etc.), but are out of the scope of this paper.

3   Data Collection, Pre-processing, Dissemination and Storage in MASSIF

In order to overcome limits mentioned above, MASSIF project proposes an enhanced SIEM deployed as a logical overlay on the monitored system, in this case a CI. In particular, the solution presented in this paper implements a set of functionalities which address data treatment issues from the acquisition to the storage phases. The main modules of this solution are the Generic Event Translation (GET) and the Resilient Storage (RS). The GET collects data from the "Payload Machinery", which is composed of very heterogeneous and multi-layer event sources, such as legacy IT and SCADA components, service infrastructure monitors, security applications and appliances (security sensors). The collection process is complemented by security analysis of the data at the edge side of the SIEM architecture. The RS reliably stores events which contain useful information of relevant security breaches.

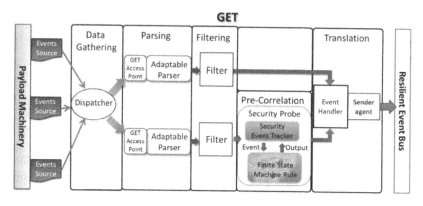

Fig. 1. Architecture of Generic Event Translation (GET) module

Cross-Layer Event Gathering, Parsing, Filtering and Translation

The GET framework is the module of the SIEM in charge of cross-layer event collection, that is gathering, parsing, filtering and translating data generated by the Payload Machinery. Such functionalities are assigned to a set of components and agents located at the edge-side of the MASSIF SIEM architecture, typically within the monitored environment. Moreover, the GET is able to manage different data formats and can be interfaced very closely to the field systems to sign information as soon as it is generated.

As depicted in Fig. 1, the first functionality offered by the GET allows to gather raw data from event sources. Typically, data are transferred to the acquisition component of the GET, namely the *Dispatcher*, by means of Syslog [19] or textual based protocols, which are by far the most widely used data transport solutions. Then, the GET extracts information from the flow of raw data (e.g., a stream of characters) previously collected. This operation, named *parsing*, is performed by components named *Adaptable Parsers (APs)*. APs adopt Compiler-compiler technology to automatically manipulate formally specified documents [20]. This approach retains a number of associated advantages including: a very large degree of expressiveness, the availability of well-known tools for the automatic processing of grammar-based artifacts, a high level of generality and technology-independence, which decouples the format definition from the underlying technology used for data processing. In particular, *Format-specific Grammar* contains the description of the event format – its syntax and semantics - and is used to generate the Adaptable Parser able to parse a specific kind of data format. Grammar parser technology has been widely used to define diversity based intrusion detectors, as presented in [21]. Additionally, AP is interfaced by means of a component named *GET Access Point (GAP)*, which associates data sources with related APs to correctly dispatch previously gathered data. In order to avoid the propagation of data irrelevant from a security perspective, *Event Filters* selectively discard events generated by the event sources. They perform a stateless process which checks a certain number of logical conditions (Event Filters) within data fields of the event messages. As data are parsed, information has to be conveyed to core services into a common and generic format. The format translation and adaptation task is assigned to a component named *Event Handler (EH)*, which complements the message with a trusted timestamp, provided by the synchronized time reference of the SIEM. Finally, the *Sender Agent* sends SIEM-formatted events to the dissemination layer of the enhanced SIEM, namely the Resilient Event Bus.

Cross-Layer Event Correlation, Aggregation and Abstraction

The part of the GET in charge of cross-layer event correlation, aggregation and abstraction is the Security Probe (SP). The SP introduces a novel level of intelligence into SIEM analysis and contextualizes it to the specific application domain. Particularly, SP is a Finite State Machine (FSM)-based event pattern detector which reduces the burden of processing the whole data at the core of the SIEM. Specifically, SPs are based on State Machine Compiler (SMC) [22] technology, which gives the possibility to separate the description of the FSM from its actual implementation, thus allowing the analyst to concentrate his/her attention on the correlation logic (and rule) instead of the implementation details. By exploiting State Patterns and FSM models, Security Probes can be instantiated to perform very different kinds of correlation (i.e. aggregation, pattern detection and abstraction), which transform the enormous volume of data generated by Payload Machinery (micro-events) into a restricted and controlled flow of semantically richer macro-events (abstraction). Security Probes operate with event sources belonging to very different layers: in order to make FSMs "evolve", Adaptable Parsers feed the SPs with proper information. The Security Event Tracker is part of the SP in charge of getting input events, identifying the FSM instance to evolve, receiving the feedback from the machine (e.g. an alert) and sending the FSM output to the EH; the FSM logic (states, transitions, …) is maintained in the Finite State Machine Rule.

As GET framework functionalities are distributed among several (edge-side) components, load distribution policies and mechanisms, such as load balancing, can be implemented: this would allow handling load peaks in different phases of the edge-side data processing and reconfiguring the usage of computational resources. Moreover, SotA security technologies have been adopted to protect data channels among GET components: for instance SSL/TLS protocols are able to guarantee CIA properties. Specifically, as new data arrive at the Dispatcher, they are signed and encrypted, so to initialize the flow protection mechanisms perpetrated throughout the whole SIEM architecture.

Resilient Storage for Forensic Support

In order to design a Resilient Storage (RS) module, we identify three main features of data storage in MASSIF SIEM: i) the "least persistence principle" which emphasizes the necessity to store exclusively data generating significant alerts; ii) forensic data access control, which emphasizes the access control to security breach information; iii) fault and intrusion tolerance, which harden the components of the resilient storage system.

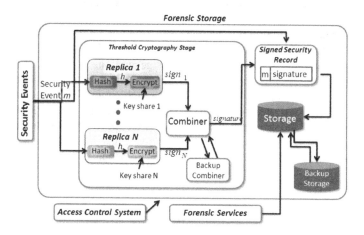

Fig. 2. Resilient Storage architecture

Key mechanism adopted to design the RS is the threshold cryptography combined to diversity and replication techniques. RS is particularly useful to criminal/civil prosecution of attackers in the post-security breach stage: in this case the main component feeding the RS is the SIEM Correlation/Rule Engine at core-side [23]. Concretely, the Resilient Storage (Fig. 2) implements threshold cryptography: it generates RSA signatures by relying on threshold signature scheme by Shoup [24]. The latter generates a valid signature from any subset of k (k is a threshold) participants out of l (l is total number of participants). This schema prevents the reconstruction of the secret key starting from the knowledge of k-1 or less shares. So, the unforgeability property holds even if less than k players are corrupted and work together to hack the system. This property increases the reliability and makes the system more intrusion tolerant. In particular, the protocol divides the secret key in l shares and distributes each piece to a different player. After the secret key is divided into shares, the incoming message (containing information about the security breach) is sent in parallel to l nodes (Replicas), which perform hash calculation and encryption. In order to increase system security, node diversity is embraced (e.g. different hardware, operating systems, and programming languages). Each Replica computes a hash function of the same message. This function returns a unique digest for this message, named "h" in Fig. 2. Then digest is encrypted in order to produce a signature share (or partial signature): for this purpose, each node has its own secret key. A component, called Combiner, is responsible for assembling all partial signatures received from the participants of the threshold cryptosystem in order to generate a full signature. Then, the full signature is attached to the original message, thus forming a signed security record, i.e. a forensic record. This new record is stored for future forensic analysis. To ensure unforgeability and preserve the records, it is common to use Write-Once-Read-Many (WORM) storage devices. Forensic Services entity provides additional services, such as storage system access control. All communications between components are protected by means of SSL and authentication protocols.

4   Implementation Details: The Dam Case Study

In order to present our solution we show the case study of a dam monitoring and control system. A dam is an infrastructure conceived for a multitude of purposes including food water supplying, hydroelectric power generation, irrigation, water sports, wildlife habitat granting, flow diversion, navigation. Dam monitoring applications use structural and geotechnical instrumentation in combination with Automated Data Acquisition Systems (ADAS) and SCADA systems. Such systems are increasingly becoming automated and remotely controlled. This fact paves the way for a new class of security induced safety issues, that is for the possibility that cyber-attacks against the IT layer of the dam, ultimately result in damage to people and environment.

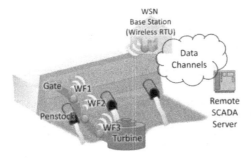

Fig. 3. WSN-based water flow monitoring in a dam

The monitoring and control system of our case study - depicted in Fig. 3 – adopts the Wireless Sensor Network (WSN) technology, which is an increasing trend [25] [26] [27] to critical infrastructure monitoring, as demonstrated by the appearance of more and more commercial products [28]. In our scenario, the water in the basin is released by opening a Gate and is conveyed through a Penstock to the Turbine of a hydroelectric power plant. The monitoring system is composed of three water flow sensors placed at different points of the penstock (WF1, WF2, WF3). Additional sensors indicate the turbine activity and the gate openness. Water flow sensors constitute the nodes of a WSN, which, at regular intervals, send their measurements to a WSN Base Station (BS) located at the dam surveillance office. The BS acts as a wireless Remote Terminal Unit (RTU) and sends measurements to the Remote SCADA server. Typically, data channels from local facility to remote control offices are heterogeneous and very resource constrained. Normally, water flows are used to control the turbine speed: for instance, if the turbine speed exceeds a specific threshold, gate openness is regulated as consequence. Indeed, high turbine speed may result in electric overload and in facility failure due to excessive rotational vibrations.

To explain the functioning of our solution we designed a storyboard for an attack closely mimic Stuxnet behavior [29]. The considered attack model is represented by means of an Attack Tree as in Fig. 4.

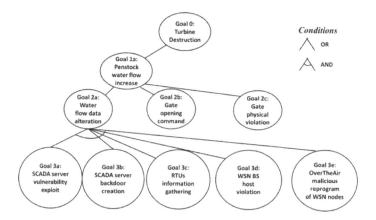

Fig. 4. Attack tree for turbine disruption

Attack trees identify actions and conditions to successfully realize an attack. The root of the tree represents the final target while branches indicate the steps to perpetrate the attack. Actions represent alternatives (OR) or necessary conditions (AND).

Assumption for the attack (precondition) is that the attacker has access to some hosts in the remote station and can plug a USB device in (e.g. he/she is an employee at the remote control facility) and has tools to exploit SCADA software and server host vulnerabilities. Goal 0 of Attack Tree indicates that the attack target is the turbine destruction. Goal 1 accomplishes Goal 0 by excessively increasing the water flow in the Penstock. Goal 2 indicates three alternatives to realize this: physically breaking the gate; excessively opening the gate by sending an explicit command to the gate actuator; making the monitoring and control system measure low levels of water flows in order to solicit automatic gate opening to feed the turbine. Goal 3 indicates necessary actions to alter water flow measurements, particularly when they are collected from nodes of a WSN: usage of malicious software from a pen drive on some host in the remote facility to locate and exploit SCADA server vulnerabilities; creation of a backdoor on the SCADA server; gathering of information about RTU devices and facilities (i.e. IP address of BS host); scanning and violation of the BS host; access to the BS host and installation of a malicious Over-The-Air (OTA) program which reprograms sensors with a rogue code. Studies about intrusion detection of WSN attacks can be found in [30], where, however, the sensor nodes are the starting point of attacks.

In order to support attack detection, we observe that the three water flow sensors are related to the same physical event (penstock discharge), and measure values in the same physical range. For this reason, any physical incoherence can be highlighted and reported. In order to detect it with a traditional SIEM, we should get physical measurements and propagate them to the central engine. This results in three issues: data cannot be easily gathered and translated from sensor measurement into the SIEM format; SIEM correlation rules are not suitable to describe physical anomalies; the whole measurement data has to be propagated to the SIEM correlation engine, whose resources, instead, should be reserved to analyze relevant security facts.

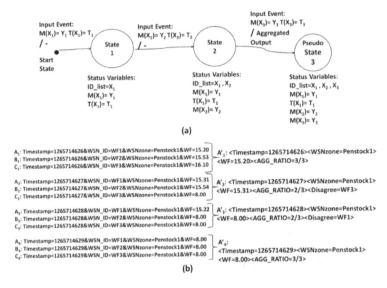

Fig. 5. (a) Finite State Machine (b) WSN sensor data and Security Probe output

In our test case we provide a Security Probe (SP) implementing a Triple Modular Redundancy (TMR) system. TMRs are widely used to generate a single output from several independent processes by adopting a majority voting scheme. The SP aggregates three measurements from sensor data and reports the number of sensors falling in the same measurement range. Any disagreement on the measurements is reported in the output. Fig. 5 (b) shows WSN data arriving at the SP (before parsing) and its output. The FSM (a) shows transitions triggered by measurement events (other inputs are not depicted, such as time ticks for timer expiration). X is the sensor ID. M(X) its measurement. T(X) its timestamp. Note that the first event is used as a reference to aggregate other inputs. State 3 is a pseudo-state as it causes the machine to come back to StartState. Aggregated Output generates the output as in (b). The sequence of events indicates what happens when the attacker tries to modify three water flow sensors by forging values under a specific threshold (8.00): initially sensor 3 is tampered, then sensors 2, 3 and finally sensors 1, 2, 3.

We observe that in case of disagreement, Disagree identity of TMR output changes two times (ID is 3 and then 2). This fact can be used for a rule at the correlation engine as depicted in Fig. 6, which shows the implementation for the OSSIM SIEM by AlienVault [31]. A case study presenting the integration of physical data sources into OSSIM is presented in [32]. In this paper, the detection rule (*Directive*) considers multi-layer events, namely: 1) a Scan warning on the central system (root rule); 2) a remote login on the WSN BS (rule 2); 3) a variation in the Disagree field of the TMR (in rule 3 and 4, "userdata1" is the Disagree field extracted from the TMR SP output).

```
<directive id="500100" name="WSN water flow sensor tampering" priority="5">
        <rule type="detector" name="Snort Portscan" reliability="2" occurrence="1" from="ANY"
            to="ANY" port_from="ANY" port_to="ANY" plugin_id="1100" plugin_sid="21">
            <rules>
                <rule type="detector" name="SSH Successful Authentication" reliability="3"
                    occurrence="1" from="1:DST_IP" to="10.0.0.1" port_from="ANY"
                    time_out="100000" port_to="ANY" plugin_id="4003" plugin_sid="7"/>
                <rule type="detector" name="TMR Security Probe Disagreement""
                    reliability="1" occurrence="1" from="ANY" to="ANY" port_from="ANY"
                    time_out="100000" port_to="ANY" plugin_id="1001" plugin_sid="1"/>
                <rule type="detector" name="TMR Security Probe Disagreement""
                    reliability="1" occurrence="1" from="ANY" to="ANY" port_from="ANY"
                    time_out="100000" port_to="ANY" plugin_id="1001" plugin_sid="1"
                    userdata1="!1:USERDATA1"/>
            </rules>
        </rule>
</directive>
```

Fig. 6. OSSIM directive of WSN attack (XML code)

The TMR SP shows three capabilities: it treats physical data from a security perspective; it places SIEM intelligence at the periphery and avoids irrelevant data to be propagated to the central system; it exploits specific knowledge of the application domain (e.g. similarity of water flow measurements in the WSN).

The "reliability" value in the rule represents the confidence of each warning. Supposing an alert threshold of 7 (they sum to 7), we observe that four warnings alone are not able to raise an alarm. In order to show the RS system, we have integrated it in OSSIM. OSSIM Server is the correlation/rule engine which is able to raise Alarms once events are correlated based on *Directives*: typically it stores them on a Database. The OSSIM SIEM allows registering multiple databases for storing security events based on their Risk level.

To integrate our RS system, we prepared a db driver and registered such a driver in the OSSIM Server to store ALARM level messages. The RS driver only supports two SQL primitives: the INPUT and the SELECT. During an INPUT the provided data is stored after the generation of the threshold cryptography based signature. During the SELECT the verification of the signature is operated and the operation fails if the signature is not verified.

#	Id	Alarm	Risk	Date	Source	Destination	Correlation Level
1	66	WSN water flow sensor tampering	5	2012-01-01 10:01:15	ANY	ANY	4
		Alarm Summary [Total Events: 4 - Unique Dst IPAddr: 2 - Unique Types: 2 - Unique Dst Ports: 1]					
1	65	TMR Security Probe Dis	1	2011-12-31 23:59:25	ANY	ANY	4
2	64	TMR Security Probe Dis	1	2011-12-31 23:59:24	ANY	ANY	3
3	63	SSH Successfull authent	1	2011-12-31 23:54:12	ANY	ANY	2
4	62	Snort Portscan	1	2011-12-31 23:49:10	ANY	ANY	1

Fig. 7. OSSIM alarm and related events (addresses are obfuscated)

In order to store only very significant Alarms, RS treats only highly risky events (Risk > Risk Threshold). Moreover, to guarantee a valid support to the forensic activity, together with the alert related event, all the events participating in the generation of the alert are sent to the RS. To this aim we used the OSSIM capability to retrieve chains of events as shown in Fig. 7.

5   Conclusions and Future Work

In this paper we have discussed main limits of current SIEM technology when deployed to secure CIs and presented the solutions developed in the context of the MASSIF project. We have focused on the framework assigned to data collection and storage, namely the Generic Event Translation (GET) and the Resilient Storage (RS) and we have tested it on the challenging case study of a dam monitoring and control system. We have presented an attack model aimed at tampering a WSN from a remote facility and have indicated how to support SIEM detection of the attack with a domain specific probe modeled on the Triple Modular Redundancy (TMR) solution. In the future we plan to: evaluate the performance of the developed SIEM solution against a complete set of misuse cased reproduced in a testbed laboratory and on top of a real dam; produce quantitative evidence of the benefits due to the adoption of the enhanced SIEM, against traditional solutions.

Acknowledgments. The research leading to these results has received funding from the European Commission within the context of the Seventh Framework Programme (FP7/2007-2013) under Grant Agreement No. 257644 (MAnagement of Security information and events in Service Infrastructures, MASSIF Project). It has been also partially supported by the TENACE PRIN Project (n. 20103P34XC) funded by the Italian Ministry of Education, University and Research.

References

1. Kim, S.H., Wang, Q., Ullrich, J.B.: A comparative study of cyberattacks. Commun. ACM 55(3), 66–73 (2012), doi:10.1145/2093548.2093568
2. Symantec ® Applied Research. Symantec 2010 Critical Infrastructure Protection Study (Global Results) (October 2010)
3. White Paper, Symantec ® Intelligence Quarterly Report: October-December. Targeted Attacks on Critical Infrastructures (2010)
4. White Paper, Global Energy Cyberattacks: "Night Dragon", McAfee ® FoundstonerProfessional Services and McAfee Labs (February 10, 2011)
5. Baker, S., Waterman, S., Ivanov, G.: In the Crossfire: Critical Infrastructure in the Age of Cyber War. McAffee© (2010), http://resources.mcafee.com/content/NACIPReport
6. Stouffer, K., Falco, J., Scarfone, K.: Guide to Industrial Control Systems (ICS) Security. National Institute of Standards and Technology (NIST), SP 800-82 (June 2011)
7. MASSIF project, http://www.massif-project.eu/
8. MASSIF project, Scenario requirements Deliverable D2.1.1 (April 2011)
9. INSPIRE project, http://www.inspire-strep.eu/
10. Zeng, W., Chow, M.Y.: A trade-off model for performance and security in secured networked control systems. In: Proc. IEEE ISIE, pp. 1997–2002 (2011)
11. Xu, Y., Song, R., Korba, L., Wang, L., Shen, W., Lang, S.: Distributed device networks with security constraints. IEEE Trans. Ind. Informat. 1(4), 217–225 (2005)
12. Landau, S.: Security and Privacy Landscape in Emerging Technologies. IEEE Security & Privacy 6(4), 74–77 (2008), doi:10.1109/MSP.2008.95
13. RSA™ Security. RSA enVision™ Universal Device Support Guide (2008)
14. AlienVault™, Available OSSIM Plugin List (2010)

15. ArcSight™, ArcSight™ Smartconnector (2009)
16. Q1Labs™, Supported devices, http://q1labs.com/products/supported-devices.aspx
17. Federal Rules of Evidence, The Committee on the Judiciary House of Representatives (December 1, 2010), http://judiciary.house.gov/hearings/printers/111th/evid2010.pdf
18. Sousa, P., Bessani, A., Correia, M., Neves, N., Verissimo, P.: Highly available intrusion-tolerant services with proactive-reactive recovery. IEEE Transactions on Parallel and Distributed Systems 21(4) (2010)
19. BSD Syslog Protocol, RFC 3164, http://www.ietf.org/rfc/rfc3164.txt
20. Campanile, F., Cilardo, A., Coppolino, L., Romano, L.: Adaptable Parsing of Real-Time Data Streams. In: Proceedings of the 15th Euromicro International Conference on Parallel, Distributed and Network-Based Processing (PDP 2007), pp. 412–418. IEEE Computer Society, Washington, DC (2007), doi:10.1109/PDP.2007.16
21. Coppolino, L., D'Antonio, S., Esposito, M., Romano, L.: Exploiting diversity and correlation to improve the performance of intrusion detection systems. In: International Conference on Network and Service Security, N2S 2009, June 24-26 (2009) ISBN: 978-2-9532-4431-1
22. Home of SMC: the State Machine Compiler, http://smc.sourceforge.net/
23. Afzaal, M., Di Sarno, C., Coppolino, L., D'Antonio, S., Romano, L.: A Resilient Architecture for Forensic Storage of Events in Critical Infrastructures. In: 2012 IEEE 14th International Symposium on High-Assurance Systems Engineering (HASE), October 25-27, pp. 48–55 (2012), doi:10.1109/HASE.2012.9
24. Shoup, V.: Practical threshold signatures. In: Preneel, B. (ed.) EUROCRYPT 2000. LNCS, vol. 1807, pp. 207–220. Springer, Heidelberg (2000)
25. Buttyan, L., Gessner, D., Hessler, A., Langendoerfer, P.: Application of wireless sensor networks in critical infrastructure protection: challenges and design options (Security and Privacy in Emerging Wireless Networks). IEEE Wireless Communications 17(5), 44–49 (2010), doi:10.1109/MWC.2010.5601957
26. Wolmarans, V., Hancke, G.: Wireless Sensor Networks in Power Supply Grids. In: SATNAC 2008. Wild Coast Sun (September 2008)
27. Bai, X., Meng, X., Du, Z., Gong, M., Hu, Z.: Design of Wireless Sensor Network in SCADA System for Wind Power Plant. In: Proceedings of the IEEE International Conference on Automation and Logistics, Qingdao, China (September 2008)
28. Minteos DamWatch, http://www.minteos.com/wp-content/uploads/2011/02/Microsoft-Word-minteos-damwatch_ita.pdf
29. Langner, R.: Stuxnet: Dissecting a Cyberwarfare Weapon. IEEE Security and Privacy 9(3), 49–51 (2011), doi:10.1109/MSP.2011.67
30. Bondavalli, A., Daidone, A., Coppolino, L., Romano, L.: A hidden Markov model based intrusion detection system for wireless sensor networks. International Journal of Critical Computer-Based Systems (IJCCBS) 3(3) (2012)
31. OSSIM AlienVault™, http://www.alienvault.com/
32. Coppolino, L., D'Antonio, S., Formicola, V., Romano, L.: Integration of a System for Critical Infrastructure Protection with the OSSIM SIEM Platform: A dam case study. In: Flammini, F., Bologna, S., Vittorini, V. (eds.) SAFECOMP 2011. LNCS, vol. 6894, pp. 199–212. Springer, Heidelberg (2011)

PDR: A Prevention, Detection and Response Mechanism for Anomalies in Energy Control Systems

Cristina Alcaraz and Meltem Sönmez Turan

National Institute of Standards and Technology, Gaithersburg, MD
{mariacristina.alcaraz,meltem.turan}@nist.gov

Abstract. Prevention, detection and response are nowadays considered to be three priority topics for protecting critical infrastructures, such as energy control systems. Despite attempts to address these current issues, there is still a particular lack of investigation in these areas, and in particular in dynamic and automatic proactive solutions. In this paper we propose a mechanism, which is called PDR, with the capability of anticipating anomalies, detecting anomalous behaviours and responding to them in a timely manner. PDR is based on a conglomeration of technologies and on a set of essential components with the purpose of offering situational awareness irrespective of where the system is located. In addition, the mechanism can also compute its functional capacities by evaluating its efficacy and precision in the prediction and detection of disturbances. With this, the entire system is able to know the real reliability of its services and its activity in remote substations at all times.

Keywords: Detection, Energy Control Systems, Industrial Wireless Sensor Networks, MANET, Prevention, Response, The Internet, and Wide-Area Situational Awareness.

1 Introduction

Modernisation of our critical energy control infrastructures is bringing a set of unexplored and unsolved challenges. Most of them are mainly related to the need to find a desirable trade-off between operational performance in (almost) real-time, and protection against serious threats. These threats do not necessarily have to be cyber-attacks [1]. They can be associated with unforeseen or abrupt changes registered within the system, such as a power surge in generators or a voltage reduction in transmission lines. If these unexpected situations are not controlled properly, they may trigger a serious effect that may lead to local, regional or national outages and/or blackouts, with the possibility of spreading on its own to other countries. This is the case of the well-known blackout of August 14, 2003 that occasioned an economic and social crisis between two countries; U.S. and Canada. Unfortunately, this kind of event has not been the only one that has happened in recent years [2].

Considering the application domain and its sensitive nature, this protection should consist of proactive and reactive solutions based on dynamic and automatic methods. The reason lies in that the vast majority of energy control subsystems (e.g. substations) are distributed at distant-geographic locations in which the control is normally limited

B. Hämmerli, N. Kalstad Svendsen, and J. Lopez (Eds.): CRITIS 2012, LNCS 7722, pp. 22–33, 2013.

to a few human operators in the field. This need was also identified by NIST in [3], and NIST classified this need as one of the eight priorities to be taken into account when protecting Critical Infrastructures (CIs). This priority, known as *Wide-Area Situational Awareness* (WASA), focuses on supervising and controlling the performance of underlying systems located over large geographic areas in (almost) real-time. This includes anticipating, detecting and responding to problems before they can cause disruptions.

Given this, we present a dynamic solution that tries to cover some of the stated points for WASA, such as prevention, detection and response. The proposed approach, called here as PDR, is based on four main technologies; Industrial Wireless Sensor Networks (IWSNs), Mobile Ad-Hoc Networks (MANETs), the Internet and the ISA100.11a standard [4]. We have selected these technologies as each one of them offers an attractive set of benefits for local and remote protection [5,6]. Moreover, the architecture suggested for PDR is also able to evaluate by itself the level of precision of the schemes proposed for detection and prevention. Any information from the system has to be reported sooner or later to the Supervisory Control and Data Acquisition (SCADA) Center so that it can be made aware of the accuracy and functionality of the approach, and to remotely control the situation at all times and any time.

Although there are currently some similar works to this proposal, there are also important differences that should be stressed here. For example, Roman et al. [7] presented a lightweight situation awareness mechanism based on a WSN and on a set of statistical and collaborative techniques. Similarly, He et al. [8] presented a situational awareness mechanism based on the multivariate times series association technique to observe the functionality of a set of sensors. However, none of them ensures preventive and reactive capacities that enable the system to take the control against incidents, faults or threats such as we try addressing in this paper. This means that there are a special research lack within this area, and effort to deliver dynamic and intelligent solutions based on WSNs should be still needed.

The paper is organised as follows. Section 2 introduces the general architecture of PDR together with the technologies that play a special role within our approach. The details of the components that comprise the architecture are described in Section 3, whilst three proactive and reactive methods are discussed in the remainder of the same section. Section 4 concludes the paper and outlines future work.

2 PDR: General Architecture and Technologies

The architecture proposed for PDR is mainly based on IWSNs, MANETs, the Internet, and ISA100.11a. Figure 1 illustrates an example of the collaboration and cooperation of such technologies for control and supervision of energy generation and distribution systems. This figure also represents, in a general way, the operation in the field and energy distribution from bulk generations systems (e.g. nuclear systems, hydroelectric systems, wind farms, and others) to urban areas [3].

For electricity production, the majority of generation systems have to be connected to generators to induce mechanical energy into electric energy to a low voltage. To increase the level of voltage and its transmission over long distances, the system makes use of large electricity transmission lines with transformers (transmission system).

To distribute the power to urban areas, the voltage load must be downloaded into substations reducing its level of voltage (distribution system). Both transmission and distribution substations are based on transformers, control devices (e.g. Remote Terminal Units (RTUs)), industrial meters, sensors and industrial engineering devices. Any activity in the field must be supervised, either locally or remotely, and any information produced or sensed must be sent to a centralised system for purposes of control and register. All of this control system is commonly known as a SCADA System.

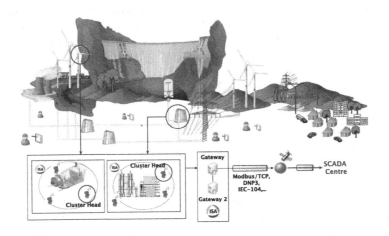

Fig. 1. General Architecture of the PDR mechanism

Unfortunately, this complex circuit of power generation and distribution is quite sensitive to unexpected events. This means that one fault registered in a local point of the system could trigger a change in its normal behaviour, probably leading to a cascading effect towards other CIs [9]. To control and coordinate these types of unforeseen situations, we distribute IWSNs and MANETs throughout the entire system and close to its more sensitive parts, such as energy generators, motors, turbines, industrial engines, transformers, and others. In order to understand their functionalities in the field, we describe in detail their particular characteristics and services below.

An IWSN [10] is composed of small and smart devices with the capability (4MHz-32MHz micro-processor, 8KB-128KB RAM, 128KB-192KB ROM) for sensing real states of an object or its surroundings. These states are associated with physical events in the context, such as temperature, pressure, voltage, vibration, etc. To measure these types of events, sensor nodes should be deployed close to the supervised target, for example, generators or motors of wind turbines (See Fig. 1). As conventional sensor nodes, industrial sensor nodes are also autonomous devices capable of processing and transmitting information to a base station. In our case, this base station is a powerful gateway device. Industrial sensor nodes can also offer services of auto-configuration, auto-organisation, self-monitoring and self-healing, detection, warning and tracking of anomalous behaviours or threatening situations such as peaks in voltage in electrical pylons or abrupt changes of temperature registered in industrial engines, as well as querying and reporting on-demand. All of these features and services have encouraged both industry and government to modernise their CIs. Indeed, the industrial sector is aware of the advantages and opportunities of this technology to increase its levels of competitiveness, productivity and efficiency [10]. On the other hand, the government needs the technology to find a way to protect many of our CIs. According to the last report of the American Recovery and Reinvestment Act (ARPA) of 2009 [3], the U.S. already aims to invest in new information and communication systems in order to automate, for example, substations with smart sensors. The reasoning behind this investment is to find ways to avoid or mitigate disturbances and instabilities generated in remote locations.

Having commented this, we are not saying that IWSNs intend to replace traditional wired industrial systems, such as RTUs. Instead, they try to offer a complementary tool for maximizing automation tasks and ensuring protection. As mentioned above, this protection includes all of the potential capabilities for prevention, detection and response against anomalous events of the system. An anomalous event is defined by the Oxford dictionary as *"something that deviates from what is standard, normal, or expected"* [11]. For our case, we identify two types of anomalies; *infrastructural anomalies* and *control anomalies*. The former type is related to the deviations associated with normal behaviour of the observed infrastructure, such as high/low voltage level, strong stress, high/low temperature, corrosion, gas/oil leaks, etc. In contrast, the latter type refers to the normal behaviour of the control network; i.e. the IWSN. This technology is quite sensitive to many type of threats (from hardware threats to application threats [12,7]). This is due to its mesh topology and their wireless-channels, in where harsh industrial conditions (e.g. vibration or noise) could also break their links and cause unreliable communication. For simplicity reasons, we particularly focus in this paper on time-related threats (i.e., delayed packets or do not reach their destination at all) and availability threats (i.e., physical unavailability of a sensor), such as de-synchronisation (deSync) in the communication channels (i.e., the communication between two nodes is deviated from the initial configuration), loss of information, information relay or exhaustion of energy.

Continuing with the architecture of PDR, it also includes MANET networks as a self-configuring technology of mobile devices connected by wireless links. This kind of communication enables human operators to locally manage the systems, allowing their mobility in the field and collaboration with other human operators. Any information acquired from sensors can be visualised by their hand-held interfaces (e.g. a PDA). These interfaces facilitate the automation tasks by managing; (i) measurements, i.e. physical events, (ii) alarms with relevant data on real states from the observed infrastructure, or (iii) commands with a particular action. For communication from/to sensors, it is currently possible to apply wireless industrial communication protocols, such as ZigBee PRO [13], WirelessHART [14] or ISA100.11a. We focus our attention on the ISA100.11a standard for several reasons. First of all, it is an extended version of WirelessHART and was intended for industrial environments. Thus, it provides a set of useful services to address the coexistence with other technologies, communication reliability (e.g. use of hopping and blacklisting methods) and alarm management based on priorities. Second, it improves some of the security services of the ZigBee PRO, such as the key negotiation process in commissioning phase [6]. Another advantage of ISA100.11a is its flexibility for configuring wireless networks.

We believe that a good approach for our architecture is a hierarchical configuration; i.e. a network based on clusters of sensors. For each cluster, a trustworthy sensor is selected, which is known as the Cluster Head (CH) with a unique ID_{CH}. The main reasons of selecting this configuration are several. This conformation of clusters does not only reduce computational costs in sensors, but it also facilitates a rapid location of a problem by knowing the sensor deployment and the affected area. In addition, the studies made in [15] clearly highlight the effectiveness and suitability of the technology for awareness situational within Smart Grid contexts, since the most of the current SCADA wireless communication protocols (e.g., Zigbee or ISA100.11a) can be configured following a star topology and the use of the gateway enables the underlying system to establish connectivity with other networks (e.g., MANETs, Bluethooth). However, there is a problem that should be stressed here: CHs may be susceptible to threats or failures, putting the supervision of a neighbourhood at risk/isolation. A possible solution would be to perform re-clustering techniques or deployment of redundant nodes [16].

Nonetheless, and to simplify the architecture of our approach, we consider that CHs are trustworthy nodes and they are not threatened. They are responsible for (i) filtering and aggregating measurements (inherent tasks of any CH), (ii) receiving alarms from its sensors, and (iii) resending any information to the gateway. Here, the gateway acts as a powerful interface between the acquisition world and the SCADA Center, with the capability for processing data and translating different types of messages. For reasons of simplicity, we assume that the communication link 'sensor-sensor' and 'sensor-gateway' are protected by using security services of ISA100.11a, and communication 'gateway-hand-held' and 'gateway-SCADA Center' are protected through security services of the TCP/IP standard and/or virtual private networks.

Table 1 summarises the advantages of building a proactive and reactive system based on IWSNs, MANETs, ISA100.11a and the Internet. Note that this table is based on the needs identified for WASA and on the studies done on WSNs, MANETs and the Internet in [5]. When combining technologies, different types of advantages are obtained, such as *monitoring*, *prevention*, *detection*, *alerting*, *response*, *collaboration* and *mobility*. Given this, the next step is to present the approach using the mentioned technologies.

Table 1. Advantages of using IWSNs, MANETs, ISA100.11a and the Internet for WASA

	Technologies	Monitoring	Prevention	Detection	Alert	Response	Collaboration	Mobility
A	*IWSN & ISA100.11a*	$\sqrt{} - local$	$\sqrt{}$	$\sqrt{}$	$\sqrt{}$		$\sqrt{} - local$	
B	*MANETs*	$\sqrt{} - local$				$\sqrt{} - local$	$\sqrt{} - local$	$\sqrt{}$
C	*The Internet*	$\sqrt{} - remote$					$\sqrt{} - remote$	
D	*A & B & C*	$\sqrt{} - local/remote$	$\sqrt{}$	$\sqrt{}$	$\sqrt{}$	$\sqrt{}$	$\sqrt{} - local/remote$	$\sqrt{}$

3   PDR in Wide-Area Situational Awareness

As mentioned in Section 2, the sensor network follows a hierarchical configuration where CHs take on a special role within our approach. Each CH is configured with four main modules; a *Normalisation* module, a *Behaviour Pattern* module, a *Filtration-Aggregation* module and an *Alarm Manager* module (See Fig. 2). Any reading value of voltage, $volt_i$, from sensors must be normalised by the Normalisation module in order to format and standardise their contents. The normalised message is later processed by the Behaviour Pattern module so as to identify normal or abnormal states. Normal states refer to those acceptable voltage reading values that are inside permitted thresholds, $[V_{min}, V_{max}]$. For these states, each CH has to (i) filter and aggregate the new value through the Filtration-Aggregation module, and (ii) send the aggregated values to the gateway. When the message is received by the gateway, it re-sends the message to the SCADA Center for supervision purposes, accountability or future analyses.

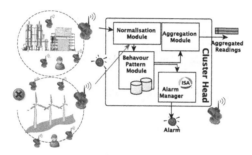

Fig. 2. Cluster Head: Dissemination and Warning

For unacceptable states ($volt_i \notin [V_{min}, V_{max}]$), it is essential to differentiate and classify different kind of states that could happen in our application context. One way to classify it would be to (i) consider the six levels of priority offered by the ISA100.11a standard [4], namely *normal, journal, low, medium, high* and *urgent* signalled with 0 to 5 respectively (such a value is denoted here as v_i), and (ii) define priority thresholds for each state. These thresholds not only depend on the security policies, but also the established policies for each country/organization.

Depending on the v_i and priority thresholds, the CH, through the Alarm Manager, will have to generate a particular type of alert with a specific label; *journal, low, medium, high* and *urgent*. The alert has to be sent to the gateway. For generation of the alert, the manager makes use of ISA100.11a objects. In particular, these objects come from the ARMO (Alert Reporting Management Object) class, and they have to be received and processed by a unique device in the system (in our case, the gateway), which contains the ARO (Alert Receiving Object) class of ISA100.11a. When alarms arrive to the gateway, the system is expected to respond to them properly and in a timely manner. For this reason, we deal with the prevention, detection and response in this section.

Our intention is to anticipate infrastructural anomalies, detect suspicious behaviours in the control network and provide a rapid response to face incidents. These three activities will be configured inside the gateway using a set of interconnected modules (See Fig. 3). In particular, five main modules; an *ARO Manager* module, a *Prevention* module, a *Detection* module, a *Diagnostic* module, and an *Alarm Manager* module.

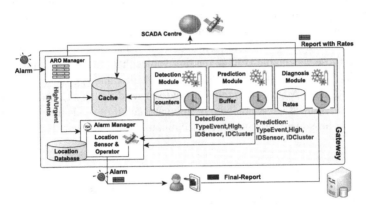

Fig. 3. Architecture of the Gateway: Incidents Management and Warning

Any incident from the control network has to be received by the ARO Manager. It is in charge of queuing incidents according to their priorities and handling critical alarms [4,5]. These alarms have to be forwarded to the Alarm Manager Module so that it can locate the nearest staff in the field immediately. For localisation of human operators, it is necessary to depend on the global positioning technologies and an updated database with information relative to deployment knowledge of sensors and human operators' availability according to their contracts. Both tasks are performed by the sub-module *Location Sensor & Operator*. Lastly, and continuing with the ARO Manager, any non-critical evidence must be temporally stored in a cache memory for purposes of prevention, detection and response. Given that these three aspects are relevant topics within our approach, we will discuss them in-depth in the following sections.

3.1   Prevention of Infrastructural Anomalies through a Forecasting Model

Deviations in system attributes such as temperature or voltage levels are the main indicators of infrastructural anomalies. In this section, we propose a forecasting model to prevent these anomalies, particularly focusing on the voltage measurements. However, the model can easily be extended to other attributes as well.

As mentioned in previous sections, ISA100.11a classifies voltage measurement using six criticality levels ([0-5]). Receiving voltage measurements with level 4 or 5 requires the attention of the operators within a short time period. The forecasting algorithm may detect an anomaly before receiving a critical alarm (e.g. about 20 minutes ahead), and this enables the operator to have more time to resolve the problem.

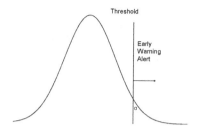

Fig. 4. Early warning alert and threshold value

The forecasting model aims to predict the occurrence of the critical alarms based on the assessment of previously received signals. To this end, the CH_s collect the signals from sensors and send them to the gateway to be temporarily stored in a cache memory, which stores the voltage measurements received over the last $\Delta_{Twindow}$ minutes. Note that the Prediction module exports all the information with priority [0-3] from this cache to a internal buffer stored by ID_{CHj} and ID_{si}. This buffer is applied for analyzing the behaviour of the system in the following minutes. Exportation is done each time period (denoted here as $\Delta_{TdiagnosticPrevention}$), the value of which is defined by the security policies.

Evaluation of the values in cache memory is done independently for each sensor. When the system is stable, we assume that these measurements follow an independent discrete probability distribution with $Pr(v = i) = p_i$ for $i = 0, 1, \ldots, 5$, with $p_0, p_1, p_2, p_3 \geq 0$ and $p_4 = p_5 = 0$, where v is the voltage measurement level. It should be noted that the distribution of v should be estimated based on previous signals received when the system is in stable position. Moreover, the estimated distribution should be tested periodically, especially after making some infrastructural changes to the system. When there is an incident in the system, the distribution of v starts to deviate from the original distribution. The measurements tend to increase and eventually the sensors generate critical alarms, i.e. p_4 and p_5 are no longer zero.

Table 2. False alarm probabilities and corresponding threshold values for D_1 and D_2 depending on k previous values

	α	T for D_1	T for D_2		α	T for D_1	T for D_2
	0.01	14	9		0.01	15	23
$k = 5$	0.05	11	7	$k = 10$	0.05	12	20
	0.10	10	6		0.10	11	19

Let $(v_1, v_2, \ldots, v_k)$ be the measurements corresponding to a particular sensor in the temporary cache memory that are received in the last $\Delta_{Twindow}$ minutes. The evaluation of the forecasting algorithm is based on the summation of v_i values, $S_k = v_1 + v_2 + \ldots + v_k$. Whenever the summation is greater than a threshold value, the algorithm sends an early warning alert for the corresponding sensor. The threshold value T is selected so that $Pr(S_k \geq T) \approx \alpha$, where α is an acceptable false alarm probability, i.e. the probability that the forecasting unit incorrectly outputs an early warning (See Fig. 4).

Calculation of this probability requires the distribution of the S_k, which can be determined by induction, using the facts (i) the distribution of S_1 is equal to the distribution of v_i's, and (ii) the distribution of $S_k = S_{k-1} + v_k$. Table 2 provides threshold and false alarm probabilities for two example distributions, D_1 and D_2, where D_1 is the discrete uniform distribution i.e., $p_i = 0.25$ for $i = 0, \ldots, 3$ and D_2 satisfies $p_i \approx 2p_{i+1}$, for $i = 0, 1, 2$, i.e., $p_0 = 0.5335$, $p_1 = 0.2667$, $p_2 = 0.1333$ and $p_3 = 0.0665$.

3.2 Detection of Control Anomalies

As mentioned above, the Detection module is in charge of detecting suspicious anomalies in the sensor network. These anomalies are related to relays, deSync and loss of sensitive information, as well as the presence of dead nodes. To control these threatening situations, we use four counters for each sensor; C_{relay}, C_{deSync}, $C_{lossInf}$ and $C_{deadNode}$. These counters should be frequently initialised when a given time for diagnosis, $\Delta_{T\,diagnosticDetection}$, is attained.

For diagnostic, the Detection module needs to evaluate the time-stamp of each message received. If the time-stamp of a specific message is outside of an established maximum time for receiving messages (T_{MAX}), then the module may deduce that such a message was lost within the network, increasing the value of the counter $C_{lossInf}$. It is also possible that the time-stamp is within the required time, but a relay threat or a deSync threat are happening in the field. To detect a relay threat, a correlation process should be carried out so as to check evidence streams with information stored in the cache, the entries of which should be ordered by the time-stamp so as to speed up the process of search and correlation of values. In this way, if a specific sensor s_i with ID_{si} already sent a message with time-stamp$_{si}$ in the past, then the Detection module may infer that a relay attack is starting within the system, increasing its C_{relay}. Similarly, we require configuration information related to each sensor, such as the expected time to receive an evidence, to detect a deSync threat. If a sensor s_i with ID_{si} sends messages outside expected time period, the Detection module increases the counter C_{deSync}. This also means that it is important to take into account the network configuration, as ISA100.11a offers the possibility of configuring the time division multiple access with specific a time-slot for the data link layer, in addition to providing a customizable hopping method for 16 channels. Note that two further situations may arise when a deSync threat is frequently produced within the network; (i) hardware or software problems, or (ii) the presence of a delay attack. A delay attack refers to forwarding information in a desynchronized manner in order to provoke delays in the reception of messages.

However, none of the previous measures control the presence of a dead node, which could be caused by a physical attack, energy exhaustion or a Denial of Service (DoS) attack. To this end, we use a diagnostic procedure, which is frequently executed when $\Delta_{T\,diagnosticDetection}$ is reached. This procedure checks the cache memory in order to see whether a particular sensor s_i with ID_{si} temporally stopped its activity in the field. If so, the Detection module has to update the counter $C_{deadNode}$. When four counters exceed their respective prescribed thresholds, the Detection module will have to warn of the situation immediately. The notification must include CH_j-ID_{CHj}, s_i-ID_{si}, the type of event and the priority of the detected event. The events can range from 'relay-threat', 'deSync-threat', 'lossInf-threat' to 'dead-node'. To complete the functionality of this part of the approach, we recommend to consider for a future other further detection measures (e.g., jamming, hardware failure, node subversion, tampered, manipulation), many of which are extensively analysed in [6,7].

3.3 Response to Anomalies and Evaluation

After the resolution of incidents in the field, human operators should provide the system with enough feedback on the situation to be able to evaluate the level of precision (either of the prediction module or the detection module) (cf. Section 3.1 and Section 3.2). This feedback consists of three simple values; *good, bad* and *undetected*, and they have to be introduced through authorised hand-held interfaces and sent back to the gateway. When this feedback is received by the gateway, it has to be managed by the Diagnostic module to rate the final behaviour of the Prediction module and the Detection module. Given that we predict infrastructural anomalies and detect control anomalies, such feedback also has to include the type of resolution; i.e. an infrastructural issue or a control issue. With all of this information, the Diagnostic module has to compute a set of counters, which are declared as follows:

- Two counters of *True Positive* ($C_{PredictionTP}$ and $C_{DetectionTP}$) are incremented whenever a suspicious threat was properly predicted/detected by the system, and the human operator's feedback indicates a 'good' value.
- Two counters of *False Positive* ($C_{PredictionFP}$ and $C_{DetectionFP}$) are incremented whenever a suspicious threat was not correctly predicted/detected, and the human operator's feedback signals it as a 'bad' value.
- Two counters of *False Negative* ($C_{PredictionFN}$ and $C_{DetectionFN}$) are incremented whenever the human operator's feedback indicates the presence of an undetected critical situation (an 'undetected' value), and the approach was not able to detect it.
- Two counters of *True Negative* ($C_{PredictionTN}$ and $C_{DectionTN}$) are incremented whenever a valid situation (e.g. $volt_i \in [V_{min}, V_{max}]$) happens within the system and it was properly classified by the system as innocuous.

Considering all these variables, the Diagnostic module has to find the way to evaluate the precision of our mechanism throughout its entire life-cycle. To this end, a set of metrics and measures of contingency described in [17] have been considered for our mechanism. These metrics consist of estimating the 'precision' by eventually computing the equations of Table 3.

Table 3 also shows us a set of thresholds, namely $T_{PredictionFP}$, $T_{PredictionFN}$, $T_{DetectionFP}$, $T_{DetectionFN}$, which should be defined to control the real level of precision of the modules. Note that the threshold for false negative rates should be much more restrictive with respect to the rest, since it is unacceptable that a control system cannot be able to predict/detect undesirable situations. Thus, when a false negative rate (either $C_{PredictionFN}$ or $C_{DectectionFN}$) is higher than its prescribed threshold, a report should be generated to warn the SCADA Center of the situation immediately. In this case, the organisation will have to analyse, for example, the possibility of extending the value of $\Delta_{Tdiagnostic}$ for detection or changing the probabilities of the transition between states for prediction. In contrast, a high false positive rate is not really a problem for critical

Table 3. Precision Levels of the Prevention and Detection modules

Rate	Prevention	Detection
True Positive	$\dfrac{C_{PredictionTP}}{C_{PredictionTP}+C_{PredictionFP}}$	$\dfrac{C_{DetectionTP}}{C_{DetectionTP}+C_{DetectionFP}}$
False Positive	$\dfrac{C_{PredictionFP}}{C_{PreventionFP}+C_{PreventionTN}} \leq T_{PredictionFP}$	$\dfrac{C_{DetectionFP}}{C_{PreventionFP}+C_{PreventionTN}} \leq T_{DetectionFP}$
False Negative	$\dfrac{C_{PredictionFN}}{C_{PreventionFN}+C_{PreventionTP}} \leq T_{PredictionFN}$	$\dfrac{C_{DetectionFN}}{C_{PreventionFN}+C_{PreventionTP}} \leq T_{DetectionFN}$

environments given that this fact does not imply a loss of critical warnings. Lastly, it is worth stressing that the Prediction and Detection modules maintain a narrow relationship with each other. If the Detection module is not able to detect a delay attack, it is possible that the Prediction module increases its $C_{PredictionFN}$, since critical alarms may be delayed. Similarly, if a relay attack appears within the network, the values sequence may change the value of $C_{PredictionFN}$ or the $C_{PredictionFP}$ by re-sending messages with priority [0,2] or [3], respectively.

4   Conclusion

In this paper we have modelled a preventive and reactive system based on four main types of technologies: IWSNs, MANETs, the Internet and the ISA100.11a standard. With this, we aim to show the capabilities of these technologies for prevention, detection and response in critical environments, and of course, cover some still pending challenges for WASA. As a result, the proposed system is able to warn of an emergency situation in advance, detect anomalous behaviours and respond against crisis situations in order to minimise security risks and avoid a cascading effect. On the other hand, the solution, called here PDR, is also able to evaluate by itself the level of precision of its components of prevention and detection. This process will help the SCADA Center to maintain an exhaustive report corresponding to the functionality and reliability of the control service in the field and at any time.

Lastly, it is essential to continue advancing in this research area since there are a lot of open issues that need to be dealt with, such as security and connectivity problems when heterogeneous devices are being connected. For this reason, our next goal is to research how to connect sensors to the Internet [18] when gateways are not working, and how alarms and measurements can reach the SCADA Center in emergency situations in a secure manner. Likewise, it would also be interesting to (i) provide location privacy mechanisms so as to protect the deployment of sensors and their visibility with respect to external threats [19]; and (ii) design and adapt lightweight computational intelligence techniques (e.g., expert systems or learning mechanisms) that may substitute the presence of human operators in the field.

References

1. Alcaraz, C., Lopez, J.: Analysis of Requirements for Critical Control Systems. In: Sixth IFIP WG 11.10 International Conference on Critical Infrastructure Protection. National Defense University, Washington DC (2012)
2. Atputharajah, A., Saha, T.K.: Power System Blackouts - Literature Review. In: International Conference on Industrial and Information Systems (ICIIS), pp. 460–465 (2009)
3. NIST. NIST Framework and Roadmap for Smart Grid Interoperability Standards, Release 2.0. NIST Special Publication 1108R2 (February 2012)
4. ANSI/ISA-99.02.01-2009 Standard. Security for Industrial Automation and Control Systems Part 2: Establishing an Industrial Automation and Control Systems Security Program (2009)
5. Alcaraz, C., Lopez, J., Zhou, J., Roman, R.: Secure SCADA Framework for the Protection of Energy Control Systems. Concurrency and Computation Practice & Experience 23(12), 1414–1430 (2011)
6. Alcaraz, C., Lopez, J.: A Security Analysis for Wireless Sensor Mesh Networks in Highly Critical Systems. IEEE Transactions on Systems, Man, and Cybernetics, Part C: Applications and Reviews 40(4), 419–428 (2010)
7. Roman, R., Lopez, J., Gritzalis, S.: Situation Awareness Mechanisms for Wireless Sensor Networks. IEEE Communications Magazine 46(4), 102–107 (2008)
8. Weisong, H., Hongmei, X.: Large-scale wireless sensor networks situation awareness using multivariate time series association rules mining. In: 2010 International Conference on Communications, Circuits and Systems (ICCCAS), pp. 95–97 (2010)
9. Peerenboom, J., Fisher, R.: Analyzing Cross-Sector Interdependencies. In: HICSS, pp. 112–119. IEEE Computer Society (2007)
10. Güngör, V., Lu, B., Hancke, G.: Opportunities and Challenges of Wireless Sensor Networks in Smart Grid. IEEE Transactions on Industrial Electronics 57(10), 3557–3564 (2010)
11. Oxford Dictionary. Anomaly, http://oxforddictionaries.com/definition/anomaly (retrieved on March 2012)
12. Zhou, Y., Fang, Y., Zhang, Y.: Securing Wireless Sensor Networks: a Survey. IEEE Communications Surveys Tutorials 10(3), 6–28 (2008)
13. ZigBee Alliance. ZigBee PRO, http://www.zigbee.org/ (retrieved on March 2012)
14. HART. WirelessHART Technology, http://www.hartcomm.org (retrieved on March 2012)
15. Ebrahimi, M.S., Daraei, M.H., Behzadan, V., Khajooeizadeh, A., Behrostaghi, S.A., Tajvidi, M.: A novel utilization of cluster-tree wireless sensor networks for situation awareness in smart grids. In: Innovative Smart Grid Technologies Asia, pp. 1–5 (2011)
16. Gupta, G., Younis, M.: Fault-tolerant Clustering of Wireless Sensor Networks. IEEE Wireless Communications and Networking 3, 1579–1584 (2003)
17. Salfner, F.: Event-based Failure Prediction An Extended Hidden Markov Model Approach. PhD thesis, Humboldt-Universitätzu Berlin (2008)
18. Lopez, J., Alcaraz, C., Najera, P., Roman, R.: Wireless Sensor Networks and the Internet of Things: Do We Need a Complete Integration? In: First International Workshop on the Security of the Internet of Things (SecIoT 2010), Tokyo, Japan (2010)
19. Zhu, W., Xiang, Y., Zhou, J., Deng, R., Bao, F.: Secure Localization with Attack Detection in Wireless Sensor Networks. IJIS 10, 155–171 (2011)

Embedded Cyber-Physical Anomaly Detection in Smart Meters

Massimiliano Raciti and Simin Nadjm-Tehrani

Department of Computer and Information Science, Linköping University
SE-581 83 Linköping, Sweden
{massimiliano.raciti,simin.nadjm-tehrani}@liu.se

Abstract. Smart grid security has many facets, ranging over a spectrum from resisting attacks aimed at supervisory and control systems, to end user privacy concerns while monitored by the utility enterprise. This multi-faceted problem also includes vulnerabilities that arise from deployment of local cyber-physical attacks at a smart metering location, with a potential to a) manipulate the measured energy consumption, and b) being massively deployed aiming at destabilisation. In this paper we study a smart metering device that uses a trusted platform for storage and communication of metering data, and show that despite the hard core security, there is still room for deployment of a second level of defence as an embedded real-time anomaly detector that can cover both the cyber and physical domains.

1 Introduction

Limitations of today's power networks, combined with the need for sustainable energy resources has led to promotion of smart grid architectures [1]. These promise higher reliability due to the inherently distributed nature of production and distribution, higher efficiency due to incorporation of mass scale sensors and faster management dynamics, and fine-grained adaptation to local failures and overloads. The large scale deployment of such networks is, however, dependent on exploitation of standard (IP-based) protocols, commodity sensors and actuators, and the ability of vendors to create a trusted environment on which adaptations of supply and demand can be based. The notion of cyber-physical systems, aiming to cover the "virtually global and locally physical" [2] is nowadays used even to encompass smart grids as an illustrating example.

Security is one of the less developed attributes in the cyber-physical domain. While security is indeed part of the grand challenges facing large scale development of cyber-physical systems, the focus of smart grid security is increasingly on threats to control systems [3], or serving the privacy of the end user while being subject to monitoring [4]. In this paper we address the risk of manipulations at the end-user level, even when a trusted infrastructure is assumed to be present at the smart metering end points.

B. Hämmerli, N. Kalstad Svendsen, and J. Lopez (Eds.): CRITIS 2012, LNCS 7722, pp. 34–45, 2013.
© Springer-Verlag Berlin Heidelberg 2013

The contributions of this paper are as follows:

1. We analyse the design of a smart meter which uses trusted computing technology to enforce strong security requirements, and we show the existence of a weakness in the forthcoming end-nodes, justifying real-time anomaly detection.
2. We propose an architecture for embedded anomaly detection for both the cyber and physical domains in smart meters and create an instance of a clustering-based anomaly detection algorithm in a prototype under industrial development.
3. We illustrate the detection of cyber attacks, which in principle can be script-based and massively deployed, and provide the infrastructure owner with reliable alerts.

The rest of the paper is organised as follows: Section 2 discusses the related work in this field, Section 3 presents the smart metering infrastructure, Section 4 discusses our proposed anomaly detection architecture and Section 5 shows the detection results on some cyber-attacks performed on a prototype of a smart meter.

2   Related Work

Smart grid cyber security has been a hot topic in recent years, with both researchers, industry and organisations involved in the definition of security requirements and standard solutions [5–7].

The Advanced Metering Infrastructure (AMI) is particularly vulnerable to cyber attacks, and careful attention has been given to its specific security requirements analysis [8]. Confidentiality, privacy, accountability, integrity and availability are critical requirements for accurate electricity billing and real-time power demand estimation. Cleveland [8] points out that encryption alone is not the solution that matches all the requirements, and automated diagnostics, physical and cyber intrusion detection can be means of preventing loss of availability.

Intrusion detection has been considered as a possible defence strategy in AMIs. Berthier et al. [9, 10] highlight the need for real-time monitoring in AMI systems. They propose a distributed specification-based approach to anomaly detection in order to discover and report suspicious behaviours during network or host operations. The advantage of this approach, which consists of detecting deviation from high-level models (specifications) of the system under study, is the effectiveness on checking whether the system follows the specified security policies. The main disadvantages are the high development cost and the complexity of the specifications.

Kush et al. [11] analyse the gap between conventional IDS systems and the specific requirements for smart grid systems. They find that an IDS must support legacy hardware and protocols, be scalable, standard compliant, adaptive to changes, deterministic and reliable. They evaluate a number of existing IDS approaches for SCADA systems, the approach by Berthier et al. and few conventional IDS systems that could be applied to AMIs, and they verify that none of them satisfies all the functional requirements.

Beside cyber attacks, physical attacks are also a major cause of concern. Electricity theft is the main motivation that induces unethical customers to tamper with the meters, and the minimisation of energy theft is a major reason why smart metering practice has been initiated. McLaughlin et al. [12, 13], however, show that smart meters offer even more vulnerabilities compared to the old electromechanical meters. Physical tampering, password extraction, eavesdropping and meter spoofing can be easily performed with commodity devices.

An approach for discovering theft detection with smart metering data is discussed in Kadurek et al. [14]. They devise two phases: during the first phase the energy balance at particular substations of the distribution systems is monitored. If the reported consumption is different from the measured one, an investigation phase aims as locating the point where the fraud is taking place.

In our environment the security requirements for AMI are fulfilled using trusted computing technology, complemented by our proposed embedded anomaly detection architecture that takes into account both the cyber and the physical domain.

3   The Trusted Smart Metering Infrastructure

The Trusted Sensor Network (TSN) [15] is a smart metering infrastructure defined as a use case within the EU FP7 SecFutur Project [16]. The main goal of this solution is to ensure authenticity, integrity, confidentiality and accountability of the metering process in an environment where multiple organisations can operate and where legal calibration requirements must be fulfilled [15]. This goal is achieved by a careful definition of the security requirements supported by trusted computing techniques. As depicted in Figure 1, a Trusted Sensor Module (TSM) is located in each household. The energy measurements produced by one or more sensors are encrypted and certified by the TSM, which sends them to a Trusted Sensor Module Collector (TSMC). This component gathers the data coming from several TSMs and relays it to the operator server infrastructure

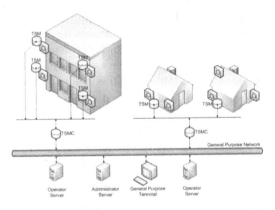

Fig. 1. Trusted Smart Metering Infrastructure [15]

for its storage. Through the general purpose network several organisations can get remote access to the functionality of the metering system for installation, configuration and maintenance, but strict access policies and accountability of the actions are enforced.

A smart meter in this architecture is called Trusted Meter (TM), and it can be composed of one of more physical sensors, one or more TSMs and one TSMC. A detailed description of the architecture is presented elsewhere [15].

MixedMode^{TM}, a partner company within the SecFutur project, has developed a prototype of a Trusted Meter, described in the next section.

3.1 Trusted Meter Prototype

The prototype of a TM is composed of one physical sensor and includes the functionalities of a TSM and a TSMC. The sensor is an ADE7758 integrated circuit, which is able to measure the accumulated active, reactive and apparent power. The functionality of the sensor is accessible via several registers that can be read or written through its interface to the Serial Peripheral Interface (SPI) bus. There is a variety of registers that can be accessed for reading out energy measurements, configuring the calibration parameters, operational states etc.

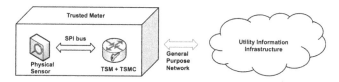

Fig. 2. Trusted Meter

The sensor is then interfaced with an OMAP 35x system where the functionalities of the TSM and TSMC are implemented in software, with the addition of specialised hardware, namely Trusted Platform Module (TPM), that provides the trusted computing functionalities. The system, running Ångström Linux, uses secure boot to ensure that the hardware and software modules are not corrupted and encryption is used to send out the readings to the operator servers.

3.2 Threats

After a careful study of the security requirements of the system, the applied security mechanisms and the design of the meter prototype, we came up with the following observations:

- The consumption measurements, certificates, and credential recorded in the processor module (OMAP 35x) will not be subject to change by malware or external applications due to the use of TPM technology, which also prevents typical smart meter vulnerabilities reported in an earlier work [12].
- The metering data that is sent out to the operator servers is encrypted by the application, hence secure while in transmission.

– The weakest point in the system is represented by the unprotected physical connection between the sensor and the OMAP 35x system where the TSM and TSMC functionalities are implemented.

The main threat is hence represented by potential man-in-the middle attacks on the SPI bus that affect the values of data or commands transmitted, as depicted in Figure 3.

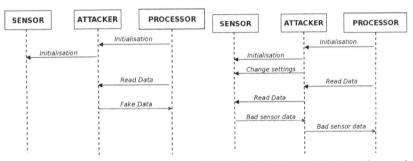

(a) Manipulation of consumption val-(b) Manipulation or injection of control
ues   commands

Fig. 3. Possible attack on the communication bus

A possible solution would be again based on encryption of the messages prior to the transmission on the SPI bus. This could be applicable in the cases when the sensor and the TSM are two physically separate modules, but when it comes to an embedded system, encryption would dramatically increase the complexity of the sensor circuitry, that must be kept cheap due to the large scale deployment.

The above analysis shows the need for real-time monitoring for intrusion detection is still present although trusted platforms offer higher level of protection than earlier solutions. This motivates proposing an embedded anomaly detection as potential technology to explore.

4   Embedded Anomaly Detection

The proposed embedded anomaly detection architecture is devised to be included in the functionality of the Trusted Meter. Figure 4 illustrates the main components of the architecture. It consists of five modules: a data logger, a data preprocessor, two anomaly detection modules and an alert aggregator. The data logger is in charge of listening for communication events and data exchange through the sensor-TSM channel. It will record both the cyber domain information, i.e. packet headers or connections, as well as the physical energy measurements.

The data preprocessor is in charge of transforming the raw signals detected on the channel into feature vectors that can be fed to the anomaly detection modules for evaluation of current state.

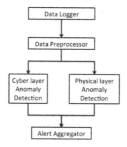

Fig. 4. Proposed Cyber-Physical Anomaly Detection Architecture

Anomaly detection consists of two modules: one is used for the cyber layer, i.e. the communication protocol on the SPI bus in the prototype meter, while the second is used to detect anomalies on the physical layer, the actual energy consumption that is reported by the sensor. The motivation for this distinction is the need for having two different time scales on the state estimation in the two domains: while the cyber communication can be monitored and suspicious events detected within seconds, anomalies on the physical domain need to be discovered in the order of days or weeks. This is due to the fact that load profiles change detection is only meaningful when based on a sufficiently long time window. The two modules complement each other: while command injection on the bus can be detected by the cyber layer anomaly detector, consumption data manipulation leading to changing consumption statistics can be detected by the physical layer anomaly detector.

The last component of the architecture, the alert aggregator, takes as input the alarms generated by the two anomaly detector modules and decides whether anomalous behaviour should be reported to the central system.

In the following sections we will describe the modules in depth and present their implementation in our current test system.

4.1 Data Logger

In the prototype meter, the unprotected communication channel between the sensor and the TSM+TSMC module is the SPI bus. The SPI communication is always initiated by the processor (in the OMAP 35X system) who writes, in the communication register of the sensor, a bit that specifies whether the operation is a read or a write command, followed by the address of the register that needs to be accessed. The second part of the communication is the actual data transfer from or to the addressed register of the sensor. The application that implements the TSM and TSMC functionalities performs an energy reading cycle every second, sending calibrations or configuration commands when required.

Our bus logger records the following information: the timestamp of the operation, the command type (read or write), the register involved in the operation of the value that is read or written. In our experimental setup, as described later, the data logged at the driver level of the SPI interface of the TSM+TSMC side sufficed for our evaluation. However, bus messages should be sniffed and logged by an external element in order to record all the commands received by the ADE7758 sensor, and its deployment will be considered in the design of the next version of the prototype.

4.2   Data Preprocessing and Feature Extraction

The data preprocessor receives records in the format presented in the previous section, and produces vectors of features that will be processed by the anomaly detectors. A common data preprocessor for both domains avoids processing the received data twice. The features selected are numerical variables that together represent the normal operation of the system. For the cyber domain, these are based on information regarding the frequency and types of operations carried out on the SPI bus during a period of observation time I. There are three categories of features:

- **Operation Type:** percentage of number of read or write operations performed in the period of observation I. An additional feature counts the number of times the read-only registers are accessed, which is useful to capture the fact that most of the time (every second in our case) the communication is performed to read out energy measurements.
- **Category Type:** percentage of the number of times the registers of the following categories are accessed in the period of observation I: *reading, configuration, interrupt, calibration, event, info*. The first category includes registers used for accumulation of active, reactive and apparent energy accumulation for the three different phases. Register categorised as *configuration* are those used for configuring different operational parameters of the energy measurement. Registers in the category *interrupt* are interrupt status flags. Registers included in the *event* category are used to store information on events such as voltage or current peak detection etc. The category *calibration*, groups the important registers used to calibrate the different parameters of the sensor. Finally, the *info* category groups registers where checksums and the version of the sensor are stored.
- **Register Frequencies:** usage frequency of each individual register addressed in the period of observation I.

These features are designed to characterise the typical communication patterns, therefore anomalous communication sequences or register access rates should be discovered by the anomaly detector.

In the physical domain, commonly used indices for customers characterisation, based on load profiles, can be utilised as features. These include daily indices, as the widely used indices proposed in Ernoult et al. [17], such as the non-uniformity coefficient $\alpha = \frac{P_{min}}{P_{max}}$, the fill-up coefficient $\beta = \frac{P_{avg}}{P_{max}}$, the modulation coefficient at peak hours $MC_{ph} = \frac{P_{avg,ph}}{P_{avg}}$ and the modulation coefficient at non-peak hours $MC_{oph} = \frac{P_{avg,oph}}{P_{avg}}$, where P_{min} is the minimum power demand reported during the day, P_{max} is the maximum power demand, P_{avg} is the average power demand,

$P_{avg,ph}$ is the average power demand during the peak hours and $P_{avg,oph}$ is the power demand during the off-peak hours. More refined indices that take into account weekly patterns (working days and weekends) can be added, as those described in Chicco et al. [18].

4.3 Cyber-Layer Anomaly Detection Algorithm

The sensor-processor communication is based on a series of messages exchanged through the bus. In this context, the set of possible combinations is not very large, due to the fact the set of registers accessible is bounded. The behaviour in terms of the commands sequences, captured by the features selected, can be considered as data points that fall into certain regions of the multidimensional features space. In order to identify the good behaviour, an algorithm that is able to identify these regions and consider them as the normality space would be needed.

Therefore, we have adopted and embedded an instance of a clustering-based anomaly detection algorithm [19] that uses a smart indexing strategy and is therefore computationally efficient. Section 5 presents the evaluation of this algorithm.

4.4 Physical-Layer Anomaly Detection Algorithm

The features available for modelling the physical domain suggest that when the load profile changes due to an eventual attack, the statistics over a long period would be affected. A lightweight change detection algorithm can therefore be embedded into the smart meter. A statistical anomaly detector using the indicators described in Section 4.2 has been developed. However, due to absence of long term data and ability to train and test the anomaly detector on consumed electricity profiles, we have focused development and tests on the cyber level attacks.

4.5 Alert Aggregator

The last component of the architecture is in charge of collecting the alerts generated by the anomaly detector modules, and performing aggregation in order to reduce the number of alarms sent to the central operator. The alert aggregation module can gather additional information in order to provide statistics that show the evidence of an attack or the anomalous conditions. This creates a smart meter health although individual analysis would still require a lot of effort and privacy concerns would hinder its "careless" deployment. However, this can be useful when investigating areas in which non-technical losses (i. e. losses that are not caused by transmission and distribution operations) are detected, supporting for example localisation strategies as in [14]. Future works include further investigations and privacy-aware development of this module.

5   Evaluation

In this section we present the evaluation of the anomaly detection on a number of attacks performed in the cyber domain. We start presenting the methodology to collect the data for evaluation. Then we introduce the cyber attacks we performed and finally we show the outcomes of the clustering-based anomaly detection algorithm.

5.1   Data Collection

In order to obtain data for training and testing the anomaly detection algorithm, the trusted meter prototype has been installed in a household and real energy consumption measurements have been collected during a period of two weeks in January 2012. Although this frame of time is not long enough to capture normality for the physical domain, it is representative enough for the cyber domain, where a 187MB data log file has been collected. The log, produced by the data logger module as explained in section 4.1, is composed of bus communication transactions that involve several registers for energy reading, sensor configurations, calibration commands and sensor events. The energy reading operations are performed with a period of one second, and they are predominant in the dataset. The data preprocessor, as presented in section 4.2, gathers the transactions during a period of observation I which has been set to 10 seconds, and produces a feature vector that is processed by the anomaly detection algorithm.

5.2   Cyber Attacks and Data Partitioning

Four types of attack have been implemented:

1. **Data Manipulation Attack:** In this scenario, the attacker performs a man-in-the-middle attack in which the values of the registers involved in the energy measurement are lowered. This can be easily done by overwriting the signal on the bus on every reading cycle.
2. **Recalibration Attack:** This commands is injected on the bus in order to change the value of some registers that hold calibration parameters, causing the sensor to perform erroneous measurement adjustments during its operation.
3. **Reset Attack:** This command causes the content of the energy accumulation registers to be wiped out. It has to be executed within every reading cycle in order to reduce the reported energy consumption. In our scenario, we executed it with a period of one second, interleaving it with the period of the measurement process.
4. **Sleep Mode Attack:** This command puts the sensor into sleep mode, e.g. no measurements are taken. While in sleep mode, the sensor SPI interface still replies to the commands executed by the processor module, but the energy consumption is not accumulated by the sensor.

In our evaluation, we tested the attacks 2 to 4, since attack 1 does not produce new messages on the bus and it would only be detectable by the physical layer anomaly detector. The attacks were first implemented at application level, through the SPI interface drivers of the processor module. Since the data was collected in an attack-free scenario, a script has been implemented to weave the attack information into the clean data. Our traces consist of two weeks of logs in which 2/3 of the data represent normal conditions, and the remaining 1/3 is affected by one attack at a time. Thus 3 different testing traces were generated. However, a physical hardware that can implement such attacks on the bus (SecFat) is under development in the SecFutur project.

The anomaly detector algorithm is therefore trained with the feature vectors obtained by the first third of the data, while we tested with 3 traces in which half of the trace contains the remaining one third of normal data and the rest the normal data interleaved with an attack. When the data preprocessor computed the feature vectors, we manually set an oracle bit to indicate whether the features are affected by an attack or not. This will be helpful for comparison when evaluating the outcomes of the anomaly detection algorithm.

5.3   Results

During our evaluation, we have tuned the two classical parameters of the clustering-based anomaly detection algorithm which need to be configured manually in order to create a good normality model and optimise the search efficiency. These are the maximum number of clusters (M), and a cluster centroid distance threshold (E), that is used when determining whether a new data point falls within its closest cluster or not. The optimal number of clusters typically depends on the distribution of the input data into the multidimensional space. The threshold is also important, since during real-time monitoring it determines whether a new feature vector belongs to any pre-existing cluster or not. Therefore, in order to select a suitable combination of the two parameters, the outcomes of the detection were explored with M ranging from 10 to 100, and E ranging from 1 to 2.5.

The metrics used for evaluating the detection algorithm were the detection rate (DR), calculated from the percentage of feature vectors during the attack that are correctly classified as anomalous, and the false positive rate (FPR), which measures the percentage of normal observations that are erroneously classified as anomalous.

Our results show that the algorithm does not build a correct partitioning of the normality data when M is set to 10 and 20 with all the possible combinations of E. In the detection phase, all the observations (with or without attacks) are classified as anomalous, leading to 100% DR but with a 100% FPR rate. An optimal partitioning of the normality data is found when M is set to at least 30. In this case, the algorithm uses 18 clusters to model the data, and for every configuration of E in the range between 1 and 2 we get 100% DR with no false positives for all three types of attacks. In the cases when E is over 2 we allow a very large threshold and the detection rate is reduced to zero for the recalibration attack, since it is the attack type that is more similar to normal conditions where recalibration takes place in the training period. The results are similar when increasing M up to 100. This means that the algorithm finds 18 clusters to be the best number for modelling the normality data.

6   Conclusion and Future Work

In this paper we have analysed the vulnerabilities of a recently designed smart metering infrastructure. Although confidentiality, authenticity, accountability, integrity and privacy are provided by the use of TPM technology embedded into smart meters, some vulnerabilities persist and real-time monitoring for cyber and physical tampering attacks is still a security solution that must be considered when designing new smart meters. Therefore, we have explored deployment of a lightweight embedded anomaly detection architecture that takes into account both cyber and physical domains and implemented and evaluated part of this architecture on a smart meter prototype. The evaluation performed on attacks in this psuedo-real settings has shown that the algorithm is able to efficiently detect several types of attacks without emitting any false positive.

Further development will target the physical layer anomaly detector and the module that combines the outcomes of the detection on both domains and provides a smart meter health indicator to provide the utility company with a more accurate non-technical loss analysis.

Acknowledgments. This work has been financially supported by the Swedish National Graduate School in Computer Science (CUGS) and the EU FP7 SecFutur Project. Support by Niklas Carstens and Maurits Broxvall, from MixedMode, collaborating in the SecFutur project, is gratefully acknowledged.

References

1. Fang, X., Misra, S., Xue, G., Yang, D.: Smart grid-the new and improved power grid: A survey. IEEE Communications Surveys Tutorials PP(99), 1–37 (2011)
2. Rajkumar, R.R., Lee, I., Sha, L., Stankovic, J.: Cyber-physical systems: the next computing revolution. In: Proceedings of the 47th Design Automation Conference, DAC 2010, pp. 731–736. ACM (2010)
3. Alcaraz, C., Fernandez, G., Carvajal, F.: Security aspects of SCADA and DCS environments. In: Lopez, J., Setola, R., Wolthusen, S.D. (eds.) Critical Infrastructure Protection. LNCS, vol. 7130, pp. 120–149. Springer, Heidelberg (2012)
4. NISTIR 7628: Guidelines for Smart Grid Cyber Security. Privacy and the Smart Grid, vol. 2, http://csrc.nist.gov/publications/nistir/ir7628/nistir-7628_vol2.pdf (accessed June 2012)
5. NISTIR 7628: Guidelines for Smart Grid Cyber Security Requirements, http://csrc.nist.gov/publications/nistir/ir7628/introduction-to-nistir-7628.pdf (accessed June 2012)

6. Pallotti, E., Mangiatordi, F.: Smart grid cyber security requirements. In: 2011 10th International Conference on Environment and Electrical Engineering (EEEIC), pp. 1–4 (2011)
7. Lu, Z., Lu, X., Wang, W., Wang, C.: Review and evaluation of security threats on the communication networks in the smart grid. In: Military Communication Conference, MILCOM 2010, pp. 1830–1835 (2010)
8. Cleveland, F.: Cyber security issues for advanced metering infrastructure (ami). In: 2008 IEEE Power and Energy Society General Meeting - Conversion and Delivery of Electrical Energy in the 21st Century, pp. 1–5 (July 2008)
9. Berthier, R., Sanders, W., Khurana, H.: Intrusion detection for advanced metering infrastructures: Requirements and architectural directions. In: 2010 First IEEE International Conference on Smart Grid Communications (SmartGridComm), pp. 350–355 (October 2010)
10. Berthier, R., Sanders, W.: Specification-based intrusion detection for advanced metering infrastructures. In: 2011 IEEE 17th Pacific Rim International Symposium on Dependable Computing (PRDC), pp. 184–193 (December 2011)
11. Kush, N., Foo, E., Ahmed, E., Ahmed, I., Clark, A.: Gap analysis of intrusion detection in smart grids. In: Valli, C. (ed.) 2nd International Cyber Resilience Conference, Secau - Security Research Centre, pp. 38–46 (August 2011)
12. McLaughlin, S., Podkuiko, D., McDaniel, P.: Energy theft in the advanced metering infrastructure. In: Rome, E., Bloomfield, R. (eds.) CRITIS 2009. LNCS, vol. 6027, pp. 176–187. Springer, Heidelberg (2010)
13. McLaughlin, S., Podkuiko, D., Miadzvezhanka, S., Delozier, A., McDaniel, P.: Multi-vendor penetration testing in the advanced metering infrastructure. In: Proceedings of the 26th Annual Computer Security Applications Conference. ACSAC 2010, pp. 107–116. ACM (2010)
14. Kadurek, P., Blom, J., Cobben, J., Kling, W.: Theft detection and smart metering practices and expectations in the netherlands. In: 2010 IEEE PES Innovative Smart Grid Technologies Conference Europe (ISGT Europe), pp. 1–6 (2010)
15. Broxvall, M.: Metering devices with legal calibration requirements, Deliverable D2.1, http://www.secfutur.eu/WP2/Deliverables/D2.1/Deliverable_D2_1.pdf (accessed May 2012)
16. EU SecFutur FP7 Project, http://www.secfutur.eu (accessed June 2012)
17. Ernoult, M., Meslier, F.: Analysis and forecast of electrical energy demand. In: Revue générale de l'électricité, vol. 4 (1982)
18. Chicco, G., Napoli, R., Postolache, P., Scutariu, M., Toader, C.: Electric energy customer characterisation for developing dedicated market strategies. In: 2001 IEEE Porto Power Tech Proceedings, vol. 1, p. 6 (2001)
19. Burbeck, K., Nadjm-Tehrani, S.: Adaptive real-time anomaly detection with incremental clustering. Information Security Technical Report - Elsevier 12(1), 56–67 (2007)

Improving Control System Cyber-State Awareness Using Known Secure Sensor Measurements

Ondrej Linda, Milos Manic, and Miles McQueen

Abstract. This paper presents design and simulation of a low cost and low false alarm rate method for improved cyber-state awareness of critical control systems - the Known Secure Sensor Measurements (KSSM) method. The KSSM concept relies on physical measurements to detect malicious falsification of the control systems state. The KSSM method can be incrementally integrated with already installed control systems for enhanced resilience. This paper reviews the previously developed theoretical KSSM concept and then describes a simulation of the KSSM system. A simulated control system network is integrated with the KSSM components. The effectiveness of detection of various intrusion scenarios is demonstrated on several control system network topologies.

Keywords: Cyber-Security, Critical Control Systems, State-Awareness.

1 Introduction

Resiliency and enhanced state-awareness are crucial properties of modern control systems. Especially critical infrastructures, such as energy production and industrial systems, would significantly benefit from being equipped with intelligent components for timely reporting and understanding of the status of the control system. This goal can be achieved via complex system monitoring, real-time system behavior analysis and timely reporting of the system state to the responsible human operators [1].

In [2] a resilient control system was defined as follows: "... one that maintains state awareness and an accepted level of operational normalcy in response to disturbances, including threats of an unexpected and malicious nature". Here, the enhanced state-awareness is understood as a set of diverse performance criteria such as cyber or intelligent analysis that is used to maximize the adaptive capacity of the system to respond to threats.

Falsification of physical system state can pose significant danger to the operation of a control system. During system state falsification, an intelligent adversary attempts to deceive the operator with the intention to achieve desired manipulation of the control system without early detection. An intuitive way for achieving this task is modification of physical measurement values sent to the operators by injecting false information. Hence, protection of measurement values is of high importance. There exist crypto graphic techniques that provide sufficient level of information protection [3], [4]. However these techniques require increased computational cycles, increased power, and higher available network bandwidth, which might not be available on many currently deployed control systems.

B. Hämmerli, N. Kalstad Svendsen, and J. Lopez (Eds.): CRITIS 2012, LNCS 7722, pp. 46–58, 2013.

To address these issues, a novel low cost, low false alarm rate, and high reliability detection technique for identifying manipulation of critical physical process and falsification of system state was previously proposed [5], [6]. This technique, called Known Secure Sensor Measurements (KSSM), uses the idea of obtaining a randomly selected subset of encrypted (i.e. known secure) physical measurements that are sent in sequence after the plain-text (i.e. insecure and unencrypted) measurements used for control. The subsequent comparison of the randomly selected plain-text and the KSSM values reveals potential system falsification. By randomly modifying this selected subset of KSSM sensors, a complex cyber-state awareness of the control system and falsification of system state can be maintained while imposing as little additional computational and bandwidth cost as desired. Hence, by utilizing the physical measurements themselves for aiding cyber-security, the KSSM method differs from traditional approaches to network system security such as anomaly or signature detection systems [7]-[10].

This paper describes the design and simulation of the KSSM method. First, the overall architecture of the system is presented, followed by description of the two major components, Sensor Selector and Signal Analyzer. The Sensor Selector uses an algorithm to perform pseudo-random sensor selection based on multiple criteria. The Signal Analyzer contains a buffer of requested KSSM values and performs measurement comparison and system state falsification detection. The designed KSSM system architecture was integrated with a virtual control system communication network. The performance of the system is demonstrated on several test scenarios.

The rest of the paper is organized as follows. Section 2 reviews the previously proposed KSSM concept, followed by description of the design and simulation of the KSSM enabled control system in Section 3. Experimental testing is presented in Section 4 and the paper is concluded in Section 5.

2   Known Secure Sensor Measurement Concept

The concept of Known Secure Sensor Measurements was previously proposed in [5]. The KSSM technique constitutes a novel low cost, low false alarm rate, and high reliability detection technique for identifying malicious manipulation of critical physical processes and the associated falsification of system state. The fundamental idea of the method is to obtain a randomly selected subset of encrypted (known secure) physical measurements that are sent in sequence after the plain-text (unencrypted) measurements used for control. The comparison of the randomly selected plain-text and KSSM values reveals potential falsification of system state.

The developed KSSM concept was targeted for critical infrastructure control systems that lack robust crypto graphic techniques and have limited computational and communication bandwidth resources. It is important to note here that most critical infrastructures fit well within this targeted group. Hence, the KSSM method is widely applicable.

The fundamental assumption of the KSSM method is that the intelligent attacker is able to compromise any of the components in the information layer of the control system. The information layer is a communication layer which communicates physical process measurements to the process control layer, where they are presented to the operator. Fig. 1 depicts an exemplary hybrid energy production system with highlighted physical,

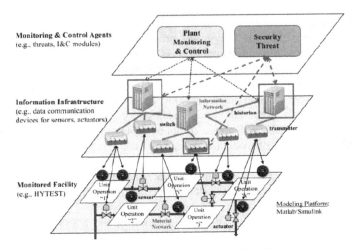

Fig. 1. Hybrid energy production facility [5]

information and process control layers. In addition, it is assumed that the attacker will not be detected in the system as long as no transmitted measurements values are modified or blocked. It is important to emphasize here that the KSSM concept is intended not to detect anomalous process activity or whether the system functions within its normal operation envelope. Instead, the KSSM concept is designed to verify the system state information presented to the operator and reject system state falsification due to adversarial sensor measurement value corruption.

The main hypothesis of the KSSM concept is the idea that a small subset of sensor measurements, which are known to be secure (i.e. cannot be falsified in the physical layer), has the potential to significantly improve the observability of adversarial process manipulation due to cyber-attack. Furthermore, randomly selecting this small subset of known secure sensors can harden the detection mechanism because which sensor measurements are being secured at particular time cannot be predicted by the attacker. Finally, it is assumed that there is only limited communication bandwidth available and the size of the selected KSSM sensor subset can be selected such that the real-time control of the system is not disrupted.

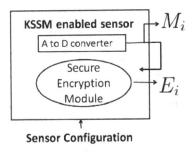

Fig. 2. Schema of a KSSM-enabled sensor [5]

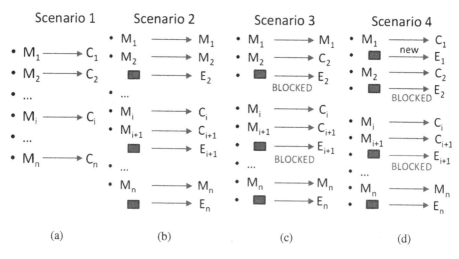

Fig. 3. Communication scenarios

In order to allow protection against an intelligent adversary, it must be possible to trust specific components of the system. In the KSSM system a cryptographic sensor module constitutes this trusted component as depicted in Fig. 2. The cryptographic sensor may be KSSM enabled with software or hardware as a means to forward the plain-text measurement value M_i through a secure encryption module to produce a KSSM value E_i. If the particular sensor is part of the randomly selected subset of KSSM sensors, the encrypted measurement value E_i is sent to the control room after the plain-text measurement M_i.

The KSSM control module resides in the control room of the plant. The module is responsible for performing selection of the random subset of KSSM-enabled sensors. In addition, the control module also compares the received KSSM values with the plain-text measurements in order to detect falsification of the system state.

Fig. 3 schematically depicts the considered system state falsification scenarios and the counter-measures used by the KSSM system. The plain system state falsification is demonstrated in Fig. 3(a). Here, the sensor measurements M_i are potentially corrupted by the attacker within the information layer. The falsified measurement values Ci reach the control operator. The basic idea of the KSSM system is depicted in Fig. 3(b), where a subset of the KSSM-enabled sensors is requested to report encrypted measurement values E_i to the control room. In this specific example, there will be a mismatch between values C_i and the decoded value of E_i. Further, an attacker aware of the KSSM protection system might attempt to deceive the system by blocking the encrypted values E_i from reaching the control room, as shown in Fig. 3(c). However, the KSSM system randomly modifies the subset of KSSM-enabled sensors, thus making it increasingly difficult for the attacker to design an attack with reliable detection delay. This is shown in Fig. 3(d), where the values C_1 and E_1 from the newly selected KSSM-enabled sensor would produce a mismatch and indicate a presence of system state falsification.

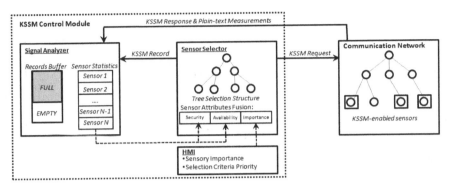

Fig. 4. Architecture of the KSSM system

3 Known Secure Sensor Measurement System Simulation

This section describes the design and simulation of the KSSM-equipped control systems. First the overall architecture is presented. Next its major components of Sensor Selector and Signal Analyzer are described in more detail.

3.1 KSSM System Architecture

The overall KSSM system architecture is depicted in Fig. 4. The system is composed of two major parts, the KSSM control module and the communication network, which connects the control module with those sensors that are KSSM-enabled. The KSSM control module is composed of two main components, the Signal Analyzer and the Sensor Selector. All components monitor the network traffic in the control system and communicate among each other to perform effective system state falsification detection while minimizing the impact on the system's communication bandwidth.

The Sensor Selector component is responsible for selecting a subset of KSSM-enabled sensors every time iteration. The sensor selection is performed using a tree-like sensor selection data structure, which resembles the known network topology. The Sensor Selector uses several criteria, including subjective human input to calculate the selection weight of each sensor. A randomization algorithm is then applied to ensure representative sensor selection from the communication network. Every time a subset of sensors is selected by the Sensor Selector a KSSM request is sent to the sensors and a KSSM record about the selection is stored in the Signal Analyzer.

The Signal Analyzer is responsible for monitoring both the plain-text unencrypted and the KSSM encrypted network messages. Everytime a KSSM record about sensor selection is received from the Sensor Selector, the Signal Analyzer stores the record in a record buffer. Upon receiving the previously requested KSSM message from the network, the KSSM value is paired with its plain-text value stored in the record buffer and their values are compared. The Signal Analyzer also keeps track of important network traffic statistics such as sensor availability and response latency, which are used for adjusting the sensor selection process.

3.2   KSSM Sensor Selector

The main task of the Sensor Selector is to perform randomized sensor selection every time iteration. To achieve this, the Sensor Selector contains an approximate model of the network topology in a form of a tree data structure. The root of the tree corresponds to the main communication node of the control system network. Branches connect the root node to possibly multiple-levels of nodes. Each node corresponds to a sub-network in the real network system. Finally, leafs of the tree structure correspond to individual KSSM-enabled sensors. It should be noted that it is not required for the tree structure to exactly match the real communication network topology. Rather, the branches of the tree should correspond to logical units in the control system network, in order to achieve evenly distributed sensor selection.

The process of sensor selection is performed by randomly descending from the root of the tree to particular leaf. All branches in the selection tree emanating from particular node are assigned a specific selection probability, which guides the random descending process. This method is repeated until the the new subset of KSSM enabled sensors has been selected. The branch selection probabilities are updated after selection of each sensor, so that more probability is distributed to the branches that were not assigned. The pseudo-code of this randomized sensor selection algorithm can be summarized as follows:

Step 1: Initialize the sensor selection probabilities p_{ij} of each branch in the selection tree.

Step 2: Repeat for all k KSSM sensors.

Step 2.1: Set current node n_i as root.

Step 2.2: Repeat, until current node n_i is a leaf.

Step 2.2.1: Randomly select j^{th} branch of current node n_i based on branch selection probabilities p_{ij}.

Step 2.2.2: If there exist unselected leafs in the sub tree connected to the jth branch descend to the jth children of current node n_i.

Step 2.3: Return the index of the sensor in the selected leaf.

Step 2.4: Repeat until current node n_i is a root

Step 2.4.1: For all siblings of current node n_i compute the new branch selection probability from their parent as:

$$p_{kj} = \begin{cases} p_{kj} = p_{kj}(1-\alpha), & k = i \\ p_{kj} = p_{kj} + \dfrac{\alpha \, p_{ij}}{(K-1)}, & k \neq i \end{cases}$$

$$(1)$$

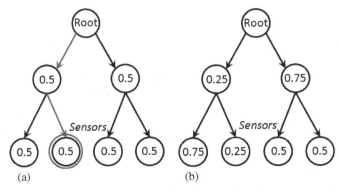

Fig. 5. Sensor selection tree before (a) and after selection (b). The sensor selection   is denoted by red color.

Step 2.4.2: Ascent to the parent of node n_i.

Coefficient α used in **Step 2.4.1** controls the spatial diversification of the selected sensors. Values close to 1 will result in large spatial diversification (e.g. sensors sampled in different areas of the network), while values closer to 0 will result in selected sensors being more likely to be close to each other (e.g. in the same sub-network). Parameter k denotes the cardinality of the selected KSSM sensor subset.

This process of KSSM enabled sensor selection and selection weight updates is depicted in Fig. 5. Due to the re-distribution of branch selection weights, the subset of sensors is more likely to be distributed throughout the network. Hence, KSSM and plain text message loss rate due to random component failures in parts of the communication system can be reduced.

After the subset of KSSM enabled sensors has been specified the Sensor Selector re-computes the initial branch selection probabilities in the selection tree to reflect the most current behavior of the communication system. These recomputed branch selection probabilities are used to initialize the tree parameters in **Step 1**. This process for computing the initial branch selection probabilities is composed of three parts: 1) sensor selection weight calculation, 2) bottom-up selection weight propagation, and 3) top-down selection probabilities normalization.

The sensor selection weight is calculated for each KSSM-enabled sensor based on a weighted average of three parameters: availability, security and importance. The availability can be computed as the inverse value of the averaged time interval of obtaining the requested KSSM value from the particular sensor. When the sensor response time increases, its availability is decreased and the sensor will be selected less often to ease the work-load of the particular sensor and its part of the network.

The security is computed as the averaged time-interval between receiving two mismatching KSSM-values and plain text values. Because random noise might corrupt the KSSM messages, single mismatch should not immediately raise an alarm. However, when the frequency of mismatched messages is significantly increased the security is increased, which results in sensor being selected more often to quickly converge to final detection. Here, a significant increase is considered to be an increase above the normal frequency of mismatched measurement values due to ordinary communication noise.

Finally, the importance attributed to a sensor is a subjective value provided by the operator, which can help to fine-tune the selection algorithm (e.g. some sensors might be more important for the control and thus should be sampled more often). In addition, the operator can specify the weighting coefficients for the weighted average of these attributes.

The bottom-up selection weight propagation proceeds in a recursive manner and its purpose is to propagate the sensor selection weights up the tree. The algorithm reads the selection weight from all children into their common parent, the weights are summed and recursively propagated to the higher level until the root node is reached.

In the final stage, the selection weights need to be converted into branch selection probabilities. This is achieved by descending from the tree root to individual leafs and normalizing the selection weights for all branches emanating from each node. The normalization procedure ensures that all branch selection probabilities sum up to 1 for each node.

3.3   KSSM Signal Analyzer

The main task of the Signal Analyzer is to monitor the network traffic and detect potential falsification of system state. Every time a KSSM request is sent to a particular sensor a record about this is stored in the record buffer in the Signal Analyzer. Upon receiving the KSSM measurement value, the corresponding plain-text measurement is looked up in the record buffer. The KSSM measurement is decrypted and compared to the plain-text value. A measurement mismatch can be used to indicate a potential presence of an intelligent adversary in the information layer of the system.

The intelligent adversary who is aware of the KSSM system might attempt to avoid detection by preventing the KSSM values from reaching the Signal Analyzer. For this reason, the record buffer contains an upper limit on the number of active KSSM records. When a KSSM message is blocked its plain-text counterpart will not be removed from the record buffer and the capacity of the buffer will be decreased. When this capacity reaches the specified threshold, an indication of potential attempt to falsify the system can be reported.

The Signal Analyzer also gathers important network traffic attributes, which are used to adapt the KSSM system to the specifics of the current network traffic. First, the time interval of requesting and receiving a KSSM value is computed for each sensor. This information is used to calculate the availability of individual KSSM-enabled sensors. Next, the time interval between obtaining two mismatched plain-text and KSSM values for each sensor is being monitored. This information is used to calculate the security of individual sensors and used for sensor selection. Finally, the Signal Analyzer stores the response time of obtaining the plain-text measurements, which can be used to monitor and adjust the appropriate size of the requested KSSM sensor subset so that the response of the control system is not affected. This adaptive mechanism is explained below.

The Signal Analyzer monitors the maximum response time of any plain-text sensors and compares that to the requested allowed response time. For example, if the sensor values should be reported to the control room once every second than the maximum allowed response time can be set to 0.8 seconds to create a safety buffer. The difference between maximum and the allowed response time creates a feedback signal that could be used to adjust the number of sampled KSSM sensors so that the real-time system response is not affected. When the maximum response time is below the allowed threshold for a certain period of time, the number k of sampled KSSM sensors is increased by one. Similarly, when the maximum response time is above the allowed threshold for certain amount of time, the number k of sampled KSSM sensors is decreased in order to preserve the real-time response of the system.

4   Experimental Results

This section first describes the implemented virtual communication network used as an experimental test-bed. Next, a set of testing scenarios is used to demonstrate the performance of the proposed KSSM system.

4.1   Experimental Test-Bed

In order to validate the performance of the designed KSSM system a virtual communication network was implemented. The network simulator models packet-based traffic in control system communication networks. The network is composed of communication nodes and sensor nodes. The communication nodes are equipped with packet buffers and routing tables. The packet buffer dispatches packets on first-in first-out basis. The sensor nodes can generate the plain-text measurement value as well as its encrypted version upon request.

The network simulator can simulate various deterministic as well as stochastic properties of the network. For example, the desired through-put can be set for individual network nodes as well as stochastic packet loss rates or packet corruption rates.

The KSSM Control module is connected to the communication network interface, where KSSM requests can be passed into the network and plain-text and KSSM messages can be received.

For the purpose of experimental testing a simple control system communication network has been constructed. The network gathers measurements from 9 sensors, which are grouped into 3 sub-networks as depicted in Fig. 6.

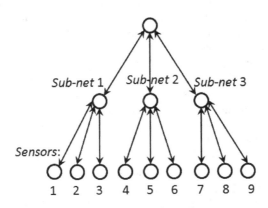

Fig. 6. Testing network topology

4.2   Sensor Selection

The purpose of the first testing scenario was to demonstrate the automatic adaptation of the sensor selection algorithm to reflect the current behavior of the observed network traffic. In this scenario, the control system is run for 10,000 seconds and the sensor data are gathered once every second. In addition, $k=2$ KSSM values are requested every second. The communication network is initialized with uniformly distributed time delay and packet loss and corruption rates throughout the entire network. Also, all of the selection criteria for individual sensors are weighted equally. Three events are used to simulate various changes of the environment to demonstrate the adaptation mechanism of the Sensor Selector.

Event 1: At time t = 2500s a possible cyber-attack is simulated on sensor 9. This attack is implemented as an increased packet corruption rate for the communication node of sensor 9, leading to increased number of mismatched plain-text and KSSM messages from sensor 9.

Event 2: At time t = 5000s the network traffic in sub-network 1 becomes congested, which is implemented as decreased through-put of particular communication nodes. Hence, the availability of sensors 1-3 is decreased.

Event 3: At time t = 7,500s the operator decides to adjust the sensor selection mechanism via the HMI by assigning weight 1.0 to the importance attribute and decreasing the weight of the security and availability attributes to 0.1. In addition, the operator subjectively increases importance of sensor 5 to its maximum value of 1.0.

Event 1 affects the security of sensor 9. The increased probability of obtaining an incorrect KSSM message from sensor 9 causes the time interval of receiving two mismatching plain-text and KSSM messages from sensor 9 to decrease. Hence, the security of this sensor is increased. This fact can be clearly observed in Fig. 7(a).

Event 2 affects the availability of sensors 1-3. After the time delay for messages from sub-network 1 was increased, the response time of the KSSM messages from sensors 1-3 were increased. This resulted in decreased availability of sensors 1-3 as shown in Fig. 7(b).

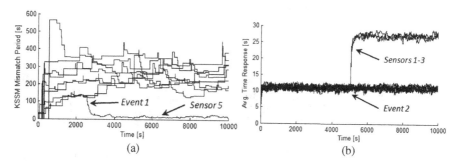

(a)   (b)

Fig. 7. KSSM values mismatch period (a) and average time response for various KSSM sensors (b)

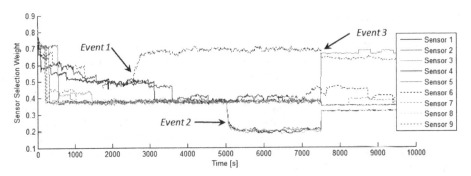

Fig. 8. Selection weight for different sensors during the test scenario

Fig. 8 shows the evolution of the sensor selection weight for individual sensors. It is apparent how the sensor selection weights are converging to a uniform distribution during the first 2,500s of the simulation. The diverse selection weights at the start of the simulation are due to the stochastic sampling process, which must be first averaged over certain amount of time to obtain good initial results. Next, it is apparent that the increased security of compromised sensor 9 when event 1 occurs leads to its increased selection weight. It can also be seen that the decreased availability of sensors 1-3 when event 2 occurs leads to their lower selection weight.

Finally, Event 3 at time 7,500s can be observed when the operator overrides the selection criteria importance and modifies the selection weight, which increases the weight of sensor 5 due to its higher importance.

To verify the influence of the sensor selection weight on the KSSM sensor sampling process, Fig. 9 shows histograms of sensor selection for the four quarters of the simulation. It can again be observed that the increased value of the security parameter leads to more frequently selecting sensor 9 in Fig. 9(b) and the decreased availability of sensors 1-3 leads to their less frequent selection in Fig. 9(c). Finally, the higher importance of sensor 5 results in its more frequent sampling together with sensor 9, which was likely compromised by an attacker, as shown in Fig. 9(d). In summary, Fig. 9 demonstrates that the KSSM system adjusts the sensor selection algorithm to obtain more samples from likely compromised sensors and to obtain less samples from congested parts of the network.

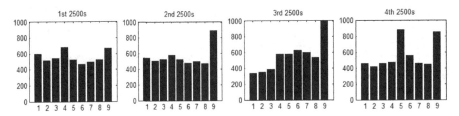

Fig. 9. Sensor selection histograms for different intervals of the simulation

4.3   Variable Network Bandwidth

The following test scenario was designed to demonstrate the automatic update of the number k of sampled KSSM messages. The essential property of the KSSM system is that it should use the available communication bandwidth in the control system network without compromising its real-time response. In this scenario, the identical communication network as shown in Fig. 6 was used. The network was simulated for 1,000s and the sensor measurements have been reported once every second.

In order to achieve the requested real-time response of obtaining sensor measurements once every second, a maximum desired response for plain-text measurement was set to 0.8s. For the initial 300s, the network was simulated with low average time-delay for individual network nodes (0.05s average latency of network node per packet). At time 300s the average time delay on the network nodes was increased to 0.1s. Finally, at time 600s the average time delay was increased to 0.15s. Note that the actual time delay for a specific packet was computed using a uniform distribution with standard deviation of 0.02s centered at the average time delay value.

Fig. 10 demonstrates this behavior of the system. First, Fig. 10(a) depicts the maximum observed response time of the plain-text measurements. It is apparent how this maximum response time increases at times 300s and 600s. Next, Fig. 10(b) shows the number k of selected KSSM sensors. The algorithm starts with k=0 KSSM sensors and first observes the maximum response time of the plain-text measurements. When this maximum response time is found to be below the desired threshold of 0.8s, the number k of selected KSSM messages is incrementally increased up to the maximum value of all 9 sensors sending encrypted messages.

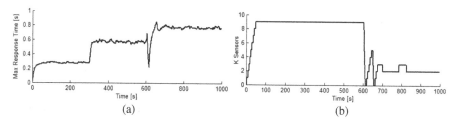

Fig. 10. Maximum response time of plain-text measurements (a) and the number of selected KSSM values (b)

The first increase in time-delay at time 300s increased the maximum response time (~0.6s) but did not yet exceed the desired performance. However, when the time-delay was again increased at time 600s, some of the plain-text measurements were not reported in the desired time and the KSSM system quickly decreased the number k of KSSM sensors, in order not to compromise the real-time response of the control system. Next, the KSSM control module attempted to increase the number of KSSM samples and observe its impact on network response time. Eventually, the number of KSSM values stabilized at k=2, which provided the maximum level of cyber-state awareness given the available communication bandwidth.

5   Conclusion

This paper presented a design and simulation of a low cost, low false and high reliability alarm rate method for improved cyber-state awareness of critical control systems - the Known Secure Sensor Measurements mechanism. The KSSM method relies on the physical measurements to detect malicious falsification of the control system's state. The KSSM technique can be incrementally integrated with already installed control systems for enhanced resilience.

First, the previously developed theoretical KSSM concept was reviewed and then its simulation was described. A virtual control system communication network was used to demonstrate the performance of the system. It was shown that the KSSM system can adapt its parameters to specific network behavior including the operator's request. Furthermore, it was demonstrated that the number of selected KSSM sensors can be automatically adapted to provide the maximum amount of cyber-state awareness while minimizing the impacts on the real-time performance of the control system.

The presented work constitutes a first step towards successful demonstration of the feasibility of the KSSM concept. The future work will be focused on additional experimental testing and implementation of the KSSM concept and on improving the sensor selection algorithm via computational intelligence techniques.

References

1. Linda, O., Manic, M., McJunkin, T.R.: Anomaly Detection for Resilient Control Systems Using Fuzzy-Neural Data Fusion Engine. In: Proc. IEEE Symposium on Resilient Control Systems (August 2011)
2. Rieger, C.G., Gertman, D.I., McQueen, M.A.: Resilient Control Systems: Next Generation Design Research. In: Proc. 2nd IEEE Conf. on Human System Interactions, Catania, Italy, pp. 632–636 (May 2009)
3. Stamp, M.: Information Security, ch. 3-5, 9, 2nd edn. John Wiley and Sons (2011)
4. Ferguson, N., Schneier, B., Kohno, T.: Cryptography Engineering, ch. 3-7 (2010)
5. McQueen, M., Giani, A.: 'Known Secure Sensor Measurements' for Critical Infrastructure Systems: Detecting Falsification of Systems State. In: Troubitsyna, E.A. (ed.) SERENE 2011. LNCS, vol. 6968, pp. 156–163. Springer, Heidelberg (2011)
6. Giani, A., Bitar, E., McQueen, M., Khargonekar, P., Poolla, K.: Smart Grid Data Integrity Attacks: Characterization and Countermeasures. In: Proc. of IEEE SmartGridComm (October 2011)
7. Linda, O., Vollmer, T., Manic, M.: Neural Network based Intrusion Detection System for Critical Infrastructure. In: Proc. IJCNN 2009 (June 2009)
8. Linda, O., Manic, M., Vollmer, T., Wright, J.: Fuzzy Logic Based Anomaly Detection for Embedded Network Security Cyber Sensor. In: Proc. of IEEE Symposium on Computational Intelligence, pp. 202–209 (April 2011)
9. Yang, D., Usynin, A., Hines, J.W.: Anomaly-Based Intrusion Detection for SCADA Systems. In: 5th Intl. Topical Meeting on Nuclear Plant Instrumentation, Control and Human Machine Interface Technologies (NPIC&HMIT 2005), Albuquerque, NM, November 12-16 (2006)
10. Zhong, S., Khoshgoftaar, T., Seliya, N.: Clustering-based network intrusion detection. Intl. Journal of Reliability, Quality and Safety 14(2), 169–187 (2007)

The Effects of Network Link Unreliability for Leader Election Algorithm in a Smart Grid System

Stephen Jackson and Bruce M. McMillin

Computer Science Department,
Missouri University of Science and Technology, Rolla, MO 65409, USA
{scj7t4,ff}@mst.edu

Abstract. Cyber-physical systems (CPS) can improve the reliability of our critical infrastructure systems. By augmenting physical distribution systems with digital control through computation and communication, one can improve the overall reliability of a network. However, a system designer must consider what effects system unreliability in the cyber-domain can have on the physical distribution system. In this work, we examine the consequences of network unreliability on a core part of a Distributed Grid Intelligence (DGI) for the FREEDM (Future Renewable Electric Energy Delivery and Management) Project. To do this, we apply different rates of packet loss in specific configurations to the communication stack of the software and observe the behavior of a critical component (Group Management) under those conditions. These components will allow us to identify the amount of time spent in a group, working, as a function of the network reliability.

Keywords: cyber-physical systems, critical infrastructure, reliability, leader election, stability.

1 Introduction

Historically, leader elections have had limited applications in critical systems. However, in the smart grid domain, there is a great opportunity to apply leader election algorithms in a directly beneficial way. [1] presented a simple scheme for performing power distribution and stabilization that relies on formed groups. Algorithms like Zhang, et. al's Incremental Consensus Algorithm [10], begin with the assumption that there is a group of nodes who coordinate to distribute power. In a system where 100% up time is not guaranteed, leader elections are a promising method of establishing these groups. A strong cyber-physical system should be able to survive and adapt to network outages in both the physical and cyber domains. When one of these outages occurs, the physical or cyber components must take corrective action to allow the rest of the network to continue operating normally. Additionally, other nodes may need to react to the state change of the failed node. In the realm of computing, algorithms for managing and detecting when other nodes have failed is a common distributed systems problem known as leader election.

B. Hämmerli, N. Kalstad Svendsen, and J. Lopez (Eds.): CRITIS 2012, LNCS 7722, pp. 59–70, 2013.

This work observes the effects of network unreliability on the the group management module of the Distributed Grid Intelligence (DGI) used by the FREEDM smart-grid project. This system uses a broker system architecture to coordinate several software modules that form a control system for a smart power grid. These modules include: group management, which handles coordinating nodes via leader election; state collection, a module which captures a global system state; and load balancing which uses the captured global state to bring the system to a stable state.

It is important for the designer of a cyber-physical system to consider what effects the cyber components will have on the overall system. Failures in the cyber domain can lead to critical instabilities which bring down the entire system if not handled properly. In fact, there is a major shortage of work within the realm of the effects cyber outages have on CPSs [7] [9]. In this paper we present a slice of what sort of analysis can be performed on a distributed cyber control by subjecting the system to packet loss. The analysis focuses on quantifiable changes in the amount of time a node of the system could spend participating in energy management with other nodes.

2 Background Theory

2.1 FREEDM DGI

The FREEDM DGI is a smart grid operating system that organizes and coordinates power electronics and negotiates contracts to deliver power to devices and regions that cannot effectively facilitate their own need.

To accomplish this, the DGI software consists of a central component, the broker, which is responsible for presenting a communication interface and furnishing any common functionality needed by any algorithms used by the system. These algorithms are grouped into modules.

This work uses a version of the FREEDM DGI software with only one module: group management. Group management implements a leader election algorithm to discover which nodes are reachable in the cyber domain.

2.2 Broker Architecture

The DGI software is designed around the broker architecture specification. Each core functionality of the system is implemented within a self contained module which is provided access to core interfaces which deliver functionality such as scheduling requests, message passing, and a framework to manipulate physical devices, including those which exist only in simulation environments such as PSCAD[2] and RSCAD[8].

The Broker provides a common message passing interface which all modules are allowed access to. This interface also provides the inter-module communication which delivers messages between software modules, effectively decoupling them outside of the requirement for them to be able to recognize messages addressed to them from other modules.

Several of the distributed algorithms used in the software require the use of ordered communication channels. To achieve this, FREEDM provides a reliable ordered communication protocol (The sequenced reliable connection or SRC) to the modules, as well as a "best effort" protocol (The sequenced unreliable connection or SUC) which is also FIFO (first in, first out), but provides limited delivery guarantees.

We elected to design and implement our own simple message delivery schemes in order to avoid complexities introduced by using TCP in our system. During development, we noticed that constructing a TCP connection to a node that had failed or was unreachable took a considerable amount of time. We elected to use UDP packets which do not have those issues, since the protocol is connectionless. From there, we were able to implement and develop our lightweight protocols which are very best effort oriented to deliver messages as quickly as possible within the following requirements.

Sequenced Reliable Connection. The sequenced reliable connection is a modified send and wait protocol with the ability to stop resending messages and move on to the next one in the queue if the message delivery time is too long. When designing this scheme we wanted to achieve several criteria:

- Messages must be accepted in order - Some distributed algorithm rely on the assumption that the underlying message channel is FIFO.
- Messages can become irrelevant - Some messages may only have a short period in which they are worth sending. Outside of that time period, they should be considered inconsequential and should be skipped. To achieve this, we have added message expiration times. After a certain amount of time has passed, the sender will no longer attempt to write that message to the channel. Instead, he will proceed to the next unexpired message and attach a "kill" value to the message being sent, with the number of the last message the sender knows the receiver accepted.
- As much effort as possible should be applied to deliver a message while it is still relevant.

There one adjustable parameter, the resend time, which controls how often the system would attempt to deliver a message it hadn't yet received an acknowledgment for.

Sequenced Unreliable Connection. The SUC protocol is simply a best effort protocol: it employs a sliding window to try to deliver messages as quickly as possible. A window size is decided, and then at any given time, the sender can have up to that many messages in the channel, awaiting acknowledgment. The receiver will look for increasing sequence numbers, and disregard any message that is of a lower sequence number than is expected. The purpose of this protocol is to implement a bare minimum: messages are accepted in the order they are sent.

Like the SRC protocol, the SUC protocol's resend time can be adjusted. Additionally, the window size is also configurable, but was left unchanged for the tests presented in this work.

2.3   Group Management Algorithm

Our software uses a leader election algorithm, "Invitation Election Algorithm" written by Garcia-Molina and listed in [4]. His algorithm provides a robust election procedure which allows for transient partitions. Transient partitions are formed when a faulty link between two or more clusters of DGIs causes the groups to temporarily divide. These transient partitions merge when the link is more reliable. The election algorithm allows for failures that disconnect two distinct sub-networks. These sub networks are fully connected, but connectivity between the two sub-networks is limited by an unreliable link. We have included the timeout we have set (the names are taken directly from [4]) in our tests in Table 1.

Table 1. Group Management Timeouts

Timeout	Duration
Proportional Timeout	10 - 30 seconds
Ready Timeout	10 seconds
Invite Timeout	5 seconds
Check Timeout	15 seconds
Timeout Timeout	10 seconds

The elected leader is responsible for making work assignments and identifying and merging with other coordinators when they are found, as well as maintaining a up-to-date list of peers for the members of his group. Likewise, members of the group can detect the failure of the group leader by periodically checking if the group leader is still alive by sending a message. If the leader fails to respond, the querying node will enter a recovery state and operate alone until they can identify another coordinator to join with.

2.4   Network Simulation

Network unreliability is simulated by dropping datagrams from specific sources on the receiver side. Each receiver was given an XML file describing the prescribed reliability of messages arriving from a specific source. The network settings were loaded at run time and could be polled if necessary for changes in the link reliability.

On receipt of a message, the broker's communication layer examine the source and select randomly based on the reliability prescribed in the XML file whether or not to drop a message. A dropped message was not delivered to any of the sub-modules and was not acknowledged by the receiver. Using this method we were able to emulate a lossy network link but not one with message delays.

2.5   System Implementation

The FREEDM DGI software uses a Broker Architectural pattern. This design is realized in C++ using the Boost Library[3]. We have also make use of other languages such as Python to provide bootstrapping and start-up routines for the software.

2.6   How the Network Reliability Simulator Fits into the Communication Stack

Because the DGI's network communication is implemented using UDP, there is a listener class which is responsible for accepting all incoming messages on the socket the system is listening on. This component is responsible for querying the appropriate protocol's class to determine if a message should be accepted. To do this, when a message is received, the message is parsed by the listener. At this point the network simulation will halt processing the message if it should be discarded based on the defined random chance in the configuration file. Otherwise, it is delivered to the addressed module.

3   Experimental Design

Tests were the system were completed by applying network settings and then running the nodes in the prescribed configuration for ten minutes (using the UNIX timeout command). At this point the test was terminated and the group management system appends statistics to an output file. New settings were applied and the next test was begun.

3.1   Tools Used, Systems Used

The application of settings and the initiation of tests was completed using a custom script written in Python. This script used a library, Fabric [5], to start runs of the system by the secure shell (SSH). This was run on one of the machine and monitored the I/O of all nodes to ensure everything was behaving correctly.

Our experimental software also provided for "bussing," where a group of edges would have the same reliability and were iterated together, and "fixing," which allowed for edges that would not change reliability across any of the runs.

All tests were run on four Pentium 4 3GHz machines with 1GB of RAM and Hyper-threading. Tests were run on an ArchLinux install using a real-time kernel, however, the snapshot of the FREEDM software used to run the tests does not feature a real-time scheduler.

The testing software was responsible for initializing instances, allowing them to run and then terminate after a fixed time limit. Additionally it provided an iterative object which generated network settings which were copied to the target machines before each test began.

Table 2. Tests Performed

Test No.	Test Type	Protocol	Resend Time	Window Size
1	2 Node	SRC	200ms	N/A
2	2 Node	SUC	200ms	8
3	2 Node	SRC	100ms	N/A
4	2 Node	SUC	100ms	8
5	Transient	SRC	200ms	N/A
6	Transient	SUC	200ms	8
7	Transient	SRC	100ms	N/A
8	Transient	SUC	100ms	8

Each node recorded its own state information, which was appended to a log file at termination of the run. This data was then coupled with the experimental procedure data to create the tables and charts in the results.

For each run of the system, the first 60 seconds of the system were not logged to filter out transients. This leads to a maximum recordable in-group time of nine minutes.

3.2   Tests Performed

Our experiments considered two configurations of the system which can be considered highly characteristic of most other scenarios. The first, a two node configuration was intended to observe a slice of the behavior of the system when two nodes (a leader and a group member) struggle to communicate with one another.

The second configuration was a four node configuration with a transient partition, where the nodes were divided into pairs. Each pair of nodes could reliably communicate with each other, but reliable communication across pairs was not guaranteed. We would vary the reliability of the connection between the pairs and observe the effects on the system.

For both tests, we ran the system using both our sequenced reliable protocol as well as our sequenced unreliable protocol. Additionally, we varied the amount of time between resends for both protocols. A full list of the tests we performed are listed in Table 2.

In each test, we recorded the number of elections which began, the number that completed successfully, the amount of time spent working on elections, the amount of time spent in a group, and the mean group size. Using these metrics, we hoped to capture a good representation of what kind effects network problems could have on the stability of the groups formed.

4   Results

All results are the average of the statistics captured by each node participating, and have been grouped similarity.

4.1   Tests 1 and 2

Test one featured the sequenced reliable (SRC) protocol in a two node configuration with a 200ms resend time, and another run with the the unreliable protocol (SUC) with a window size of 8. The system was configured with two DGI nodes with a transient link between them. The mean group size is presented in Figure 1, and the amount of time in group is shown in Figure 2.

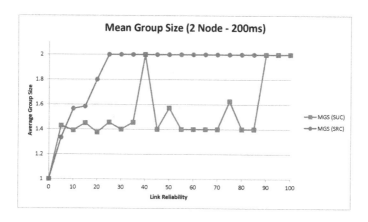

Fig. 1. Average size of formed groups for two node system with 200ms resend time

4.2   Test 3 and 4

Tests 3 and 4 follow the same experimental setup as tests one and two, but the resend time has been reduced to 100ms. The mean group size is presented in Figure 3, and the amount of time in group is shown in Figure 4.

4.3   Test 5 and 6

Tests five and six are the first to use the transient partition setup. The system is setup with four nodes. Two pairs of nodes are selected. Each pair of nodes can communicate without issue to each other. However, the reliability of the link between the two pairs was varied for each step of the test. These tests used a 200ms resend time. Both SRC and SUC protocols are shown here. As in the previous tests, the window size remained at 8 for the SUC protocol.

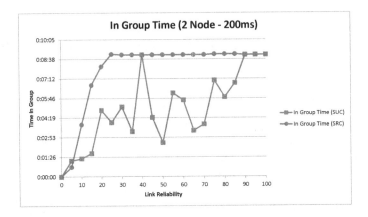

Fig. 2. Total time spent in group of at least size two for two node system with 200ms resend time

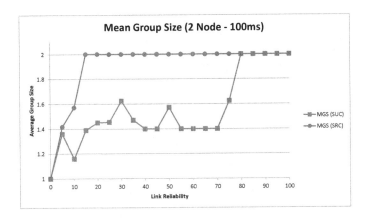

Fig. 3. Average size of formed groups for two node system with 100ms resend time

4.4   Tests 7 and 8

Tests seven and eight were run with the same setup as Tests 5 and 6, however the resend time was reduced to 100ms.

5   Observations

As one would expect the mean group size increases with the stability of the link. This observation can be directly made from the data we collected. However, our measurements often included outliers such as the major one observed in Figure 6. To confirm these points as outliers we re-ran the case (Reliability 40 with Test 2, shown in Figures 1 and 2) multiple times and collected the same measurements. We collected these into Figure 9.

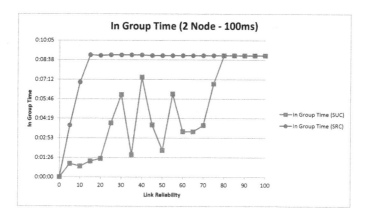

Fig. 4. Total time spent in group of at least size two for two node system with 100ms resend time

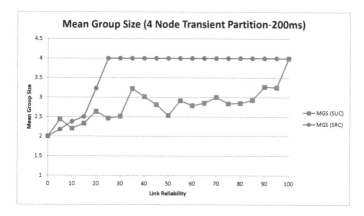

Fig. 5. Average size of formed groups for a four node system with a transient partition and 200ms resend time

The points in Figure 9 are centered around 4m18s which is where the expected value should be based on the approximate trend of those tests. Based on further examination, we believe points like these (since they tend to only occur with the SUC protocol) to be cause by two factors. The first factor is that SUC will ignore packets that don't arrive in increasing order, which makes situations where many messages are being passed (such as the election) more difficult to complete. The second factor is the relative stability of the formed group. The timeout for a leader or a member detecting that the other is unreachable is fairly long and given there is a relatively low amount of traffic when it is being delivered, it is much more likely to arrive and keep the formed group alive. The outlier in Figures 1 and 2 is simply a case where a group formed, and the relative ease of sustaining a group kept it alive for the duration of the test. Other cases can explained similarly.

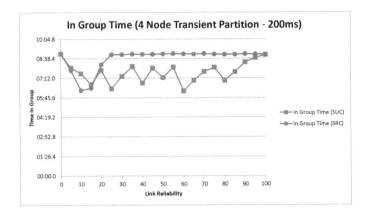

Fig. 6. Total time spent in group of at least size two for a four node system with a transient partition and 200ms resend time

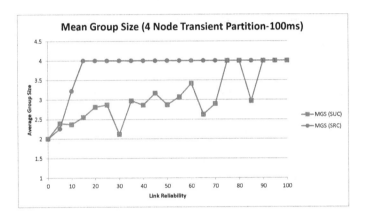

Fig. 7. Average size of formed groups for a four node system with a transient partition and 100ms resend time

We had originally selected these two protocols to evaluate their potential in our software. As our development continued we used the SRC protocol as the default (although it is simple to switch between them). The advantages of this are obvious. As presented in nearly every test, even with fairly low link reliability very stable groups formed. However, it does have limitations: send and wait can be slow. Although it was not relevant in these tests, with a sufficient number of messages in the system, the protocol is not capable of delivering messages fast enough to empty its waiting message queue, even with full reliability.

One of our most noteworthy observations can be made based on our transient partition cases. When the partition completely separates the two nodes, the in group time is at its maximum value. As the reliability increases however, the transient partition causes the in group time to decrease, since the two sides of the partition are attempting to form groups with each other. This raises

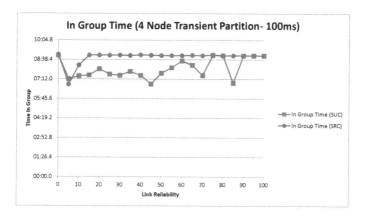

Fig. 8. Total time spent in group of at least size two for a four node system with a transient partition and 100ms resend time

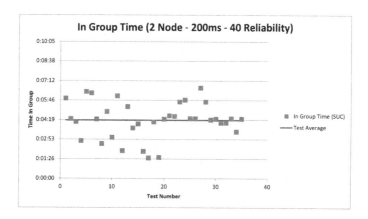

Fig. 9. Total time spent in group of at least size two for the two node node system with the SUC protocol, 200ms resend, and 40 reliability. The average of all points is the solid line.

questions as to what happens to the underlying physical system when this happens. [6] showed that sometimes the ideal cyber network does not mimic the physical network. Then however, we have to wonder what happens when the cyber network has link failures or lost messages? Are there circumstances where a group is coordinating using a bus shared with nodes that are not in the same group allows for interactions that destabilize the system?

In the circumstances where the transient link causes an overall decrease in in group time, groups of many different sizes can form. In our case alone, groups of anywhere from one to four members can exist. In a system where coordination is made based on flow contracts [1], what issues can arrive when a contract is formed with a node who leaves the group shortly thereafter? Will the effect compound if there are also physical link failures in the system?

6 Conclusion

In this work we have examined an application of leader election algorithms in a cyber-physical system. We showed that while there are definite benefits and uses for leader election algorithms in cyber-physical systems, they generate a flurry of new problems for system designers to deal with. We have shown that network instability can cause disruptions to the amount of service the cyber system can provide. In our analysis we questioned what the effect of transient partitions and link failures would be on the physical system, especially when the two networks are isomorphic. Our work shows that with the selection of an appropriate protocol under certain failure models, a good quality of service can be achieved in general. The transient partition case, by contrast, creates problems with group stability and is an issue to be investigated further with respect to its effect on CPSs.

Acknowledgements. The authors acknowledge the support of the Future Renewable Electric Energy Delivery and Management Center, a National Science Foundation supported Engineering Research Center under grant NSF EEC-081212, and the United States Department of Education GAANN program.

References

1. Akella, R., Meng, F., Ditch, D., McMillin, B., Crow, M.: Distributed power balancing for the FREEDM system. In: 2010 First IEEE International Conference on Smart Grid Communications (SmartGridComm), pp. 7–12 (October 2010)
2. Centre, M.H.R.: Pscad.com (May 2012), http://pscad.com
3. Dawes, B., Abrahams, D., Rivera, R.: Boost c++ libraries (May 2012), http://www.boost.org
4. Garcia-Molina, H.: Elections in a distributed computing system. IEEE Transactions on Computers C-31(1), 48–59 (1982)
5. Hansen, C.V., Forcier, J.E.: Fabric (May 2012), http://fabfile.org
6. Kubler, S., Pahwa, S., Schulz, N., Scoglio, C.: A simulative analysis of the robustness of smart grid communication networks. In: North American Power Symposium (NAPS), pp. 1–7 (August 2011)
7. Singh, C., Sprintson, A.: Reliability assurance of cyber-physical power systems. In: 2010 IEEE Power and Energy Society General Meeting, pp. 1–6 (July 2010)
8. Technologies, R.: Power systems simulator software: Rscad software suite (May 2012), http://www.rtds.com/software/rscad/rscad.html
9. Yan, Y., Qian, Y., Sharif, H., Tipper, D.: A survey on smart grid communication infrastructures: Motivations, requirements and challenges. IEEE Communications Surveys Tutorials PP(99), 1–16 (2012)
10. Zhang, Z., Chow, M.Y.: Incremental cost consensus algorithm in a smart grid environment. In: 2011 IEEE Power and Energy Society General Meeting, pp. 1–6 (July 2011)

Distributed Generation
and Resilience in Power Grids

Antonio Scala[1,2,3], Mario Mureddu[4,5],
Alessandro Chessa[1,5], Guido Caldarelli[2,1,3], and Alfonso Damiano[6]

[1] ISC-CNR Physics Dept., Univ. "La Sapienza" Piazzale Moro 5, 00185 Roma, Italy
[2] IMT Alti Studi Lucca, piazza S. Ponziano 6, 55100 Lucca, Italy
[3] London Institute of Mathematical Sciences, 22 South Audley St.
Mayfair London W1K 2NY, UK
[4] Department of Physics, University of Cagliari, Italy
[5] Linkalab, Complex Systems Computational Laboratory, 09129 Cagliari, Italy
[6] Dipartimento di Ingegneria Elettrica ed Elettronica, Università di Cagliari, Italy

Abstract. We study the effects of the allocation of distributed generation on the resilience of power grids. We find that an unconstrained allocation and growth of the distributed generation can drive a power grid beyond its design parameters. In order to overcome such a problem, we propose a topological algorithm derived from the field of Complex Networks to allocate distributed generation sources in an existing power grid.

Keywords: distributed generation, AC power model, complex networks, pagerank.

1 Introduction

Distributed Generation from renewable sources is having a deep impact on our power grids. The difficult task of integrating the stochastic and often volatile renewable sources into a the grid designed with a power-on-demand paradigm could perhaps solved leveraging on distributed storage [5]; nevertheless, massive and economic power storage is not yet readily available. In the meanwhile, power grids are nowadays required to be robust and smart, i.e. systems able to maintain, under normal or perturbed conditions, the frequency and amplitude variations of the supplied voltage into a defined range and to provide fast restoration after faults. Therefore, many studies have concentrated on the dynamic behaviour of Smart Grids to understand how to ensure stability and avoid loss of synchronization during typical events like the interconnection of distributed generation. The large number of elements present into real grids calls for simplifications like the mapping among the classic swing equations [23] and Kuramoto models [17,18,16] that allows to study numerically or analytically the synchronization and the transient stability of large power networks.

Even simple models [15] akin to the DC power flow model [25] show that the network topology can dynamically induce a complex size probability distributions of blackouts (power-law distributed), both when the system is operated

B. Hämmerli, N. Kalstad Svendsen, and J. Lopez (Eds.): CRITIS 2012, LNCS 7722, pp. 71–79, 2013.

near its limits [11] or when the system is subject to erratic disturbances [22]. New realistic metrics to assess the robustness of the electric power grid with respect to the cascading failures [26] are therefore needed.

Smart grids are going to insist on pre-existing networks designed for different purposes and tailored on different paradigms and new kind of failures are possible: therefore a careful transition is needed. One possible approach could be the use of advanced metering infrastructure (AMI) not only for implementing providers and customers services, but also to detect and forecast failures; nevertheless an ill-designed network will never be efficient.

Our approach will not concentrate on the instabilities but will focus instead on the condition under which, in presence of distributed generation, the system can either be operated or controlled back within its design parameters, i.e. it is *resilient*. It is akin in spirit to the approach of [13], that by applying DC power flow analysis to a system with a stochastic distribution of demands, aims to understand and prevent failures by identifying the most relevant load configurations on the feasibility boundary between the normal and problematic regions of grid operation.

To model power grids, we will use the more computational intensive AC power flow algorithms as, although DC flows are on average wrong by a few percent [24], error outliers could distort our analysis.

To model distributed renewable sources, we will introduced a skewed probability distribution of load demands representing a crude model of reality that ignores the effects like the correlations (due for examples to weather conditions) between different consumers or distributed producers.

2   Methods

2.1   AC Power Flow

The AC power flow is described by a system of non-linear equations that allow to obtain complete voltage angle and magnitude information for each bus in a power system for specified loads [19]. A bus of the system is either classified as Load Bus if there are no generators connected or as a Generator Bus if one or more generators are connected. It is assumed that the real power PD and the reactive power QD at each Load Bus are given, while for Generator Buses the real generated power PG and the voltage magnitude $|V|$ are given. A particular Generator Bus, called the Slack Bus, is assumed as a reference and its voltage magnitude $|V|$ and voltage phase Θ are fixed. The branches of the electrical system are described by the bus admittance matrix Y with complex elements Y_{ij}s.

The power balance equations can be written for real and reactive power for each bus. The real power balance equation is:

$$0 = -P_i + \sum_{k=1}^{N} |V_i| |V_k| (G_{ik} \cos \theta_{ik} + B_{ik} \sin \theta_{ik})$$

where N is the number of buses, P_i is the net real power injected at the ith bus , G_{ik} is the real part and B_{ik} is the imaginary part of the element Y_{ij} and θ_{ik} is the difference in voltage angle between the ith and k^{th} buses. The reactive power balance equation is:

$$0 = -Q_i + \sum_{k=1}^{N} |V_i| \, |V_k| \, (G_{ik} \sin \theta_{ik} - B_{ik} \cos \theta_{ik})$$

where Q_i is the net reactive power injected at the ith bus.

Real and reactive power flow on each branch as well as generator reactive power; the output can be analytically determined but due to the non-linear character of the system numerical methods are employed to obtain a solution. To solve such equations, we employ Pylon [2], a port of MATPOWER [1] to the Python programming language.

A requirement for the stability of the load and generation requirements is the condition that all branches and buses operate within their physical feasibility parameters; going beyond such parameters can trigger cascades of failures eventually leading to black outs [21].

In the present paper a topological investigation on the power grid has been developed in order to evaluate the effects of distributed generation on the voltage and power quality. Hence, a steady state analysis has been carried out and the transient phenomena connected to the power flow control have been neglected. Under this hypothesis the frequency variation connected to power flow control has been considered stabilized and the system has been considered characterized by a constant steady state supply voltage frequency. Therefore, if all the nodes are near their nominal voltage, it is much easier to control the system and to avoid reaching infeasible levels of power flow. Consequently, to measure the effects of power quality of a power grid under distributed generation we measure the fraction F of load buses whose tension goes beyond $\pm 5\%$ of its nominal voltage. Notice that real networks are often operated with some of the buses beyond such parameters so that (especially for large networks) it is expected to be $F \neq 0$ under operating conditions. The maximum of the resilience for a power grid (intended as the capability of restoring full feasible flows) is expected to be for $F = 0$.

2.2   Distributed Generation and Skew-Normal Distribution

We will consider distributed generation due to erratic renewable sources like sun and wind; therefore, we will model the effects of "green generators" on a power grid as a stochastic variation the power requested by load buses. Load buses with a green generator will henceforth called green buses. We will consider the location of green buses to be random; the fraction p of green buses will characterize the penetration of the distributed generation in a grid.

If the power dispatched by distributed generation is high enough, loads can eventually become negative: this effect can be related to the efficiency of green generators. We model such an effect by considering the load on green buses described by the skew-normal distribution [4], a pseudo-normal distribution with a non-zero skewness:

$$f(x, \alpha) = 2\phi(x)\Phi(\alpha x)$$

where α is a real parameter and

$$\phi(x) = \exp\left(-x^2/2\right)/\sqrt{2\pi} \qquad \Phi(\alpha x) = \int_{-\infty}^{\alpha x} \phi(t)\, dt$$

The parameter α will characterize the level of the distributed generation: to positive α correspond loads positive on average, while for negative α green nodes will tend to dispatch power.

Our model grids will therefore consist of three kind of buses: N_G generators (fixed voltage), N_l pure loads (fixed power consumption) and N_g green buses (stochastic power consumption) with $N_G + N_l + N_g = N$ the total number of buses and $N_g + N_l = N_L$ the number of load nodes. The fraction $p = N_g/N_L$ measures the penetration of renewable sources in the grid.

2.3   Complex Networks and Page Rank

The topology of a power grid can be represented as a directed graph $G = (V, E)$, where to the i-th bus corresponds the nodes n_i of the set V and to the k-th branch from the i-th to the j-th bus corresponds the edge $e_k = (i, j)$ of the set E. In Power System engineering, it is custom to associate to the graph G representing a power networks its *incidence* matrix B whose elements are

$$B_{ik} = \begin{cases} 1 & if \ e_k = (i, \_) \in E \\ -1 & if \ e_k = (\_, i) \in E \\ 0 & otherwise \end{cases}.$$

An alternative representation of the graph much more used in other scientific fields is its *adjacency* matrix A whose element are

$$A_{ij} = \begin{cases} 1 & if \ (i, j) \in E \\ 0 & otherwise \end{cases}$$

While Graph Theory has an old tradition since Euler's venerable problem on Koenigsberg bridges [6], Complex Networks is the new field investigating the emergent properties of large graphs. An important characteristic of the nodes of a complex network is their centrality, i.e. their relative importance respect to the other nodes of the graph [10]. An important centrality measure is Page Rank, the algorithm introduced Brin and Page [7] to rank web pages that is at the hearth of the Google search engine. The Page Rank r_i of the i-th node is the solution of the linear system

$$r_i = \frac{1 - \rho}{N} + \rho \sum \frac{A_{ij} r_j}{d_j^o}$$

where N is the number of buses (nodes), $d_i^o = \sum_i A_{ij}$ is the number of outgoing links (out-degree) and $\rho = 0.85$ is the Page Rank damping factor. In studying power grids, we will employ Page Rank as it is strictly related to several invariants occurring in the study of random walks and electrical networks [14].

3 Results

3.1 Effects of Distributed Generation

We have investigated the effects of our null model of distributed generation on the 2383 bus power grid of Poland, 1999. Starting from the unperturbed network, we have found an initial fraction $F_0 \cong 1.6\%$ of load buses beyond their nominal tension. We have therefore varied the penetration p at fixed distributed generation level α's; results are shown in Fig. 1.

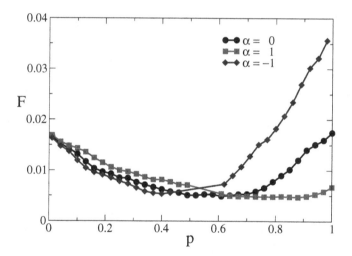

Fig. 1. Effects of the penetration p of distributed generation on the resilience of the Polish power grid at different values α of the green generators. Notice that for $\alpha = 0$ renewable sources satisfy on average the load requested by the network, while for $\alpha < 0$ there is a surplus of renewable energy. Lower values of the fraction F of buses operating near their nominal tension correspond to a higher resiliency. Notice that the penetration of distributed generation initially enhances resiliency. At higher values of p, resilience worsens; in particular, it is severely impaired if distributed generation produces on average more energy than the normal load requests ($\alpha = -1$). It is therefore advisable to keep levels of renewable energy production below the normal load request ($\alpha = 1$).

We find that the behaviour of the fraction F of buses operating near their nominal tension does not follow a monotonic behaviour. Initially (low values of p), the penetration of distributed generation enhances resiliency (i.e. decreases F).

At higher values of p, F grows and resilience worsens. Such an effect is particularly severe if green nodes introduce a surplus ($\alpha < 0$) of power respect to the normal ($p = 0$) operating load requests. On the other hand, keeping the levels of renewable energy production below ($\alpha > 0$) the normal load request delays the point beyond which the penetration of distributed generation worsens the resiliency.

Notice that when distributed generation is ancillary ($\alpha > 0$) and not predominant in the power supplied of the network, full penetration ($p = 1$) of renewable sources lead to more stable state than the initial ($p = 0$) one.

3.2 Targeted Distributed Generation

Beside their natural application to web crawling, the Page Rank algorithm can be applied to find local partitions of a network that optimize conductance [3]. We therefore investigate what happens in a power network if distributed generation is introduced with a policy that accounts for the pagerank of load nodes. In other words, for a level of penetration p, we choose the first $n_g = pN_L$ load nodes in decreasing pagerank order to become green nodes. The effects of such a choice are shown compared to the random penetration policy in Fig. 2.

We find that, for low penetration levels, the pagerank policy reduces the number of nodes operating beyond their nominal tension both for positive and for negative α's. Again, the excess of power production ($\alpha < 0$) comparatively reduces the resilience of the network.

Preliminary results show that Page Rank is the best behaved among centralities in enhancing power grid resilience; such study will be the subject of a future publication.

4 Discussion

We have introduced a model base on the AC power flow equation that allows to account for the presence of erratic renewable sources distributed on a power grid and for their efficiency. By defining the resilience of the grid as a quantity related to the possibility of controlling the power flow via voltage adjustments (hence returning within the operating bounds of its components), we have studied the penetration of distributed generation on a realistic power grid.

We have found that while the introduction of few "green" generators in general enhances the resilience of the network by decreasing the number of nodes operating beyond their nominal voltage, a further increase of renewable sources could decrease the power quality of the grid. Anyhow, if distributed generation is ancillary and not predominant in the power supplied of the network, the grid at full penetration ($p = 1$) of renewable sources is in a more stable state than the starting grid ($p = 0$).

Our finding that a surplus of production from renewable sources is also a source of additional instabilities is perhaps to be expected in general for networks that have been designed to dispatch power from their generators to their loads

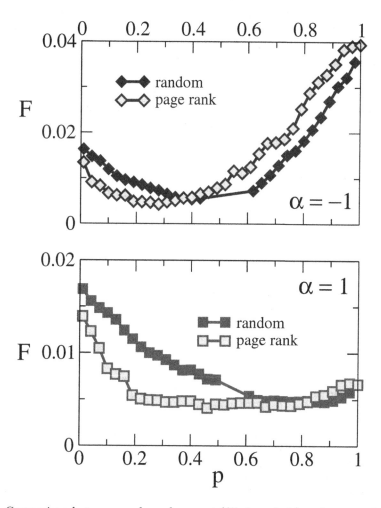

Fig. 2. Comparison between random placement (filled symbols) and page-rank placement (empty symbols) of green generators in the Polish grid, both for surplus production of renewable energy (upper panel, $\alpha = -1$) and for levels of renewable energy production below the normal load request (lower panel, $\alpha = 1$). The page-rank placement of renewable sources allows to attain lower values of the fraction F of buses operating near their nominal tension (and hence a higher resiliency) at lower values of the penetration p. The best case is realized for levels of renewable energy production below the normal load request, where a plateau to low values of F is quickly attained.

and not to produce energy "locally". While we have found that in an isolated grid instability possible increases with the penetration, what happens when more grids are linked together is an open subject. Power grids are typical complex infrastructural systems; therefore they can exhibit emergent characteristics when they interact with each other, modifying the risk of failure in the individual systems [12]. As an example, the increase in infrastructural interdependencies could either mitigate [8] or increase [20,9] the risk of a system failure.

Finally, we find that a policy of choosing the sites where to introduce renewable sources according to Page Rank allows to increase the resilience with a minimal amount of green buses. Such policy does not take into account other factors and should therefore be integrated in a multi-objective optimization to consider the environmental, economical and social constraints.

Acknowledgements. We thank US grant HDTRA1-11-1-0048, CNR-PNR National Project Crisis-Lab and EU FET project MULTIPLEX nr.317532 for support. The contents do not necessarily reflect the position or the policy of funding parties.

References

1. matpower, http://www.pserc.cornell.edu/matpower/
2. pylon, http://pylon.eee.strath.ac.uk/pylon/
3. Andersen, R., Chung, F., Lang, K.: Local graph partitioning using pagerank vectors. In: Proceedings of the 47th Annual IEEE Symposium on Foundations of Computer Science, FOCS 2006, pp. 475–486. IEEE Computer Society, Washington, DC (2006)
4. Azzalini, A.: The skew-normal distribution and related multivariate families. Scandinavian Journal of Statistics 32(2), 159–188 (2005)
5. Baghaie, M., Moeller, S., Krishnamachari, B.: Energy routing on the future grid: A stochastic network optimization approach, pp. 1–8 (October 2010)
6. Berge, C.: Théorie des graphes et ses applications. Collection Universitaire de Mathématiques, II, Paris, Dunod (1958)
7. Brin, S., Page, L.: The anatomy of a large-scale hypertextual web search engine. Comput. Netw. ISDN Syst. 30(1-7), 107–117 (1998)
8. Brummitt, C.D., D'Souza, R.M., Leicht, E.A.: Suppressing cascades of load in interdependent networks. Proceedings of the National Academy of Sciences (2012)
9. Buldyrev, S.V., Parshani, R., Paul, G., Stanley, H.E., Havlin, S.: Catastrophic cascade of failures in interdependent networks. Nature 464(7291), 1025–1028 (2010)
10. Caldarelli, G.: Scale-free Networks. Oxford University Press (2007)
11. Carreras, B.A., Lynch, V.E., Dobson, I., Newman, D.E.: Critical points and transitions in an electric power transmission model for cascading failure blackouts. Chaos: An Interdisciplinary Journal of Nonlinear Science 12(4), 985–994 (2002)
12. Carreras, B.A., Newman, D.E., Gradney, P., Lynch, V.E., Dobson, I.: Interdependent risk in interacting infrastructure systems. In: Proceedings of the 40th Annual Hawaii International Conference on System Sciences, HICSS 2007, p. 112. IEEE Computer Society, Washington, DC (2007)
13. Chertkov, M., Pan, F., Stepanov, M.G.: Predicting failures in power grids: The case of static overloads. IEEE Trans. Smart Grid 2(1), 162–172 (2011)

14. Chung, F., Zhao, W.: Pagerank and random walks on graphs,
    http://www.math.ucsd.edu/~fan/wp/lov.pdf
15. Dobson, I., Carreras, B., Lynch, V., Newman, D.: An initial model for complex
    dynamics in electric power system blackouts. In: Proceedings of the 34th Annual
    Hawaii International Conference on System Sciences (HICSS-34), HICSS 2001,
    vol. 2, p. 2017. IEEE Computer Society, Washington, DC (2001)
16. Dorfler, F., Bullo, F.: Synchronization and transient stability in power networks
    and non-uniform Kuramoto oscillators. SIAM Journal on Control and Optimization
    (2012) (to appear) (submitted October 2011)
17. Filatrella, G., Nielsen, A.H., Pedersen, N.F.: Analysis of a power grid using a
    kuramoto-like model. The European Physical Journal B - Condensed Matter and
    Complex Systems 61(4), 485–491 (2008)
18. Fioriti, V., Ruzzante, S., Castorini, E., Marchei, E., Rosato, V.: Critical information
    infrastructure security, pp. 14–23. Springer, Heidelberg (2009)
19. Grainger, J., Stevenson, W.: Power System Analysis. McGraw-Hill, New York
    (1994)
20. Laprie, J.C., Kanoun, K., Kaâniche, M.: Modelling interdependencies between the
    electricity and information infrastructures. CoRR abs/0809.4107 (2008)
21. Pahwa, S., Hodges, A., Scoglio, C., Wood, S.: Topological analysis of the power grid
    and mitigation strategies against cascading failures. ArXiv e-prints (June 2010)
22. Sachtjen, M.L., Carreras, B.A., Lynch, V.E.: Disturbances in a power transmission
    system. Phys. Rev. E 61, 4877–4882 (2000)
23. Stagg, G., El-Abiad, A.: Computer Methods In Power System Analysis. McGraw-
    Hill Education (April 1968)
24. Stott, B., Jardim, J., Alsac, O.: Dc power flow revisited. IEEE Transactions on
    Power Systems 24(3), 1290–1300 (2009)
25. Wood, A.J., Wollenberg, B.F.: Power Generation, Operation and Control. Wiley,
    New York (1984)
26. Youssef, M., Scoglio, C., Pahwa, S.: Robustness measure for power grids with re-
    spect to cascading failures. In: Proceedings of the 2011 International Workshop
    on Modeling, Analysis, and Control of Complex Networks, Cnet 2011. ITCP,
    pp. 45–49 (2011)

Breaking Nondeducible Attacks
on the Smart Grid

Thomas Roth and Bruce M. McMillin

Computer Science Department, Missouri University of Science and Technology,
Rolla, MO 65409, USA
{tprfh7,ff}@mst.edu

Abstract. The evolution of the electric power infrastructure into a
smart grid carries with it the potential for residential homes to become
malicious attackers on global state estimation. This paper presents an
attack model where a distributed cyber controller in a smart grid exe-
cutes an internal attack to falsify its advertised generation. This differs
from current attack models in that the attacker is an active element of
the system that participates in its normal operation. Through the use of
information flow properties, the attack is proven to be nondeducible and
thus unidentifiable in a current smart grid architecture. An adaptation
of mutual exclusion is then applied to break the nondeducible attack.

Keywords: power grid, cyber-physical, information flow security.

1   Introduction

The future smart grid proposes the use of distributed cyber intelligence to manage energy resources such as generators and loads at the residential level. This
differs from the current power infrastructure in that it shifts the responsibility
for power generation onto household consumers. Through distributed management of energy resources, the grid would become more reliable with houses able
to utilize their neighbors should their connection to the wider power grid be
compromised. Economic optimization of residential power usage would also be
improved through the use of intelligent cyber algorithms for power management.
These benefits have made the smart grid a topic of considerable research in the
critical infrastructures community.

One underdeveloped aspect of smart grid research is the security of proposed
smart grid models. Current research on smart grid security focuses on external attacks which compromise a subset of the smart meters in the system. Such
attacks generate false reports on the power usage of each house and cause the system to transition into an incorrect state. Significant contribution has been made
to investigate these false data injection attacks [6,7]. Prior work has also investigated the privacy of metered data, both with respect to the power utility [3]
and external observers [5]. Combined, these works address the basic security
concerns of data integrity and data confidentiality against external attackers.

B. Hämmerli, N. Kalstad Svendsen, and J. Lopez (Eds.): CRITIS 2012, LNCS 7722, pp. 80–91, 2013.

A less explored aspect of smart grid security is attack models which consider the attacker to be a household within the system. One key smart grid feature is that each house has some degree of local generation used to produce its own power. A house can impact system-wide generation through manipulation of its local energy resources. The current power infrastructure restricts control over generation to the centralized power utility, a trusted entity in the system, with no concern over malicious use of generation. However, with generation at individual households, the notion of trust is no longer relevant and new potential for attack arises in the malicious use of energy resources at the residential level.

Internal attack models have become more relevant in the wake of the Stuxnet worm, which resulted in wide-spread infection of Siemens programmable logic controllers [4]. Stuxnet was able to fake process control signals in the infected system and appear indistinguishable from normal system operation. This attack occurred within the system, with system components driven by the fake signals of a malicious controller, and requires a different attack model to analyze than those used for false data injection attacks. Prior work has shown that such an attack cannot be detected when it occurs in a smart grid [2], but no solutions to prevent such an attack have been proposed.

Unlike most prior work which consider how to protect the system from an external adversary, this work phrases an internal attack model against the current smart grid architecture. Information flow theory is then applied to determine if the attack, itself, is nondeducible to the system, and a method to break the nondeducibility and restore system security is introduced. Section 2 presents the required background information and Sect. 3 details the formal system model. The attack is then analyzed in Sect. 4 and a potential solution is proposed in Sect. 5. Section 6 summarizes the contribution of this work.

2   System Overview

This section presents the system model based on a smart grid architecture under development by the FREEDM Systems Center [1]. It then summarizes the attack model, and presents the information flow property used to analyze the attack.

2.1   Smart Grid Architecture

The smart grid architecture consists of the houses in a neighborhood, each with its own energy production and consumption, connected by a shared distribution line. This distribution line connects to the wider power grid and can be used to share power with other neighborhoods or the power utility. Figure 1 shows the structure of a neighborhood in a smart grid, with a supply house providing power to a demand house through a special transaction called a power migration. Renewable energy resources such as solar and wind provide the generation at each house, whereas the load comes from household appliances.

Each house has the ability to draw power from the distribution line to satisfy its internal demand. This capability exists in the current grid infrastructure

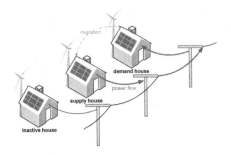

1. Supply house advertises its excess generation
2. Demand house requests power from supplier
3. Supply house and demand house start a migration
3a. Supply house increases its local generation
3b. Demand house increases its local load

Fig. 1. Power Migration in a Smart Grid   **Fig. 2.** Power Migration Steps

where power flows from the centralized power utility into individual houses. Each house also has the ability to push some of its excess power to the shared line. This capability, unique to the smart grid, represents a house using its local generation to satisfy the demand of other houses in the system.

Pushes and pulls of power are governed by distributed cyber intelligence. Each house has an embedded cyber controller which communicates with the other controllers in the system. Migration contracts are formed between controllers which migrate some amount of power from one house to another. A migration is a sequence of a push from a supplier followed by a pull from a house in demand. The physical representation of this transaction would be that a supplier turns on its generator, causing power to flow into the shared distribution line, and then a demand house plugs in some power-consuming device. This creates a natural flow of power from the supply house to the demand house. Figure 2 lists the sequence of events for a successful power migration.

2.2 Attack Model

This paper will not consider purely physical attacks where an attacker manipulates its energy resources without participation in the cyber communication protocol. Such an attack would bypass the cyber layer and fail to highlight the cyber-physical vulnerabilities of the system. An attacker will instead attempt to fake a migration contract. The goal of the attack is to trick other houses into thinking that the attacker has greater supply or greater demand than its current local state. This will cause other houses to form migration contracts with the attacker that cannot be satisfied. With respect to normal sequence of events in Fig. 2, an attacker will omit either step 3a or step 3b during the migration. Figure 3 illustrates an attack from a fake supplier with no local generation. The actual power for this migration contract is siphoned from other legitimate transactions in the system.

The attack hinges on the observation that physical power cannot be tracked. It is impossible to determine the origin of power on the shared distribution line. Therefore, the owner of a power injection cannot be determined through mere observation of the physical layer. In this attack model, the attacker will claim

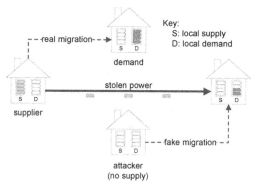

Fig. 3. Fake Supply Attack Model

to inject power into the system and use the power generated by other suppliers to fulfill its outstanding migration contracts. Through this manner, its peers are unable to determine whether the power on the distribution line originated from the attacker or some other supplier. The following sections show that this attack is effective if the attacker can time its migrations to be concurrent with other migrations in the system. Note that security mechanisms such as cryptography and authentication are not sufficient to prevent this internal attack model, and alternative methods must be employed to counter the attack.

2.3   Nondeducibility

An information flow property will be used to analyze this attack model and determine if the attack reveals enough information to identify the attacker. If the attacker cannot be identified, then the attack is successful and cannot be prevented. Sutherland proposed a model of information which described information flows between different views of a system [9]. The security of the system could then be defined in terms of the legal and illegal information flows. Let a system be defined as a set of worlds W, where a world $w \in W$ represents a single execution of the system. Let two information functions $f_1(w)$ and $f_2(w)$ define a view over each world. A system is secure with respect to the Sutherland definition if:

$$(\forall z : f_2^{-1}(z) \neq \emptyset)(\forall w \in W)(\exists w' \in W : f_1(w) = f_1(w') \wedge f_2(w') = z). \quad (1)$$

In terms of more familiar security terminology, $f_1(w)$ defines the high-level security domain and $f_2(w)$ defines the low-level domain. Equation (1) states that, for each low-level observation z, over every high-level command sequence w, there exists some execution w' where the high-level command sequence w and the low-level observation z coexist. This means that it is possible to pair each low-level observation with each high-level command sequence and still have a valid system execution. This definition of security is known as nondeducibility.

Equation (1) can be relaxed to consider, rather than system-wide security, trace-level security in which a single low-level observation is considered to determine whether that observation leads to deducible information. Given a low-level observation of z, this modifies (1) to:

$$(\forall w \in W)(\exists w' \in W : f_1(w) = f_1(w') \wedge f_2(w') = z). \tag{2}$$

Equation (2) is satisfied if all possible high-level command sequences are able to result in a low-level observation of z. If a single high-level sequence cannot produce the low-level observation of z, it is deducible that at least one command sequence was impossible, and the Sutherland definition does not hold.

3   System Model

A formal system model for a smart grid can be represented by a sequence of state transitions. Henceforth, the system will be considered a microgrid that consists of a single neighborhood. The houses of the neighborhood will be referred to as nodes of the system. Each node i has two state variables, P_i and $\hat{P}_i$. P_i represents the amount of excess generation at node i and can be calculated as $P_i = generation_i - load_i$. This state variable is sufficient to model both excess and deficit generation, where a value of $P_i < 0$ indicates that node i is in demand and requires $|P_i|$ units of power supplied by an external source. $\hat{P}_i$ represents the advertised generation of node i broadcast to the system by the embedded cyber controller. The distinction between these variables is that P_i is the actual generation at node i whereas $\hat{P}_i$ is the external view seen by other nodes.

Suppose a system contains n nodes, then a state of the system Q is defined as the set $Q = \{\hat{P}_1, \ldots, \hat{P}_n, P_1, \ldots, P_n P_B\}$ where P_i and $\hat{P}_i$ abide by the above definitions and P_B represents the amount of power on the shared distribution line. A lattice of security levels is defined that segregates the state variables into different security domains. For each node i, a security level L_i is created to represent its internal state. An additional level labeled *system* is used to represent the state knowledge shared by all nodes in the system. These security levels follow a partial order such that $(\forall i : 1 \leq i \leq n)(system \leq L_i)$. This allows a node i to view both its private level L_i as well as the shared *system* level, but restricts nodes other than node i from viewing its internal state. Figure 4 depicts the security lattice for a system of n nodes.

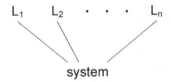

Fig. 4. System Security Lattice

State variables are assigned to security levels such that, for each node i in the system, $P_i \in L_i$ and $\hat{P}_i \in system$. Such an assignment has the natural meaning that the amount of generation at a given node is private data known only to that node, and the rest of the system must rely on its view of the advertised value $\hat{P}_i$. This represents the reality of a smart grid where a house is not allowed direct access to a meter in their neighbor's house. The final state variable P_B is assigned to *system* since each node can measure the amount of power on the shared distribution line.

A state transition $Q \to Q'$ occurs when a node performs a command drawn from a pool of legal system commands. Each command modifies the original state Q to produce a new state Q' where state variables in Q' are represented by prime notation. A partial list of system commands, annotated with their security level, is presented in Table 1. Note that commands issued by demand nodes to increase and decrease local load are omitted. This omission is for the sake of brevity since the security analysis will not include demand nodes.

Table 1. List of State Transition Commands

command	level	description
select(i,j)	*system*	supplier i forms a migration contract with demand node j $\hat{P}_i' \leftarrow \hat{P}_i + 1$
increase(i)	L_i	node i increases its local generation by one unit if $P_i < \hat{P}_i$ then $P_i' = P_i + 1$ and $P_B' = P_B + 1$

An assumption made on the system model is that each node participates in the communication protocol. It is therefore an invariant on the system that each *increase* command follow a *select* command. A guard is included in the command description as an *if* statement to satisfy this requirement in Table 1. This assumption is made because the focus of this work is on the cyber-physical interactions of the system rather than purely cyber or purely physical security.

A supplier forms a migration contract with the command sequence *select* $\to$ *increase*. The goal of an attacker is to replace this transaction with a 'bad' transaction that results in an incorrect state assessment of the attacker in the view of its peers. The 'bad' transaction for this attack model would be to lie about the creation of a contract and never provide the promised power. This would leave a demand node waiting for power that that would never arrive. Henceforth, this attack will be referred to as the fake supply attack.

4   Attack Analysis

This section will analyze the attack model and prove that the fake supply attack is nondeducible. The attack will be evolved over several iterations that begin with a naive, deducible attack and conclude with a sophisticated, nondeducible attack. Various remarks will be made on each variation to demonstrate key points regarding the security of the system.

Proposition 1. *The fake supply attack fails if the attacker acts in isolation as the sole supply node in the system.*

Proof. Table 2 shows the command sequence and state transitions for this attack when executed by node 1. Let the high-level domain $H = L_1 \cup L_2 \cup L_3 \cup L_4$ and the low-level domain $L = system$. If information flows from H to L, then *system* would be able to deduce the high-level commands and thus deduce the attacker.

Table 2. Attack in Isolation

cmd	P_1	$\hat{P}_1$	P_2	$\hat{P}_2$	P_3	$\hat{P}_3$	P_B
init	0	0	0	0	0	0	0
select(1,3)	0	1	0	0	0	0	0

Given the formulation of H and L, the low-level view consists of states with the form $\{\hat{P}_1, \hat{P}_2, \hat{P}_3, P_B\}$. For the command sequence in Table 2,

$$view_L = \{0,0,0,0\} \rightarrow \{1,0,0,0\}. \tag{3}$$

If the command sequence were nondeducibility secure, then this low-level trace could be paired with any sequence of high-level commands by Equation 2. One such arbitrary sequence is $c_H = \{increase(3)\}$ in which node 3 increases its local generation. However, this command sequence would result in

$$view_L = \{0,0,0,0\} \rightarrow \{0,0,0,1\} \tag{4}$$

which does not correspond to (1). Furthermore, this trace is invalid since the guard for the increase command is not enabled in the initial state. Therefore, the system can deduce the original command sequence was not c_H and at least one high-level sequence has been ruled out. The system is able to deduce the attacker, and as such, the attack has been shown to fail.   □

Remark 1. Observe that the attack is deducible because at least one high-level command is not enabled and therefore at least one command sequence is not possible. In fact, all traces that contain a high-level node i whose $\hat{P}_i$ remains 0 will be deducible since $increase(i)$ would not be enabled. This observation means that the attacker belongs to the subset of nodes where $\hat{P}_i > 0$. This first case demonstrates two key points. First, it shows how nondeducibility can be used to analyze a low-level observation and determine whether an attacker can be identified. Second, it illustrates the format that used for the remaining analysis.

Proposition 2. *The fake supply attack fails if the attacker acts after another migration transaction has been completed.*

Proof. Table 3 shows the command sequence for the attack when performed by node 1. The previous remark states that it is possible to deduce the attacker belongs to the subset of nodse where $\hat{P}_i > 0$. Henceforth, the set of high-level nodes will be restricted to the set of nodes active in the system. For this command sequence, node 1 and node 2 both issue commands and are thus considered active. This makes the high-level domain $H = L_1 \cup L_2$ and the low-level domain $L = system$.

Table 3. Attack after Other Migration **Table 4.** Attack during Other Migration

cmd	P_1	$\hat{P}_1$	P_2	$\hat{P}_2$	P_3	$\hat{P}_3$	P_B
init	0	0	0	0	0	0	0
select(2,3)	0	0	0	1	0	0	0
select(1,3)	0	1	0	1	0	0	0
increase(2)	0	1	1	1	0	0	1

cmd	P_1	$\hat{P}_1$	P_2	$\hat{P}_2$	P_3	$\hat{P}_3$	P_B	T
init	0	0	0	0	0	0	0	0
pass(2)	0	0	0	0	0	0	0	2
select(2,3)	0	0	0	1	0	0	0	2
select(1,3)	0	1	0	1	0	0	0	2
increase(2)	0	1	1	1	0	0	1	2

For the command sequence in Table 3,

$$view_L = \{0,0,0,0\} \rightarrow \{0,1,0,0\} \rightarrow \{0,1,0,1\} \rightarrow \{1,1,0,1\}. \qquad (5)$$

The set of possible high-level commands is restricted for this view because at each point in the trace only a subset of the high-level commands are enabled. In particular, $increase(1)$ is not enabled during the second state transition $\{0,1,0,0\} \rightarrow \{0,1,0,1\}$ since node 1 has not issued a $select$ command and the guard $\hat{P}_1 > P_1$ is not satisfied. This observation immediately discards a valid high-level command sequence where node 1 issues the $increase$ command. Thus the command sequence is deducible and the attack fails.   □

Remark 2. The reason the attack fails in this command interleaving is that the attacker node 1 has not issued its select command by the time the increase is performed, and thus is not eligible for action. If it is known that a power increase occurs only after a select message, it can be deduced that node 1 did not perform the power increase since its select message had not arrived in time.

Lemma 1. *The fake supply attack succeeds if the attacker acts concurrently with some other migration in the system.*

Proof. Table 4 shows the relevant command sequence for an attack performed by node 1. Given the previous formulation of $H = L_1 \cup L_2$ and $L = system$,

$$view_L = \{0,0,0,0\} \rightarrow \{0,1,0,0\} \rightarrow \{1,1,0,0\} \rightarrow \{1,1,0,1\}. \qquad (6)$$

Note that although it is possible to deduce both of the $select$ commands for this sequence, these commands are issued at the $system$ level and therefore do not reveal high-level information. Therefore, this trace is further restricted to consider only the last state transition $\{1,1,0,0\} \rightarrow \{1,1,0,1\}$. If this state transition is deducible, then the system can determine which high-level node performed the $increase$ command and deduce which node performed the attack.

The possible high-level commands for this state transition are $increase(1)$ and $increase(2)$. Both commands are enabled since the guard $\hat{P}_i > P_i$ holds for both $i = 1$ and $i = 2$. Both commands also result in the same final state $\{1, 1, 0, 0, 1\}$. Therefore, it is possible for either of the commands to be issued and still result in the same low-level trace. This abides the definition of nondeducibility: the low-level trace can be paired with any of the high-level commands. Thus the final state transition is nondeducibility secure, the attack itself is nondeducible, and the attack succeeds.   □

Remark 3. This case demonstrates that, if an attacker acts between a *select* message issued by another supplier and its associated *increase*, the attacker can pose as a supply node without the *system* being able to determine which of the two nodes increased its generation. The attacker therefore succeeds to fake its supply for a single attack. Note that the tight timing suggested by this interleaving is not as severe as it seems, as although the attacker must inject itself between the select message and corresponding increase, and although these two messages may happen in very quick succession, it is difficult to place a causal order between events in a distributed system. Therefore, even if the attacker responds far after the increase message, and the actual command sequence is that of Table 3, it is still possible given communication delays for other nodes to be unable to order the events. This uncertainty on event order strengthens the attack since it increases the attacker's time window.

Theorem 1. *An attacker who launches repeated fake supply attacks against a system such that the attack is always concurrent with another migration made by the same supplier is nondeducible and thus unidentifiable.*

Proof. Table 5 extends Table 4 into a second attack that targets the same supplier twice. The first attack produces the trace

$$view_L = \{0, 0, 0, 0\} \to \{0, 1, 0, 0\} \to \{1, 1, 0, 0\} \to \{1, 1, 0, 1\} \qquad (7)$$

and the second attack produces the trace

$$view_L = \{1, 1, 0, 1\} \to \{1, 2, 0, 1\} \to \{2, 2, 0, 1\} \to \{2, 2, 0, 2\} \qquad (8)$$

Similar to the analysis for Lemma 1, the state transitions of interest are the ones caused by an *increase* command. These are $\{1, 1, 0, 0\} \to \{1, 1, 0, 1\}$ and $\{2, 2, 0, 1\} \to \{2, 2, 0, 2\}$. There are four permutations of high-level commands: $\{increase(1), increase(1)\}\{increase(1), increase(2)\}\{increase(2), increase(2)\}$ and $\{increase(2), increase(1)\}$. Note that the first command refers to the first state transition, and the second command refers to the second state transition. Also observe that each of these sequences produces the same low-level observation, and thus will only be deducible if one sequence is not valid because its commands are not enabled. However, during the first state transition, both $increase(1)$ and $increase(2)$ are enabled from application of Lemma 1. Likewise, they are enabled for the second state transition. Therefore, all commands are enabled during both state transitions, all command sequences are valid, and the system is nondeducibility secure.   □

Table 5. Nondeducible Repeated Attack   **Table 6.** Attack with Mutual Exclusion

cmd	P_1	$\hat{P}_1$	P_2	$\hat{P}_2$	P_3	$\hat{P}_3$	P_B
init	0	0	0	0	0	0	0
select(2,3)	0	0	0	1	0	0	0
select(1,3)	0	1	0	1	0	0	0
increase(2)	0	1	1	1	0	0	1
select(2,3)	0	1	1	2	0	0	1
select(1,3)	0	2	1	2	0	0	1
increase(2)	0	2	2	2	0	0	2

cmd	P_1	$\hat{P}_1$	P_2	$\hat{P}_2$	P_3	$\hat{P}_3$	P_B	T
init	0	0	0	0	0	0	0	0
pass(2)	0	0	0	0	0	0	0	2
select(2,3)	0	0	0	1	0	0	0	2
pass(1)	0	0	0	1	0	0	0	1
select(1,3)	0	1	0	1	0	0	0	1
pass(2)	0	1	0	1	0	0	0	2
increase(2)	0	1	1	1	0	0	1	2

Remark 4. The goal of an attacker is to disrupt the system, and as such the attacker will seek to perform repeated attacks to continue to disrupt normal system operation. Therefore, an actual attack on the system will produce a trace similar to Table 5 rather than the single case considered by Lemma 1. Also note that this is a strong attack model in which the attacker always chooses to act during migrations made by a single supplier. It is possible to use a weaker attack model, in which the attacker acts during migrations made by any arbitrary supplier regardless of prior attack history, but the analysis would depend on other variables such as the number of attackers in the system.

5   Token Solution

The nondeducible attack succeeds when the attacker forms a migration at the same time as another supplier in the system. One approach to detect this attack would be to utilize mutual exclusion to prevent concurrent access to the critical section, in this case the formation of a migration contract. This would force suppliers to behave in a manner consistent with Table 3 in which each supply node must wait for the previous migration contract to complete before it can form its own contract. The simplest approach to add mutual exclusion to the system model is to utilize a token mechanism where a supplier can only issue its commands when it has the token. This mechanism can utilize a simple token-ring implementation where the token has a fixed iteration path, and nodes that do not need to form a migration simply pass the token. A more sophisticated algorithm, such as Raymond's tree algorithm [8], could also be implemented to improve access time to the critical section.

The use of a token introduces a new token-holder state variable T which stores the index of the node that has the token. An additional command *pass(i)* must be introduced which updates the token-holder variable. This variable is shared state information available at the *system* level. The system commands are then modified to guard against the token-holder as shown in Table 7.

Theorem 2. *The introduction of a token-based mutual exclusion algorithm to the system model makes the repeated fake supply attack fully deducible.*

Proof. Table 6 presents the nondeducible attack from Lemma 1 with the addition of a token. The command sequence has been modified to include the *pass*

Table 7. Modified State Transition Commands

command	level	description
pass(i)	*system*	node i obtains possession of the token $T' = i$
select(i,j)	*system*	supplier i forms a migration contract with demand node j **if** $T = i$ **then** $\hat{P}_i' \leftarrow \hat{P}_i + 1$
increase(i)	L_i	node i increases its local generation by one unit **if** $T = i$ **and** $P_i < \hat{P}_i$ **then** $P_i' = P_i + 1$ **and** $P_B' = P_B + 1$

commands needed for the sequence to be a valid system trace. Note that, consistent with the analysis for Lemma 1, the state transition of interest will be the final transition from $\{1, 1, 0, 0, 2\} \rightarrow \{1, 1, 0, 1, 2\}$ with states in $view_L$ appended to include the state variable T. In Lemma 1, both high-level commands of $increase(1)$ and $increase(2)$ were enabled which made the attack nondeducible. However, after the introduction of a token, only the node with an index equal to the token-holder value $T = 2$ is allowed to issue the $increase$ command. Therefore, $increase(1)$ is not enabled during the final state transition through mere observation of the value for T. Since one possible set of high-level commands has been discarded, the attack is deducible and fails. □

Remark 5. The facet that breaks nondeducibility is that a token identifies the source of a change in the shared distribution line. When an $increase$ in P_B occurs in $view_L$, the origin of the $increase$ can be determined by observation of T. In this way, although power cannot be watermarked in the physical layer, the cyber layer can be used to uniquely identify the $increase$ commands.

Observe that the system does not require the token mechanism for its normal operation. The token is only used to break a nondeducible pair in the system and determine the origin of an attack. Therefore, the system does not need to use a single token and serialize the migration contracts. Instead, the initial system state can contain no tokens. Then, when a nondeducible attack occurs, the system can generate a new token that applies only to the nodes active during the nondeducible attack. This defines a new critical section and applies the token mechanism to a subset of suspicious nodes in the system. In this way, the token-based mechanism can be used to break a nondeducible attack at runtime without the performance overhead of a full mutual exclusion implementation.

6   Conclusion

This work presented a nondeducible attack against a current smart grid architecture, proved that the attack is nondeducible if the attacker performs concurrent migrations with another supplier, and presented a token-based mechanism to break the nondeducibility. The main theoretical contribution of this work is demonstration of how information flow properties such as nondeducibility can be used to analyze the security of an attack rather than the security of a system. Such application of information flow properties gives rise to the notion of deducible and nondeducible attacks, where a deducible attack is detectable and thus preventable while a nondeducible attack cannot be prevented. This work has also presented a system design that is resilient against at least one form of nondeducible attack through use of mutual exclusion.

Future work will extend the model to consider alternative attack models and expand the token-based mechanism into a generalized method of breaking nondeducible attacks on arbitrary systems.

Acknowledgment. The authors acknowledge the support of the Future Renewable Electric Energy Delivery and Management Center; a National Science Foundation supported Engineering Research Center, under grant NSF EEC-081212.

References

1. Akella, R., Meng, F., Ditch, D., McMillin, B., Crow, M.: Distributed power balancing for the freedm system. In: First IEEE International Conference on Smart Grid Communications, SmartGridComm, pp. 7–12 (October 2010)
2. Akella, R., McMillin, B.M.: Information flow analysis of energy management in a smart grid. In: Schoitsch, E. (ed.) SAFECOMP 2010. LNCS, vol. 6351, pp. 263–276. Springer, Heidelberg (2010)
3. Efthymiou, C., Kalogridis, G.: Smart grid privacy via anonymization of smart metering data. In: First IEEE International Conference on Smart Grid Communications. SmartGridComm, pp. 238–243 (October 2010)
4. Falliere, N., Murchu, L., Chien, E.: W32. stuxnet dossier (February 2011), http://www.symantec.com/content/en/us/enterprise/media/security_response/whitepapers/w32_stuxnet_dossier.pdf
5. Gamage, T.T., McMillin, B.M., Roth, T.P.: Enforcing information flow security properties in cyber-physical systems: A generalized framework based on compensation. In: Proceedings of the 2010 IEEE 34th Annual Computer Software and Applications Conference Workshops, COMPSACW 2010, pp. 158–163. IEEE Computer Society, Washington, DC (2010)
6. Lin, J., Yu, W., Yang, X., Xu, G., Zhao, W.: On false data injection attacks against distributed energy routing in smart grid. In: IEEE/ACM Third International Conference on Cyber-Physical Systems, ICCPS, pp. 183–192 (April 2012)
7. Liu, Y., Ning, P., Reiter, M.K.: False data injection attacks against state estimation in electric power grids. In: Proceedings of the 16th ACM Conference on Computer and Communications Security, CCS 2009, pp. 21–32. ACM, New York (2009)
8. Raymond, K.: A distributed algorithm for multiple entries to a critical section. Information Processing Letters 30(4), 189–193 (1989)
9. Sutherland, D.: A model of information. In: Proceedings of the 9th National Computer Security Conference, pp. 175–183 (September 1986)

CPS-CSH Cyber-Physical Analysis and Design

Dale Fitch[1], Sahra Sedigh[2], Bruce McMillin[3], and Ravi Akella[3]

[1] School of Social Work, University of Missouri-Columbia,
Columbia, MO 65211, USA
fitchd@missouri.edu
[2] Department of Electrical and Computer Engineering,
Missouri University of Science and Technology, Rolla, MO 65409, USA
sedighs@mst.edu
[3] Computer Science Department, Missouri University of Science and Technology,
Rolla, MO 65409, USA
ff@mst.edu, ravi.akella@mail.mst.edu

Abstract. Existing methodologies to assess cyber-physical systems (CPSs) are hampered by their diverse nature and complexity. This paper proposes a model for cyber-physical systems design and analysis rooted in the social science approach to complex system analysis, Critical System Heuristics (CSH). The model affords an analysis at both the level of abstraction of functionality and the type of functionality within a CPS. The CPS-CSH model is developed and examples from reliability for electric smart grid systems and security for water distribution systems are presented.

Keywords: Cyber-Physical, Modeling, Security, Reliability, Analysis.

1 Introduction and Motivation

Cyber-physical systems (CPSs) are the integration of computation, as manifested by embedded computers and communication networks, with physical processes that often involve people. Control interactions, safety, liveness, security, fault tolerance, reliability, and human factors are among the many challenges in the development and analysis of CPSs, which must take into account the complex ways in which the cyber, physical, and social components interact [1]. Such systems include the electric power grid, water distribution systems, smart houses, and air traffic management, to name a few.

It is tempting to draw boundaries around individual components of such systems in an attempt to assemble a CPS, compositionally. Unfortunately, this is a significant challenge, as the cyber and physical components are inexorably intertwined; CPSs exhibit significant reliance on both their physical infrastructure and the cyber infrastructure by which it is governed. Thus, a view of a larger system boundary of increased complexity and scope is necessary. However, cyber and physical component properties are useful within the system boundary in comprising the overall system description. To address this challenge, structured analysis techniques in which system functions and system guarantees are

B. Hämmerli, N. Kalstad Svendsen, and J. Lopez (Eds.): CRITIS 2012, LNCS 7722, pp. 92–105, 2013.

quantified show promise in aiding system understanding. We expect that the structured analysis will be able to address questions of (1) what design aspects must be addressed within a CPS, (2) how do CPS components relate to each other, and (3) where do functionalities within a CPS occur?

This paper rises to the challenge of CPS modeling by developing a cyber-physical ontology that embraces both the physical and cyber system semantics in a meaningful, unified, way. Such an ontology aids in applying a structured system approach to assessment and modeling of not only reliability, but also safety, liveness, fault tolerance, security, and human aspects of CPSs. The approach to ontology generation applies Critical Systems Heuristics (CSH) [2] to CPS systems. CSH has been applied to social systems to understand their interactions, governance, and world view. Given the deep embedding of people in a CPS-CSH is a natural choice.

The outline of this paper is as follows. Section 2 presents related modeling literature from both science/engineering and the CSH model from the social sciences. Section 3 proposes the combined model, CPS-CSH. Section 4 applies the model to power grid infrastructure reliability modeling. Section 5 applies CPS-CSH to water transportation system security modeling. Section 6 discusses how to engage the full spectrum of CPS stakeholders: future CPS designers; users of these systems, e.g., utility and other companies; and those affected by these systems, e.g., utility and consumer boards.

2   Background and Related Literature

The paper bridges i) engineering and computer science and ii) the social sciences to develop a modeling framework for CPSs. This section presents concepts from each category that serve as the foundation of our research and contrasts this paper with related literature.

2.1   Related Concepts and Studies from Engineering and Computer Science

CPSs manage cyber, physical, and network resources to accomplish a task. Qualitative modeling on interdependencies among these various resources has been reported, based primarily on interdependencies [3, 4] among the cyber, physical, and network infrastructures. In particular, the EU Critical Utility Infrastructural Analysis initiative (CRUTIAL) aims to understand interdependencies among the power and information infrastructures [5–7]. While extensive, in these studies it is not always clear how the interactions are determined and at what level of system abstraction, can they be addressed.

Reliability and the Electric Power Grid. The advanced electric power grid, which as envisioned by the US Department of Energy [8], promises a self-healing infrastructure. One of the means through which this vision can be achieved is the use of cyber-coordinated power flow control devices that maintain the functionality of the physical power grid and ensure its adaptability to changes in loading conditions. The cyber and physical networks interact in nontrivial ways, and there is no one-to-one correspondence between their respective components.

Reliability of the physical infrastructure of the power grid has been the topic of decades of research. These studies are vital to analysis of modern power distribution systems, however, they give less consideration to cyber control, computation, or communication issues, and as such, their application to intelligent networks is limited. In [9], Kazemi and Billinton present reliability assessment of an automated power distribution system, in which control equipment is added to isolate earth faults and short-circuit faults from the rest of the system. The behavior of the system when such faults occur, and the probabilities of fault occurrence were used to determine the failure rates and repair times of system components. Even though this study analyzes the effect of adding control to the power grid it falls short of modeling and assessing system level effects.

This paper goes beyond the physical infrastructure to explore interdependencies among the cyber and physical components of CPSs with regard to their interdependencies among entities at different levels of the system hierarchy. Our goal is the development of a quantitative reliability model that captures such interdependencies.

Security. Security forms a non-functional aspect for CPSs, as does reliability. Security concerns include all entities of the CPS plus an observer/attacker. Security encompasses three aspects of confidentiality, availability, and integrity. The complex interactions within cyber-physical systems increase the difficulty of ensuring system security. Some of the reasons that pose additional risk to the electric power grid include increased complexity of the grid due to interconnected networks leading to an increased number of entry points for potential adversaries and the impact of coordinated cyber-physical attacks. A Department of Energy publication [10] discussed existing cyber security standards, focusing specifically on control systems used in critical infrastructures. The standards help identify requirements for secure communication protocols and systems.

While standards exist they are insufficient to ensure the security of CPSs given the evolution of a wide range of threats exploiting the vulnerabilities of these systems. The US Department of Homeland Security [11] identified essential challenges for protecting cyber infrastructures - i) appropriate integration, protection, detection, and response mechanisms to construct CPSs that are resilient to both accidental failures, malicious attacks or manipulations, and surreptitious monitoring, and ii) verification and validation of interconnected and interacting control system components for the overall process by developing models, theories, and tools that account for a system's cyber and physical components in an integrated, unified way. With so many stakeholders in security, it is not always understood what is being protected, and from whom.

2.2   Related Concepts and Studies from the Social Sciences

This paper proposes the use of Critical Systems Heuristics (CSH) to develop a qualitative ontological model of CPSs. CSH is a methodological approach to facilitate boundary setting when analyzing systems [2]. The resulting boundary judgment produces a "reference system" that defines the boundary issues and boundary categories; i.e., what is to be considered and what is to be left out. In sum, the boundary judgments determine the context of the application and deem assertions made about objects within the boundary to be valid. Conversely, no valid assertions can be made regarding objects outside the boundary of the reference system.

The determination of the scope of the context is crucial, because the scope defines what the content can entail and how data or information about that content is to be analyzed or assessed. As such, value assumptions are explicit in the CSH process. Implicit value assumptions often result in errors of logic, analysis, or the generalization of findings. These value assumptions are a key component of social systems in the sociotechnical system. Without explicit value statements, attributes of either the cyber system, the physical system, and/or the cyber-physical system may be misapplied; resulting in unforeseen consequences.

Drawing system boundaries is not an easy process. As soon as a boundary is drawn then claims are made that either "too much" or "not enough" was considered. Therefore Ulrich developed "heuristics" based upon Habermas' emancipatory discourse [12] in which four boundary issues are discussed: sources of 1. motivation, 2. power, 3. knowledge, and 4. legitimation. The first three constitute those involved in the system and the last constitutes those affected. Taken together they become the "reference system." Each of these four issues has three categories: 1. stakeholder - those involved or concerned by a situation, 2. the specific concern relevant to the stakeholder, and 3. difficulties regarding the concern because concerns compete with each other. Taken together, the four issues are examined by each of the three categories, resulting in twelve boundary questions. These twelve questions are framed within a CPS context and are represented in Table 1, the left column indicating the Ulrich heuristics, and the right, the proposed CPS-CSH model (further articulated in Section 3).

Jeppesen [13] used CSH to analyze a sustainable transportation system containing the interdependent components of land-use, urban design, and infrastructure along social, economic and environmental dimensions. These latter dimensions are reflective of CSH #12, Worldview, and capture the different visions of improvement that needed to be considered. Jeppesen found CSH to be helpful in delineating the different levels of the system to be analyzed. Germane to this paper was that regardless of policies implemented at the highest level of the system, the national level, if the local level found no legitimacy in the claims (CSH #12), then they were disregarded. Stated otherwise, if the lowest level of the system does not function as purposed, then higher system levels will not be able to achieve their purpose either. Maru and Woodford [14] used CSH to examine the strategic planning process for natural resource sustainability. Of particular importance to this paper is that their application of CSH revealed

Table 1. CSH in the CPS context

Societal Sources of Motivation	Cyber-Physical Objects
1. Who is the client or customer or that which is acted upon?	Controlled Object
2. What is the purpose of that which is acted upon?	Regulated Object Functionality
3. What is the measure of improvement or success for this client or customer or that which is acted upon?	Improved Operational Element
Sources of Power	**Cyber-Physical Environment**
4. Who or what is the decision maker or controller?	Control Element
5. What resources are controlled by the decision maker?	Actor on Object and State Information
6. What does the decision maker not control or what is the environment?	Cyber-Physical Environment
Sources of Knowledge	**Cyber-Physical Expertise**
7. Who is to be considered a professional or expert in the situation?	Domain Expert
8. What expertise do these professional's hold? That is, what is considered relevant knowledge? Which methodologies do they use?	Domain Knowledge
9. What is the guarantor of success? That is, upon what axioms or algorithms do the professionals rely?	System Correctness
Sources of Legitimation	**Cyber-Physical Requirements**
10. Who or what is a witness to the interests of those affected but not involved? That is, who or what can observe the actions of the decision makers upon the client or customer or that which is acted upon?	Embedded Monitor
11. What secures the emancipation of those affected from the premises or assertions made by those involved? That is, how can unanticipated adverse consequences be minimized?	Evaluation of the Methodology used (#8) or the resulting Guarantee (#9)
12. What worldview pervades? That is, what different visions of improvement should be considered?	Protects Against Requirements Invalidation

the need for epistemological pluralism; i.e., not all sources of knowledge (CSH #7-9) were equally recognized. Furthermore, a measure of improvement suitable for one level of the system rarely worked at a higher level of the system.

3 Development of CPS-CSH Model Architecture

The overarching objective of this work is to develop a system modeling architecture that facilitates assessment, prediction, and eventually certification of the dependability of cyber-physical critical infrastructures. This section presents the development of the CPS-CSH model architecture.

Applying CSH to a CPS presents a challenge in identifying boundary aspects #1-12. While CSH was developed for human systems, it has strong analogs in CPSs. Referring to Table 1, in a CPS, guarantors (#9) may be cyber and not human resources. A decision-make (#4) becomes a cyber or physical control element. Witnesses (#10) become embedded monitors. Purposes (#2) become mathematical expressions for (#3) regulation and improvement.

Crucial for the application of CPS-CSH is that the discourse related to Legitimation (CSH #10-12) is conducted by entities meta to or apart from the decision maker or controller (CSH #4). In a sense, CSH #1-9 might be viewed as a subsystem of CSH #10-12. Moving back and forth between determining exactly what is the reference system will always result in drawing different system boundaries. Thus, what may be considered a system at one level of discourse or analysis may become a subsystem when the boundaries are redrawn. Moving back and forth between these system boundaries, or moving up or down between systems and subsystems, is analogous to different hierarchial levels of the system. Therefore, moving down one level of hierarchy is akin to examining the components or subsystems of an overall system. Conversely, moving up one level of hierarchy is to examine a larger system, which, in turn, may always be considered a part of still a larger system. Going back and forth between system hierarchy levels unwittingly becomes extremely problematic regarding Sources of Knowledge, because what constitutes knowledge and its attendant logic at one level of the hierarchy cannot by definition be the same guarantor of knowledge at a different level of hierarchy. For example, an algorithm that assesses the reliability (CSH #9) of a physical system (or separately a cyber system) cannot be the same algorithm used to assess the reliability of a cyber-physical system. The attendant logic requires a fundamentally different mathematical or semantic representation.

4   Application of CPS-CSH to Power Systems Reliability

The following two tables apply CSH to the advanced electric power grid system at two levels of the hierarchy, that of the Power Flow Control (PFC) device, and then at a higher layer of the hierarchy - the entire CPS as seen by the utility operator. Different than CSH in the social sciences, a CPS has mathematical constraints for certain boundary aspects #1-12.

The system is a graph of devices, $PFC_i, i = 1, ...n$ interconnected by a_{ij} with power flows $f(a_{ij})$.

System states are denoted as $S_k, k = 1, ..., N$, each of which can be classified as "operational" or "failed" to facilitate assessment of reliability. Each PFC (depicted in Figure 1) contains an embedded computer that runs a Long Term Control (LTC) that provides control settings to Power Electronics (PE) and has an embedded Monitor (M). Both the Monitor and the Long Term Control

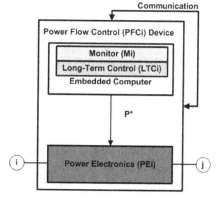

Fig. 1. Power Flow Control Device

Table 2. CPS-CSH Analysis with Boundary at the PFC

	CSH Boundary Categories	PFC Devices	Constraint
	Societal Sources of Motivation	**Cyber-Physical Objects**	
1.	Controlled Object	Power Line, a_{ij}	
2.	Regulated Object Functionality	To Regulate Power Flow $f(a_{ij})$ in a line a_{ij}	
3.	Improved Operational Element	Regulated Power Flow $f(a_{ij}$ in a line $a_{ij})$	
	Sources of Power	**Cyber-Physical Environment**	
4.	Control Element	Long Term Control, LTC_i	Capacity Constraints: $f(a_{ij}) < Max_{ij}$
5.	Actor on Object and State Information	Power Electronics, PE_i, line flows, $f(a_{ij})$, messages from Neighboring PFC devices, PFC_k, $k \neq i$ Information from Generators and Loads	$f(P_i^* = f(a_{ij})$ $(S_i =$ "operational")
6.	Cyber-Physical Environment	Neighboring PFC devices, PFC_k, $k \neq i$ Generators and Loads	
	Sources of Knowledge	**Cyber-Physical Expertise**	
7.	Domain Expert	Electrical Engineers and Computer Scientists	
8.	Domain Knowledge	Max Flow Algorithms, PE design	
9.	System Correctness	Methodology that produced design	
	Sources of Legitimation	**Cyber-Physical Requirements**	
10.	Embedded Monitor	M_i	
11.	Evaluation of the Methodology used (#8) or the resulting Guarantee (#9)	Evaluating methodology and design	
12.	Protects Against Requirements Invalidation	Protects against malfunction	

communicate with other PFCs to run a maximum flow algorithm (Max Flow) to determine these settings. The PFC controls line a_{ij}.

4.1 Model Queries for Reliability

Preliminary work in CPS reliability showed that a cyber-physical system's reliability is not a composition of individual reliability models, but is a system-level aspect [15]. Reliability is initially identified in CPS-CSH at the Advanced Power Grid level as a measure of improvement. As such, while reliability is not composable, aspects of reliability measurement, such as fault injection occur at lower levels of the hierarchy than the system.

The work of Avizienis et al. [16] provides insight into a process by which one traverses downward from the system level of the hierarchy to the "atomic" component level; i.e., the point where no further internal structure can be delineated.

However, they do not describe how different levels of systems function within and between each other. To the extent that any given system may interact with other systems; i.e., at the interfaces, this interaction is not differentiated between system to system vs. subsystem to system in their taxonomic model. What is needed is a general algorithm to determine the appropriate level of the system hierarchy for meaningful assessment of reliability or other metrics.

Such an algorithm is motivated by analysis within CSH. For example, assume that we have a PFC device (#4 Decision Maker) that is designed to handle power line overloads (#2 Purpose) and the algorithm designed for that purpose (#4) has been tested and validated through research methodology (#9 Guarantee). However, we may have a power grid manager who believes that the PFC device can also detect hacker intrusions (a different #2 Purpose). As soon as he/she asserts that the use of the device can do so, then the system would reject that use because the PFC device was not designed for that purpose and it does not carry the associated guarantee.

As a second example, if dependability is deemed to be the "measure of improvement" (CSH #3) for a system, then attributes such as availability and maintainability are specific to controlled objects (CSH #1), chosen by a decision maker (CSH #4) for a specific purpose based upon what professionals (CSH #7) who employ certain methodologies (CSH #8) have determined to be the best solution for that given purpose (CSH #9). Once the controlled object changes, then the controller for that object changes, along with all the guarantees.

CSH, alone, indicates that the guarantees that a system will work as designed are derived from research studies. CPS-CSH refines this analysis to CPSs; guarantees become algorithms and mathematical/logical constraints (as in Table 1).

Stated conversely, if system designers identify the guarantees (CSH #9) upon which a system is based, then one should be able to infer the types of decision makers (CSH #4) for which that guarantee might be used. Furthermore, once the decision makers are identified, we should then be able to infer what types of objects they can control and for what purpose. At any point, if there is any nonequivalence between any of these elements, then an error of logic has occurred. In sum, once we translate the CSH heuristics into ontological classes, each heuristic/class will have various attributes dependent upon what it is that needs to be controlled, e.g., a PFC or valve. The task is to explore various controllers and derive the CSH attributes for each heuristic. Once identified, we can then ascribe the constraints (or mathematical algorithms) that can be used in an automated system.

4.2   Using Results of CPS-CSH to Guide Fault Injection

Assessment of reliability of a system entails (at minimum) enumeration of "operational" and "failed" system states. More sophisticated measures of dependability, such as survivability (fraction of system functionality that is maintained after failure and before repair), performability (composite metric that reflects performance and reliability) consider partial functionality. This will require us to evolve the model to consider "degrees of functionality," rather than a binary notion of functional and failed states.

Table 3. CPS-CSH Analysis with Boundary at the Advanced Power Grid

CSH Boundary Categories	Advanced Power Grid	Constraint
Societal Sources of Motivation	**Cyber-Physical Objects**	
1. Controlled Object	Physical grid (collection of lines)	G_{Phys}
2. Regulated Object Functionality	Prevent overload across the grid	$\forall a_{ij}, G_{Phys} f(a_{ij}) < c(a_{ij})$
3. Improved Operational Element	Reliability of grid, no cascading failures	$R_n = (\mathbf{\Pi_0})^T (\prod_{l=1}^{n} \mathbf{\Lambda}_l)\mathbf{u}$
Sources of Power	**Cyber-Physical Environment**	
4. Control Element	Collective PFC devices Devices	Run the max flow algorithm
5. Actor on Object and State Information	Devices $\forall PE_i, i = 1, \ldots, N$ Electrical lines $\forall_{xy} f(a_{xy}$	
6. Cyber-Physical Environment	Generators, Loads	
Sources of Knowledge	**Cyber-Physical Expertise**	
7. Domain Expert	ECE/CS People/Operations Managers	
8. Domain Knowledge	Systems Design	
9. System Correctness	Methodology that produced the design	
Sources of Legitimation	**Cyber-Physical Requirements**	
10. Embedded Monitor	$M_i, i = 1, \cdots, N$	
11. Evaluation of the Methodology used	Evaluating Design Methodology of all PFCs	Flow Balance: $\sum_{x,y \in V} f(a_{ix}) + f(a_{yj}) = 0$ Capacity Constraints: $\forall_{xy} f(a_{xy}) < Max_{xy}$
12. Protects Against Requirements Invalidation	Protect against malfunction	

Fault injection can facilitate classification of system (or component) states; one or more faults are triggered, in hopes of observing what happens in the course of actual system failure (whether accidental or maliciously induced). CPS-CSH analysis helps us determine the lowest level of the system hierarchy where faults can be injected. Furthermore, the CPS-CSH model can facilitate tracking the propagation of failures caused by the induced fault through the system hierarchy, and can identify the entity responsible for detecting or mitigating the failure.

Returning to the CPS-CSH model of Table 3, there are several possibilities for the boundary at which to inject faults to effect the Measure of Improvement (CSH#3). While Customer (CSH#1) or Purpose (CSH#2) are possible levels to inject faults such as line overloads or disconnections, it is not until Emancipation, CSH#11, in which disruption of the overall system flow can take place. A mathematical model for system-level reliability of this grid corresponding to Emancipation at this CPS-CSH level is the Markov chain Imbeddable Structure (MIS), where the state of a system composed of n components is represented by an n-dimensional binary vector, S. Each of the 2^n possible states of this vector represents one combination of component failures for the system. At this level, software faults are injected to represent failures in the cyber infrastructure [15]. Physical failures are concurrently represented, creating integrated cyber-physical failure scenarios at the system boundary.

5 Application to CPS-CSH to Water Systems Security

Impetus for CPS-CSH in the security field is provided by [17] which discusses security modeling and information flow (confidentiality) for CPSs in gas and power networks. Security analysis of CPSs done by Shastry's team; [18] tested the vulnerability of a SCADA system with an irrigation canal system. In these studies vulnerabilities were found such that a malicious attack could effectively hide in the error term of the SCADA control algorithm. As such, these attacks change the behavior of the underlying physical system in CPSs. In such systems, the state of the physical system is monitored by a network of sensors placed at specific locations on the physical system. The physical system is modeled as a composition of control input sequences, output sequences and output estimates calculated from the sensor data. Their argument is that "if we know how the output sequence, $y(k)$ of the physical system at a time instance, k should react to the control input sequence, $u(k)$, then any attack to the sensor data can be potentially detected by comparing the expected output $\overline{y(k)}$ with the received (possibly compromised) signal $y(\tilde{k})$." Depending on the quality of the estimate $\overline{y(k)}$, there could be false alarms indicating something wrong with the state of the system. It was assumed that since the signal sent by the sensors to the control center lies within specific bounds of measurement, at any specific time the signal coming from the attack sensors can be made to fall within the same range. These attack models also assume that the attacker has a knowledge of: (1) the exact linear control model of the physical system, (2) the time to detect an attack and the probability of a false alarm, and (3) the control command signals (range of $y(k)$).

The depth and breadth of knowledge required to create and defend against this attack illustrates several CSH aspects. Table 4 depicts a CPS-CSH analysis of a CPS Water System (middle column). The CPS Water System Regulates (CSH #2) water lines (CSH #1) to control the water flow through a hydraulic system. Water management is the actor on the water and state information (CSH #5) that meets a guarantee of success (CSH #9), essentially a functional water system that delivers water flow at adequate pressure. As such, they were not designed for the purpose of detecting malicious water removal. The operational element (CSH #3) improves water flow regulation. All of these are functional aspects of the CPS Water System.

To introduce intrusion detection into the CPS Water System requires examining (CSH #9) more closely. While a functional water system is a functional guarantee of success, it is not necessarily the same as that for security and the controller (CSH #4) must now compare the expected output $\overline{y(k)}$ with the received (possibly compromised) signal $y(\tilde{k})$. Technologically, this controller is an embedded monitor (CSH #10) that monitors security aspects rather than

Table 4. CSH in the CPS context

	CPS-CSH Boundary	CyberPhysical Water System	Hydraulic Intrusion Detection System
	Societal Sources of Motivation	**Cyber-Physical Objects**	
1.	Controlled Object	Individual lines and collection of water lines and associated cyber controllers	Water system
2.	Regulated Object Functionality	Monitor and control the water flow $(y(k))$, capable of responding to faults, in order to deliver water	To detect malicious intrusions; capable of responding to attacks
3.	Improved Operational Element	Regulated water flow	Minimize $\overline{y(k)} - \tilde{y}(k)$
	Sources of Power	**Cyber-Physical Environment**	
4.	Control Element	SCADA devices and human supervisors	Plant manager; Intrusion Detection system operator
5.	Actor on Object and State Information	Information from other devices and monitors(RTUs), water management devices and equipment	SCADA systems; other monitoring systems
6.	Cyber-Physical Environment	Systems/events external to the water plant/system	Maliciously introduced catastrophic events, e.g. large scale supra system events, e.g., nuclear events
	Sources of Knowledge	**Cyber-Physical Expertise**	
7.	Domain Expert	Hydraulic engineers; Computer scientists; Hydraulic system engineers	Cyber-security specialists; Hydraulic engineers; Computer scientists, Sociologists
8.	Domain Knowledge	Hydraulic and CS Algorithms; hydrodynamic models	Intrusion Detection algorithms; Hydraulic system algorithms; Sociological Theories
9.	System Correctness	Methodologies that produces the water system design and make it functional	Sequential detection theory; sequential probablity ratio test(SPRT); cumulative sum statistic(CUSUM), anomoly detection
	Sources of Legitimation	**Cyber-Physical Requirements**	
10.	Embedded Monitor	Water utility commissions	Local/regional emergency management commission
11.	Evaluation of the Methodology used (#8) or the resulting Guarantee (#9)	Evaluative Methodology; Review hearings	Due diligence; disaster scenario simulations
12.	Protects Against Requirements Invalidation	Protects against malfunctions; affordable, potable water	Protects against malicious saboteurs

functional aspects. Correspondingly, the measure of improvement (CSH #3) becomes a secure water system.

Continuing with the CPS-CSH analysis, the research that demonstrates the effectiveness of SCADA systems (CSH #9) is not the type of research that demonstrates the effectiveness of intrusion detection systems. These two types of systems will require different types of researchers (CSH #7) who possess different kinds of expertise (CSH #8). The resulting CPS-CSH model is shown in column 4 of 4.

Returning to the analysis of [18], the authors identify that while the embedded monitor can detect short-term attacks, it cannot detect longer-term attacks. They appeal to a human operator (CSH #9) to make the final determination on security, thus providing the impetus for developing a higher level of the system. As such, the final determination of security falls outside of the CPS, and, ultimately, the CPS becomes governed again by society, returning to the original CSH model as humans become involved.

6   CPS-CSH: Education and Discourse

It is envisioned that discourse will have a positive impact on outreach to society by moving beyond the technical-instrumental rationality of what systems do to the normative rationality of discussing the means to what ends. Doing so requires a communicative discourse that allows the exploration of values, assumptions, and worldviews that recognizes that CPSs reside in organizational and social systems hence the resulting situational complexity is comprised of both subjective as much as technical rationalities. The implication is that an adequate understanding of such systems cannot be achieved without involving those concerned, i.e., stakeholder groups [19].

The ultimate source of system validity can only be deemed by these stakeholders, the witnesses (CSH #10-12). Witnesses are easily conceptualized at the subsystem level in that the system functions as the witness. However, moving up one level beyond the CPS places the system in the social realm, i.e., a power or water utility serving the larger public. From this perspective, witnesses observe the workings of CPSs. Some of these witnesses become formalized (CSH #10) to delineate what the system should do (CSH #11) as a reflection of these larger social values (CSH #12), e.g., a public utility commission. In addition, one might consider environmental, economic or other political groups, e.g., legislators.

CPS-CSH can facilitate discussion among these stakeholder groups by reviewing CSH #1-9 with them and eliciting from them the values and worldviews that need to be considered when articulating CSH #1-9. For example, different measures of improvement related to reliability and security can be discussed along with their attendant costs and consequences. Ultimately, witnesses may have an opinion as to what should ultimately be served (CSH #1) by any given system weighing consumer and resource constraints.

7   Summary

The proposed CPS-CSH model is a fundamentally different approach to CPS systems analysis that draws on social science analysis of complex systems coupled with cyber-physical systems aspects. CPS-CSH was applied to system-level reliability and security analysis. It shows great promise in identifying salient features of complex CPSs, showing where functionality must be implemented, and showing where it cannot be implemented.

Acknowledgment. The authors acknowledge the support of the Future Renewable Electric Energy Delivery and Management Center; a National Science Foundation supported Engineering Research Center, under grant NSF EEC-081212.

References

1. Lee, E.: Cyber physical systems: Design challenges. In: 2008 11th IEEE International Symposium on Object Oriented Real-Time Distributed Computing (ISORC), pp. 363–369 (May 2008)
2. Ulrich, W.: Beyond methodology choice: Critical systems thinking as critically systemic discourse. Journal of the Operational Research Society 54(4), 325–342 (2003)
3. Dueas-Osorio, L., Craig, J.I., Goodno, B.J.: Probabilistic response of interdependent infrastructure networks. In: Proceedings of the 2nd Annual Meeting of the Asian-pacific Network of Centers for Earthquake Engineering Research (ANCER), Honolulu, Hawaii (July 2004)
4. Laprie, J.C., Kanoun, K., Kaaniche, M.: Modelling interdependencies between the electricity and information infrastructures. In: Proc. of the Int'l Conf. on Computer Safety, Reliability and Security (SAFECOMP), pp. 54–67 (September 2007)
5. Dondossola, G., Garrone, F., Szanto, J., Fiorenza, G.: Emerging Information Technology Scenarios for the Control and Management of the Distribution Grid. In: Proc. of the 19th Int'l Conf. on Electricity Distribution (2007)
6. Geer, D.: Security of Critical Control Systems Sparks Concern. Computer 39(1), 20–23 (2006)
7. Deconinck, G., Belmans, R., Driesem, J., Nauwelaers, B., Lil, E.V.: Reaching for 100% Reliable Electricity Services: Multi-system Interactions and Fundamental Solutions. In: Proc. of the DIGESEC-CRIS Workshop 2006 Influence of Distributed Generation and Renewable Generation on Power System Security, Magdeburg, Germany (December 2006)
8. Office of Electric Transmission and Distribution: "Grid 2030": A National Vision for Electricity's Second 100 Years (2003)
9. Kazemi, S., Fotuhi-Firuzabad, B.R.: Reliability assessment of an automated distribution system. IET Generation, Transportation and Distribution 1(2), 223–233 (2007)
10. A summary of control system security standards activities in the energy sector. Technical report, Department of Energy, Office of Electricity Delivery and Energy Reliability, Washington, DC (2005)

11. Final report on workshop on future directions in cyber-physical systems security. Technical report, Department of Homeland Security (2010)
12. Habermas, J.: Communication and the evolution of society. Beacon, Boston, MA (1979)
13. Jeppesen, S.: Exploring an explicit use of the concept of sustainability in transport planning. Systemic Practice and Action Research 24(2), 133–146 (2011)
14. Maru, Y., Woodford, K.: Enhancing emancipatory systems methodologies for sustainable development. Systemic Practice and Action Research 14(1), 61–77 (2001)
15. Faza, A., Sedigh, S., McMillin, B.: Integrated cyber-physical fault injection for reliability analysis of the smart grid. In: Schoitsch, E. (ed.) SAFECOMP 2010. LNCS, vol. 6351, pp. 277–290. Springer, Heidelberg (2010)
16. Avizienis, A., Laprie, J.C., Randell, B., Landwehr, C.: Basic concepts and taxonomy of dependable and secure computing. IEEE Transactions on Dependable and Secure Computing 1(1), 11–33 (2004)
17. Akella, R., Tang, H., McMillin, B.: Analysis of information flow security in cyber-physical systems. International Journal of Critical Infrastructure Protection 3-4, 157–173 (2010)
18. Amin, S., Litrico, X., Sastry, S., Bayen, A.M.: Stealthy deception attacks on water SCADA systems. In: HSCC, pp. 161–170 (2010)
19. Ulrich, W.: Operational research and critical systems thinking-an integrated perspective part 1: OR as applied systems thinking. Journal of the Operational Research Society, 1–20 (2011)

Modeling Emergency Response Plans with Coloured Petri Nets

Manuel Cheminod, Ivan Cibrario Bertolotti,
Luca Durante, and Adriano Valenzano

CNR-IEIIT, C.so Duca degli Abruzzi 24, I-10129 Torino, Italy
{manuel.cheminod,ivan.cibrario,luca.durante,
adriano.valenzano}@ieiit.cnr.it

Abstract. Critical Infrastructures are constantly affected by threats of various nature. Contingency planning in this context is needed in order to ensure an adequate management of emergencies. In particular, emergency response plans define the interactions and operations to be performed inside the infrastructure and among different systems during the occurrence of emergencies. The criticality of these systems need a proper methodology for the analysis of the designed emergency plans. In this paper we propose the Coloured Petri Net formalism as the basis for modeling and analysis of emergency response plans.

Keywords: Critical Infrastructure, Contingency Plan, Emergency Response, Coloured Petri Net.

1 Introduction

The modern society heavily depends on the reliable production and distribution of vital goods like water, electricity, gas and oil and on the availability of transportation networks (road, air, rail, and so on). The infrastructures responsible for such vital resources are, in fact, called Critical Infrastructures. These systems are constantly under the menace of several threats of different nature: human threats, environmental threats and cyber threats [13].

The needs and requirements that these critical systems are asked to satisfy have constantly increased in the latest years. This fact has directly influenced the complexity of the infrastructures themselves to the point that, now, we have several systems that are tightly connected through a network of dependencies and interdependencies [7].

The importance of critical infrastructures is particularly evident taking into consideration the effects of failures in such systems: because of the strict connections and strong dependencies among different infrastructures, a failure in one system is likely to start a cascading effect that causes failures in other systems. Eventually, this propagation will result in severe damages that can be quantified in terms of extensive monetary losses but also in terms of human lives [15].

For these reasons, the protection of critical infrastructures is of utmost importance [9] and several methodologies have been developed to deal with this

B. Hämmerli, N. Kalstad Svendsen, and J. Lopez (Eds.): CRITIS 2012, LNCS 7722, pp. 106–117, 2013.
© Springer-Verlag Berlin Heidelberg 2013

problem [12,14,17]. The first step in the protection of critical systems is the identification of threats and risks and the design and application of countermeasures
able to remove or reduce such risks. This process is usually referred to as "risk
management". However, residual risks are always present and must be managed
by carefully planning what to do in case of incidents. In particular *emergency
management systems* (EMS) have to be designed properly in order to quickly
and effectively react to incidents and to recover the infrastructure's normal state
of operations. Given the already mentioned complexity of these infrastructures
it is important to have the support of precise methodologies able to verify and
validate the correctness of the procedures and plans prepared by the EMS. In
this paper, we present a modeling approach that leverages the well known Petri
Net formalism in order to describe the system and it's interactions with the
EMS.

The rest of the paper is organized as follows: Section 2 describes what is
an emergency management system and what information it includes, Section 3
presents a subset of a realistic case study involving oil&gas transportation, Section 4 demonstrates how the procedures included in the emergency management
system can be translated in a formal model through the Petri Net formalism, Section 5 shows how the formal model can be analysed, Section 6 presents some of
the alternative approaches to the modeling of emergency management systems,
Finally, Section 7 draws some conclusions.

2   Emergency Management

Several types of emergencies can occur during the lifetime of a system. In general an emergency is the result of the occurrence of an unexpected event or a
combination of unforeseen events like, for instance, a human error or a technological error or a natural event like a flood or an earthquake. Moreover, some
emergencies can, in turn, cause other incidents to occur, like in the case of an
uncontrolled fire affecting different environments.

In general, the scope of an emergency system is to identify, anticipate and
respond to catastrophic events in order to reduce the potential effects to the
system. It is possible to identify four phases in an emergency management system: mitigation, preparedness, response, recovery [11]. The mitigation phase is
usually supported by the risk analysis process that combines the identification of
risks with their mitigation by means of the most appropriate countermeasures.
The preparedness phase involves the identification of possible emergencies and
the design of the procedures that all the agents involved must follow in case of
actual emergency occurrence. Usually, the procedures are organized in (semi) formal documents known as contingency plans. A contingency plan includes all the
policy and procedures designed to respond and overcome incidents and recover
the functionality of the critical infrastructure. There is not a unique standardized
way to fill a contingency plan, each organization has its own. Nonetheless, several type of information are shared among different plans. A contingency plan,
in fact, must describe the different foreseen incident scenarios and must define

the procedures able to identify the correct scenario in case of incident. Moreover, given that a critical infrastructure includes interactions among internal agents but also between internal and external entities (e.g. governmental agencies) it is mandatory to define precisely the responsibilities: who is in charge of what, who must communicate or interact with external entities and so on. The contingency plan includes also *emergency response plans*, that is documents describing what is to be performed in the system in order to react to incidents. Ideally, it is possible to identify three different parts in an emergency response plan: a detection part, an identification part and a response part [5]. The detection part is responsible to define which of the system events are to be monitored and forwarded to the identification part. This one, in turn, defines the conditions that are to be satisfied in order to clearly identify an incident scenario. The response part, instead, describes operatively the actions to be performed in the system.

3   Case Study

A case study is provided as an example of an emergency response plan. The case study involves the transportation of oil and gas from the compressor station of a producing country to the receiving terminal of the consuming one through offshore pipelines. Several agents are involved in this scenario but, for sake of conciseness, in this work we focus only on the offshore part of the pipeline system.

The contingency plan includes the identification of risks and of potential accidental events. In the case study here presented the major risk is the release of fluid running inside the pipelines. Potential accidental events are related to several different possible causes: corrosion of the pipelines, natural hazards, interaction with ship traffic (for instance, a sinking ship) or other (like human malicious actions).

The potential occurrence of unwanted events directly implies the need for an emergency response plan able to deal with the leak of fluids. The detection part of this plan identifies the information that need to be monitored in order to identify the emergency. Several sources of information are available in a typical critical infrastructure: external warnings (e.g. from external authorities), geological events, results from internal inspections, unexpected deviations of process parameters. These information pass through the detection part of the ERP which triggers the identification operations and, in particular situations, can trigger the actions defined in the response part.

In this work we focus on the monitoring of process parameters. In particular the parameters to keep under control are the pressure at the compressor station and the flow rate at the receiving terminal (values are exchanged through a communication system). If a pressure drop is detected and if the value is below a specific threshold then the first operation to perform is to check the status of the various instruments involved. If the instruments are not working then the first action to be commanded to the system is the request for repairing the instruments. On the other hand, if the instruments are correctly working then the ERP has to check the flow rate at the receiving station. If the flow

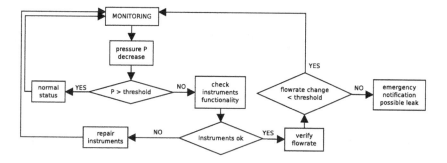

Fig. 1. Flowchart for emergency identification and notification

rate is decreasing more than a given threshold then a possible leak is identified and the proper activities are to be triggered (like, for instance, warning the correct authorities). The procedure here described is depicted by the flowchart of Figure 1.

4 Modeling

The verification and analysis of a critical infrastructure's emergency response plan is a complex task that cannot be successfully performed by hand. The amount of information available requires an approach based on models. Three elements must be translated into a formal model: the system description, the emergency response plan and the interaction between the two. The proposal of this work is to leverage the Coloured Petri Net formalism both for the modeling and for the subsequent analysis.

4.1 Coloured Petri Nets

Petri Net (PN) formalism is a well known graphical formalism able to represent processes. A system modeled as a PN is represented by a directed graph with two kind of nodes: places and transitions. Places are occupied by tokens which represent resources or states of the system. The transitions, and the rules that enable each transition to fire, represent the behaviour of the system. This formalism is powerful enough to build models for several kinds of processes. Coloured Petri Nets (CPN) (standardized in [4]) introduce extensions in the formalism that enable the description of custom data types for tokens and the definition of complex functions and constraints controlling the transitions. The enhanced expressiveness implies more compact and comprehensive resulting models.

In Figure 2 a small CPN is shown. The transition T is designed to consume tokens from three places: I, next and ID. From place I only tokens with the (i,p,v) signature are consumed where i, p and v are variables of custom types INT, P and V. Moreover, the guard [v>10] of the transition T effectively lets T to fire only if the consumed token has specific values (for variable v). This type

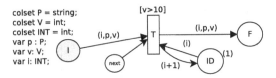

Fig. 2. Basic CPN

of token will be widely used in the rest of the paper and represents the value of some parameter: the variable p is a string (e.g.: "press", "flow") that identifies one parameter of the system (e.g.: pressure, flow rate) while the variable v states its actual value. The variable i is an incremental counter used to maintain the temporal order of the tokens.

This small Petri Net "transfers" tokens from the input place I to the place F, preserving the order dictated by variable i. This operation is constrained by two factors: the transition is enabled only if a token is present in the next place and if the i value of I matches the one of place ID (which starts with a value of 1 and is increased each time the transition fires).

4.2   Example

We provide now the CPN model for the emergency response plan described in Section 3. The response plan identifies the parameters that need to be monitored in order to identify possible emergencies. In particular, the sensible parameters are: pressure at compression station (*press*), instruments functionality (*instr*), flow rate at receiving terminal (*flow*). The actual values of these parameters are acquired from the system, are then elaborated and the proper actions are taken depending on the values read.

In Figure 3 a general schema depicting the interactions between the ERP model and the system model (from a high level point of view) is provided. The ERP model gets the parameters values from the system model through the input place I. The actions requested by the ERP model are then forwarded to the system model through the output place O. The two places I and O, in fact, can be seen as the *interface* to the system model.

From the high level view it is possible to proceed with the formalization of the operations described in the flowchart of Figure 1. The first operation encountered is the evaluation of the pressure value. Figure 4 shows how this operation can be formalized in a CPN. Transition T1 is actually *filtering* the tokens from input place I as the only tokens that can be consumed by T1 are those with the specific signature (i,'press',v) that represents one value of the pressure parameter. The accepted tokens are then stored in the place P preserving the temporal order by means of the architecture shown in Figure 2. Two possibilities arise: either the value of v (representing the pressure value) is *above* a certain threshold th or it is *below*. In the first case the token is consumed by transition T2 and put in the place OK. In the second case the transition T3 is the one to fire and the

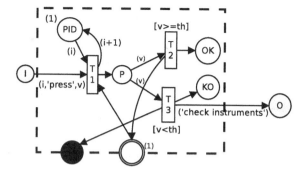

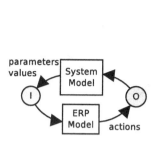

Fig. 3. High level interactions

Fig. 4. Pressure value check

token is put in the place KO (to represent that a problem has been identified) while a 'check instruments' token is sent to the output place.

This CPN can be seen as a module that takes inputs from the place I and produces outputs in O, that is it interacts with the system model. The boundaries of the modules are represented in Figure 4 with a dashed line. This module is designed so to be able to operate in concert with other modules. The two particular places visible along the bottom boundary of Figure 4 are designed to control the interaction with the other modules: the left one (filled in black) acts like an enabling signal for the next module while the right one (not filled) acts like a receptor for the module itself. The proper combination of signal and receptors among modules controls their interactions, as will be shown in the following. In case of anomalous pressure value the ERP model instructs the system to check the status of the instruments. The ERP then waits for the response and proceeds with the instruments check formalized with the CPN in Figure 5.

In case the instruments are reported to be unavailable (because of some problem/fault) then a request 'repair instruments' is sent to the system. On the other hand, if the instruments are reported to work correctly (v=1) then a 'check flow' request is issued instead. This will start the flow rate check operation depicted in Figure 6 where flow rate changes are monitored in order to detect sudden decreases of values. Two subsequent values are compared and the difference is checked against a threshold. If the difference is *not* greater than the threshold then the system is working correctly, otherwise (if the drop in the measured flow rate·is larger than the accepted threshold) a notification of a potential leak is sent to the system and this, in turn, will result in further checks and procedures to be triggered.

The comparison of two flow rate values is shown in Figure 6 where the transition T_f.1 filters the tokens from the input place I accepting only those tokens with the (i,'flow',v) signature (which carries the value v of the flow rate). The ERP model must acquire two sequential flow rate values to assess the trend of the flow rate variable. The place B acts as a buffer with a token whose initial value is (0,0). The first flow rate value gathered from input I is stored in place F. Since the token in B has the initial value of (0,0) then only the T_f.3

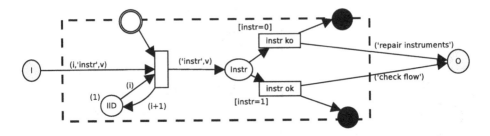

Fig. 5. Instruments check

transition is allowed to fire. This triggers two different actions. The first is to store a new token (1,v) in the place B which now contains the first value for the flow rate variable. The second action is to issue another 'check flow' request to the system. This request will cause another flow rate value to became available in place I and subsequently in place F. This time the value of the token in B enforces the transition T_f.2 to fire. This transition has two inputs: the value v from place F and the value pv from place B. The transition is thus able to produce a new token whose value is the difference between the old and current flow rate (v - pv). This value is stored in place delta and it is checked against a threshold by means of the T_f.4 and T_f.5 transitions. If the value is within the accepted threshold than the system is in a normal state. On the contrary, if the value is above the accepted threshold, an incident is reported and notified to the system through the output place O. In both cases the initial (0,0) token is restored in place B.

The combination of the described modules is shown in Figure 7. It is worth noting how the modules are connected to each other (the places connected by a thick line are in fact *collapsed* into a single place). The combination reflects the behaviour described in the flowchart of Figure 1 (i.e. each pair stands for a single "interface" place between two modules).

5 Analysis

The petri net formalism provides well assessed methodologies for the analysis of the behaviour of the system. Two kind of analysis are here considered: simulation and exhaustive analysis, both supported by the automatic tool "CPN tool" [1], used in this work. Simulation is useful to quickly get a first assessment of the behaviour of the system. It is possible to provide the initial state of the model (i.e. the initial marking) and let the tool produce one of the resulting states after the execution of the CPN. The main limitation of the simulation process is related to the way transitions are executed. Given the situation in which two transitions, namely T1 and T2, can be fired at the same time, the simulation process performs a decision about which transition to actually fire. So, if the simulator decides to trigger T1 and then T2 (in this very specific order) then the scenario where T2 is triggered before T1 is lost. On the contrary, exhaustive

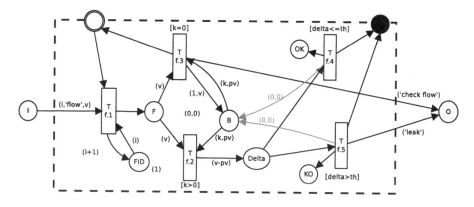

Fig. 6. Flow rate check

analysis takes into account every possible scenario an produces all the possible states in which the system can evolve. In the example before, the exhaustive analysis would have produced at least two results. In case of simple models the exhaustive analysis is feasible in little time, however, as the complexity of the model increases, the exhaustive analysis can generate a great number of states consuming a lot of resources in term of computational power and execution time.

The simulation is useful to check the results given a specific initial condition. With reference to the case study, the simulation can verify if the ERP triggers the expected actions given a specific list of input values (for pressure, flowrate and instruments availability). This gives initial confidence about the correctness of the ERP model. The complete validation is, however, provided only by leveraging the exhaustive analysis.

5.1   Test Case Simulation

The modeled test case has been analysed by means of both simulation and exhaustive analysis. The modeled ERP is driven by the value of parameters in the system model provided through the input place I in Figure 7. For this reason, the analysis requires the explicit list of all the tokens that represent parameters values. In fact, as explained in the previous sections, the system model must also react to requests coming from the ERP. For instance, the 'check instruments' request issued by the ERP involves a response from the system model in terms of a (i,'instr',v) token. Similarly for the 'check flow' request. In this work we have neither built nor analysed the complete system model. The focus has been on the interactions with the ERP model. For this reason the system model has been simplified into the CPN represented in Figure 8 which completely defines the input tokens provided to the ERP model. In particular, the pressure values have been described as initial tokens in the I place while instruments status and flow rates are provided through *buffers* of tokens. This architecture enables the simplified system model to provide the proper token in the place I as a reaction to a request token in the place O. The complete ERP model (Figure 7) and

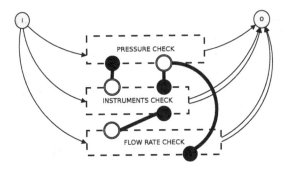

Fig. 7. Complete ERP model

the simplified system model (Figure 8) give the complete implementation of the high-level schema of Figure 3. The complete definition of input tokens enable the simulation of the ERP model. The scenario described by the value in Figure 8 is a pressure drop, followed by a sudden change in the flow rate. The simulation of the CPN resulted in a (`'leak'`) token in the O place, representing the ERP detection of a leak in the pipeline system, as expected.

5.2   Test Case Exhaustive Analysis

The simulation provides one result given an explicit set of parameters values. However, it is possible to leverage the exhaustive analysis to assess automatically the behaviour of the ERP model given all the possible combinations of values built from a set of predefined parameters values.

The CPN in Figure 2 explained how to constrain a transition to consume tokens in a specific order. A simple change in the network relaxes this constraint enabling the tokens to be consumed in an *unspecified* order. Figure 9 shows the new network. Leveraging this architecture throughout all the complete CPN of Figure 7 and by means of the exhaustive analysis behaviour it has been possible to produce all the possible system final states given all the possible combinations of parameters values. The analysis of the resulting graph of states has demonstrated the correctness of the ERP model with respect to the intended behaviour.

5.3   Scalability Considerations

The complexity of the analysis directly depends on the size of the considered CPN and its inputs. Two analysis have been here proposed: the simulation, with a specific sequence of input values, and the exhaustive analysis, with a set of input values. In the first case the complexity is $\mathcal{O}(nm)$ where n is the number of input values and m the size of the CPN. The simulation, in fact, is fast and is suitable for very large nets. On the other hand, the case of the exhaustive analysis is on a completely different level: a set of input values that

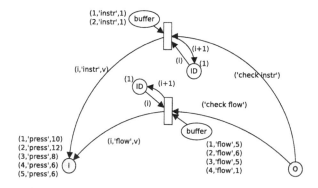

Fig. 8. System model

can be consumed without a specific order leads to a worst case complexity that is exponential on the size of the input set $\mathcal{O}(e^n)$. This hinders the feasibility of this kind of analysis with large networks. It is possible, however, to split the network in several meaningful modules and proceed with the analysis of each part in isolation reducing the term n. Of course, this is not equivalent to the analysis of the whole CPN but it is effective for the kind of scenario proposed here.

6   Related Work

The modeling of emergency management system can be addressed from several perspectives. In [2] and [10] a theoretical framework based on discrete-event dynamical systems has been proposed for the modeling and analysis of EMS. In [2], in particular, a Petri Net has been used to model and analyse an industrial fire management process. The model, however, lacks a clear definition of the conditions that can trigger the transitions.

In [8] it is recognized that resources play a critical role in the management of emergencies and possibilistic Petri Nets have been proposed as the formalism for modeling resources in an agent-based system. The focus has been on the single resources rather than on the overall emergency management system. In [16] a particular attention has been dedicated to the workflow of resources and their consumption during an emergency.

The exchange of information is an important resource during emergencies. [3] presented an hierarchical sub-division of an emergency response system in order to facilitate the management and analysis of the information exchange. At the low level they presented a model (based on CPN) of patients flow in an emergency medical department. Although colours have been used to distinguish among different patients and resources, the flow of the model is linear and does not present alternative paths. [18], instead, stressed the importance of reliable communication channel during emergencies to ensure the correct information flow among operating agents. An information flow model has been presented.

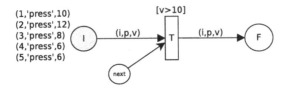

Fig. 9. Unconstrained transition

In [6] the focus is on the importance of knowledge management as support for better decision taking in case of incidents. The approach focuses on the modeling and management of information rather than behaviour of the response system.

In [19] Petri Nets have been used to measure the performances of an urban emergency system. The Petri Net model has been designed expressively for performance analysis based on probability of transition rather than detailed modeling of the system events.

The analysis we have proposed in this paper is an offline analysis which supports the design of the emergency response plan. A different approach has been proposed in [5] in which a live simulation of emergency response system is proposed to improve the coordination of agents during the occurrence of an emergency. [14] proposed a more holistic approach in the modeling of a disaster management system. Their proposal, in fact, is based on the adoption of model-based systems engineering (MBSE) implemented by the SysML language. This work is more comprehensive but on a higher level of abstraction.

7   Conclusion

In this paper we have stressed the criticality of emergency response plans in the context of contingency planning in critical infrastructures. We have proposed a modeling approach based on the coloured petri net formalism and we have shown the feasibility of this approach building a model starting from an actual emergency response plan. Finally we have introduced the possible analysis methodologies that can leverage the formalism used.

Acknowledgment. This work was supported by the INMOTOS project, funded with support from the European Commission. This publication reflects the views only of the author, and the Commission cannot be held responsible for any use which may be made of the information contained therein.

References

1. CPN tools (2011), http://cpntools.org
2. Bammidi, P., Moore, K.: Emergency management systems: a systems approach. In: 1994 IEEE Int. Conf. on Systems, Man, and Cybernetics, vol. 2, pp. 1565–1570 (1994)

3. Dilmaghani, R., Rao, R.: A systematic approach to improve communication for emergency response. In: 42nd Hawaii Int. Conf. on System Sciences (HICSS), pp. 1–8 (2009)

4. ISO/IEC: Systems and software engineering – High-level Petri nets – Part 1: Concepts, definitions and graphical notation. Int. standard ISO/IEC 15909, ISO/IEC, Geneva, Switzerland, 1st edn. (2004)

5. Jain, S., McLean, C.: Simulation for emergency response: a framework for modeling and simulation for emergency response. In: 35th Winter Simulation Conference (WSC), pp. 1068–1076 (2003)

6. Jennex, M.E.: Modeling emergency response systems. In: 40th Hawaii Int. Conf. on System Sciences (HICSS), p. 22 (2007)

7. Kröger, W.: Critical infrastructures at risk: A need for a new conceptual approach and extended analytical tools. Reliability Engineering & System Safety 93(12), 1781–1787 (2008)

8. Liu, K.F.: Agent-based resource discovery architecture for environmental emergency management. Expert Systems with Applications 27(1), 77–95 (2004)

9. Merabti, M., Kennedy, M., Hurst, W.: Critical infrastructure protection: A 21st century challenge. In: 2011 Int. Conf. on Communications and Information Technology (ICCIT), pp. 1–6. IEEE (2011)

10. Moore, K., Abraham, J.: An architecture for intelligent decision support with applications to emergency management. In: 1994 IEEE Int. Conf. on Systems, Man, and Cybernetics, vol. 2, pp. 1571–1576 (1994)

11. Neal, D.: Reconsidering the phases of disaster. Int. Journal of Mass Emergencies and Disasters 15(2), 239–264 (1997)

12. Rinaldi, S.: Modeling and simulating critical infrastructures and their interdependencies. In: 37th Hawaii Int. Conf. on System Sciences (HICSS), p. 8 (2004)

13. SANS Institute: CIA confirms cyber attack caused multi-city power outage. SANS NewsBite 10(5) (2008)

14. Soyler, A., Sala-Diakanda, S.: A model-based systems engineering approach to capturing disaster management systems. In: 4th Annual IEEE Systems Conf., pp. 283–287 (2010)

15. Vespignani, A.: Complex networks: The fragility of interdependency. Nature 464, 984–985 (2010)

16. Wang, J., Tepfenhart, W., Rosca, D.: Emergency response workflow resource requirements modeling and analysis. IEEE Transactions on Systems, Man, and Cybernetics 39(3), 270–283 (2009)

17. Yang, F., Deng, L., Xue, D.: The construction and analysis of the universal model of emergency response. In: 18th Int. Conf. on Geoinformatics, pp. 1–5 (2010)

18. Zhang, Z., Zhou, Y., Cui, J., Meng, F.: Modelling the information flows during emergency response. In: 19th Int. Conf. on Geoinformatics, pp. 1–5 (2011)

19. Zhong, M., Shi, C., Fu, T., He, L., Shi, J.: Study in performance analysis of china urban emergency response system based on petri net. Safety Science 48(6), 755–762 (2010)

Distributed Identity Based Private Key Generation for SCADA Systems

Görkem Kılınç[1] and Igor Nai Fovino[2]

[1] Izmir Institute of Technology,
Computer Eng. Dept., Gulbahce, Urla Izmir 35430, Turkey
gorkemkilinc@iyte.edu.tr
[2] Global Cyber Security Center, Viale Europa 174, Rome, Italy
igor.nai@gcsec.org

Abstract. The security of the ICT (Information Communications Technology) components of industrial systems is gaining great importance in the context of their criticality for society at large. There is an urgent need for the consideration of security in their design, and for the analysis of the related vulnerabilities and potential threats. The high exposure of industrial critical infrastructure to such threats is mainly due to the intrinsic weakness of the communication protocols used to control the process network. The peculiarities of the industrial protocols (low computational power, large geographical distribution, near to real-time constraints) make hard the effective use of traditional cryptographic schemes and in particular the implementation of a effective key management infrastructure supporting a cryptographic layer. In this paper we present the first working prototype of a distributed key generation infrastructure for SCADA systems based on the well known identity based crypto-paradigm.

Keywords: SCADA protocols, SCADA security, Key Management, Identity Based Cryptography, Distributed Private Key Generation.

1 Introduction

Modern industrial critical infrastructure are, on average, exposed to traditional computer attacks and threats. Moreover, as described by Nai et. all [1], such infrastructures are also exposed to ad-hoc created attacks aiming at interfering with, and in some case, taking the control of the process network of the industrial installation.

A relevant role in SCADA systems is played by the communication protocols used to send commands and exchange information between field devices and masters. Such protocols (e.g. Modbus, DNP3, PROFIBUS etc.) were designed decades ago for "serial communication" between SCADA master and slaves. With the advent of the modern ICT era, several vendors ported those protocols over TCP/IP, assuring the compatibility with the legacy application and, of course, offering more flexible and cheaper solutions to end users. This fact has opened

B. Hämmerli, N. Kalstad Svendsen, and J. Lopez (Eds.): CRITIS 2012, LNCS 7722, pp. 118–129, 2013.

new possibilities to attackers motivated to cause damages to target industrial systems. In particular these protocols:

1. Do not apply any mechanism for checking the integrity of the command packets sent by a master to a slave and vice-versa.
2. Do not perform any authentication mechanism between master and slaves, i.e. everyone could claim to be the "master" and send commands to the slaves.
3. Do not apply any anti-repudiation or anti-replay mechanisms.

These security shortcomings can be used by malicious users for performing different kind of cyber-attacks.

We defend the need to introduce efficient and safe authentication and integrity mechanisms in those communication protocols. The introduction of these mechanisms, per se, in not sufficient; in an environment heterogeneous, geographically sparse and composed potentially by thousands of elements (as many as the number of the PLCs/RTUs involved in the system) a prominent role is played by the Key Management Architecture adopted.

In this work, we focus our attention on the key management architectures for SCADA systems, proposing the use of an identity based signature scheme with completely distributed key generation. We present a working prototype of the architecture and the results of the tests carried out in our industrial testbed.

2   Related Work

A relevant part of the vulnerabilities of SCADA systems is due to the specialized communication protocols they use to communicate with the field devices (e.g. ModBUS, DNP3, Fieldbus etc.). Some work has been done about the security of such specialized communication protocols: for example, Majdalawieh, Parisi-Presicce and Wijesekera [2] presented an extension of the DNP3 protocol, called DNPsec, which tries to address some of the known security problems of such master/slave control protocols (i.e. integrity of the commands, authentication, non repudiation etc.). At the same way, the DNP3 User group proposed a "Secure DNP3" implementing authentication mechanisms for certain type of commands and packets. This approach is extremely close to the one adopted in the IEC 62351-5 standard. Nai et al. [3] presented a secure implementation of the ModBUS protocol aimed at introducing integrity, authentication and anti-replay mechanisms in the control flows based on the ModBUS protocol. With respect to the key management architectures in SCADA systems, Cheryl, Donald, Willian and Mark [4] adopted a classical PKI infrastructure with certification authority deputed to generate keys. If from one hand this approach relies on a very well established scheme, on the other hand the power computation required and the efficiency have been pointed out as not negligible problems by other authors. Robert et al. [5] present SKMA (Scada Key Management Architecture). The proposed architecture is designed for managing AGA-12 keys. In their work the authors make use of a KDC (Key Distribution Center) to maintain a long term key for each node in the system. If from one side this simplify the management of the whole architecture, on the other side the KDC constitutes a single point of failure that in some circumstances and for some critical infrastructures cannot be ignored. Lambert et al. [6] proposed the use of ECC (elliptic curve cryptography) and KMA in SCADA systems. In the context of ECC, but at theoretical level and without any connection with SCADA systems, in 1984 A. Shamir [7] put forward the term identity based cryptography. He introduced a cryptographic scheme which enables users to communicate securely and to verify each other's signature without exchanging private or public keys and without keeping a key directory. Although it does not require a certification authority it has a weakness which is key escrow problem. Boneh and Franklin [8] suggested distributed private key generation (DPKG) to minimize the risk of failure because of this problem. In their scheme they used Shamir's [9] secret sharing algorithm. A. Kate and I. Goldberg [10] improved Boneh's and Franklin's approach and they also included the proactive security and forward secrecy of the master key and they designed a DPKG protocol in an asynchronous communication model . As it will be described in the following we adopted this approach to build the first distributed identity based key management architecture for SCADA systems.

3   Identity Based Cryptography and Distributed Private Key Generation

To mitigate the vulnerabilities briefly described in section 1 a cryptographic layer using well established crypto-mechanisms such as SSL, IPv6 features etc. could be deployed. Unfortunately, the peculiarities of PCS systems (Low power computation, low memory resources, Near to real-time constraints)make the use of these general purpose mechanisms unlikely usable. As in the work of Lambert et al. [6], we decided to take in consideration a schema making use of ECC cryptography. However, even having a lightweight cryptographic schema, still there is a problem to consider: several SCADA systems are very sparse (let take into consideration for example a gas pipeline) and composed by thousand of elements, making the key management process extremely complex and resource consuming. The use of certification authorities and the use of centralized repositories for public key management etc. result generally too heavy on the management side to be considered a valid solution for low level distributed SCADA systems. In the scientific literature, an interesting paradigm, named identity based signature scheme, was proposed by Shamir [7] in 1984.

In an identity based cryptographic system, unlike the other public key cryptographic systems, a publicly known string such as e-mail address, domain name, a physical IP address or a combination of more than one strings is used as public key. Shamir's scheme enables users to communicate securely and verify signatures without exchanging any private or public key. Consequently, there is no need for a certification authority to verify the association between public keys and users. As for SCADA communication confidentiality is not relevant, we concentrate our attention on the signature process.

Figure 1 shows how the identity based signature scheme works. When node A wants to send a signed message to node B, it uses its own private key to sign the message. Note that, if it doesn't have, node A should ask private key generator for its private key to be able to sign a message. Private key generation is the same as the encryption - decryption scheme.

After receiving the signed message SM, node B can use the hashed value of A's identity string to verify the signature. Verification of the signature doesn't require any certification authority or other trusted third parties.

If private key generation is considered in three steps as *setup, distribution* and *extraction* then it can be said that setup and distribution steps are only performed in such cases like the establishment of the system, adding a new generator node to the system or whenever a renewal of master key pair is needed. Extraction step, on the other hand, is performed when a client needs its private key or when a new client joins the system. The possibility to provide the low

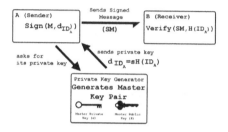

Fig. 1. Identity Based Signature Scheme

level devices of SCADA infrastructures (PLCs) with a mechanism allowing to obtain automatically a private key for signing their own network packets while limiting at minimum the interactions with the external world to verify a signed packet, is extremely appealing. Moreover, in the SCADA systems exist already an information known by everybody in the system that is also unique, the PLC ID, normally used as reference address. This fact make using identity based approach in SCADA systems very advantageous.

3.1 Key Escrow Problem

Although an identity based cryptographic system does not require a certification authority, there is a need for private key generator. Basically, a trusted third party signs user's publicly known string using its own private key (master private key) in order to generate a private key for the user. Since the private key generator (PKG) can generate private key for users, it can sign or decrypt a message for any user or it can make users' private keys public. This problem about private key generation is called the key escrow problem. DPKG is an effective solutions to the key escrow problem. In both schemes [8], [10] secret sharing methods are used for distributing private key generation among multiple PKGs.

3.2   Secret Sharing

Secret sharing is a method of distributing a secret among multiple players as no player knows the whole secret but each player has a share for the secret. The secret can be reconstructed only if a sufficient number of shares are retrieved. In SCADA system, by adopting this approach would be possible to have a completely distributed key generation system. In 1979 Shamir put forward a scheme called (k, n) threshold scheme[9]. The scheme is based on polynomial interpolation. Given k points in the form (x_i, y_i) where each x_i is distinct , there is only one polynomial $f(x)$ of degree $k - 1$ such that $f(x_i) = y_i$ for all i.

Verifiable secret sharing was first introduced by Chor, Goldwasser, Micali, and Awerbuch in 1985 [16]. In such a scheme each player can verify its share. Feldman's verifiable secret sharing scheme [11] is based on Shamir's scheme and it improves Shamir's scheme by including verifiability.

3.3   Distributed Private Key Generation for Identity Based Cryptography

In this work we tried to generate private keys securely and in a distributed approach. Our aim is to use identity based signature scheme to provide authenticity for SCADA systems. The most important step is the generation of private keys. As we explained in section 3.1 the problem about identity based scheme is the key escrow problem. In order to eliminate this problem, we performed a DPKG scheme. The formal model and an analysis of the used scheme is presented in [12].

In a DPKG there is a number of PKG nodes participating while they share the responsibility equally. In this section, we examine DPKG in three steps: setup, distribution and extraction.

Setup. This step is a preparation step to create the system parameters and to get ready for creating the master key pair distributively and extraction of private keys. It is performed by the Bulletin Board application.

Algorithm 1. Bulletin Board setup

```
Require: security parameter K and cryptographic hash function H : {0, 1}* → G*
   q ← generate prime of size K
   G ← choose elliptic curve group of order q
   G_T ← choose cyclic multiplicative group of order q
   g ← x find a generator of G
   choose pairing function e : G × G → G_T
   C[nk] ← createcommitments()
   for i = 0 → n do
      for j = 0 → k do
         C[ij] ← 0
      end for
   end for
   f_C[k] ← createfinalcommitment()
   for i = 0 → k do
      f_C[i] ← 0
   end for
   while system is on do
      broadcast(q, G, G_T, e, H, g)

   end while
```

Algorithm 2. PKGi Distribution

Require: i
Require: system parameters (q, G, G_T, e, H, g) are broadcasted on Bulletin Board
  //create a polynomial $f_i(x) = a_{i0} + a_{i1}x + a_{i2}x^2 + \ldots + a_{i(k-1)}x^{(k-1)}$
  for $j = 0 \to k - 1$ **do**
    $f_i[j] \leftarrow$ random element( )
  end for
  //calculate commitments to be broadcasted on Bulletin Board
  for $j = 0 \to k - 1$ **do**
    $C_i[j] \leftarrow f_i[j]g$
  end for
  send C_i to Bulletin Board
  for $j = 1 \to n$ **do**
    subshare[j] $\leftarrow$ evaluate (f_i, j)
  end for
  for $j = 1 \to n$ **do**
    if $j \neq i$ **then**
      send(PKGj, subshare[j])
    end if
  end for
  while not receive all **do**
    wait for subshares from other PKG nodes
  end while
  subshares from n-1 PKG nodes are received
  //subshares[k] is the set of subshares received
  //num[k] is the set of PKG numbers. i.e. subshare[3] is sent by PKG num[3]
  $s_i \leftarrow 0$
  for $j = 1 \to n$ **do**
    $s_i \leftarrow$ add(s_i, $subshare_j$)
    //where $subshare_j$ was calculated by PKGj for PKGi
  end for
  check1 $\leftarrow s_i g$
  check2 $\leftarrow 0$
  for $j = 0 \to k - 1$ **do**
    check2 $\leftarrow$ add(check2, $i^j f\_C[j]$
  end for
  if check1 = check2 **then**
    //share s_i is correct
  else
    for $m = 0 \to n$ **do**
      check1 $\leftarrow subshare[m]g$
      check2 $\leftarrow 0$
      for $l = 0 \to k - 1$ **do**
        check2 $\leftarrow$ add(check2, $i^l C[num[k][l]]$
      end for
      if check1 = check2 **then**
        //share $subshare[m]$ is correct
      else
        //PKG num[m] sent incorrect subshare
        //ask PKG num[m] again
        //or mark PKG num[m] as malicious exclude it and repeat distribution
      end if
    end for
  end if

Distribution. In this step, n PKG nodes create a master private key together without using any dealer in a way that the key cannot be reconstructed without retrieving k shares from these n PKGs. To do this, an improved version of (n, k) Feldman's secret sharing scheme stated in [10] was used in this study.

Since the private key generation for a client means to sign client's hashed ID with the master private key, noone is allowed to have access the master private key. Thus, we distribute master private key among PKG nodes in a way nobody knows it by using secret sharing approach. The idea behind secret sharing without a dealer is to make each PKG node create a secret of their own and calculate subshares to distribute among other PKG nodes. At the end, each PKG node will have n subshares including the one it calculated for itself . The sum of these subshares will be the share of the PKG node for the master private key.

The following steps are performed by every node PKG_i where $i = 1, 2, \ldots, n$.

Bulletin Board collects commitments from all n PKG nodes then it updates final commitment f_C for each PKGi as $f\_C[j] = f\_C[j] + C_i[j]$ $j = 0, 1, \ldots, k-1$. After all the commitments are collected and final commitment is calculated, Bulletin Board broadcasts all commitments.

Note that, the master secret key is $s = \sum_{i=1}^{n} a_{i0}$ but none of the PKG nodes knows it since each of them has only its own secret, a_{i0}. Master public key is $Pub = \sum_{i=1}^{n} a_{i0}g = C_0$. Public key share for the node PKG_j is $Pub_j = \sum_{l=0}^{k-1} j^l C_l$ C_l, C_{il}, Pub and Pub_i must be known by all the PKG nodes, where $i = 1, 2, \ldots, n$ and $l = 0, 1, \ldots, k-1$. These are broad casted by bulletin board application.

Keeping the threshold number (k) constant while incrementing the number of nodes increases the reliability of the system as well. Indeed a client has a wide range of available PKG nodes to choose the k needed to compute its private key.

Extraction. Let $\mathcal{O}$ be the set of available PKG nodes and g, e, H, Pub, Pub_i are known by both PKG nodes and clients where $i = 1, 2, \ldots, n$.

A client with identity string ID contacts k alive nodes from $\mathcal{O}$. Each node PKG_i returns a private key piece as $s_i H(ID)$ over a secure and authenticated channel. After receiving k pieces from k available PKG nodes, client A constructs its private key by following the algorithm 3.

Algorithm 3. Client Extraction

```
Require: O, k pieces, g, e, H, Pub[n] to be known, where i = 1, 2, ..., n and master public key Pub.
Require: PKG numbers are known
    //s[k] is the set of pieces received
    //num[k] is the set of PKG numbers which sent a piece to the client
    //s[1] is the piece received from PKG num[1]
    d ← ∑_{PKG_i ∈ O} λ_i s_i H(ID_A)

    // where λ_i = ∏_{PKG_j ∈ O\{i}}  j/(j-i)

    check1 ← pairing_e(d, g)
    check2 ← pairing_e(H(ID), Pub)
    if check1 = check2 then
        //the key is verified
    else
        //key is not verified find the malicious node
        m ← 0
        for j = 0 → k − 1 do
            check1 ← pairing_e(s[j]H(ID), g)
            check2 ← pairing_e(H(ID), Pub[num[j]])
            if check1 ≠ check2 then
                //PKG num[j] sent malicious piece
                m ← num[j]
            end if
        end for
        if m ≠ 0 then
            //ask PKG node m to send the piece again and repeat calculation of d
            // or exclude PKG node m and start again
        else
            // repeat extraction starting from asking to k PKG nodes for pieces
        end if
    end if
```

In the algorithm e is a bilinear pairing function. As a result of bilinearity property of the pairing function, the dishonest node can be recognized by observing an inequality in the pairing checks.

Whenever a new node is included to the system it performs this extraction part to have a private key so that it can start communicating with the other system nodes. However when the system requires a change of the master key, all three steps (setup, distribution, extraction) have to be executed from the beginning.

4   Prototype Overview

The DPKG prototype is implemented in three layers. The lowest layer inherits the structures and the low level functions of two libraries: Pairing Based Cryptography (PBC) [13] and the GNU Multiple Precision Library (GMP) [14]. The middle layer consists of all the mathematical functions needed to implement DPKG. This layer is completely independent from the SCADA implementation and it is highly portable and reusable with other systems and protocols. The third and the highest layer is the part which includes the SCADA system components and performs DPKG on them using the lower layers.

The prototype is implemented in C on the Linux operating system in order to maintain a high compatibility with the PBC and the GMP libraries. TCP/IP is used for the communication between the system components. The DPKG prototype is composed of three parts: *the Bulletin Board (BB), the Private Key Generator (PKG) nodes and the clients simulating the PLCs of the SCADA system.*

The communication layer is based on traditional TCP sockets. PKG nodes and BB having to perform many tasks simultaneously, they use dedicated threads to follow every request and answer.

In the startup phase the system must be configured with an XML file containing the following information available to all the entities:

- **Nodes:** the number of active PKG nodes
- **Threshold:** the number of nodes needed to reconstruct the key.
- **Cryptography Parameters:** the underlying cryptographic parameters.
- **Network Information:** the network topology information.

The bulletin board loads the parameters and choose a generator for the elliptic curve group. This value is public and is stored in a file shared by the entire system and will never change for the entire uptime. During the distribution phase and extraction phase the nodes and the BB must know the network information. A file containing the name, the ip-address and the listening port of each node is pre-shared. The PLCs are simulated through software PLCs as those used by Nai et al. in [15].

5   Experimental Tests

To verify the efficiency and the validity of our approach, several comparative tests were performed in a protected environment which reproduces the network of a typical Gas Power Plant. The test was organized in three steps: *Distribution, Estraction and Signature.*

We used PBC (Pairing-Based Cryptography) library [13] together with GMP (The GNU Multiple Precision Arithmetic) library [14] for elliptic curve arithmetics and pairings. As cryptographic hash function we used SHA-256.

5.1   Setup and Distribution

In order to measure the time required for completing the distribution phase with different numbers of PKG nodes, we performed several tests by keeping all other system parameters constant. More specifically, we changed the number of nodes (n) from 6 to 18 while keeping the threshold number (k) and other system parameters constant in order to see how the number of nodes effects the start-up time (time for completing the setup and the distribution steps).

# of PKG	Avg. Time
6	399
7	457
8	496
9	585
10	630
11	723
12	790
15	1322
18	2092

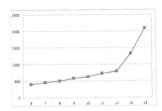

Fig. 2. Distribution phase performance test (Time in ms.)

The graph shows how the time increases exponentially with the number of nodes (n). PKGs exchange $n \times n$ messages during setup and distribution steps. Considering that this setup phase needs to be executed only during system establishment or when master key renewal is needed, an average time of 2 seconds is considered acceptable.

5.2   Extraction

In this test phase we focused on the time required by the client for extracting its private key. We changed the threshold number (k) from 2 to 8 while keeping the number of nodes (n) and the other system parameters constant. Changing the threshold value, the number of PKG nodes that the client needs to contact for key extraction changes. The value showed in the figure 3 indicates the total extraction time together with the network delay.

This test shows that the performance of the key extraction phase mostly depends on the network delay. The time increases logarithmically with the threshold value. In fact the client has to contact k PKG nodes and every signed piece ($s_i(H(ID))$) retrieval increases the total time. Keeping the threshold value too low will cause the system to be more exposed to an attacker trying to capture the user's private key, while keeping it too high will slow down the key extraction process. When the threshold value is higher than $k = \lfloor n/2 \rfloor + 1$ we also sacrifice reliability considering the case that some of the PKG nodes crashes.

By using a (n, k) threshold scheme for secret sharing which is summarized in section 3.2 with $n = 2k - 1$ we get a robust key management scheme. Even if $\lfloor n/2 \rfloor = k - 1$ of the n pieces are destroyed, we still can recover the original key. On the other hand, our opponents cannot reconstruct the key even if they retrieve $\lfloor n/2 \rfloor = k - 1$ of the remaining k pieces.

# of PKG	Avg TIme
2	162
3	225
4	283
5	313
6	329
7	341
8	350

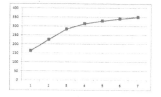

Fig. 3. Key extraction phase performance test (Time in ms.)

According to our practical analysis, we can say that the selection of n between 7 - 14 and k between 4 - 7 complying with the equation $n = 2k - 1$ is acceptable and applicable in terms of security, reliability and speed.

In most environment, many PLCs and masters can be turned on or connected to the system simultaneously. In order to verify the performance of the DPKG system we performed several test increasing the number of clients that simultaneously communicate with the DPKG system.

The results show how there is not an explicit limit to the simultaneous requests. The implicit limits are only due to the computational resources of the machines. In the next test different numbers of clients contact the DPKG system simultaneously to extract their private keys. This test is performed by contacting 8 DPKG nodes.

Client	Time
2	346
3	338
8	352
16	418
32	461

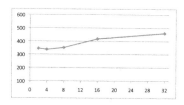

Fig. 4. Simultaneous answer performance test (Time in ms.)

5.3 Signature and Verification

The goal of this test is to present some preliminary values of a signature implementation between two SCADA entities: master and slave (PLC). The communication is performed through the Modbus protocol. In particular a master signs a ModBus package by using the private key generated in the previous step and sends it to a slave. The client verifies the data integrity and sender's identity by following the identity based signature scheme described in Section 3.

Throughout the testing phase we used type A elliptic curves. This type of curve is described by the equation

$$y^2 = x^3 + x. \tag{1}$$

The curve is defined over the field $\mathbb{F}_q$ for some prime $q = 3 \mod 4$. The order r is some prime factor of $q + 1$. Moreover, we used a symmetric pairing where $\mathbb{G}_1$ and $\mathbb{G}_2$ are the set of points $E(\mathbb{F}_p)$.

The test is performed in two parts as:

- Master sends ReadCoilsRequest to the slave and waits ReadCoilsResponse;
- Master sends WriteCoilsRequest to the slave and waits WriteCoilsResponse.

Tables below show the total time (in msec) for signing and verifying Modbus packets according to the length (in bits) of selected security parameters r and q where $q + 1 = r * h$.

Read Coils	r=150 q=160	r=80 q=224	r=160 q=512	Write Coils	r=150 q=160	r=80 q=224	r=160 q=512
Req-Sign	36.51	49.10	286.64	Req-sign	35.64	49.30	281.93
Req-Ver	15.91	15.75	202.57	Req -ver	15.75	15.80	202.03
Resp-Sign	31.71	47.07	281.25	Resp-sign	30.65	49.13	280.00
Resp-Ver	20.34	35.26	211.78	Resp-ver	17.67	16.95	200.50

As it is possible to see the total time introduced rages from a minimum of 17 msec to a maximum of 380 msec. Taking into account that we used a non optimized prototype, we can consider these results quite promising.

6   Conclusion

In this paper, after proposing the use of an identity based signature scheme to secure SCADA protocols, we presented a completely distributed architecture for generating and distributing identity based keys to the entities involved in a SCADA system. The advantages of this approach are not negligible. The adoption of identity based signatures in fact makes the use of certificates and certification authorities unnecessary, as well as it makes the use of centralized repositories for storing public keys also unnecessary, eliminating an important single point of failure. The presented distributed architecture provides robustness to ICT attacks and finds its perfect application in those SCADA systems geographically sparse and composed by a huge amount of active elements. The tests presented in section 5 show how this approach is effectively applicable in SCADA environment in terms of security, reliability and time. As future works we foresee to deploy the presented schema in a production system, to study with field applications the impact of its use on real systems.

References

1. Fovino, I.N., Marcelo Masera, R.L.: Ict security assessment of a power plant, a case study. In: Second Annual IFIP Working Group 11.10 International Conference on Critical Infrastructure Protection, Arlington, USA (2008)
2. Majdalawieh, M., Parisi-Presicce, F., Wijesekera, D.: Distributed network protocol security (dnpsec) security framework. In: 21st Annual Computer Security Applications Conference (2005)
3. Igor Nai Fovino, A.C., Masera, M.: Secure modbus protocol, a proof of concept. In: Proceedings of the 3rd IFIP Int. Conf. on Critical Infrastructure Protection (2009)

4. Beaver, C., Donald Gallup, W.N., Torgerson, M.: Key management for scada. Technical report, Cryptography and Information Systems Surety Department Sandia National Laboratories (2002)
5. Robert, D., Colin, B., Dawson, E., Juan, M.: Skma a key management architecture for scada systems. In: Proceedings of the Proceedings of the 4th Australasian Information Security Workshop, vol. 54 (2006)
6. Lambert, R.J.: Ecc and scada key management. In: Proceedings of S4 (SCADA Security Scientific Symposium) Conference (2007)
7. Shamir, A.: Identity-based cryptosystems and signature schemes. In: Blakely, G.R., Chaum, D. (eds.) CRYPTO 1984. LNCS, vol. 196, pp. 47–53. Springer, Heidelberg (1985)
8. Boneh, D., Franklin, M.: Identity-based encryption from the weil pairing. In: Kilian, J. (ed.) CRYPTO 2001. LNCS, vol. 2139, pp. 213–229. Springer, Heidelberg (2001)
9. Shamir, A.: How to share a secret. Commun. ACM 22(11), 612–613 (1979)
10. Kate, A., Goldberg, I.: Asynchronous distributed private-key generators for identity-based cryptography. IACR Cryptology ePrint Archive 2009, 355 (2009)
11. Feldman, P.: A practical scheme for non-interactive verifiable secret sharing. In: Proceedings of the 28th Annual Symposium on Foundations of Computer Science, SFCS 1987, pp. 427–438. IEEE Computer Society, Washington, DC (1987)
12. Kilinc, G., Igor Nai Fovino, C.F., Koltuksuz, A.: A model of distributed key generation for industrial control systems. Technical report, E.C. Joint Research Centre, Institute for the Protection and Security of the Citizen (2012)
13. pairing-based cryptography, http://crypto.stanford.edu/pbc/
14. Gnu multiple precision library, http://gmplib.org/
15. Genge, B., Igor Nai Fovino, C.S., Masera, M.: Analyzing cyber-physical attacks on networked industrial control systems. In: Butts, J., Shenoi, S. (eds.) Critical Infrastructure Protection V. IFIP AICT, vol. 367, pp. 167–183. Springer, Boston (2011), doi:10.1007/978-3-642-24864-1_12
16. Chor, B., Shaft Goldwasser, S.M., Awerbuch, B.: Verifiable secret sharing and achieving simultaneity in the presence of faults. In: Proceedings of 6th IEEE Symposium on Foundations of Computer Science, pp. 383–395 (1985)

A Trusted Computing Architecture
for Secure Substation Automation*

David Guidry, Mike Burmester, Xiuwen Liu, Jonathan Jenkins,
Sean Easton, and Xin Yuan

Florida State University, Tallahassee, FL 32306, USA
{dguidry,burmester,liux,jenkins,easton,xyuan}@cs.fsu.edu

Abstract. Most critical infrastructure systems can be modeled as cyber-physical systems whose cyber components control underlying physical processes so as to optimize specified system objectives based on physical properties, physical constraints, and the current and estimated state of the system. Such systems usually require support for security and performance guarantees: wrongly received or missed commands can render the entire system unstable. Yet, securing cyber-physical systems with heterogeneous components is still an open and challenging problem. In this paper, we propose techniques for resilient substation automation of power utility systems with security based on the trusted computing paradigm. By using trusted platform module (TPM)-enabled components and a novel access control structure that enforces *need-to-get-now* (availability) policies, we show how to develop IEC/TR 61850-90-5 compliant substation automation systems that are resilient. We demonstrate the feasibility of our approach by analyzing and experimenting with an open source IEC/TR 61850-90-5 implementation.

Keywords: Cyber-physical systems, critical infrastructures, electricity grid, IEC/TR 61850-90-5.

1 Introduction

Due to the potential significant impact of critical infrastructure failures on our society, it is essential that such systems are properly secured. Most critical infrastructures such as the electricity grid can be modeled as cyber-physical systems, where cyber and physical components are closely coupled. One of the key characteristics of such systems is that timing is essential, where "correct" commands issued at the "wrong" time relative to the state of the underlying physical system may have disastrous consequences.

Developing efficient and secure cyber-physical systems for controlling and monitoring the electricity grid is extremely challenging due to the propagation speed of electricity, which imposes stringent time constraints for processing and communicating data and control commands. Traditional security techniques are

---

* This material is based upon work supported by the National Science Foundation Grant No. 1027217.

B. Hämmerli, N. Kalstad Svendsen, and J. Lopez (Eds.): CRITIS 2012, LNCS 7722, pp. 130–142, 2013.
© Springer-Verlag Berlin Heidelberg 2013

developed for cyber systems, where the criteria are confidentiality, integrity and availability, in *this* order. Most approaches do not address the availability issue, which renders them unsuitable for securing cyber-physical systems such as the electricity grid. On the other hand, critical infrastructures also offer unique features that can be used to enhance security. For example, by their very nature, critical infrastructures have components that require physical verification. This fact can be utilized to enhance security beyond what could be achieved in systems with cyber-only components.

In this paper, we propose techniques for securing substation automation systems, a fundamental building block of the electricity grid, that utilize the unique characteristics of electricity grids. Our scheme incorporates the trusted computing paradigm supported by trusted-platform module (TPM)-enabled components, and utilizes an access control structure for need-to-get-now policies to meet the stringent time constraints of the system. Built-on an open source implementation of IEC/TR 61890-5, we have established a networked testbed to test and evaluate the proposed techniques. The feasibility of our approach is demonstrated by analyzing and experimenting with the open source IEC/TR 61850-90-5 implementation. The contributions of this work include the following:

- We show how the trusted platform module (TPM) technology can be used to secure cyber-physical applications.
- We propose an access control structure that enforces need-to-get-now policies for cyber-physical systems where availability is a primary concern.
- We show how IEC/TR 61850-90-5 compliant, resilient substation automation systems can be developed based on the proposed techniques.
- We demonstrate the feasibility of our approach by analyzing and experimenting with an open source IEC/TR 61850-90-5 implementation released by SISCO [10].

The rest of the paper is organized as follows. In Section 2, we briefly introduce the Technical Report IEC/TR 61850-90-5, a newly introduced transmission protocol specification standard for substation automation. We describe the trusted computing paradigm in Section 3. A novel access control structure that enforces need-to-get-now policies is presented in Section 4. Section 5 discusses how resilient cyber-physical systems can be developed based on the proposed approach. Section 6 describes our testbed and experimental results. We conclude the paper in Section 7.

2   IEC/TR 61850-90-5

IEC/TR 61850-90-5 [6] is a current technical report for communication networks and systems that support power utility automation. It provides substation automation for heterogeneous intelligent electronic device (IED) platforms. The objective is to achieve low cost wide area monitoring, protection and control (WAMPAC) for power utility systems. IEC/TR 61850-90-5 specifies the use of the IP transport protocol (either IP multicast or unicast) for exchanging data between phasor measurement units (PMU) and phasor data concentrators (PDC). Exchanged data is encapsulated in IP packets whose payloads are either sampled values from the PMUs called *Sample Values* (SV), or control packets, called *Generic Object Oriented Substation Events* (GOOSE). Such packets allow the reporting/control information to be distributed in wide area network environments. To multicast SV or GOOSE packets over IP, the packet profiles are modified, resulting in *multicast* SV *control blocks* (MSVCB) and GOOSE *control blocks* (GoCB). IEC/TR 61850-90-5 does not address security issues.

The Technical Specifications IEC 62351-6 document [7] addresses some security issues of networked substations: it specifies appropriate cryptographic mechanisms for network applications, and addresses the security for some IEC/TR 61850-90-5 protocols. However security, which is critical for the safe operations of networked substations, is not fully addressed. True automation for power utility systems requires comprehensive security. The IEC/TR 61850-90-5 will need to offer real-time security, with assured and trusted communication. In particular, it will need to address comprehensively *availability, integrity* (and *authentication*), and when needed *confidentiality*. It must provide confidence in message delivery, in the authenticity of the sender and receiver, and in the integrity of data sent before, during, and after unexpected or extreme events, e.g. faults, rolling blackout, voltage collapse. Key to this, is assured communication.

There are several security issues that must be addressed before an effective and open standard can be established so that vendors can provide WAMPAC. In this paper our goal is to address these issues. We present techniques that support assured and trusted communication via trusted computing technologies with the focus on the availability aspect of security that is often ignored in traditional security mechanisms.

Figure 1 illustrates a substation with IEC/TR 61850-90-5 products. The IEDs communicate with each other and outside the substation through the router while IED communication to high voltage (HV) equipment is through specialized components. The router is in charge of the trust of the devices on its LAN. If a device is untrusted then the router will prevent any individual and/or substation from communicating with the device, causing it to be quarantined. The router is the substation representative for all trusted communication.

To achieve real-time security, both the reporting SV packets and the control GOOSE packets are received in real-time, when they are needed. We define the *active time* of a packet to be the time it takes: (*a*) to prepare the packet (*e.g.*, from synchrophasor data), plus (*b*) the time it takes to transmit it, plus (*c*) the time it takes to receive and verify it. If the packet is dropped then its active time is ∞. IEC/TR 61850-90-5 specifies a threshold for the active time of packets that should be less than 4 milliseconds.

3   Trusted Computing

Trusted Computing (TC) as defined by the Trusted Computing Group (TCG) [11] is a technology for securing distributed systems by using *real-time trust*

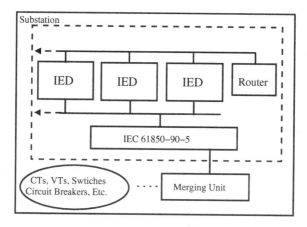

Fig. 1. An illustration of a substation in which the communication between IEDs is IEC/TR 61850 compliant

engines called *roots of trust*, that: allow the system to (*a*) attest to its integrity (*remote attestation*), (*b*) enable the system to protect keys and stored data (*sealed storage*) and (*c*) support cryptographic mechanisms.

The following technical details define the structure of a TC system. Key to the protection of the system is a trusted platform module (TPM), a real-time trust engine that acts as a *root of trust* for all security operations of the system. The functionality requirement for the TPM is to guarantee that the system will behave in a well defined manner (as expected) for the intended purpose.

3.1   The Trusted Platform Module

A Trusted Platform Module (TPM) [13] has two basic capabilities: remote attestation and sealed storage, and provides a range of cryptographic primitives including: a random number generator; hashing functions; asymmetric encryption/decryption; two unique asymmetric non-migratable key pairs (set at the time of manufacture): an attestation identity key pair for signing data originating at the TPM, and an endorsement key pair for decrypting owner authorization data and messages associated with the attestation key creation; symmetric keys to bind small amounts of data (typically keys) and to authenticate transport sessions. The TPM also has a small amount of storage (mainly for keys).

There are (at least) three roots of trust in a TPM: a root of trust for measurement (RTM) for making reliable integrity measurements, a root of trust for storage (RTS) to protect keys and data entrusted to the TPM, and a root of trust for reporting (RTR) to (a) expose shielded locations for storage of integrity measurements and (b) attest to the authenticity of stored values (based on trusted platform identities).

Security is based on an integrity protected boot-up process in which executable code and associated configuration data is measured before it is executed—this requires that a hash of the BIOS code is stored in a platform configuration

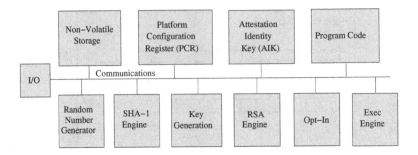

Fig. 2. The components of a Trusted Platform Module

register (PCR). For remote attestation the TPM uses an attestation identity key (AIK) to assert the state of its current software environment and its state to a third party—by signing its current PCR values. For sealed storage, encryption/decryption/authentication keys are released from protected storage, conditional on the current software state (using the current PCR values).

Figure 2 illustrates the components of a TPM that support RTR (reporting) and RTS (storage) engines. The I/O manages data flows over the communication buses (internal and external) by encrypting/decrypting data. Non-volatile storage is used for persistent keys. The PCR can be implemented in volatile or non-volatile memory. The Program Code contains firmware for measuring platform devices. Opt-In is used to customize TPM modules. Exec Engine runs program codes: it performs TPM initialization and takes measurements. The other components were discussed earlier.

A TPM can be implemented as hardware, software or an embedded software device. The TCG requires that TPM implementations are physically protected from tampering. This includes binding the TPM to other physical parts of the platform (*e.g.*, the motherboard) so it cannot be transferred to other platforms. TPM implementations have a unique (asymmetric) endorsement key (EK) that is created at the time of manufacture of the TPM. This key, is used together with an endorsement key credential (EKC), to secure all transactions and assert that the holder of the private part of the EK is the corresponding TPM, thus conforming to the TCG specifications. Before a TPM can be used a *take ownership* procedure must be performed to bind the usage of the TPM to a specific application device/user. For more details on the architecture of TPM the reader is referred to [13].

3.2   TC Compliant Cyber-Physical Systems

Cyber-Physical Systems (CPS) combine computation and communication with physical processes. They monitor and control physical processors in real time, usually with feedback loops. Typically, a Control Center manages a network of CPS (substations).

We consider CPS architectures in which a TPM microprocessor is used to protect trusted applications. We distinguish three components.

1. **The secure kernel**, that contains trusted hardware and the TPM that provides the necessary cryptographic mechanisms to platforms for program attestation and sealed storage via the RTR, RTM and RTS engines. The RTM engine is also used for trusted boot-up and the RTS engine for remote attestation. The kernel logically separates execution from upper layer applications.
2. **The sealed storage**, used for storing sensitive data and keys: access to it requires the release of keys from the TPM (via the RTS engine).
3. **The Sensing and Control Unit and the Applications.** All internal communication between the sensing and control devices and the applications, and external communication with other CPS is protected by using the RTR and RTS engines (point-to-point encrypted and authenticated). Access control policies are enforced using credentials and certificates.

3.3   The Trusted Network Connect

The Trusted Network Connect (TNC) [12] is a TC platform interoperability architecture for trusted access control that is based on the TPM module. What distinguishes the TNC from other interoperability architectures is the requirement that the configuration of the OS of the client and server (and associated configuration data) is checked prior to a communication channel being established. More specifically, a (trusted) link between a client and server is established only if:

1. The identity of the client and the server is trusted. For this purpose we need a Public Key Infrastructure in which Certifying Authorities issue certificates that establish trust-links between a Root Authority (a Trusted Third Party) and the TPMs of the client/server.
2. The client is allowed access to the server. For this purpose an access control system (typically RBAC [9]) with credentials is used.
3. The identities of the client and server are authenticated. This requires a root of trust engine to be invoked on the TPM of both sides to release the required keys for a handshake protocol [12] to be executed. The TPM will only release keys if the current configuration state of the OS of the parties allow for this.
4. The handshake protocol is properly executed. The TPM will enforce the integrity of communicated data (by releasing appropriate message authentication keys), and depending on the application, the confidentiality of communicated data.

3.4   Trusted Substation Automation Systems

The network of a power utility system (a *region*) has several *zones*, each one of which has several substations. For trusted interoperability, the TNC platform is used.

Substation-to-substation communication within a zone is over an intranet (controlled by the power utilities). Secure substation automation system (SAS) communication is crucial since it allows one substation to contact another substation to increase the output of backup generator after a primary generator is already running at maximum capacity. For secure station-to-station communication the communication must be trusted: (a) the sender must trust its own components before sending any information, and (b) the receiver must ensure that the information sent comes from a trusted sender. This is achieved by having each substation of the SAS to be TC-compliant. The same approach is used for trusted zone-to-zone communication. However here the communication is over an open network (the Internet).

4   An Access Control Structure for Need-to-Get-Now Policies

Access control systems are trust infrastructures for managing resources of distributed systems in a secure way. Security typically involves *confidentiality, integrity* and/or *availability*. For cyber systems (such as computer or network systems) the security focus is typically privacy and/or integrity. The Bell-LaPadula [1] model describes an access structure that captures *need-to-know* security requirements (confidentiality). The Biba [2] access control model captures integrity requirements. However for cyber-physical systems, and in particular critical infrastructure systems, the primary security concern is typically availability.[1]

In this section we present an access control structure for managing the resources of a cyber-physical system, for which the primary security goal is availability, with secondary goal integrity, and tertiary goal confidentiality. This captures need-to-get-now policies as opposed to need-to-know policies. Our access control structure is based on information flow models (see e.g., [5]), adapted for our particular application.

An *access control communication structure* is a tuple $\mathcal{A} = (N, L, P, \succeq)$, where N is a set of nodes, L a set of links, P a partially ordered set of security labels for resources and links, called packet *priorities* or channel *congestion levels*, and "$\succeq$" a *flow relation* defined on P. For this relation, a packet m with priority $p \in P$ is allowed to be transmitted over a channel of L with congestion $p' \in P$ if, and only if, $p \succeq p'$. That is, the network system will transmit m via a network channel if, and only if, the priority of m dominates the congestion level of the channel.[2] We take P to be a linearly ordered set $\{hi = p_k \succ p_{k-1} \succ \cdots \succ p_1 = lo\}$,[3] and the need-to-get-now (availability) policies are: (i) *packets*

---

[1] There are exceptions: *e.g.*, for medical cyber-physical systems the primary security concern is, typically, confidentiality.

[2] The general communication model also involves a *class combining operator* "$\oplus$" that specifies, for any pair of operand classes, the class in which the result of any binary function on values from the operand classes belongs. For our SAS application classes cannot be combined.

[3] In general, there should be at least $k = 3$ priorities to allow for a more flexible control of traffic flows–see Section 4.3.

are transmitted via a network channel if, and only if, their priority dominates the congestion level of the channel, (*ii*) packets that are not transmitted are dropped. These policies guarantee real-time availability for *hi* priority packets. For substation automation systems (SAS), the priorities of packets are static, defined by their profile, while the congestion level of the links is dynamic, defined by the prevailing traffic flow (see Section 4.2).

Remark 1. The following argument justifies our approach. Assume that the network system is designed to guarantee communication availability when only (authorized) *hi* priority packets are transmitted. This requires that there must be a bound on the flow of such packets and that the network system is designed to have sufficient redundancy to cope with this traffic. Since SAS network systems are: (*a*) TPM-enabled (Section 3.1) and (*b*) private (controlled by the power utility organization (Section 3.3)), availability is only impacted when authorized flow traffic is congested, resulting in packet bits getting lost/corrupted. When this happens the congestion level of the network channels is raised, in the extreme case to *hi*: this restricts the traffic to *hi* priority packets. As a consequence the transmission time is reduced and we get real-time availability.

For our application the communication network of a SAS contains two types of traffic: *reporting* traffic in which phasor measurements collected by phasor measurement units (PMU) are sent using sample value (SV) packets to a control center for *situational awareness*, and *control* traffic for *event driven communication* (*e.g.*, for critical control applications) in which generic object oriented substation event (GOOSE) packets are used to regulate the SAS.

4.1   The Security Priority of a Packet

The header frame of a packet has several components. These include the security priority of the packet, a packet identifier, and a message authentication code (MAC). The packet identifier is typically an increasing counter value (that will identify dropped packets); and the MAC authenticates the source and the target, and confirms the integrity of the payload. Additionally, the header may include an error detection code (*e.g.*, a *cyclic redundancy code*) or the payload may be encoded using an error correcting code (e.g., a *Reed-Solomon code* [8]). *hi* priority packets are restricted to this structure. For lower priority packets the payload is encrypted. When these packets are received, the payload must first be decrypted, and then decoded (if an error correction code was used), and finally its integrity verified using the message authentication code.

4.2   The Congestion Level of a Link

The congestion level of a link is determined by its traffic flow. This is established dynamically by a *real-time intelligent agent* that monitors traffic flows. When the traffic flow exceeds a certain threshold, the congestion level of the link is raised. The effect of this is to reduce the traffic flow rate to a level for which availability is guaranteed (*e.g.*, when only *hi* priority packets are allowed to be transmitted.

Remark 2. Given a payload, a network node can construct a packet with *hi* priority (*e.g.*, by not encrypting the payload) or *lo* priority, so that its priority will always dominate the congestion level of the channel, which guarantees that it will be transmitted. That is, nodes control both the generation and the transmission of packets. This is not a violation of the *separation of duties* security requirement because network nodes are TPM-compliant and different roots of trust are used for each duty (the root of trust for measurement (RTM) and the root of trust for reporting (RTR)–Section 3.1). As a consequence, when the congestion level is elevated no *lo* priority packet is transmitted. This guarantees real-time communication availability.

4.3 SV Packets and GOOSE Packets

Sample Value (SV) packets and Generic Object Oriented Substation Event (GOOSE) packets have essentially the same structure. From a security point of view however, availability for GOOSE packets can be critical (their payload contains control information), while the redundancy in SV packets makes them less critical. Therefore, it may be desirable to have two high level classes: $hi1 = \ell_k \succeq hi2 = \ell_{k-1}$, with $hi1$ requiring error detecting codes for GOOSE packets and $hi2$ requiring error correction codes.

4.4 Relationship to Existing Mechanisms for Supporting Availability

Traditionally, network availability can be achieved with Quality-of-Service (QoS) support. For example, Internet QoS mechanisms including Integrated Services (Intserv) [4] and Differentiated Services (DiffServ) [3] can both guarantee network availability. IntServ guarantees end-to-end services by reserving bandwidth along all links in the path from source to destination while DiffServ allows different bandwidth for different types of traffic on each link. Our access control structure for need-to-get-now policies is somewhat similar to DiffServ. The main difference is that DiffServ differentiates the services to different types of traffic at any time while our scheme only differentiates services when the network is under the congestion condition: when the link is not congested, our scheme treats all packets the same.

5 Resilient Cyber-Physical Systems

In this section we show how to achieve resiliency in real-time for substation automation systems (SAS) of a power utility that conforms to IEC/TR 61850-90-5 (Section 2), by using TPM-engines (Section 3.1) and an access control infrastructure that enforces need-to-get-now policies (Section 4).

First, note that, as pointed out earlier in Remark 1, we must assume that the network has sufficient redundancy so that, we get real-time resilience when only *hi* priority (authorized) packets are transmitted. This is necessary because otherwise it would be impossible to achieve real-time resilience even when no packets get corrupted or dropped. This can be achieved if we assume that there is a bound on the flow of such packets and that the SAS network system is designed with sufficient redundancy to cope with this traffic.

Next, observe that since the power utility conforms to IEC/TR 6150-90-5, the communication network of the SAS consists of traffic involving either reporting SV packets or control GOOSE packets. We also assume that the SAS is TPM-enabled (Section 3.1). This means that all actions by network nodes are managed by *trust engines* that attest to the integrity of the nodes, that protect stored data, and that prevent nodes from behaving in an unauthorized way (compromised nodes will be prevented by their trust engine). Furthermore, the adversary cannot use the SAS nodes as proxies for DoS or DDoS attacks, because their trust engines (the roots of trust for reporting) will not provide the required keys for authenticating unauthorized packets (remote attestation will prevent faulty PMU generating SV packets).

Finally by using an access control infrastructure that enforces need-to-get-now policies to manage the SAS network traffic (Section 4), we make certain that whenever the traffic flow is high and packets may get dropped, then the congestion level of the network links gets elevated, which implies that only higher priority traffic can use the network—this guarantees real-time resilience (by our first assumption).

6 Emulations and Empirical Study

In order to study the feasibility of the proposed scheme, we have set up a testbed consisting of networked machines capable of operating both Windows 7 and Ubuntu Linux; these machines are used as intelligent electronic devices connected via a Cisco Catalyst 3560G series PoE 48 switch. For the experiments reported here, all machines were configured to run Ubuntu Linux. To carry out the experiments, we started with an open source IEC/TR 61850-90-5 implementation released by SISCO [10]; we made substantial modifications to the implementation, including porting the implementation from a Windows-only to a POSIX compatible implementation, and extending support for authentication and cryptographic protocols.

Our modified version of SISCO's package implements the IEC/TR 61850-90-5 APIs, as well as additional security components. There are five major phases of communication in the implementation: (1) Software initialization which must be performed before any communication can be achieved across the network: by parsing the configuration file, we determine the role of a node in the simulation as a publisher, subscriber, or both, and prepare the necessary components to receive and/or transmit information. (2) Key Distribution Center (KDS) registration, wherein credentials necessary to communicate with the KDC and with nodes on the network are created and distributed. (3) Transmit, wherein packets are created, then encoded, a process which includes encryption (if desired), authentication and sending packets. (4) Receive, wherein packets are received, decoded (which refers to verification of the authenticity and decryption), and processed. Finally, (5) Termination, which must be carried out prior to shutting down the system: this process ensures proper unsubscription from multicast sessions and deallocation of resources dedicated to the service during operation.

To verify the feasibility of our approach, it is necessary to monitor the ability of the network to transmit SV and GOOSE packets effectively, and to understand the impact of various cryptographic functions on the ability of the network to meet the requirements of our need-to-get-now policy. To accomplish this we added a meta-framework to the implementation which saves timing information at key stages during the operation of the system. Specifically, on the publisher a time-mark is saved: (a) at the time when the packet is initially built, (b) directly before it is encrypted, (c) directly before it is HMACed for authentication, and (d) directly before it is sent. On the subscriber, the time is recorded: (e) when the packet is first received, (f) directly before it is authenticated, (g) directly before it is decrypted, and (h) finally again when the packet is fully processed by our system. Using these timestamps we were able to observe the entire transmission time for each packet, as well as the time required for sub-elements within the transmission and receiving sequences; these observations allowed us to evaluate the ability of our framework to fulfill the timing constraints of IEC/TR 61850-90-5, while providing the additional security components necessary to achieve trusted communication.

In the experiments, the session keys were generated using the TPM on the sender and then the keys were shared with all receivers in the multicast group. While this introduces weak security links, it was used because multi-cast is used in IEC/TR 61850-90-5 implementations. From a security point of view, multiple unicasts should be used instead if stronger security is desired.

6.1   Experiment Results

To simulate the heterogeneity of deployed systems, we report the results using three machines, one publisher and two subscribers. The processor of the publisher was an Intel Xeon E5405 2.00GHz x8 with 4 GB of memory; the processor of the first subscriber an Intel Xeon 5120 1.86GHz x2 with 2 GB of memory, and of the second receiver an Intel Xeon E5506 2.13GHz x4 with 6 GB of memory.

Figure 3(a) shows the HMAC computation time on the three machines. On the publisher, the average computation time for HMAC (SHA1) was 0.0298 millisecond with a standard deviation of 0.00028 millisecond. On the first subscriber, the average computation time for HMAC was 0.038 millisecond with a standard deviation of 0.00033 millisecond; on the second subscriber, the average computation time for HMAC was 0.041 millisecond with a standard deviation of 0.0026 millisecond. While the computation time for HMAC is not constant, as it is affected by other system activities, the time is fairly consistent. Note that for substation automation, where the required processing time is within 4 milliseconds, depending on the machine, the HMAC computation time does not have a substantial impact. Among the three machines, the worst was about 1% of the required time. However the HMAC computation time varied significantly

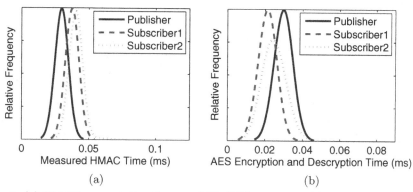

Fig. 3. (a) HMAC computation time, and (b) AES encryption/decryption time on the 3 machines

among the three machines with the largest difference being about 37%. The results show that different types of machines can have different processing times. This is a practical issue that must be addressed in the real-time communication in a large interconnected system where machines are heterogeneous.

We have measured the time required for privacy (confidentiality) using AES. Figure 3(b) shows the encryption on the publisher and decryption on the two subscribers. The subscribers were more efficient in AES computation than the publisher. The mean time for AES on the subscribers was 0.0213 millisecond and 0.0248 millisecond respectively, while it was 0.030 millisecond on the publisher. Clearly newer processors are optimized for AES-like computation. This highlights the importance of developing systems that work on heterogeneous platforms as trusted infrastructures are likely to be deployed incrementally. For PMU measurements and GOOSE packets, since the packet size is fairly small, AES encryption and decryption was fairly efficient. While these estimates need to be further verified, they were fairly consistent for over 500 packets.

We have measured the transmission time and the total required time to process each packet. The average transmission time is 0.0494 millisecond for receiver 1 and 0.0476 millisecond for receiver 2; clearly the transmission time here is smaller compared to typical substation processing times. The average total time for each packet was 0.6837 millisecond and 0.8057 millisecond. These results indicate that the active time of a packet in an IEC/TR 61850-90-5 enabled system was less than 1 millisecond. To meet the IEC/TR 61850-90-5 time constraint of 4 millisecond end-to-end time, more than 3 milliseconds can be allocated to packet transmission. Consequently, by using our access control structure that guarantees delivery for high priority packets (since the queuing delay at each router/switch is bounded) we achieve availability. Integrity of packets is provided by the HMAC and confidentiality by the AES. It follows that our approach/techniques will secure substation automation for power utility systems.

7   Conclusion

In this paper we propose techniques for resilient cyber-physical systems that are directly applicable to secure substation automation for power utility systems. A distinctive feature of our approach includes (1) incorporating TPM-enabled trusted computing technologies, and (2) enforcing need-to-get-now policies that support the time-sensitive nature of critical infrastructures, especially the electricity grid. The feasibility of our approach is demonstrated through analyzing and experimenting with an open source IEC/TR 61850-90-5 implementation.

References

1. Bell, D.E., LaPadula, L.J.: Secure Computer Systems: Mathematical Foundations. MITRE Corporation (1973),
   `http://www.albany.edu/acc/courses/ia/classics/belllapadula1.pdf`
2. Biba, K.J.: Integrity Considerations for Secure Computer Systems. MITRE Corporation, Technical Report, ESD-TR-76-372, MTR-3135 (April 1977)
3. Blake, S., Clark, D., Carlson, M., Davies, E., Wang, Z., Weiss, W.: An Architecture for Differentiated Services. RFC 2475 (December 1998)
4. Braden, R., Clark, D., Shenker, S.: Integrated Services in the Internet Architecture: an Overview. RFC 1633 (June 1994)
5. Denning, D.E.: A lattice model of secure information flow. Commun. ACM 19(5), 236–243 (1976)
6. International Electrotechnical Commission. IEC/TR 61850-90-5, Edition 1.0 2012-05, Technical Report, Power systems management and associated information exchange – Data and communications security (May 2012),
   `http://webstore.iec.ch/preview/info_iec61850-90-5%7Bed1.0%7Den.pdf`
7. International Electrotechnical Commission. IEC/TS 62351-1, First edition 2007-05, Technical Specifications (May 2012),
   `http://webstore.iec.ch/preview/info_iec61850-90-5%7Bed1.0%7Den.pdf`
8. Reed, I.S., Solomon, G.: Polynomial Codes Over Certain Finite Fields. SIAM Journal of Applied Math. 8, 300–304 (1960)
9. Sandhu, R., Coyne, E., Feinstein, H., Youman, C.: Role-based access control models. IEEE Computer 29(2) (1996)
10. SISCO. Cisco and SISCO Collaborate on Open Source Synchrophasor Framework, Press Release (2011),
    `http://www.sisconet.com/downloads/90-5_Cisco_SISCO.pdf`
11. Trusted Computing Group (TCG), `http://www.trustedcomputinggroup.org/`
12. Trusted Network Connect Architecture for Interoperability (TNC), Specification 1.3. Revision 6 (April 2008)
13. Trusted Platform Module (TPM) Structures, Level 2, Version 1.2. Revision 116, Communication Networks and Systems for Power Utility Automation (March 2011),
    `http://www.trustedcomputinggroup.org/resources/tpm_main_specification`

Probabilistic Model Checking
of CAPTCHA Admission Control
for DoS Resistant Anti-SPIT Protection

Emmanouela Stachtiari[1], Yannis Soupionis[2], Panagiotis Katsaros[1],
Anakreontas Mentis[1], and Dimitris Gritzalis[2]

[1] Dependability & Security Group Dept. of Informatics,
Aristotle Un. of Thessaloniki, Greece
{emmastac,katsaros,anakreon}@csd.auth.gr
[2] Information Security And Critical Infrastructure Protection Research Group,
Dept. of Informatics, Athens Univ. of Economics and Business, Athens, Greece
{jsoup,dgrit}@aueb.gr

Abstract. Voice over IP (VoIP) service is expected to play a key role
to new ways of communication. It takes advantage of Internet Protocols by using packet networks to transmit voice and multimedia data,
thus providing extreme cost savings. On the other hand, this technology
has inherited drawbacks, like SPAM over Internet Telephony (SPIT).
A well-established method to tackle SPIT is the use of CAPTCHAs.
CAPTCHAs are vulnerable to Denial of Service (DoS) attacks, due to
their excessive demands for bandwidth. We suggest that anti-SPIT protection should be combined with appropriate admission control policies,
for mitigating the effects of DoS attacks. In order to identify how effective
is this technique, we quantify the costs and the benefits in bandwidth
usage through probabilistic model checking four different admission control policies. We conclude with comments on how appropriate is each
policy in tackling DoS attacks.

Keywords: admission control, DoS, CAPTCHA, probabilistic model
checking.

1 Introduction

Voice over IP (VoIP) offers a low-cost and high-quality service of multimedia data
transmission over Internet Protocol networks, such as the Internet. Inevitably
though, VoIP has "inherited" a major threat of internet communication service
abuse that is widely known as SPAM over Internet Telephony SPIT [15]. Key
VoIP service providers have recognized SPIT as a critical issue that undermines
IP telephony growth and they develop increasingly sophisticated mechanisms to
tackle this threat [19,13].

Most of the systems that provide protection against SPIT adopt basic principles and design considerations from the area of IT Security [11,6,12]. A widespread

B. Hämmerli, N. Kalstad Svendsen, and J. Lopez (Eds.): CRITIS 2012, LNCS 7722, pp. 143–154, 2013.
© Springer-Verlag Berlin Heidelberg 2013

approach is to develop policy-based mechanisms based on predetermined conditions. These conditions can be formalized as a structured security policy implemented by a set of rules defined by the user organization. Anti-SPIT protection policies include all decisions and actions to perform, in order to provide effective protection. However, it is true that under certain circumstances such a policy cannot identify whether a VoIP communication originates from software robots ("bots") or humans. A common technique to manage those VoIP sessions is the use of audio CAPTCHAs (Completely Automated Public Turing Test to Tell Computer and Humans Apart) [18].

A CAPTCHA is a test that most humans should be able to pass, but computer programs should not. Even though audio CAPTCHA is a well-established technology, as an anti-SPIT protection mechanism it is susceptible to Distributed Denial of Service (DDoS) attacks, due to the computer resources demands associated with the CAPTCHA challenges. DDoS attacks against VoIP servers are notoriously difficult to be countered [16]. They are launched by taking control of numerous machines that belong to unaware users. These machines are used to force a victim server into instantly delivering a huge bulk of CAPTCHA challenges that can exhaust the available bandwidth [9]. Such a bandwidth consumption attack may render the server unavailable for legitimate users.

We propose that anti-SPIT protection should be combined with appropriate admission control policies for mitigating the effects of DDoS attacks. In a VoIP server under attack the vast majority of service requests causing CAPTCHA challenges comes from incoming attack traffic. Admission control filters all service requests according to some bandwidth preservation criterion and therefore opens a possibility to prevent legitimate CAPTCHA challenges. In effect, a cost for bandwidth preservation is induced.

We quantify the costs and the benefits in bandwidth usage through probabilistic model checking of a server model handling DDoS traffic. We opted for a Continuous Time Markov Chain (CTMC) representation developed within the PRISM [7] model checking toolset and parameterized based on data from real audio CAPTCHA implementations [12]. The obtained results provide analytic estimates of appropriate cost and benefit metrics for comparing cost-effectiveness of four admission control policies, namely simple sum [8], cutoff scheme [10], fractional guard [14] and a threshold-based [3] policy. Our cost and benefit metrics are expressed as reward properties quantified over all possible paths of the CTMC reachability graph. Our comparative results have been validated by extensive sensitivity analysis over different combinations of parameter ranges.

The paper is organized as follows. First, in Section 2 we give a short background on probabilistic model checking and the PRISM tool. Section 3 discusses the examined admission control policies and the attack scenario we consider. In Section 4, we provide the details of the performed probabilistic analysis and the developed PRISM models, along with the adopted cost and benefits metrics. Section 5 presents the obtained model checking results and interprets the shown trends. Section 6 refers to the related work for probabilistic analysis of bandwidth abuse. The paper concludes with a review on the findings and a discussion on their contribution towards the improvement of anti-SPIT protection and our future work plans.

2 Probabilistic Model Checking

Probabilistic model checking is an algorithmic formal verification technique for analyzing systems with probabilistic behavior. The PRISM model checking toolset [7] generates models from a high-level description of the system's behavior with guarded commands. These commands are grouped into modules and each module's behavior is defined by local variables and transitions of the form:

$$[l]g \rightarrow \phi_l : u_1 + \ldots + \phi_n : u_n; \tag{1}$$

The guard g is a predicate over model variables and constants, whereas each update u_i specifies how new values are assigned to local variables. Transitions can occur with some likelihood or frequency depending on the specified model type. We opted a CTMC for faithfully representing the contention for a limited amount of bandwidth provided in a VoIP system. For CTMCs, ϕ_i is the transition's rate, the parameter of a negative exponential distribution that governs the waiting time of the transition, provided that the guard is true. Optional label l is used for explicit synchronization with other transitions. The rate of synchronized transitions is the product of the rates of the individual transitions.

Our CTMC model possesses the fundamental Markov property, which is also presumed in [4] for analyzing bandwidth usage: the conditional probability distribution of future states depends only upon the present state. This assumption is justified by the fact that bandwidth sharing, under the common assumption of Poisson session arrivals, is insensitive to the flow size and the session arrival process.

PRISM implements a series of graph-theoretic algorithms for reachability analysis and iterative numerical solvers for computing/checking probabilistic properties expressed in Probabilistic Computation Tree Logic (PCTL). It is also possible to compute reward properties based on some reward structure defined over the model. Path formulas in PCTL consist of temporal operators, such as F (eventually) or G (always) and predicates that can be true or false in the reached states. Models can be queried with properties of the form $P =?[prop]$ about the probability to satisfy a path formula $prop$. Reward structures are used to accumulate reward or cost values when certain states or transitions are observed. Properties of the form $Rr =?[prop]$ query the model for the expected value of the reward r along paths satisfying $prop$. In CTMCs, probabilistic and reward-based properties can be bounded by time t, if a transient analysis is required. In this case, a reward property takes the form $(C \leq t)$.

3 Admission Control Policies

Let us consider the following scenario: a client group of legitimate users is served by the VoIP infrastructure, while at the same time new legitimate clients and intruders that generate attack traffic are requested to answer CAPTCHAs. Requests for multimedia services and CAPTCHA resources demand a non-negligible amount of bandwidth and they can be granted process time, as long as the bandwidth has not been exhausted. In a DDoS attack, the number of malicious requests is rapidly increased in order to cause bandwidth exhaustion. The attack succeeds, if the incoming malicious requests consume all the available bandwidth, before a legitimate request for service or a CAPTCHA resource can be accepted.

When a policy is applied for admission control, the available bandwidth is preserved by distinguishing the CAPTCHA challenges that will be served. This is a sufficient way to prevent bandwidth abuse, since the bandwidth for the provided VoIP services can be utilized only by legitimate users (we assume that attackers cannot break/pass the CAPTCHA test and therefore they cannot dispatch directly requests for multimedia services).

We focus on parameter-based admission control policies, as opposed to measure-based policies that cannot be analyzed by a model-based approach. More precisely, we study the following policies: the simple sum [8], the cutoff scheme [10], the fractional guard [14] and a threshold-based [3] policy. In order to discuss the policy approach, we have adopted the following notation:

1. κ representing the consumed bandwidth at a certain instant
2. β referring to the total link capacity
3. ρ denoting the expected bandwidth for a service request, and
4. c the expected bandwidth consumed for transferring a CAPTCHA challenge

In all policies, a service request is accepted provided that there is available bandwidth to serve it ($\kappa + \rho < \beta$). The applied control approach for admission of the arrived CAPTCHA requests is as follows:

Simple Sum: a CAPTCHA challenge is delivered only if $\kappa + c < \beta$. This means that a new request is accepted, only if the available bandwidth suffices for the expected CAPTCHA challenge needs in bandwidth.

Cutoff Scheme: requests by already authorized users have a higher priority than the incoming CAPTCHA requests. In effect, a portion of the bandwidth is reserved for assuring that user needs will be always accommodated. The question regarding the ratio of bandwidth that should be reserved poses a significant trade-off. If too much bandwidth is reserved, then new users requesting access to services are likely to be discarded even when the bandwidth is underutilized. On the other hand, underestimation of the bandwidth needed for providing VoIP services can lead to the rejection of VoIP service requests. A CAPTCHA request is accepted if $max(\kappa, \delta) + c < \beta$, where δ is the bandwidth reserved for authorized users.

Fractional Guard: CAPTCHA requests are accepted with a probability that depends on the bandwidth consumption. This policy can be expressed by the equation $\pi * rand(0, 1) > \kappa$, where $rand$ returns a uniform positive value less than one and π is a parameter that influences the acceptance rate.

Threshold Based: this policy is an adapted version of the call bounding scheme, described in [3]. During a fixed period of time τ at most λ CAPTCHA requests are accepted. All other requests are rejected until the expiration of the time period, when the number of received requests is set to zero.

4   VoIP System Model and Cost Benefit Analysis

4.1   PRISM Model Description

Four models have been developed in PRISM, with each of them representing a VoIP server under DDoS attack with one of the mentioned admission control policies. The applied policy affects the model's behavior regarding whether an arriving CAPTCHA request can be accepted or not. CAPTCHA requests are generated from one legitimate and one malicious source with different rates, thus representing a race for acquiring the still available bandwidth resource. We consider that if a legitimate CAPTCHA request is admitted, the model's execution ends with an attack failure. If a legitimate CAPTCHA request cannot be accepted due to bandwidth exhaustion, then the malicious traffic results in a DDoS success. Since the period of time needed to solve a CAPTCHA challenge (5-15 seconds) exceeds the time period in which an attack success is observed (<1 second), it is reasonable to take into account the additional bandwidth consumption by all accepted CAPTCHA requests, until reaching the model's final state. The following model variables are used to encode state information for the described VoIP system.

- *captchas*, the number of CAPTCHA challenges currently in progress
- *established_legitimate*, becomes true if a legitimate CAPTCHA request has been accepted
- *successful_attack*, becomes true if the malicious traffic has consumed all available bandwidth
- *captcha_counter*, a counter used in the threshold-based policy for the number of accepted CAPTCHA requests. It is periodically set to zero.

Table 1 highlights the model parameters, with some of them being common in all models. We vary the *malicious_requests* parameter to represent DDoS attacks of various intensities. All other parameters are assigned constant values. The *clients_rate* and *new_clients_rate* parameters are assigned values, such that on average one CAPTCHA request is expected among 20 service requests from legitimate users. This happens due to the fact that most anti-SPIT techniques have the CAPTCHA mechanism as the last obstacle against SPIT attacks [5] and consequently only a portion of SPIT attacks are challenged by CAPTCHA. The *captcha_size* parameter represents bandwidth consumption for transferring the CAPTCHA challenge's audio file and is set to 200 kbps [18]. We assume that the *service_size* is 83 kbps of Session Initiation Protocol (SIP) trunk bandwidth per service request [1], considering the G.711 wave-format codec. We set the *link_capacity* to 5 Mps for a VoIP server with a total bandwidth of 10 Mps, out of which 5 Mps are devoted for servicing already authorized clients.

Table 1. Model Parameters

Name	Description
All models	
malicious_requests	Rate of malicious requests. (1-100.000 req/sec)
clients_rate	Rate of requests arriving from authorized clients. (200 req/sec)
new_clients_rate	Rate of requests arriving from unauthorized clients. (10 req/sec)
captcha_size	Bandwidth requirements for a CAPTCHA challenge. (200 kbps)
service_size	Bandwidth requirements for serving authorized clients. (83 kbps)
link_capacity	Total available bandwidth (5 Mbps)
Cutoff scheme	
bandwidth_reserved	Percentage of available bandwidth reserved for serving service requests
Fractional guard	
acceptance_parameter	A value such that the probability of accepting a CAPTCHA is given by $acceptance\_parameter * k$, where k is the currently available bandwidth
Threshold-based	
initialize_rate	Frequency of setting the counter of accepted CAPTCHA requests to zero.
captcha_limit	Threshold of the counter accepted CAPTCHA so that CAPTCHA requests are still accepted.

The decision of whether a request will be accepted or not is made based on two PRISM formulas, namely AdmitService and AdmitCAPTCHA. While the AdmitService formula has the form $consumed\_bandwidth + service\_size \leq link\_capacity$ in all models, the AdmitCAPTCHA formula varies for each policy, as it is shown in Table 2.

Table 2. The variants of the AdmitCAPTCHA formula in each policy

Policy name	AdmitCAPTCHA variants
simple sum	$consumed\_bandwidth + captcha\_size \leq link\_capacity$
cutoff scheme	$consumed\_bandwidth + captcha\_size \leq link\_capacity$
fractional guard	$consumed\_bandwidth + bandwidth\_reserved * link\_capacity + captcha\_size \leq link\_capacity$
threshold-based	$(captcha\_counter < captcha_l imit)\&(consumed\_bandwidth + captcha\_size \leq link\_capacity)$

The main transitions of the VoIP system model are:

- *admit_malicious*: admit a malicious CAPTCHA request. Occurs with rate *malicious_requests*, if the AdmitCAPTCHA formula evaluates to true.
- *reject_malicious*: drop a malicious CAPTCHA request. Occurs with rate *malicious_requests*, if the AdmitCAPTCHA formula evaluates to false.

- *admit_new_client*: admit a CAPTCHA request from legitimate user. Occurs with rate *new_clients_rate*, if the AdmitCAPTCHA formula evaluates to true.
- *reject_new_client*: drop a CAPTCHA request from legitimate user. Occurs with rate *new_clients_rate*, if the AdmitCAPTCHA formula evaluates to false.
- *admit_service*: admit a service request. Occurs with rate *service_rate*, if the AdmitService formula evaluates to true.
- *reject_service*: drop a service request. Occurs with rate *new_clients_rate*, if the AdmitService formula evaluates to false.

In the fractional guard policy, the typical rate for an accept request transition is multiplied by *accept_parameter* $*$ (*link_capacity* $-$ *consumed_bandwidth*)/*link_capacity*, where *accept_parameter* is the value of π. Similarly, the typical rate for a drop request transition is multiplied by $1 - ($*accept_parameter* $*$ (*link_capacity* $-$ *consumed_bandwidth*)/*link_capacity*$)$

4.2   Costs and Benefit of Admission Control

The probability of DDoS attack success against a CAPTCHA anti-SPIT mechanism is only one aspect of admission control effectiveness. Evaluating other aspects of bandwidth usage is also very important. For example, an extremely rigid policy that discards most CAPTCHA requests is not vulnerable to DDoS, but it also fails to serve the legitimate users who generate CAPTCHA requests.

A more complete view for the admission control cost-effectiveness is obtained by considering all metrics related to costs and benefits in bandwidth usage, while avoiding to quantify strongly correlated properties such that we will not take into account the same effects twice. Then, it will be possible to compare the different policies based on their net benefit.

We assigned costs and benefits to specific model events by attaching the following reward structures:

- Accepted (A_S) and rejected (R_S) service requests: they compute respectively the expected number of accepted and rejected service requests. Both of them take values in the range of $[0, 1]$, since the server model receives at most one service request at each execution path.
- Accepted (A_N) and rejected (R_N) new clients: they compute the expected number of accepted and rejected CAPTCHA requests from new legitimate clients. They also take values in the range of $[0, 1]$ for the same reason as the previous structures.
- Available bandwidth (A_B) while the system is under DDoS attack: this reward computes the expected bandwidth percentage that remains available during the attack.

We defined the cost and benefit metrics from the server's viewpoint as shown in Table 3. The probability to accept an incoming service request should be as high as possible and therefore we consider it as a benefit metric. On the other hand, the probability to reject a request initiated by a new client, as well as the percentage of unexploited bandwidth upon a DDoS attack is a cost that admission control should minimize. The net benefit is calculated by

$$netbenefit = 2 * B_1 - C_1 - C_2 \tag{2}$$

The benefit is weighted twice as much as each of the costs. The appropriate weights depend on the optimization priorities that are specific to the context of the performed analysis.

Table 3. Cost and benefit metrics for the analysis

Cost		Benefit	
Metric	Value	Metric	Value
Probability of rejecting an incoming request from a new client (C_1)	$R_N/(A_N + R_N)$	Probability of accepting an incoming service request (B_1)	$A_S/(A_S + R_S)$
Percentage of unexploited bandwidth upon DDoS (C_2)	A_B		

The goal of our analysis is to rank the policies according to their net benefit, at each grade of attack intensity. Since the choice of parameters affects the ranking, we assumed the best net benefit for each policy with some specific attack intensity. By having ran the models with different parameters, we discovered the higher net benefit for increasing numbers of malicious requests.

5   Experimental Results

The experimental results for a wide range of malicious requests rate using various model parameters are summarized in Fig. 1. In simple sum, the net benefit decreases exponentially as the malicious requests become more frequent. Specifically, the benefit converges to zero and the probability to reject a new client's request increases at higher attack rates. On the other hand, the available bandwidth is zero for all rates of malicious requests. Cost outperforms benefit when the attack rates are higher than 13.000 requests per second.

The cutoff scheme offers greater net benefit as the reserved bandwidth shrinks, as long as it is more than the percentage of bandwidth occupied by service requests, which we assume to be 0.5. Reserving 60% of bandwidth, as compared to 80%, leads to less unexploited bandwidth and to a higher probability of accepting new clients' requests. On the other hand, accepting an incoming service request is guaranteed in both cases. The maximum net benefit was achieved by setting the reserved bandwidth parameter to 0,51.

In fractional guard, the higher the accept parameter value is, the higher the net benefit for up to 10.000 malicious requests is. At larger attack rates, a smaller accept parameter is optimal and it achieves better results after 14.000 malicious requests. When the attack rate is low, a small accept parameter leads to a significantly higher possibility of dropping new client requests and a larger percentage of unexploited bandwidth. On the other hand, fractional guard offers a higher probability of serving a service request, which is maintained for very high attack rates. Generally, the net benefit decreases slower for small accept parameters.

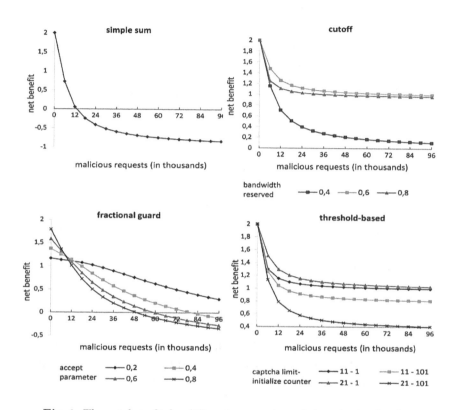

Fig. 1. The net benefit for different parameters of the examined policies

The series of net benefit in the threshold-based policy are associated with sets of the CAPTCHA limit and initialization rate parameters. When the initialization rate equals to 1, setting the CAPTCHA limit to 21 yields better net benefit. A requirement for the CAPTCHA limit is to be smaller than the maximum CAPTCHA sessions that the bandwidth can handle. For an initialization rate of 101, bigger CAPTCHA limit leads to better net benefit. This is observed because the more frequent the initialization of the accepted CAPTCHA counter happens, the smaller the counter threshold is. The best net benefit was achieved by setting the initialization rate to 1 and the CAPTCHA limit to 24, which is the maximum number of CAPTCHA that the bandwidth can accommodate, while at the same time it has enough space to serve a service request.

It is concluded that the threshold-based policy gave the best results in the cost-benefit analysis at all attack rates as Fig. 2 displays. On the other hand,

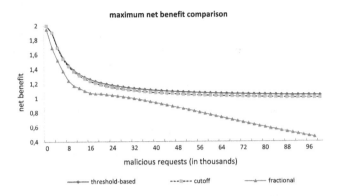

Fig. 2. Maximum net benefit achieved by policies

the cutoff policy ranks second, having a very small difference from the first one. This policy requires knowledge of the expected arrival rate of legitimate requests, which is susceptible to change. Fractional guard did not perform very well due to our choice of evaluation metrics. This policy does not provide enough guarantees for serving legitimate requests and randomized decision of accepting CAPTCHA requests can have flaws that are revealed by model checking (all possible results of these decisions are taken into account).

6   Related Work

A game-theoretic framework for analyzing the effectiveness of bandwidth attacks is presented in [17]. The game consists of an attacker launching an attack using IP spoofing and a defender, who attempts to detect the attack using coarse-grained statistical filtering. The authors examine various strategies for such games and evaluate the payoffs. Their results show that statistical methods are a promising means for revealing bandwidth abuse attacks. They also pose the idea to use statistical filtering for identifying suspicious groups in the server's traffic, towards directing resource-consuming filtering techniques only to those groups.

In [8], the authors define the evaluation criteria to compare one parameter-based and tree measure-based admission control policies. Parameter-based policies make decisions based on a priori knowledge of the server's traffic, while measure-based policies rely on actual measurements of load. They evaluate simulation results based on the criteria of the probability for guaranteed service to clients and the level of network utilization. However, model checking provides higher confidence for policy effectiveness than simulation-based approaches, because the results characterize all possible system execution scenarios, as opposed to only a limited number of simulation traces.

PRISM is used in [2] to formally analyze the bandwidth amplification attack against the Domain Name System (DNS), along with three countermeasures:

packet filtering, random packet drops, and aggressive retries of legitimate packets. The authors compute the attack probability based on CTMC representation of an attack scenario and measure the cost-effectiveness of each countermeasure, when it is used for completely eliminating the probability of attack success. Our cost-benefit analysis is based on the same principles with those applied in [2].

7 Conclusions and Further Research

Voice over IP technology becomes a popular communication system, as it is widely used for establishing and maintaining multimedia sessions over the Internet. One of the obvious potential problems of VoIP applications is the growth of the SPIT phenomenon, which is often handled with the use of audio CAPTCHA. Even though this technique is able to distinguish sessions which are initiated by human from those initiated by software (bots), it adds up a serious threat: the possibility of bandwidth abuse through DDoS attacks.

In this work we study the effectiveness of CAPTCHA admission control policies towards eliminating the DDoS threat by discarding a limited number of VoIP sessions. We provide results obtained by probabilistic model checking of a CTMC representing bandwidth consumption in a VoIP system. Costs and benefits for the analyzed policies have been quantified by appropriate reward properties defined and evaluated within the PRISM model checking toolset.

The examined policies are ranked according to the computed net benefit for a range of parameter values that provide insight for the analysis sensitivity. We show that threshold-based and cutoff admission policies offer effective defense against DDoS attacks. Two other policies, namely fractional guard and simple sum are not characterized by decent results in terms of cost-effectiveness. More specifically, it is shown that when applying the simple sum policy, the more attack sessions are initiated the less net benefit is obtained. We note that the parameters used in our analysis do not depend on hardware characteristics.

As future work prospect we aim to study how the admission policies and the use of audio CAPTCHA affect the time needed for call establishment in VoIP sessions, since there are critical timeouts set by most VoIP providers. Moreover, we plan to measure cost effectiveness not only in terms of bandwidth usage, but also in terms of CPU and memory consumption.

References

1. Cisco: Voice over ip per call bandwidth consumption. Document id 7934, Cisco Communication (February 2006)
2. Deshpande, T., Katsaros, P., Basagiannis, S., Smolka, S.A.: Formal analysis of the DNS bandwidth amplification attack and its countermeasures using probabilistic model checking. In: HASE, pp. 360–367. IEEE Computer Society (2011)
3. Fang, Y., Zhang, Y.: Call admission control schemes and performance analysis in wireless mobile networks. IEEE Transactions on Vehicular Technology 51(2), 371–382 (2002)

4. Fred, S.B., Bonald, T., Proutiére, A., Régnié, G., Roberts, J.W.: Statistical bandwidth sharing: a study of congestion at flow level. In: SIGCOMM, pp. 111–122 (2001)

5. Gritzalis, D., Marias, G.F., Rebahi, Y., Soupionis, Y., Ehlert, S.: Spider: A platform for managing sip-based spam over internet telephony (spit). Journal of Computer Security 19(5), 835–867 (2011)

6. Gritzalis, S., Gritzalis, D.: A digital seal solution for deploying trust on commercial transactions. Inf. Manag. Comput. Security 9(2), 71–79 (2001)

7. Hinton, A., Kwiatkowska, M., Norman, G., Parker, D.: PRISM: A tool for automatic verification of probabilistic systems. In: Hermanns, H., Palsberg, J. (eds.) TACAS 2006. LNCS, vol. 3920, pp. 441–444. Springer, Heidelberg (2006)

8. Jamin, S., Shenker, S., Danzig, P.B.: Comparison of measurement-based call admission control algorithms for controlled-load service. In: INFOCOM, pp. 973–980 (1997)

9. Kandula, S., Katabi, D., Jacob, M., Berger, A.: Botz-4-sale: Surviving organized DDoS attacks that mimic flash crowds. In: NSDI. USENIX (2005)

10. Lin, Y.B., Mohan, S., Noerpel, A.: Queueing priority channel assignment strategies for PCS hand-off and initial access. IEEE Transactions on Vehicular Technology 43(3), 704–712 (1994)

11. Marias, G., Dritsas, S., Theoharidou, M., Mallios, J., Gritzalis, D.: Sip vulnerabilities and anti-spit mechanisms assessment. In: ICCCN, pp. 597–604 (2007)

12. Mitrou, L., Gritzalis, D., Katsikas, S.K., Quirchmayr, G.: Electronic voting: Constitutional and legal requirements, and their technical implications. In: Secure Electronic Voting. Advances in Information Security, vol. 7, pp. 43–60. Springer (2003)

13. Quittek, J., Niccolini, S., Tartarelli, S., Stiemerling, M., Brunner, M., Ewald, T.: Detecting spit calls by checking human communication patterns. In: ICC, pp. 1979–1984. IEEE (2007)

14. Ramjee, R., Towsley, D., Nagarajan, R.: On optimal call admission control in cellular networks. Wireless Networks 3, 29–41 (1997)

15. Rosenberg, J., Jennings, C.: The session initiation protocol (sip) and spam. Rfc 5039, Network Working Group (January 2008)

16. Sisalem, D., Kuthan, J., Ehlert, S.: Denial of service attacks targeting a sip voip infrastructure: attack scenarios and prevention mechanisms. IEEE Network 20(5), 26–31 (2006)

17. Snyder, M.E., Sundaram, R., Thakur, M.: A game-theoretic framework for bandwidth attacks and statistical defenses. In: LCN, pp. 556–566. IEEE Computer Society (2007)

18. Soupionis, Y., Gritzalis, D.: Audio captcha: Existing solutions assessment and a new implementation for voip telephony. Computers & Security 29(5), 603–618 (2010)

19. Soupionis, Y., Gritzalis, D.: Aspf: Adaptive anti-spit policy-based framework. In: ARES, pp. 153–160 (2011)

Reasoning about Vulnerabilities in Dependent Information Infrastructures: A Cyber Range Experiment

Adedayo O. Adetoye, Sadie Creese, and Michael H. Goldsmith

Cyber Security Centre
Department of Computer Science
University of Oxford
Oxford, OX1 3QD, UK
{adedayo.adetoye,sadie.creese,michael.goldsmith}@cs.ox.ac.uk
http://www.cybersecurity.ox.ac.uk/

Abstract. Malice aside, even the pursuit of legitimate local goals such as cost minimisation, availability, and resilience in subsystems of a critical information infrastructure (CII) can induce subtle dynamic behaviours and dependencies that endanger higher-level goals and security of services. However, in practice, the subsystems of a CII may not be entirely cooperative, potentially having different and perhaps conflicting management goals; and some subsystems may be malicious or untrustworthy. Consequently, vulnerabilities may arise accidentally or deliberately through the dependency on subsystems with conflicting goals, or systems which might contain potentially rogue elements. We have developed an analytical framework for reasoning about vulnerabilities and risks in dependent critical infrastructure. To validate the analytical framework we have carried out a series of experiments on a Cyber Range facility, simulating dependent information infrastructures. This paper presents results obtained from the experiments.

Keywords: Dependent Information Infrastructure, Analytical Tools, Cyber Range Experiment.

1 Introduction

Critical Information Infrastructures (CIIs) seldom operate in isolation. Often they are built, and sometimes they organically emerge from smaller (perhaps autonomous) subsystems. Thus, the services provided by CIIs may rely on subsystems with various degrees of quality and which have complex dependency relationships between them. Even though the typical CII will be distributed, emergent, and connected together via complex dependency relationships; from the user's perspective, the services that the CII provides must operate transparently, securely, and efficiently regardless of the structure or complexity of the underlying system. When dealing with *critical* infrastructures however, guaranteeing quality is even more important, because not meeting service requirements or violating policies can have very dire consequences.

In order to provide guarantees about services with respect to the user requirements, various subsystems of the CII may have to collaborate together. This is not always possible because the systems may fall under different administrative boundaries with

B. Hämmerli, N. Kalstad Svendsen, and J. Lopez (Eds.): CRITIS 2012, LNCS 7722, pp. 155–167, 2013.

conflicting goals. The conflicts can generate exploitable vulnerabilities, and it is essential that we discover and understand these vulnerabilities in order to plan for and mitigate the associated risks.

A major challenge arises because the interactions between information infrastructure subsystems to provide essential services are often so complex that it may be difficult to foresee the effect that local changes within a subsystem may have on global objectives such as the security and quality of services delivered by the information system. Local goals, such as policy-driven load-balancing, for example, can create transient dynamic behaviours with unexpected impacts on the goals and requirements of other dependent systems within the infrastructure. It is thus beneficial to have tools for reasoning about, and for discovering the potential impact of changes within the dependent infrastructure on a target system of interest. Such tools may help in forward-planning, for decision support during the selection of controls and remedies to risks arising from the introduction of change.

To see how benign local changes might inadvertently sabotage global goals, let us consider an example involving storage outsourcing in an open cloud storage ecosystem. Suppose that an organisation (A, as shown in Fig. 1) wishes to achieve availability of data d by outsourcing redundantly to, say three (B, C, and D), different cloud storage providers at a time t. Now suppose that the storage providers, seeking to minimise their cost of service provision, have a policy to further outsource some of their storage to other storage provider that minimises their operating costs. Now if at a later time $t' > t$ the storage provider E advertises a very favourable cost, so that the providers B, C, and D further outsource data d to E in line with their individual policies. This interaction between the pricing strategy of E and the policies at B, C, and D has led to the violation of the redundancy requirement at A because by aggregating the data at E, a single point-of-failure is established. The notation $d\phi X$ in Fig. 1 means that the labelled node is hosting the data d from the customer X. As we can see from the figure, at the time t' only the node E is hosting the data d, in violation of the requirement that d must be hosted in at least 3 different sites.

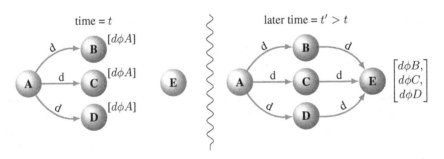

Fig. 1. The interaction of policies at B,C,D and the price changes at E leads to a violation of the redundancy objective of A at time t'

Unless A negotiates with the storage providers not to further outsource its data for storage elsewhere, it is difficult to provide any guarantee that the desired availability will not be violated by legitimate dynamic changes that might take place within the ecosystem. In fact, such changes need not be across organisations, it may be internal, involving one branch and another of the same organisation; or even at the enterprise level where the operating procedures and practices may need to change as a result of corporate acquisitions and mergers. Reasoning about the impact of such changes is a problem that we wish to tackle.

Now, as in the example above, we observe that changes within a dependent infrastructure that lead to a vulnerability or the direct violation of policies of a stakeholder need not be purely technical. Enterprise policies, the physical environment, and even events that are external to the relevant organisations can effect changes, which have consequences for the dependent stakeholders. For this reason we take a holistic approach to the modelling of dependencies across the CII ecosystem that encompasses the physical, technological, information, and the enterprise environment within our framework. So, dependencies may span technological assets, to enterprise layer policies and operating procedures and the information and physical environments as well as organisational externalities. This allows us to discover scenarios where non-traditional dependencies can impact target objectives. For example, when market and competitive conditions influences policies for supply chain selection, which in turn changes the technology environment and the overall security posture. In our experiment, which we shall present later in Section 3, the choice of outsourcing cost minimisation policies (an enterprise-level change) impacted the resilience and security requirements of the stakeholder's information assets (an information-level impact). We have adopted a layered-architecture to study how changes and dependencies across the various layers of an organisation and its organisational dependencies can impact objectives. See [1,3] for details about our layered approach.

1.1 Research Results

The primary objective of this paper is to verify and validate our dependency modelling and analytical framework via experimentation on the Cyber Range: a Cyber war-gaming environment for high-fidelity stress-testing of enterprise and information infrastructures. Having developed a dependency taxonomy within a conceptual dependency model, as well as an analytical framework (reported previously [1,3]) we wanted to investigate by carrying out specific types of experiments involving the exploitation of dependencies across multiple layers of multiple enterprises whether our model was rich enough to explain the vulnerabilities. Had this not been the case, it would have necessitated a refinement of our model. Consequently, and because of space constraints, we only presented the analysis of a single experiment scenario checking the violation of a (k, n) secret sharing policy. Other policies such as availability metrics were investigated but not presented. The validation methodology remained the same.

1.2 Related Work

Our research work focuses on dependent infrastructures. There are three main, often complementary, approaches to modelling such dependencies:

1. **Graph/Network-Based Models.** Here the interconnected infrastructure is modelled as a network or graph consisting of nodes (infrastructure components) and edges or links representing the relationship or interconnectivity between the nodes. Graph-theoretic models of dependencies have been well-studied [16,6,14,2,10,1], graph-based models can be visually compelling when presented graphically, but more importantly the graph-based model makes it possible to apply many results from network/graph theory to infrastructure analyses. In [16] the authors have develop a flexible way to describe the behaviours of nodes in the network while incorporating various models of network services. The approach is based on service dependencies between infrastructure nodes which is validated within a simulation environment. Our formalism, however, permits in addition to network nodes and services, actors from the environment such as people, natural phenomena (earthquakes, floods, etc.), and other externalities which along with their impacts can be incorporated directly into the model. This potentially allows richer scenarios to be specified and reasoned about within our model. In [11], a dependency model based on *Quality* (various properties and indicators such as *quantity*, *speed* and *reliability*), *Response* (*input* and *time*-induced variability in service output), *State* of operation (*normal*, *stressed*, *crisis* and *recovery* states) and *Environmental* factors are considered. The basic idea is to support richer models of dependencies that can capture real-world scenarios. Although we have only presented a simulation scenario in this paper, we have defined a foundational calculus of dependency [1], which can capture all the four areas identified in [11]. Our framework also features an analytical system driven by *What If?* queries for the discovery of vulnerabilities in dependent infrastructures [3].

2. **Agent-Based Simulations.** Here CII components and subsystems are modelled as autonomous agents interacting with other agents, evolving and showing emergent behaviours. Examples include [7,17,9]. The CIMS© framework is an agent-based CII modelling and simulation platform that was developed to provide a portable and highly visual tools to identify and graphically display interdependency weaknesses and vulnerabilities to the critical portions of the infrastructure or operations [7]. It allows high-level reasoning about CII states. CIMS© is a fully-fledged simulation environment which allows network nodes to be connected to external simulations or even physical sensors. Our framework allows a simulated CII to be analysed through the use of translators that can transform the simulated CII into the dependency model used by the framework.

3. **Input-Output Analyses.** Inspired by Wassily Leontief's Input-output model of the economy, [8] developed what is referred to as the Leontief-based infrastructure input-output model to enable an accounting of the intra-connectedness within infrastructures as well as the interconnectedness among them. Leontief's model enables understanding the inter-connectedness among the various sectors of an economy and forecasting the effect on one segment of a change in another. Oliva et al [12] combine the input-output and an agent-based model to overcome the limitations of agent-based models which are often difficult to validate because of lack of quantitative data and the often very abstract input-output models, but which are validated using real economic data. We do not use the input-output model.

In the arena of dependency modelling and analysis, [13] identifies four abstract problem areas that are relevant for the analysis of infrastructure dependencies and the subsequent emergent system behaviours:

1. Given a set of initiating events $\{E(a), E(b), \ldots\}$ what is the cascading impact on a subset of nodes $\{x, y, z, \ldots\}$? Here $a, b, \ldots, x, y, z, \ldots$ represent infrastructure entities of interest, and for any such node a, $E(a)$ is an event associated with a.
2. Given a set of nodes $\{x, y, z, \ldots\}$ and a desired end state, what is a set of events $\{E(a), E(b), \ldots\}$ that would cause this effect?
3. Given a set of events $\{E(a), E(b), \ldots\}$ and a set of observed outcomes of on nodes $\{x, y, z, \ldots\}$, is it possible to determine the derived dependency $(abDxyz)$? Here $(abDxyz)$ means dependency sources a and b are acting together to generate the outcomes in the target nodes x, y and z.
4. Given a set of infrastructure networks and a critical function, what is the subset of critical nodes $\{x, y, z, \ldots\}$ across all networks that will adversely impact a specific mission functionality due to direct or derived dependency?

The first two problems are captured and reasoned about under our analytical framework through an automated *What If?* reasoning interface, and the last two are captured within its analytical engine, which automatically derives dependency relationships through an event-driven semantic model. In particular, we note that our analytical framework does not require the dependency relationships to be built directly, as is typically done in simulation-based approaches [13], rather, our modelling approach derives dependency relationships by logical deductions backed up by formal axioms. Some details about how this is achieved have been reported elsewhere [1,3].

2   Architecture of Analytics

We have developed within the *SATURN* project an analytical framework, which provides an environment for modelling and reasoning about CII dependency and the associated risks. A high level software architecture of the framework is shown in Fig. 2. Currently, there are two primary ways of using the framework, namely through **SDML** (our domain-specific language for infrastructure dependency modelling) and through simulation. This paper is based the latter approach. At the core of the framework is a *dependency model*, which we have defined to capture various forms of dependency relationships between infrastructure elements and their states. The user will not typically generate the dependency model directly, rather, pluggable translators are used to derive the dependency model from a model source. For example, in this paper, the results of a CII simulation are used to generate the dependency models through a simulation event translator. Our special-purpose CII dependency modelling language, **SDML**, comes with a built-in translator within our toolset that generates the dependency model directly from the modelling language. Thus, in principle, any CII model can be analysed under this extensible framework provided there is a translator for the CII model.

The advantage of transforming a given CII model into our dependency model is that it can benefit from powerful analytics and *What If?* queries that we have developed as part of our critical infrastructure analysis framework. The analysis engine (*Analytics* in

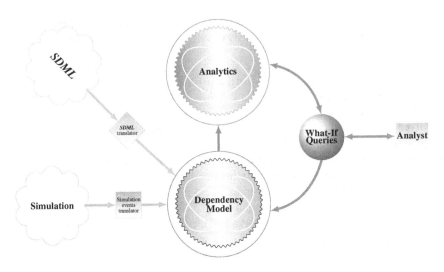

Fig. 2. The Software Architecture of *SATURN* Analytics

Fig. 2) can reason about the dependency relationships and states of the infrastructure entities as they evolve over time to discover the satisfaction of target constraints. Such constraints may be in the form of policy objective specifications that formalise when a target policy has been violated. The analytical reasoning is then carried out through a series of *What If?* queries that the analyst can issue to see how initial target configurations and events can impact target objectives. As an example, a *What If?* query may enquire about the impact on a target organisation of the failure of a set of suppliers in its supply chain. The result may be a set of processes and assets in the target organisation which loose supply of essential services, and which in turn may impact other business objectives within the target organisation. We have published preliminary versions of our analytical framework in [3], a more up-to-date description and the full semantics of the associated modelling language *SDML* is currently being prepared for publication.

3   The Cyber Range Experiment

In order to investigate how (potentially malicious) dynamic changes within an information infrastructure may violate safety and resilience requirements of dependent systems, we have developed an experiment on a *Cyber Range* facility. The Cyber Range facility has been purposefully built to conduct Cyber warfare games in a completely isolated and safe environment. The experiment set-up is the following.

The experiment was conducted on a cluster of 50 physical IBM3250 servers, internetworked by a simple low-fidelity switched LAN. In addition to the IBM3250 servers, a separate DHCP server and two workstations for controlling and monitoring the experiment were connected to the LAN. Since the objective of the experiment is not to study the impact of Cyber attacks on the supply chain, we did not mount or directly simulate any during the experiment. Each physical IBM3250 server used in the experiment ran a VMWare ESXi "bare-metal" hyper-visor, which hosted a single CentOS Linux server that we had already instrumented for the experiment. Each CentOS server hosted an *Akka*[1] actor system, which ran actors simulating cloud storage servers used in the experiment. In total, we conducted 20,020 separate experiments on the Cyber Range facility. The experiments ran uninterrupted for a total period of about five weeks before it completed. In the next section we shall describe the experiment scenario that we were investigating and the aspects of the experiment used in this paper.

3.1 Experiment Scenario

Our experiment scenario is based on an institution (let us call it *OrgX*) that wishes to outsource its data storage in an open cloud environment. For our experiment, we assume that *OrgX* requires that the storage outsourcing must conform to a (k, n) secret sharing policy, in the spirit of Shamir's [15] (k, n)-threshold cryptographic secret sharing protocol whereby a piece of secret must be broken down to n cryptographic chunks; and, in order to reconstruct the secret, at least k chunks must be present. The security guarantee that Shamir's threshold cryptographic sharing provides is that, even when the adversary has access to $k - 1$ chunks, the adversary can gain no information at all about and cannot reconstruct the original secret. Thus, in order to protect the outsourced secret data, *OrgX* requires that no single provider may have k or more chunks of the data according to the (k, n)-threshold scheme.

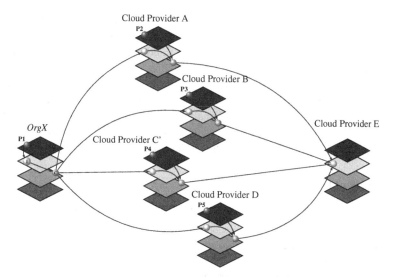

Fig. 3. Suppliers' cost-minimisation policies circumvent client's (k, n) secret sharing scheme

The scenario of Fig. 3 shows our layered model and the dependencies within and across the layers. Each organisation is represented as a stack of four layers: namely, the *Enterprise* (the blue, topmost) layer, the *Information* (yellow) layer, the *Technology* (green) layer, and the *Physical* (red, bottom) layer. The assets (represented by the

---

[1] *Akka* (http://akka.io/) is a scalable real-time transaction processing platform for building concurrent and distributed applications.

spheres here) are placed on the particular layer of the organisation that they belong to, and the assets are connected together by arrows representing some dependency relationships between the assets. For example, the Enterprise-layer policy $P1$ at $OrgX$ governs how the information I should be outsourced, and hence there is a dependency arrow from $P1$ to I representing the dependency of the processing of I on $P1$. The dependency arrow between I and the Technology-layer control C (e.g. some hardware/software processor that ensures I is chunked up and distributed according to the policy $P1$) at $OrgX$ represents the flow of information from I to the control, and the indirect dependency relationship between $P1$ and C (obtained by traversing arrows between the two entities) captures the fact that the operation of control C depends on the Enterprise-layer policy $P1$. Now let us assume that $P1$ requires a $(k, n) = (2, 4)$ secret sharing policy. The particular example of Fig. 1 demonstrates the violation of the $(2, 4)$ secret sharing policy in a small data storage supply chain. Here we lay emphasis on the fact that it is the application of the enterprise (blue) layer policies ($P2, P3, P4, P5$) at the various organisations in the supply chain that ultimately led to the violation of the information processing requirements at $OrgX$ as facilitated by the technology layer controls and the mechanisms implementing the enterprise layer policies at the supply chain organisations. See [3] for a more detailed discussion of our layered approach.

An objective of the experiment is to understand the impact of enterprise-layer policies and selection of controls within an information infrastructure supply chain on information security policy. In the experiment scenario, the enterprise-layer decision within the supply chain to minimise the cost of storage outsourcing and the consequent changes within the chain led to a violation of policies. It is thus useful from the perspective of $OrgX$ to understand its sensitivity to these changes and the impact that they might have on its own policies. We assumed in the experiment that all the cloud providers were following the same cost minimisation strategy: which was to outsource data storage to the cheapest provider in the ecosystem. This was only a simplifying choice, and not a limitation. It is possible under our *What If?* analysis set-up to specify different enterprise strategies for each cloud storage provider in the supply chain. However, the experiment considered the case where all the providers pursued a uniform goal.

3.2 Experiment Description

The following parameters were considered in the experiment (although, not all are used in this paper).

1. **The number n of chunks that data must be broken into:** this parameter is a part of the (k, n) threshold scheme.
2. **number k that sets an upper bound on the number of data that can be aggregated:** this parameter is a part of the (k, n) threshold scheme.
3. **The number (cn) of cloud storage providers:** this determined whether certain (k, n) policies are even satisfiable in the first place. For example, the $(2, 100)$ sharing policy cannot be satisfied if $cn = 80$ if all the 100 chunks are to be outsourced.
4. **Cluster size clu:** this parameter is an upper bound on the initial number of chunks that $OrgX$ can outsource to a *single* provider.
5. **The *hops* parameter:** determines the greatest number of "hops" or nodes downstream that a part of the data may be outsourced to.

6. **Finally, the parameter** *failingClouds*, which when set to *true* allows cloud providers to fail randomly.

For each experiment, a value is set for each of the parameters above. For example, for the experiment 4,722 we had the following values: $cn = 70, k = 4, n = 15, clu = 2$, $hops = 3$, and *failingClouds* = *false*. This means that the experiment considers an ecosystem made up of 70 cloud storage providers, under a $(4, 15)$ data outsourcing policy. The initial data outsourcing cluster clu=2 means that the 15 chunks are outsourced 2 each to the first seven immediate downstream storage provider and one to the last provider. The selection of the immediate downstream provider is completely random. The $hops = 3$ parameter means that *OrgX* requires that the data may be further outsourced downstream at most 3 times. To this effect a sticky policy is attached to the data, which must be decremented once the data is outsourced. Finally, the parameter *failingClouds* = *false* means that that experiment does not consider availability and resilience issues associated with the failure of storage providers.

At the beginning of the experiment, the default storage price at the storage providers is 100 units, but any of the providers may advertise a lower price at any time. This creates a dynamically changing ecosystem, in which each participant seeks to minimise its storage cost, while at the same time negotiating not to violate its own local policies and constraints. The actors in the experiment generated logs whenever events of interest, such as data outsourcing, price changes etc. occur. But in order to use the results of the experiment within our analytical framework, it must first be translated to the framework's dependency model. We do not describe this step in this paper. It suffices to say that we carried out the translation step offline once the results of the experiment were available by replaying back the log files to the translator. However, it is possible in principle to carry out such analysis in real-time, perhaps across a network. This was not possible in our case because the Cyber Range facility by its nature requires that it must be air-gapped and closed off to the Internet to prevent accidental contamination.

3.3 Reasoning about the Violation of (k, n) Policies

The following is a brief description of the experiment after translation to the *SATURN* dependency model. The outsourced data chunks are assigned a type *Secret* and the cloud storage providers are assigned the type *CloudStorage*. The assigned types are used in *What If?* queries to filter the entities. Whenever a data chunk d is outsourced to a storage provider, d is added to the set *ServicesIn* of the provider. Under the graph-theoretic description of the dependency model, *ServicesIn* is the set of incident edges to a vertex, and *Entities* refers to the set of all named objects (edges, and vertices) in the model. The *What If?* query to report whenever a storage provider violates the (k, n) policy is now shown in Fig. 4. Please refer to [3] for a more detailed description of the *What If?* construct. The query simply says that any entity of the type *CloudStorage* (*X:CloudStorage in Entities*) in the model, that is, any cloud storage provider, must be reported if the size of the secrets that it acquires is equal to or exceeds k (*size(Y|Y:Secret in x.ServicesIn)*$>= k$). This is the constraint placed on the supply chain by the (k, n) policy. Other policies are similarly specified. The *What If?* query interface allows us to reason about the entities in the model, their states and dependency relationships as they

No Storage Provider should have k or more chunks at any time

```
/**
 * Model-check whether any ''CloudStorage'' provider could have
 * k or more ''Secret'' data at any point.
 */
BeginWhatIf
  report {
    X:CloudStorage in Entities.size(Y|Y:Secret in x.ServicesIn)>= k
  }
EndWhatIf
```

Fig. 4. Reporting the violation by a CloudStorage provider of a (k, n) policy, for some k and n

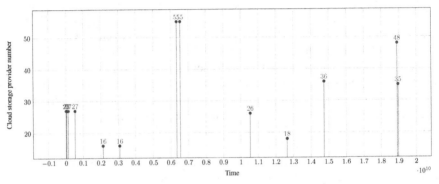

Fig. 5. Storage providers violating policy over time

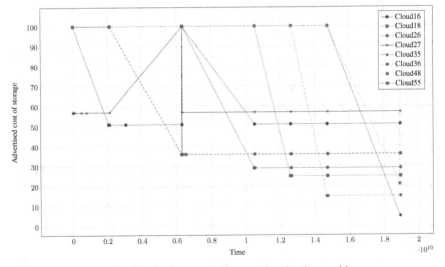

Fig. 6. Advertised storage price over time by the providers

evolve over time to give us deeper visibility and insights into the dynamics of a CII. In particular, the logical queries allow us to create "hooks" to capture events of interest, which can be a very powerful way of reason about dependent infrastructures.

We now turn our attention back to the result for experiment number 4,722 that we described earlier[2]. The graph of Fig. 5 plots the cloud storage providers against the time when the violated the $(4, 15)$ policy. The time on the x-axis has been normalised to start at 0, when the first violation occurred during the experiment. The y-axis records the cloud *ID*, so that 40 corresponds to the cloud storage provider named *Cloud40*. Thus, *Cloud27*, was the first to violate the policy, followed by *Cloud16*, and then by *Cloud55* and so on.

Now, the graph in Fig. 6 shows the advertised storage cost over time by the cloud storage providers. As may be observed from the graph, there is a very strong correlation between the provider that advertises the least cost and the one that violates the (k, n) policy. When *Cloud27* advertised its cost at 57 units against the backdrop of other providers advertising at 100 units, it was able to violate the *OrgX*'s (k, n) policy as the other providers scrambled to outsource to it. Similarly, a flurry of outsourcing ensued when *Cloud16* undercut the current cheapest by advertising a price drop to 51 units, allowing it to circumvent *OrgX*'s policy. The same follows for the other price cuts. While there was no collusion between the storage providers, the interaction of their separate enterprise policies meant that *OrgX* was vulnerable to price minimisation attacks.

4   Conclusion and Future Work

The results of the Cyber Range experiment that we have carried out demonstrate how unexpected dependencies and potential vulnerabilities might arise in enterprise relationships. In particular, the experiment shows a dependence of the (k, n) policy's violation on the cost of storage within the supply chain. Generally speaking, it will be a useful additional tool in the arsenal of the security or risk analyst to be able to discover such correlations from enterprise events. In this particular experiment, we do expect that *OrgX* will be vulnerable to a price setting attack by a rogue provider in the supply chain. In practice, however, the complexity and the dynamic nature of enterprise dependencies will make it difficult to foresee how various interactions and enterprise relationships can result in vulnerable and exploitable architectures. Thus, analytical tools such as the *SATURN* dependency platform can give very valuable insights for the discovery of potential vulnerabilities. When combined with *What If?* games, the analyst can test the impact of potential configuration changes and relationships on target objectives. A potential area of work is the integration of powerful statistical and data mining tools into the *SATURN* framework for reasoning about dependent CII events. This may help to identify subtle dependency relationships via statistical correlation of events.

We are aware that, sometimes, it may not be practical or desirable to share all the information necessary to reason about or maintain a global target property in a dependent information system. Thus a promising area of future work for us is the investigation of abstraction strategies whereby the states of an entity in the dependency graph about

---

[2] Note that this experiment was chosen arbitrarily, just for illustration. There is nothing special about it in particular.

which we do not have the requisite information are assigned values from a category of templates that is informed by a risk profiling of the entity. *What If?* scenarios can then be subsequently played out to characterise the sensitivity of target objectives on the entity's assigned profile. Note that if we assign probabilities or likelihood to an entity's state belonging to one of the predefined risk categories, then the problem would be akin to abstraction and reasoning under uncertainty, which is a well-studied subject. A related, perhaps complementary idea, which is out of scope of our current work is the use of self-stabilising algorithms to drive the system to achieve the target global objective while utilising more local information: for example, information local to a node and its immediate neighbours in the dependency graph. This is the promise of self-stabilisation [4,5], and it would be of interest to identify families of policies that may be enforced by this method in a dependent CII.

References

1. Adetoye, A.O., Creese, S., Goldsmith, M.H.: Analysis of dependencies in critical infrastructures. In: Proceedings of the 6th International Conference on Critical Information Infrastructure Security (CRITIS 2011). LNCS, Springer, Heidelberg (2011)
2. Balakrishnan, A., Magnanti, T.L., Mirchandani, P.: Connectivity-splitting models for survivable network design. Networks 43(1), 10–27 (2004)
3. Creese, S., Goldsmith, M.H., Adetoye, A.O.: A logical high-level framework for critical infrastructure resilience and risk assessment. In: 2011 Third International Workshop on Cyberspace Safety and Security (CSS), pp. 7–14 (September 2011)
4. Dijkstra, E.W.: Self-stabilizing systems in spite of distributed control. Communications of the Association of the Computing Machinery 17(11), 643–644 (1974)
5. Dolev, S.: Self-Stabilization. MIT Press, Cambridge (2000)
6. Dudenhoeffer, D.D., Permann, M.R., Manic, M.: CIMS: a framework for infrastructure interdependency modeling and analysis. In: Felipe Perrone, L., Lawson, B., Liu, J., Wieland, F.P. (eds.) Proceedings of the Winter Simulation Conference WSC 2006, Monterey, California, USA, pp. 478–485 (2006)
7. Dudenhoeffer, D.D., Permann, M.R., Woolsey, S., Timpany, R., Miller, C., McDermott, A., Manic, M.: Interdependency modeling and emergency response. In: Wainer, G.A. (ed.) Proceedings of the 2007 Summer Computer Simulation Conference, SCSC 2007, San Diego, California, USA, July 16-19, pp. 1230–1237. Simulation Councils, Inc. (2007)
8. Haimes, Y., Jiang, P.: Leontief-based model of risk in complex interconnected infrastructures. Journal of Infrastructure Systems 7, 1–12 (2001)
9. Masucci, V., Adinolfi, F., Servillo, P., Dipoppa, G., Tofani, A.: Ontology-Based Critical Infrastructure Modeling and Simulation. In: Palmer, C., Shenoi, S. (eds.) Critical Infrastructure Protection III, p. 229 (2009)
10. Neville, J., Jensen, D., Chickering, M.: Relational dependency networks. Journal of Machine Learning Research 8 (2007)
11. Nieuwenhuijs, A., Luiijf, E., Klaver, M.: Modeling Dependencies In Critical Infrastructures. In: Papa, M., Shenoi, S. (eds.) Critical Infrastructure Protection II. IFIP, vol. 290, pp. 205–213. Springer, Boston (2008)
12. Oliva, G., Panzieri, S., Setola, R.: Agent-based input-output interdependency model. International Journal of Critical Infrastructure Protection 3, 76–82 (2010)
13. Pederson, P., Dudenhoeffer, D., Hartley, S., Permann, M.: Critical infrastructure interdependency modeling: A survey of U.S. and international research. Technical Report INL/EXT-06-11464, Idaho National Laboratory, Idaho Falls, Idaho 83415 (August 2006)

14. Ragni, M., Scivos, A.: Dependency calculus reasoning in a general point relation algebra. In: Kaelbling, L.P., Saffiotti, A. (eds.) IJCAI 2005, Proceedings of the Nineteenth International Joint Conference on Artificial Intelligence, Edinburgh, Scotland, UK, July 30-August 5, pp. 1577–1578. Professional Book Center (2005)
15. Shamir, A.: How to share a secret. Communications of the ACM 22(11), 612–613 (1979)
16. Svendsen, N.K., Wolthusen, S.D.: Multigraph dependency models for heterogeneous infrastructures. In: Goetz, E., Shenoi, S. (eds.) Critical Infrastructure Protection. IFIP, vol. 253, pp. 337–350. Springer, Boston (2007)
17. Walsh, S., Cherry, S., Roybal, L.: Critical infrastructure modeling: An approach to characterizing interdependencies of complex networks & control systems. In: 2nd Conference on Human System Interactions, HSI 2009, pp. 637–641 (May 2009)

Algebraic Analysis of Attack Impacts and Countermeasures in Critical Infrastructures

Thomas Richard McEvoy[2] and Stephen D. Wolthusen[1,2]

[1] Norwegian Information Security Laboratory,
Department of Computer Science,
Gjøvik University College, Norway
[2] Information Security Group,
Department of Mathematics,
Royal Holloway, University of London, UK
{T.R.McEvoy,stephen.wolthusen}@rhul.ac.uk

Abstract. Critical infrastructure systems are distributed environments in which the mixture of technologies and interdependencies between physical and logical components lead to complex interactions. Calculating the possible impacts of attacks and the success of proposed countermeasures in such environments represents a severe problem. We propose a process algebraic technique as a means of affecting such calculations. Our approach allows us to demonstrate equivalence w.r.t. attack and defense strategies respectively. It also forms a basis for determining the efficiency and effectiveness of countermeasures. In comparison with other methods, such as attack/defense trees and attack graphs, our approach allows us to relax assumptions regarding the ordering of events by applying structural reasoning to outcomes and reducing the state space for the analysis. An obvious application is to risk management.

1 Introduction

Critical infrastructure systems – for example, ICS (Industrial Control Systems) – are highly complex, distributed environments [1]. Calculating the effect of such attacks in such environments represents a severe problem. We propose a process algebraic approach to calculating such impacts and incorporating the effects of countermeasures. In comparison with other attack/defense modeling methods, our approach allows us to relax assumptions regarding the ordering of events and to reduce the state space to be explored. We use a formal adversary capability model [2] such that an adversary may overwrite a proper subset of system processes altering data flows in the system. We use an applied π-calculus to calculate how altered data flows impact on system goals. We also use this approach to rank (and show equivalence between) attacks and interventions, leading to a basis for measuring the efficiency and effectiveness of countermeasures with obvious applications for risk management and intrusion detection.

Section 2 outlines related work. Section 3 defines our problem and outlines our approach. In section 4, we define our π-calculus variant. Section 5 sets out our

B. Hämmerli, N. Kalstad Svendsen, and J. Lopez (Eds.): CRITIS 2012, LNCS 7722, pp. 168–179, 2013.
© Springer-Verlag Berlin Heidelberg 2013

adversary capability model. Section 6 provides the method for calculating impacts and impact reductions. Section 7 provides a simple example. We conclude and set out future research directions in section 8.

2 Related Work

Attacks and countermeasures have been modeled using attack/defense trees [3,4,5]. These techniques impose a logical order of alternating attack and defense moves which counter each other. Game-theoretical approaches provide equivalent information. However, such approaches do not necessarily capture the (logical temporal) ordering of events or dependencies between sub-goals [3]. It is also possible to use attack graphs to model and calculate exposures to network attacks . However, on critical infrastructure networks, such techniques would be limited due to the requirement, in many cases, to use vulnerability scans to calculate attack reachability and creates limitations in scale and complexity for many such approaches [6,7]. Such approaches also appear to assume that the subversion of a critical host is a requirement for attack success, whereas we argue that in distributed control system the subversion of any host or network node may – due to the transitive effects of loss of data integrity, availability or confidentiality – turn out to be critical. Another approach – attack coordination graphs – addresses the issue of dealing with coordinated attacks and allow the generation of novel attacks, but again appears to ignore the possibilities offered by the transitive effects of attacks on information flows in the system [8]. Our approach is based on the formal adversary capability model and an associated applied π-calculus [9,2] used to define adversary actions algebraically.

3 Problem and Approach

Assuming an adversary subverts a process in a critical system,the process will subsequently affect the information flow in the system. In a complex system, the outcomes may not be obvious. A single change may have multiple effects (and subsequent kinetic impacts on physical processes) – in particular, because such effects may be singular, distributed, transitive, or recursive in nature. The situation may be further complicated by the simultaneous occurrence of multiple attacks, not necessarily cooperating, or interventions by operators.

To do this, we represent information flows algebraically using variable names to stand for data objects in our system. Names are sent and received between processes and hence travel from impact sources (where data subversion occurs) to impact sinks where the effect is realized. Given different attacks, different sets of names may lose different security characteristics. Hence we can rank impacts by imposing a partial order over sets and security characteristics. We can induce equivalence over impacts for different attacks and we can consider the efficiency and effectiveness of countermeasures. This information may subsequently be used by business managers or engineers expert in the system to determine business impacts or to plan defensive strategies.

A key advantage of our approach is it enables us to model the effects of attacks and countermeasures concurrently, rather than imposing a logical ordering (which is of necessity binary in action). Furthermore, compared to other approaches, we show we can reduce the state space to be searched by considering the scope of names affected by an attack, i.e., reducing our search to the key business/operational processes and communication, rather than having to consider entire semantic domains. Finally, the method may lend itself to automation [10].

4 π-Calculus Definition

The π-calculus is a formal programming language use to specify and reason about system interactions using algebraic notation. It allows the definition of processes using a set of names U which can stand for communication channels or data objects in a system. Sums (of actions) are defined by the capabilities (over names) of the calculus which are its operations and functions. In turn, processes may be defined as a sum or as a set of sub-processes acting concurrently.

We define the capabilities of our π-calculus as *send*, *receive*, perform a *function*, *silent action* and *conditional action* –

$$\pi ::= \bar{x}\langle y \rangle_c | x(z)_c | f(u) \supset v | \tau | [\mathcal{L}]\pi$$

Send and receive have the obvious meaning of sending and receiving names between processes. Functions over names are defined either informally or using an algorithm. Conditional actions refer to the exercise of capabilities based on some logical condition, normally defined in a first- order logic $\mathcal{L}$ with equivalence. We note that in our variant of the calculus, names may be associated with characteristics. Characteristics can be used to express information about data such as routing addresses.

Silent functions are actions which are invisible in the system (from the point of view of a given observer). So, for example, an operator cannot directly see a process fail. In our approach, we use silent functions to capture this kind of information and calculate its effect.

We define the processes and sums of our calculus as follows –

$$P ::= M | (P|P') | \nu z P | !P$$
$$M ::= \mathbf{0} | \pi.P | M + M' | M \oplus M'$$

A process P may be a sum M of capabilities. Processes may be concurrent. A process may be declared with new names which are restricted to the scope of the process. A process may replicate, allowing infinite action. A sum M may be null action, a strict sequence of capabilities, a sequence of capabilities which may or may not execute or a mutually exclusive sum of capabilities.

The interaction of processes and their internal functions (both observable and silent) allows us to prove a class of distributed algorithms. There are various proof methods – see [9] for details. In this context, proof by reduction is the most useful and is implemented by the axioms of reduction. A process is reduced by the interaction between sending and receiving processes, or by the exercise of a silent action. Reduction enables us to demonstrate interactions within the system as a whole.

5   Adversary Capability Model

In its simplest form, our adversary capability model is defined using the π calculus described in section 4 by equation 1 and 2:

$$\Omega := \bar{x}\langle m\rangle_c.\mathbf{0} \oplus x(z)_c.\mathbf{0} \oplus \tau.\mathbf{0}|!A \tag{1}$$

$$P := x(z) + M \oplus \omega|!P \tag{2}$$

In words, the adversary A is a process which can send a malicious message m by a channel x and receive any message by x and make decisions about the names it sends and receives by τ which is a decision making function whose internal state is not open to us. A process P may be vulnerable to exploitation, shown by ω, by a malicious message m sent by the adversary. P becomes a malicious process P' by receiving m where P' represents a process which the adversary has overwritten to suit his purposes. Each subverted process (and the adversary) will be endowed with one or more of the capabilities shown in Table 1.

SUB is the ability to create malformed messages to subvert processes. P indicates that a subverted process will not advertise its presence, but act covertly where possible. For example, it will make no egregious protocol errors. ACC intends that a process can access a subset of other processes based on the channel names available to it. COM is overt communication with other processes by known channels. CC is covert communication via channels unknown to other (legitimate) processes and the operator. SP-PAR indicates a subverted process may spawn other processes to work concurrently with it. MN means a subverted process can intercept messages sent to it. MV indicates a subvert process by substituting channels may divert messages sent to it. MP indicates a subverted process may drop any message sent to it. MR indicates a subverted process may recall and replay any message sent to it. MM indicates a subverted process may manipulate any message sent to it. MI indicates a subverted process may inject false messages into the system. Subverted processes may also make decisions about messages sent to them by D-MAT and may be updated (or update themselves) to cope with new environmental conditions by LB.

Each of these capabilities in turn can be expressed formally in the π-calculus [2]. For example, let P, Q, R be processes such that $P := \bar{x}a.\mathbf{0}$, $Q := x(a).\mathbf{0}$ and $R := y(a).\mathbf{0}$ then by MV $P' := P\{^y/_x\} := \bar{y}a$ so name a is diverted to a process R containing y instead of Q. Various attack scenarios may be built from these fundamental capabilities [ibid.].

Table 1. Adversary Capability Model

SUB	Create and send malicious messages
P	Indistinguishabilty Assumption
ACC	Reachability or access
COM	Overt Communication
CC	Covert Communication
SP-PAR	Spawn Additional Processes
MN	Message Interception
MV	Message Diversion
MD	Message Delay
MP	Message Drop
MR	Message Replay
MM	Message Manipulation
MI	Message Injection
D-MAT	Decision Making
LB	Learning Behavior

6   Impact Reachability Analysis

We show how we calculate the effects of attacks and countermeasures and consider the advantages offered by this approach for reducing state space w.r.t calculating attack/defense maneuvers.

6.1   Calculating Impacts and Countermeasures

Let S be a system consisting of N processes $P_1, P_2, \ldots, P_N$. Let U be the set of names for the system S. For each process P_i we define a set of names $u(P_i) \in U$ which are its channels and messages. We assume a subset of processes R in S, re-numbering w.l.o.g. $P_1 \ldots P_k$ for $k < N$ may be overwritten by an adversary Ω such that for a given set of runs of a system $P_i \rightsquigarrow P_i'$ where $i := [0..k]$. We make the explicit assumption that the adversary cannot subvert all processes by setting $k < N$. Each subverted process P_i' will act over the set of names U arbitrarily differently from how processes P_i act over the set of names U.

Let confidentiality, integrity, availability be the set $K = \{C.I.A\}$ of primary security characteristics which belong to a name $u \in U(P)$ for a process P. These characteristics are defined binarily.

Definition 1. Structural Impact. *We define a structural impact to be the loss of the primary security characteristics $\kappa \subseteq K$ of a name u at the point where the name is functionally required by another process.*

To calculate a structural impact, we use a silent function $\uparrow \langle \tilde{u} \rangle_\kappa$ which we call a *source function* to indicate the subversion of a set of names in a process P_i. We do not require to state immediately which characteristics are lost. We call a process containing a source function an *impact source*. We call a name which has lost one or more of its primary security characteristics a *subverted name* and we denote it u_κ.

The impact of the attack is formally calculated by a reduction over the set of all runs of the future systems states, following a subversion event. At the point where the impact is realized for a name, the process is marked by a silent function $\downarrow (\tilde{u})_\kappa$ which is the *sink function* where κ may again be any subset of $\{C, I, A\}$ which is not the empty set $\emptyset$. Let F be the set of (non-communicating) functions in S then an impact is realized when a subverted name is required by an $f \in F$. We consider that $f \in F$ may include functions belonging to an adversary process W, whose existence we assume, but which lies outside the scope of the system S. It should be noted that processes will not be aware of their own state as an impact source or an impact sink unless explicit measures are taken within the system to observe and respond to anomalies.

Impact sinks are calculated as follows:

Loss of Confidentiality – Loss of confidentiality arises where any adversary process W which exists outside the boundary of the system S receives a subverted name or copy from S. We mark the process W as the sink process and the process where the name originated as the source process and $\kappa' := \{C\}$. In fact, it is enough to consider that confidentiality is breached when any process not authorized to act over a name receives that name. For example, a subverted process can use state information to calculate an attack value.

Loss of Integrity – Loss of integrity arises where any process $P \in S$ receives a subverted name whose content has been altered by the adversary. Again, we mark the processes as source and sink appropriately and $\kappa' := \{I\}$.

Loss of Availability(Direct) – To calculate a direct loss of availability (MD or MP) we mark the name as not available, but calculate the loss of availability by sending the marked name (as though it were available) to discover the sink. Again, we mark the name with $\kappa' := \{A\}$.

Loss of Availability(Indirect) – Indirect loss of availability comes about due to multiple message injections (MI) starving a set of processes of the opportunity to send or receive legitimate names. In this case, we determine the set of processes and the set of legitimate names which are "starved" for each process and subsequently mark this set of processes and names with the appropriate source functions and proceed as before.

Transitive Effects – For cases relating to integrity and availability, it may be that the initial subverted name is used to create a new subverted name. If a sink process R receives a subverted name which is used in this way, then the calculation stops for that name, but we subsequently mark R as the source process for the new name(s) subverted by the loss of integrity or availability of the initial subverted name and continue the calculation with the new name(s). We note that the transitive effect need not be the same as the immediate effect.

For example, a loss of integrity could lead transitively to a loss of availability or confidentiality. Transitive effects may also occur where the previous name is forwarded by a process which uses it.

Recursive Effects – Recursive cases require some attention w.r.t stopping the calculation at the appropriate point. In essence, however, if a process R' receives a subverted name from a process R^* (for which it was previously an impact source, even transitively) and as a result a name already implicated in the source functions belonging to that process is re-infected then the calculation over that name terminates. This simply requires keeping track of the processes and names affected.

Various cases arise from our calculation which we sketch here (a formal treatment is reserved for future work – see section 8):

Case 1 – A source may be a sink without any further steps after subversion, that is, attack initiation has an immediate impact within a process. In this outcome, the only impacts are loss of availability and loss of integrity as the process by definition in inside the boundary of the system, so loss of confidentiality may not be considered. All the action is also within the process and there are no transitive computational effects.

Case 2 – A single source may lead to a single sink. The loss of all security characteristics may be considered. The impact is a single impact on another process.

Case 3 – A single source may lead to multiple sinks. Multiple impacts occur possibly for the loss of all security characteristics.

Case 4 – Multiple sources may lead to a single sink. This outcome gives rise to being able to consider attack variants which are equivalent w.r.t. impact or multiple attacks from independent sources which cooperate to produce a single impact.

Case 5 – Multiple sources may lead to a multiple sinks. This outcome is an obvious extension of the fourth case. Here the attack may result from breaching a distributed condition over bounds normally imposed by correct system behavior – such as breaching safety conditions.

Case 6 – A sink may transitively become an impact source (not necessarily with the same characteristics) for further sink

Case 7 – A source may act recursively becoming a sink for itself after a number of intervening steps

Case 8 – A source may act transitively resulting in a further sink acting recursively

Case 9 – An attack may result, under different orderings, in different impacts.

This outcome reveals a situation where an attack starting with apparently identical conditions can result in multiple possible impacts, depending on event ordering during the limited projection over events. Part of the strength of our approach is it enables structural reasoning over these possible outcomes by considering all orderings of events, rather than imposing an artificial order on attack and defense maneuvers.

We now define *defensive interventions* which are countermeasures, which may be static or dynamic, expressed in our algebra.

Definition 2. Defensive Intervention. *An defensive intervention is a programmed action or countermeasure by the operator which may be applied prior to or during an attack may result in an impact reduction.*

An impact reduction results in the number of names implicated (by loss of security characteristics) in an impact source or an impact sink being reduced, possibly to zero. The effect of a defensive intervention is calculated using the same method as the impact for an attack:

Confidentiality – The calculation needs to show that a set of names does not reach the impact sink in the process W which exists beyond the bound of the system.

Integrity – The calculation needs to show that the loss of integrity is explicitly detected by the system (no process may respond to a κ condition directly) and integrity is restored or compensated for.

Availability – As for integrity, the calculation needs to show that the loss of availability is explicitly detected and restored or compensated for as before.

Interventions can reduce impacts for single sinks, for multiple sinks, transitively and recursively. Hence our approach enables us to consider concurrently the effects of attacks and both static and dynamic interventions and, indeed, further interventions by the attacker.

6.2   Equivalence and Ordering

Definition 3. Attack Equivalence. *Two attacks I and J are held to be equivalent $I \sim J$ if the maximum impact of I is the same as the maximum impact of J, written $im(I) \approx im(J)$ for a given system S.*

Equivalence implies that both I and J affect the loss of the same characteristics in K for the same set of names $\tilde{n} \in L$.

We show that impacts form a partial order. Let K be the set of impacts. Let S be the set of processes. Let U be the set of names in S. Let 2^U be the power set of U and let 2^K be the power set of security characteristics. Let $G = 2^U \times 2^K$, i.e., the cross product of all possible subsets of U with all possible losses of security characteristics in K. Let K_+ be $2^K/\emptyset$. Let U_+ be $2^U/\emptyset$. Each attack I, J forms a subset of elements $\{f, g, h, \ldots\} \in G$. Let $H = \langle G, m \rangle$ be a multi set of G. We define a mapping for each attack I such that $F : I \mapsto H$ and, with some abuse of notation, $m = |I|$:

$$F(I) = \begin{cases} (\emptyset, \emptyset) = \emptyset \\ (\emptyset, L_+) = \emptyset \\ (K_+, \emptyset) = \emptyset \\ (K_+, L_+) = G' \subseteq H \end{cases} \tag{3}$$

It is easy to show that there is a partial order based on the set relation $\subseteq$ for all sets $G(I) \subseteq H$. Hence, there is a partial ordering over impacts.

As a limitation, we note that the equivalence relationship and ordering only hold for maximal impacts. The reason for the condition of considering maximal impacts only is that some event orderings may only result in a partial impact. Seeking to establish equivalence between attacks with different impact sources as a result of different event orderings is considered too fine a distinction. In other words, we only consider worst case scenarios.

A defensive intervention is considered *effective* if it reduces to zero, the impact of an attack I. Two interventions E and F are equivalent $E \sim F$, if for the same attack I on the same system $S(P)$, they achieve an identical impact reduction. That is, they prevent, possibly partially, the identical set of impact reductions on the set of names subverted by an attack I. An intervention E is considered *efficient* if it is effective for an equivalence class $[I]$ of attacks.

6.3 State Space Reduction

Although we require to explore all possible orderings following an intervention by an adversary or an operator, we show that we deal with a much reduced state space compared with techniques using attack/defense trees [4] or attack graphs [7]. We start by considering that the set of transitions α are image-finite.

Theorem 1. Image-Finiteness. *Transition relations are image finite.*

Details may be found in Sangiorgi et al. [9]. Hence we are limited per process to the names we need consider during an hostile or defensive intervention. Obviously, we can limit attacks to a particular set of processes to reduce the scope of analysis. Subsequently, we may further limit the scope to the specific category of transitions with fresh names – see section 4 – which are created new in a process (i.e. the system data).

Theorem 2. Name Boundedness. *The calculation of structural impacts is limited to the fresh names of the system.*

Proof. Let L be the fresh names of the system. Let 2^L be the power set of fresh names. We associate with each name the process in which it was generated. If we create a graph over the partial order which results from the $\subseteq$ relation for 2^L, where each node is a subset and each edge represents the relation, we may traverse each edge as follows. Starting from a single name, we traverse to any subset of names which share the same process. We call this a *functional* transition. Further we may traverse to any node which contains a name generated using the original name we started from. We call this a *generative transition*. This edgewise progress is identical to the progress of impacts through the system, ignoring communication. Considering communication, the number of possible orders is limited by the conditions on traversing an edge. Let $n = |L|$. The maximum number of reductions is bounded by the number required for the scope of a fresh name to extend beyond the perimeter of the system, else n, which represents the total number of names generated by the system which may be subject to structural impact. By assuming an average number of reductions $\bar{x}$ per transition, it is clear this is of order $\mathbf{O}(n)$.

This theorem shows that – for calculating impacts – we may focus on transitions which result in fresh names being sent and received (or not, in cases of loss of availability). Impacts are achieved by the subversion of such names (possibly in transit).

7   Application

Taking the example of a control loop in a SCADA system to illustrate our approach. A realistic control path will consist of a complex mesh of components where the control path is not just determined by interactions between the operator, the SCADA server and the RTU but other components which may intervene such as OEE (Operating Equipment Effectiveness) software or engineering workstations [1]. For example, let S be a relatively simple ICS system such as we described. We note, first, that we can clearly define multiple components as processes with some economy – see equation 4.

$$S := \nu\tilde{x}(!ADV|!OP|!HMI|!SC\,\textstyle\coprod!PLC|\,\textstyle\coprod!RTU|!NTP|!HIS|!ENG|\,\textstyle\coprod!N) \tag{4}$$

ADV is the adversary, OP the operator, HMI the human-machine interface, SC the SCADA server, $\coprod!PLC$ a set of PLCs ($\coprod$ indicates multiple processes in parallel), $\coprod!RTU$ a set of RTUs, NTP the NTP server, ENG an engineering workstation and $\coprod!N$ a set of network nodes such as routers and switches.

We focus on a set of names representing potentially critical data in the system. We can make use of Theorem 2 in relation to the names and their destination address characteristics to simplify our analysis of potential impact sources and sinks. The destination processes are clearly potential impact sinks, the processes which route our critical names to those destinations and the originating processes the potential impact sources. We can eliminate other processes from consideration during this first pass in the analysis. Considering an input signal u sent by the SCADA server to an RTU labeled r, the (subverted) system structure may be minimized as follows –

$$S' := \nu\tilde{x}(!HMI|!SC_\Omega|!PLC_r|!RTU_r|!HIS|\,\textstyle\coprod!N') \tag{5}$$

Where Ω indicates the process SC has been subverted. For the SCADA server SC, we specify its functions, channels and names.

$$SC_\Omega := MM(u) \supset u'.(\bar{h}u' + \bar{n}u'_r + \bar{m}u').SC'||SC_\Omega \qquad (6)$$

The resulting analysis identifies the sources and sinks, shown in equation 3. Note, the transitive effect of signaling the RTU on the PLC –

$$S' := \nu\tilde{x}(!HMI_{\downarrow(u)_I}|!SC_{\Omega,\uparrow(u)_I}|!PLC_{r,\downarrow(u)_I}|!RTU_{r,\downarrow(u)_I}|!HIS_{\downarrow(u)_I}| \prod !N') \quad (7)$$

Since the same names (data) are distributed to different parts of the system, a loss of integrity in one segment of the network, for example, a network node, which is an impact source, connecting the SCADA server and the Historian may not affect other parts of the system. This allows us to see that impacts may be differentiated depending on the attacker's degree of access to the system. Again, although, in this case, all parts of the system suffer an attack on data integrity, we can focus on the impact in one part of the system – to further shrink the scope – or on the overall impact of a subversion, depending on our purpose.

We may subsequently specify countermeasures using our approach. Here Theorem 2 ceases to be useful and we revert to reduction techniques, considering the interaction of processes, to determine if impact sinks and sources persist, or may be eliminated by the use of countermeasures (or operator interventions). In [11], we prove the validity of a countermeasure (an IP traceback protocol) by carrying out a reduction over processes which can be shown to undo a loss of integrity in control system signals by identifying routes between the controller and the operator which do not contain subverted nodes. If we apply our calculation to this approach, we would show that messages containing the subverted name, say u_I, would be rejected by the operator because they came via a node $N_{\uparrow(u)_I}$ which was known to be subverted from applying the IP traceback technique. Hence, a byproduct of impact segmentation is that data observations in different parts of the network may be used to check for data consistency, leading to anomaly detection applications based on data values.

8   Conclusion and Future Work

We have shown that an algebraic approach allows us to calculate the impact of attacks and countermeasures. Our approach enables us to induce both equivalence and partial ordering over impacts and countermeasures. The approach also allows us to capture (logical temporal) orderings which may be significant in impact terms and reduces the state space to be searched compared with other attack/defense models. Applications exist for risk management, intrusion detection and prevention and post-incident forensics analysis. Future work will consider extensions to the calculus will enable us to take account of latent effects such as attack timing. We will also consider attack reachability as mediated by accessibility ACC and process vulnerability ω.

References

1. Langner, R.: Robust Control System Networks. Momentum Press, New York (2012)
2. McEvoy, T.R., Wolthusen, S.D.: A Formal Adversary Capability Model for SCADA Environments. In: Xenakis, C., Wolthusen, S. (eds.) CRITIS 2010. LNCS, vol. 6712, pp. 93–103. Springer, Heidelberg (2011)
3. Mauw, S., Oostdijk, M.: Foundations of Attack Trees. In: Won, D.H., Kim, S. (eds.) ICISC 2005. LNCS, vol. 3935, pp. 186–198. Springer, Heidelberg (2006)
4. Kordy, B., Mauw, S., Radomirović, S., Schweitzer, P.: Foundations of Attack–Defense Trees. In: Degano, P., Etalle, S., Guttman, J. (eds.) FAST 2010. LNCS, vol. 6561, pp. 80–95. Springer, Heidelberg (2011)
5. Bistarelli, S., Peretti, P., Trubitsyna, I.: Analyzing Security Scenarios Using Defence Trees and Answer Set Programming. Electron. Notes Theor. Comput. Sci. 197(2), 121–129 (2008)
6. Ingols, K., Chu, M., Lippmann, R., Webster, S., Boyer, S.: Modeling Modern Network Attacks and Countermeasures Using Attack Graphs. In: Annual Computer Security Applications Conference, ACSAC 2009, pp. 117–126 (December 2009)
7. Lippmann, R.P., Ingols, K.W.: An Annotated Review of Past Papers on Attack Graphs (1998)
8. Braynov, S., Jadliwala, M.: Representation and Analysis of Coordinated Attacks. In: Proceedings of the 2003 ACM Workshop on Formal Methods in Security Engineering, FMSE 2003, pp. 43–51. ACM, New York (2003)
9. Sangiorgi, D., Walker, D.: π-Calculus: A Theory of Mobile Processes. Cambridge University Press, New York (2001)
10. Delaune, S., Kremer, S., Ryan, M.D.: Symbolic Bisimulation for the Applied Pi Calculus. J. Comput. Secur. 18(2), 317–377 (2010)
11. McEvoy, T.R., Wolthusen, S.: Agent Interaction and State Determination in SCADA Systems. In: Butts, J., Shenoi, S. (eds.) Critical Infrastructure Protection. IFIP AICT, pp. 99–109. Springer, Heidelberg (2011)

Evaluation of Resilience of Interconnected Systems Based on Stability Analysis

Angelo Alessandri[1] and Roberto Filippini[2]

[1] Department of Mechanical Engineering – University of Genoa
P.le Kennedy Pad. D, I-16129 Genova, Italy
alessandri@diptem.unige.it
[2] CERN
385 Route de Meyrin 1217 Meyrin Switzerland
roberto.filippini@cern.ch

Abstract. A modeling framework is proposed to deal with the resilience of interconnected systems. Such systems are regarded as abstract entities subject to mutual functional dependencies. Each system is identified by a node of a directed graph, whose arcs represent such dependencies. In case of malfunction in a node, the failure may propagate to the other nodes with a possible cascading effect. The system behavior under failures is analyzed in a simple case study by using well-established stability tools. Based on such results, metrics of resilience are discussed.

Keywords: systems of systems, interdependencies, cascade failures, resilience, stability.

1 Introduction

The analysis of interconnected systems is a stimulating subject of research that involves a number of challenging issues [1]. One of such issues is the representation of the so-called systems of systems (SoS) within a comprehensive modeling framework. This challenge concerns both complexity and other topics such as management and optimization, which are usually encountered, for example, in energy power grids, transportation systems, and telecommunications networks [2]. Generally speaking, the analysis based on decomposition in system components is either unfeasible or of poor utility for the understanding of their interplay and, in particular, for the difficulty of inferring the off-nominal behaviour of the overall system. When facing these problems, consolidated analysis frameworks (e.g., risk assessment) fail to return a comprehensive solution, thus motivating vast simulation campaigns as a last resort [3].

Based on either systemic or holistic view, the approaches available in the literature rely on the grounding idea of including the off-nominal behaviours within the possible modes of functioning of a system [4,5]. This has the effect of extending the scope of control to non-functional properties, such as prevention of undesired events, robustness to disturbances, and recovery from failures. The overall of such properties is referred to, in literature, as *resilience*. In the

B. Hämmerli, N. Kalstad Svendsen, and J. Lopez (Eds.): CRITIS 2012, LNCS 7722, pp. 180–190, 2013.

parlance of this research field, a resilient system is able to properly react to the occurrence of a failure that potentially propagates to other systems due to mutual interdependencies.

In this paper, we address the problem of analyzing the resilience of interconnected systems. Such systems are treated as abstract entities; we decompose them into a set of elements, interconnected by functional dependencies, and model their system response to failures of various nature. The failures considered are of two types: internal operation drifts and external cascade effects. An operation drift is the slow degradation of the nominal functioning conditions caused by either an internal malfunction or the coupling with the other systems. A cascading failure is triggered by the loss of functioning in a system that propagates to its dependent systems.

Based on the idea of developing an approach as much general as possible, we develop an abstract representation of a system as network of functional dependencies established among its components [6]. On top of this representation we associate a simple state dynamics with each system component, which are regarded as the nodes of this functional dependency network. In nominal conditions, each node behaves like a stable system, but, in case of failure, it turns into an unstable mode and such instability may propagate to the entire network. In order to discover the conditions under which failures may propagate to the other nodes, we study the network resilience in terms of simple stability properties such as invariance and attractiveness [7]. The resilience of a set of interconnected systems can be regarded as the existence of an invariant set that is attractive for all trajectories originated after the occurrence of a failure. The above concepts will be explained by referring to a simple case study.

This study has to be considered in the broader context of network system analysis, which is a topic of crucial importance nowadays, and several studies exist in literature. For example, the problem of identifying critical and vulnerable nodes in complex networks is addressed in [8]. A similar approach is followed in [9] for the study of large scale service outages. The work of [10] applies input-output inoperability models (IIM) in order to evaluate the consequences in case of cascading failures. Stochastic approaches to failure analysis in critical infrastructures are also taken into consideration in [11]. Substantial differences exist if comparing these approaches with what it is proposed here. The majority of studies consider failure pathologies in interconnected systems, as generated throughout physical dependencies, e.g., those related to the transmission and transformation of physical quantities. In this paper, the failure/recovery mechanisms are modelled and analysed at a more abstract level, and they are essentially derived from functional relationships. The advantages of such a representation are twofold. First, the resilience of systems of heterogeneous nature can be studied, thus breaking through the specific sector diversity and widening the scope of the analysis. Second, it is possible to model the system dynamics with a reduced set of parameters that account for the resilience measures of each system component, such as failure buffering and recovery.

The paper is structured as follows. In Section 2, resilience problem is addressed in quite a general framework. Section 3 is devoted to the case study for a simple topology of two interconnected systems. Conclusions are drawn in Section 4.

2   Modeling Resilience

A complex system consists of several heterogeneous elements interconnected by functional relationships of various nature (e.g., service provider/user, producer/ consumer, controller/controlled and so forth). Such relationships are of functional nature and define a network topology, which is represented by a dependency graph. An example of dependency graph in shown in Fig. 1.

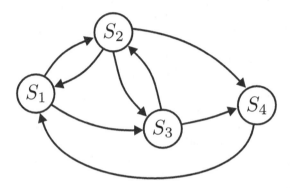

Fig. 1. Interconnections of four systems

Dependency graphs are of type directed, where nodes and edges represent systems and functional dependencies among them. More specifically, a functional dependency is an *input precondition* for a system to work in order. At the same time, it provides the direction of propagation of a *failure* in a system towards the systems that are functionally connected to it. The primary source of failure is an internal disturbance that causes an operation drift, i.e., the system leaves the initial state, while providing its service to the systems connected as descendant nodes. The change of state from functioning to non-functioning occurs if a state threshold is overdone. This threshold corresponds to the minimum *quality of service* that a system has to provide to its descendants in order to be considered as functioning. The failure propagates with cascading effects to the descendant nodes. A system is recovered to its functioning state as soon as the degradation of service level crosses a minimum threshold. In order that recovery is fully performed, it is necessary that all systems that provide input dependencies are functioning.

The resilience of a network of interconnected systems is the ability to resist to internal drift and cascading failures, and recover back to the initial operation state. Thus, resilience can be regarded as a sort of structural property.

Let us consider a set of interconnected systems, each of which is identified by a node $k \in N \overset{\triangle}{=} \{1, 2, \ldots, n\}$ with a dependency directed graph $G(N, A)$, where A is the set of the edges. We assume that a continuous state $x_k \in [0, 1]$ is associated with the system S_k of the node k and represents the percentage of service loss at this node. We model the system response to a disturbance, induced by cascading failure from a system S_i, with the service loss rate $\lambda_{ik} > 0$, which accounts for the local buffering. The recovery to the initial state after the failure caused by S_i depends on the service recovery rate $\mu_{ik} > 0$. The state threshold $\sigma_{kj} \in (0, 1)$ models the maximum tolerable percentage of service loss, beyond which the system S_k is considered to be failed for the descendant system S_j. A system is coupled to the ancestor system S_i by a coupling factor $\alpha_{ik} \in [0, 1]$, which models the adjustment to changes of interconnected systems around the respective nominal operation state. The internal disturbance is modeled with $d_k \geq 0$.

The service loss rate and recovery rate can be calculated from the service threshold and other two quantities: the time-to-failure (TTF) and the time-to-recovery (TTR) from a failure. The time-to-failure TTF_{ik} is the time a system S_k takes to cross the service threshold σ_{ik} from the assumed internal state $x_k = 0$ due to a failure in S_i. Such a relationship is expressed by the following:

$$\int_0^{TTF_{ik}} \lambda_{ik} \exp(-\lambda_{ik}t) \, \mathrm{d}t = \sigma_{ik} . \tag{1}$$

The service loss rate is derived from (1) as follows:

$$\lambda_{ik} = -\frac{\log(1 - \sigma_{ik})}{TTF_{ik}} .$$

The time-to-recovery TTR_{ik} is the time the system takes to recover from a failure in S_i and returns within the service threshold from the internal state x_k taken equal to 1. Thus, the recovery rate is given as follows:

$$\mu_{ik} = -\frac{\log(\sigma_{ik})}{TTR_{ik}} .$$

Similar indexes exist in reliability theory for the calculation of failure and recovery rates (see, for example, [12]). Given a system, in principle one can derive its model parameters related to buffering resources and recovery measures from the operational experience.

The state equations for the generic system S_k define its behaviour in nominal and failure conditions, hereafter each of which is a *system mode*. Let I_k be the set of the incoming neighbours of node k. A system is in its nominal operation mode when all the input dependencies of the systems belonging to I_k are enabled, namely, their states are within the corresponding service thresholds. In such a mode, the system is only affected by internal disturbances and coupled with the input nodes. By assuming that the service recovery rate is unique, and denoting it by μ_k, the dynamics of the system S_k is the following:

$$\dot{x}_k = -\mu_k \left(x_k - \sum_{i \in I_k} \alpha_{ik} x_i \right) + d_k \, , \; k = 1, 2, \ldots, n$$

if $x_i < \sigma_{ik}$, $\forall i \in I_k$, and $d_k \in L_\infty(\mathbb{R}_{\geq 0}, \mathbb{R}_{\geq 0})$ (i.e., non-negative bounded signals). The term d_k may account for any possible malfunction or failure that drives the state out of the nominal behaviour. The system enters the failure mode if one of the input dependencies is not enabled. In general, the service loss rate depends on the input dependencies that go out of service and so it is for the service threshold as well. If the input dependency $i \in I_k$ is failed, we have

$$\dot{x}_k = \lambda_{ik} (1 - x_k)$$

with $x_i > \sigma_{ik}$.

In a general problem setting, a system S_k will account for one nominal operation mode and $2^n - 1$ failure modes. Nonetheless, simplifications can be applied by assigning the same service loss rates and the same service thresholds in order to aggregate failure modes.

The state space of the interconnected systems taken as a whole is an hypercube $[0, 1]^n$. Such a set can be split into four disjoint subsets, denoted by *operation region, resilience region, non-resilience region*, and *out-of-operation region*. The operation region is the subset of the state space that includes the trajectories of all the systems working as expected, namely $O := [0, \sigma_1] \times [0, \sigma_2] \times \cdots [0, \sigma_n]$. The out-of-operation region corresponds to the case when all the systems have their state variables definitely over the service threshold; it will be denoted by $\bar{O}$. The resilience region R is the portion of state space for which the transient behaviour evolves into the operation region. The non-resilience region $\bar{R}$ is the portion of the state space for which the transient behaviour evolves into the out-of-operation region. Clearly, a difficulty is that of identifying R, $\bar{R}$, and $\bar{O}$.

Based on the aforesaid, we need to address the problem of devising a metric of resilience. Since the state-space hypercube can be decomposed into the disjoint subsets O, R, $\bar{R}$, and $\bar{O}$, an evaluation of the network resilience capability is given by the ratio

$$c_r := \frac{M(R)}{M(R \cup \bar{R})} = \frac{M(R)}{M(R) + M(\bar{R})} \in [0, 1] \tag{2}$$

with

$$M(Z) := \int_Z \mathrm{d}x$$

where $Z \subset \mathbb{R}^n$. (2) provides an aggregate figure of merit, which only depends on the various model parameters. The case $c_r = 1$ means perfect resilience to failures, while $c_r = 0$ corresponds to lack of resilience. In addition to the evaluation of c_r, the model may support an optimal design of the resilience region by allocating additional resources (e.g., a longer buffer or a faster recovery) to the most critical components.

3   Simple Case Study

Let us focus on two systems denoted by S_1 and S_2, as shown in Fig. 2. A simple failure propagation and recovery mechanism is assumed, based on the functional dependencies existing between the two systems [6]. Each system can counteract the failure up to a certain extent. If S_1 fails (i.e., its state threshold is exceeded), it stops providing service to S_2, which starts failing in its turn. Two scenarios exist: 1) S_1 recovers, i.e., the state of S_1 comes back within its threshold σ_1, before S_2 may fail; 2) S_2 fails before S_1 gets recovered. In the latter case, both systems will be failed and unable to recover, i.e., they enter a deadlock in which each system is waiting for the other to restore the respective service.

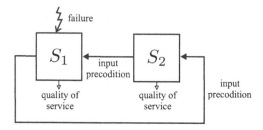

Fig. 2. System composed of two subsystems with mutual functional dependency

In this example, we analyze the system behavior in case of failure of either S_1 or S_2. Each system is characterized in terms of service loss rate, recovery rate, service threshold; the coupling factor is assumed to be zero. The two systems are initially in their operation mode, functioning and providing the service as the output. If the disturbance d_1 in system S_1 drives the state x_1 out of the service operating region (i.e., x_1 becomes larger than σ_1), the failure will propagate from S_1 to S_2. As a consequence, the state dynamics of x_1 and x_2 will switch to recovery and failure modes, respectively. While x_1 converges to 0, x_2 diverges to 1. The resilience depends on the capability of S_1 and S_2 to reenter the operating region $O := [0, \sigma_1] \times [0, \sigma_2]$. A similar reasoning holds for S_2, if affected by the disturbance d_2. The system response is described by the following switching dynamics:

$$
\begin{pmatrix} \dot{x}_1 \\ \dot{x}_2 \end{pmatrix} = \begin{cases} \begin{pmatrix} -\mu_1\, x_1 + d_1 \\ -\mu_2\, x_2 + d_2 \end{pmatrix} & \text{if} \quad 0 < x_1 \le \sigma_1, 0 < x_2 \le \sigma_2 \\[2mm] \begin{pmatrix} -\lambda_1\, x_1 + \lambda_1 \\ -\mu_2\, x_2 + d_2 \end{pmatrix} & \text{if} \quad 0 < x_1 \le \sigma_1, x_2 > \sigma_2 \\[2mm] \begin{pmatrix} -\mu_1\, x_1 + d_1 \\ -\lambda_2\, x_2 + \lambda_2 \end{pmatrix} & \text{if} \quad x_1 > \sigma_1, 0 < x_2 \le \sigma_2 \\[2mm] \begin{pmatrix} -\lambda_1\, x_1 + \lambda_1 \\ -\lambda_2\, x_2 + \lambda_2 \end{pmatrix} & \text{if} \quad x_1 > \sigma_1, x_2 > \sigma_2 \end{cases}
\tag{3}
$$

where $t \geq 0$; recall that, for S_i, $\sigma_i \in (0, 1)$ is the threshold corresponding to the maximum tolerable percentage of service loss, $\lambda_i > 0$ is the service loss rate, and $\mu_i > 0$ is the recovery rate ($i = 1, 2$). A pictorial description of the switching dynamics is shown in Fig. 3 with the four modes: an operation mode (top), two mixed failure-recovery modes (left and right), and a full-failure mode (bottom). An example of phase portrait of system (3) with $d_1 = d_2 = 0$ is presented in Fig. 4.

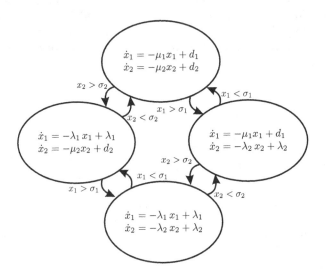

Fig. 3. Pictorial description of the second-order example with functional dependencies

Since the system cannot recover back to the operation region if its state enters to $\bar{O} := (\sigma_1, 1] \times (\sigma_2, 1]$ at a certain finite time. $\bar{O}$ is the region of unrecoverable failure scenarios. On the contrary, outside this region, it is possible for the system to come back into the operation region. Two cases exist: (i) $x_1 > \sigma_1$ and $x_2 \in [0, \sigma_2]$ and (ii) $x_1 \in [0, \sigma_1]$ and $x_2 > \sigma_2$. Let us to consider case (i), as (ii) is similar and can be inferred on the basis of the results obtained with the analysis of (i). If $d_1 = 0$, from (3) we obtain:

$$\begin{aligned} \dot{x}_1 &= -\mu_1 x_1 \\ \dot{x}_2 &= -\lambda_2 x_2 + \lambda_2 . \end{aligned} \qquad (4)$$

The state x_2 tends to diverge from the operating region as

$$x_2(t) = 1 + (x_2(0) - 1) \exp(-\lambda_2 t),$$

while x_1 converges exponentially to zero since

$$x_1(t) = x_1(0) \exp(-\mu_1 t).$$

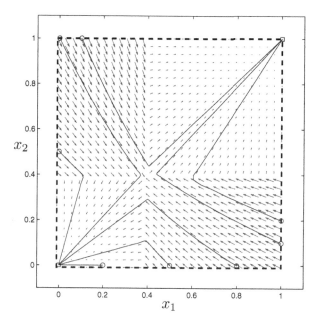

Fig. 4. Phase portrait of system (3) with $\sigma_1 = \sigma_2 = 0.4$ and $\lambda_1 = \lambda_2 = 0.5$

The trajectory limit, for the convergence of x_2 to 0, is calculated by using the reverse dynamic of (4), for all $x_1 \in (\sigma_1, 1]$ and $x_2 \in [0, \sigma_2)$ such that

$$x_1 \leq \exp(\mu_1 t)\,\sigma_1$$
$$x_2 \leq 1 + (\sigma_2 - 1)\,\exp(\lambda_2 t)$$

for all $t \geq 0$ and hence, after some computation, we obtain

$$x_2 \leq 1 - (1 - \sigma_2)\left(\frac{x_1}{\sigma_1}\right)^{\frac{\mu_1}{\lambda_2}}, \quad \sigma_1 \leq x_1 \leq 1 \tag{5}$$

for the resilience to a failure in S_2.

A similar result holds if the failure is generated in S_1. Fig. 5 shows a pictorial representation of the resulting resilience regions. It is straightforward to compute

$$c_r = \left(2 - \sigma_1 - \sigma_2 - (1 - \sigma_2)\frac{\sigma_1}{\frac{\lambda_2}{\mu_1} + 1}\left(\frac{1}{\sigma_1^{\frac{\lambda_2}{\mu_1} + 1}} - 1\right)\right.$$

$$\left. - (1 - \sigma_1)\frac{\sigma_2}{\frac{\lambda_1}{\mu_2} + 1}\left(\frac{1}{\sigma_2^{\frac{\lambda_1}{\mu_2} + 1}} - 1\right)\right) \Big/ (\sigma_1 + \sigma_2 - 2\sigma_1\sigma_2).$$

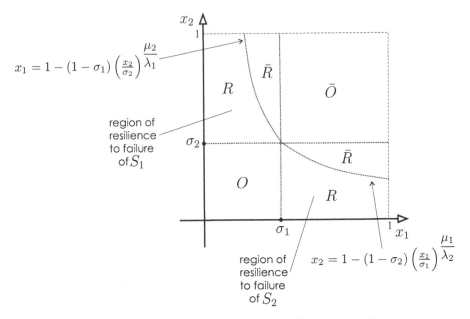

Fig. 5. Region of characterization of resilience properties

The resilience capability c_r depends on recovery and service thresholds. Obviously, c_r increases with the recovery rates, and it decreases with the service loss rates. This is in agreement with the heuristics since the longer the buffering and the faster the recovery, the higher the resilience.

The example unveils several interesting features of resilient systems. In particular, it confirms that the resilience of a system cannot be achieved locally but needs coordination, especially in the case of mutual dependencies. In the considered example, the behavior of S_2 under failure of S_1 is affected by the recovery rate of S_1 because of their interdependency. For instance, a long buffering time for S_2 will be effective only if combined with a fast recovery time of S_1.

The generalization of the resilience analysis to more complex topologies is not trivial. Nevertheless, this generalization can be done step by step, starting with simple topologies. One of these topologies is the *loop*, which generalizes the given example of mutual functional dependencies. A loop is a chain of system components, in which there is no head and no tail, e.g., S_1, S_3, and S_4 form a loop in the graph of Fig. 1. The failure propagates from the system in which the disturbance was initially generated to the other systems. If the failure completes one turn and all the systems of the loop fall in their failure modes, then the network enters a deadlock state from which it cannot escape, even though the disturbance driving the initial failure vanishes. In such a case, the out-of-operation region $\bar{O} := [\sigma_1, 1] \times [\sigma_2, 1] \times \cdots \times [\sigma_n, 1]$ is an attraction set for the state trajectories.

Another topology is the *dependency path*, which is a linear chain of system components with one head and one tail. In a dependency path, every state is recoverable to operation provided that the initial disturbance vanishes. This means that the resilience region covers the entire state space with an empty out-of-operation region. In more realistic problem settings, the recovery to operation will have to complete within given time constraints, e.g., the maximum service outage that one system may suffer from. In so doing, the resilience region will shrink progressively up to the point that it will start eroding the operation region too. In this special scenario, the resilience regions are not static but will vary in time, thus adding another complication to the global achievement of resilience.

4   Conclusions

Resilience is the capability of a complex system to absorb/counteract/recover from failures, and continue functioning properly. Only recently such a property has become of crucial importance in numerous engineering applications. We have investigated an approach for the evaluation of resilience of interconnected systems that is based on the representation in functional dependencies, from which the system response to failures is derived and analyzed. The model copes with both nominal and off-nominal (failure) behaviors and relies on a switching linear dynamics. The investigation on the resilience of interconnected systems is a preliminary goal as compared with more difficult objectives such as the design of resilient controllers. When facing scenarios that include large-scale accidents, anticipation of reaction to the occurrence of an event and coordination of the system reactions are fundamental. This mimics the principle of state awareness, i.e., the knowledge of both operation state and resilience margins of a system connected to a network, which can be the goal of future investigations.

References

1. Valerdi, R., Axelband, E., Baehren, T., Boehm, B., Dorenbos, S.J.D., Madni, A., Nadler, G., Robitaille, P., Settles, S.: A research agenda for system of systems engineering. Journal of System of Systems Engineering 1(1-2), 171–188 (2008)
2. Sousa-Poza, A., Kovacic, S., Keating, C.: Systems engineering: an emerging multi-discipline. Journal of System of Systems Engineering 1(1-2), 1–17 (2008)
3. Kroeger, W.: Critical infrastructures at risk: a need for a new conceptual approach and extended analytical tools. Reliability Engineering & System Safety 93(12), 1781–1787 (2008)
4. Hollnagel, E., Woods, D., Leveson, N.: Resilience Engineering: Concepts and Precepts. Ashgate Publishing, Aldershot (2006)
5. Jackson, S.: Architecting Resilient Systems: Accident Avoidance and Survival and Recovery from Disruptions. John Wiley and Sons, Hoboken (2009)
6. Filippini, R., Silva, A.: Resilience analysis of networked systems-of-systems based on structural and dynamic interdependencies. In: ESREL 2012, Helsinki, Finland (2012)
7. Khalil, H.K.: Nonlinear Systems. Prentice Hall, Upper Saddle River (2002)

8. Liu, Y.-Y., Slotine, J.-J., Barabasi, A.-L.: Controllability of complex networks. Nature 473(12), 167–173 (2011)
9. Schläpfer, M., Shapiro, J.L.: Modeling failure propagation in large-scale engineering networks. In: Zhou, J. (ed.) Complex 2009. LNICST, vol. 5, pp. 2127–2138. Springer, Heidelberg (2009)
10. Panzieri, S., Setola, R.: Failures propagation in critical interdependent infrastructures. Int. Journal of Modelling, Identification and Control 3(1), 69–78 (2008)
11. Bloomfield, R., Buzna, L., Popov, P., Salako, K., Wright, D.: Stochastic modelling of the effects of interdependencies between critical infrastructure. In: Rome, E., Bloomfield, R. (eds.) CRITIS 2009. LNCS, vol. 6027, pp. 201–212. Springer, Heidelberg (2010)
12. Trivedi, K.: Probability and Statistics with Reliability, Queuing, and Computer Science Applications. John Wiley and Sons, New York (2001)

System Dynamics for Railway Infrastructure Protection

Maria Carla De Maggio and Roberto Setola

Complex Systems & Security Lab., Università Campus Bio-Medico di Roma, Rome, Italy
{m.demaggio,r.setola}@unicampus.it

Abstract. The railway infrastructure represents, for its symbolic value and accessibility, a very attractive target for criminals and terrorists alike. This paper intends to address the security issues of such systems, beginning with the railway stations themselves., The peculiarities of the railway infrastructure, in terms of geographical dispersion and mass transportation, present a formidable challenge considering the ratio of limited resources against the most vulnerable components, (i.e. stations that show the largest gap between terrorist attractiveness and implemented counter-measures). To this end, we used a System Dynamics approach to model how the different factors influence the railway station target attractiveness, fragility and vulnerability. Specifically, a deep analysis of past incidents (and near incidents) allows us to quantify the effectiveness of the different elements.

Keywords: Railway Infrastructure Protection, System Dynamics, Qualitative Assessment, Sensitivity Assessment.

1 Introduction

In the last years an ever-growing attention is being paid to national and supra-national infrastructures and their protection. In fact, the technology is more and more pervasive, involving almost all aspects of life, increasingly embedding itself amongst infrastructures: this ranges from an increasing difficulty in foreseeing and preventing critical events to amplifying the effect of an incident on an infrastructure and subsequently transmitting this negative effect to other critical infrastructures. .

The discussion on Critical Infrastructure Protection (CIP) is very developed in the USA, particularly after the 9/11 events. In fact, in the USA Patriot Act of 2001 [1], for the first time "critical infrastructures" are defined as "systems and assets, whether physical or virtual, so vital for a state that the incapacity or destruction of such systems and assets would have a debilitating impact on security, national economic security, national public health or safety, or any combination of those matters".

Different Governments have listed the sectors considered as "critical" for their respective society, e.g., the USA listed 11 sectors [2] and also the European Commission in its COM(2006)787 [3] listed 11 sectors, and their sub-sectors.

Among these sectors, in all the cases, the transportation sector is one of the listed items. The importance of this sector is showed by the 2008/114/EC [4] that represents a first step towards the protection of European Critical Infrastructures (ECI), and that

B. Hämmerli, N. Kalstad Svendsen, and J. Lopez (Eds.): CRITIS 2012, LNCS 7722, pp. 191–202, 2013.
© Springer-Verlag Berlin Heidelberg 2013

invited the Member States to identify ECIs; this protocol was requested only in the sectors of energy and transportation, and their sub-sectors.

The 9/11 attacks showed us the importance of the transport sector; in particular the vulnerability of the air transport arena. But the importance of protecting other transport infrastructures cannot be neglected. In this framework large attention should be paid to the so-called mass-transportation, and especially on the railway system.

Indeed, on the base of data collected by the National CounterTerrorism Center[1], in 2010 more than 11,550 terrorist attacks took place in 72 Countries, with more than 50,000 victims, including 13,200 deaths. Considering the target of these attacks, about 500 of them (more than 3%) directly interested critical infrastructures (energy assets and transport networks in the majority of cases).

Focusing on railway framework, the peculiarity of this mass transportation system is that it is impossible to define a "perimeter" to protect, because a huge number of persons use the infrastructure; hence it should be open and the screening activity should be lighter (especially if compared to those implemented for air transportation). Another aspect that should be taken into account is the geographical "dispersion" of the railway infrastructure with the presence of thousands of potential targets. These considerations impose the development of instruments able to qualify the adequateness of the security measures in order to perform effective gap analysis and to prioritize the actions on those aspects/sites with larger gaps with respect to the actual threats.

To this end, we propose the use of a System Dynamics approach. System Dynamics was introduced by J. Forrester in 1950s [5] and is a computer-aided approach to policy analysis and design. It applies to dynamic problems arising in complex social, managerial, economic, or ecological systems – literally any dynamic systems characterized by interdependence, mutual interaction, information feedback, and circular causality. Specifically, it is generally used when the complexity of the problem at hand overcome the capability of the analyst to use quantitative approaches, but at the same time qualitative approaches are non-effective to provide adequate strategies.

In this paper we use System Dynamics to model the relationships among the different properties of a railway site in terms of functional aspects in presence of security devices and threats, in order to identify its "level of security". The large part of the paper is devoted to qualify how the different factors influence the risks of a specific site, so as how the different security strategies and devices are perceived as adequate counter-measures. Following this perspective we performed a detailed analysis of security-related incidents (and near-incidents) in order to identify correlation among railway-site characteristics, attractiveness and effects of attacks occurring worldwide in the last 30 years.

All the data collected and the approach described in this paper are part of the EC co-funded project "METRIP - MEthodological Tools for Railway Infrastructure Protection"[2], aiming to develop methodological tools to increase the protection of a critical railway infrastructure system with a focus on urban mass transportation.

---

[1] http://www.nctc.gov/

[2] http://metrip.unicampus.it/

In the following sections of the paper we will describe the peculiarities of a railway infrastructure (Section 2), we will present the analysis of data about a collection of incidents which occurred in railway assets (Section 3), and we will present the methodology of System Dynamics as a tool to verify the security level of a railway asset (Section 4).

2   Railway Infrastructure

A railway infrastructure is physically composed by stations connected by railroads, tunnels, bridges, crossings, etc. All of these elements need adequate protection against attacks. The most sensible point of a railway infrastructure, however, is the train station. The station is the point of confluence for a great number of persons, not limited to travelling passengers and workers) and goods to be shipped. The bigger stations generally provide several services, shops, and meeting points like waiting rooms. They can have a great number of railroad tracks, goods depots and systems of sorting.

The potential of attacks to railway facilities have been unfortunately demonstrated by two events which occurred a few years ago.

The Madrid train bombing is considered the worst terrorist attack in the history of Spain and Europe. An Al-Qaeda-inspired terrorist cell claimed responsibility for this attack, which occurred the 11th of March 2004, and caused 191 deaths and 2051 injured, through the explosion of 10 backpacks in 3 different regional trains.

Another tragic event is the attack of 7 July 2005 in London, which took place through a series of coordinated suicide attacks in London targeting civilians using the public transport system during the morning rush hour. Four Islamist home-grown terrorists detonated four bombs, three in quick succession aboard London Underground trains across the city and, later, a fourth on a double-decker bus. Fifty-two people, including the four bombers, were killed in the attacks, and over 700 more were injured. This attack caused the total closing of the underground and ground transportation for the day, and partially for almost a month.

Table 1. Lethality per placement by delivery/concealment (where FPD and IPD mean fatalities and injuries per device) [6]

Method	#	% of total	FPD	IPD
Concealed/left in passenger compartments	324	26.73%	3.86	14.50
Placed on railroad track or bridge, or near a train	273	22.59%	0.81	3.61
Concealed/left in stations	157	12.95%	2.44	10.10
Placed on vehicle road, bridge or in tunnel	111	9.16%	2.14	4.50
Physically thrown	84	6.93%	0.90	5.17
Carried on person	81	6.68%	6.84	34.86
Concealed in parcel or bags	59	4.87%	4.70	25.84
Placed near the bus or other target – unspecified	40	3.30%	5.38	14.56
Concealed/placed outside of stations	34	2.81%	0.35	1.87
Concealed/left at bus stop	23	1.90%	0.80	8.80
Unknown	9	0.74%	1.62	9.38
Concealed/placed in non-passenger areas	8	0.66%	2.75	0.06
Concealed in or on vehicle	5	0.41%	1.55	9.73
Concealed/placed inside of building or office	3	0.25%	0	0
Total/average	**1.211**	**100%**	**2.6**	**10.72**

The experience of these and other attacks demonstrates the importance of controlling and protecting stations, as access points to trains. This perception is confirmed by the data elaborated by the Mineta Transportation Institute (MTI) [6] showed in Table 1 which referred both to train and bus attacks: the majority of victims are via attacks to railway assets, and more than 1 in 4 is per bombing in train compartments. The MIT database collects about 522 attacks against passenger trains/stations/tracks of which 434 (83%) were explosive or incendiary attacks; among these, there were 181 attempts to derail trains with bombs or mechanical sabotage.

For these reasons, a great importance is covered by security systems owned by assets. The protection systems and devices mostly used, and thus what we considered in the classification carried out collecting data about attacks (see Section 3), are cameras, turnstiles, guards, metal detectors and canine units.

Some of these systems are functional to the station services, such as turnstiles in metro stations. Others, like CCTV surveillance, are in some cases mandatory to ensure a certain level of security to daily frequenters of the station. Moreover, camera surveillance reached a high level of technology that allows, with the support of human operators, to perform object, human, loitering and tailgating detection. Also for this reason, as we will see in the following, video-surveillance is one of the more effective security systems, especially if coupled with other devices.

3   Railway Incidents Database

The great amount of railway incidents that occurred worldwide demonstrates the vulnerability and appeal of this infrastructure.

In order to analyse the level of risk of a railway asset, we conducted research through open source information about incidents that occurred to railway stations and railroads [7] to better understand how the protection devices can avoid damages and victims, and to analyse the effect of the security systems to the risk level of an asset through the methodology described in Section 4. The database of the information collected contains data about the main incidents that occurred in railway stations or infrastructures in general from 1972 to present. All the information collected is derived from open sources, mainly from the internet; in particular from newspaper records from different countries in the world, national terrorist attacks databases and, mainly the US National CounterTerrorism Center and its Report on Terrorism of 2010 [8], containing information about terrorism worldwide. All attacks collected are detailed with their date, country, name of station, type of station (railway or metro station), type of attack, quantity of explosive (when bombing attack), description, author, number of terrorists involved, deaths, injured, attack area, and other relevant information.

The peculiarity of our database is that, in addition to information about the attack, we collected data about the station or infrastructure in which the attack took place (when available), to better understand its attractiveness, its protection level, the probability and the possible impact. In fact, for each station in which an attack took place, we listed the number of passengers and trains each day, the number of railroads, the area of the station (in m^2), and checked for the presence of security devices, such as cameras, turnstiles, metal detectors, guards, canine units.

In general, since a big station has a higher number of passengers in the day, and thus a greater amount of people circulating within it, the more the station is important and the more it is protected by different security systems in order to avoid criminal or terrorist acts. Figure 1 shows the increase in the number of victims with the number of passengers with respect to the number of daily trains. The number of dead and injured people is in fact directly dependent by the density of passengers per train in the asset.

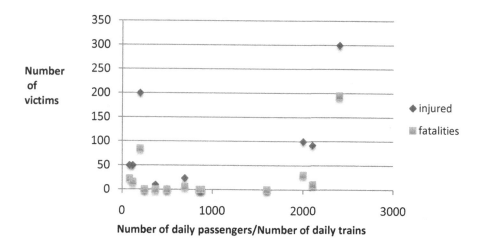

Fig. 1. Number of fatalities and injured persons per number of passengers per train

Regarding the type of attack, the majority of attacks are bombings (i.e: suicide, placed near railroads or inside trains). Other types of attack include sabotage, fire or fire bombs, firearms,   and chemical agents (Figure 2).

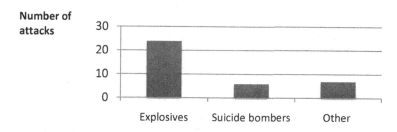

Fig. 2. Number of attacks per type

The Figure 3 shows the security systems adopted by the assets analysed: CCTV is the most highly utilized device, followed by security guards and turnstiles. Only a few assets use metal detectors and sniffer dogs. It is of great interest the analysis of the deterrence from attacks of these particular security devices; especially when compared to the normalized number of dead and injured persons that occurred in the presence of each independent security system (as shown in Figure 3b). What we observe is that the systems most effective in preventing deaths and injuries seem to be turnstiles, cameras and security guards in this order.

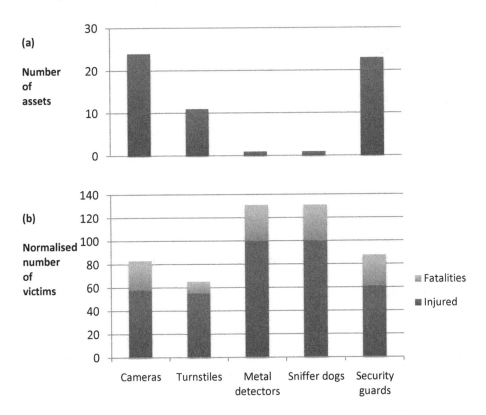

Fig. 3. Security systems used within railway assets (a) and fatalities and injured persons per attack in those assets

But it is intuitive that the coupling of more than one security device allows a higher level of security. This is confirmed in Figure 4, where the victims of attacks decrease with the increasing number of active systems. The anomaly of a great number of victims with 5 different types of security systems is due to a unique bombing attack which occurred in September 2008 in a metro station in New Delhi and resulted in 31 deaths and more than 100 injured.

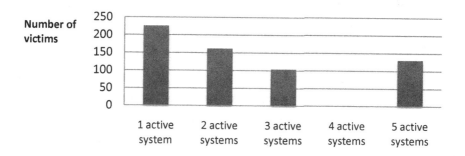

Fig. 4. Victims of attacks to stations related to the number of security systems

A further observation allows one to better understand the effect on the protection of the asset of security systems coupling, see Figure 5 (notice that the data are biased by the number of stations equipped with the different types of security devices).

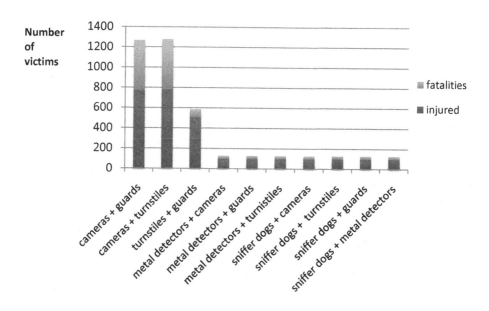

Fig. 5. Fatalities and injured persons couples of security systems

The analysis of the data, in particular the effects of attacks in the presence of differing types of security devices, allows us to apply these statistical results to the model described in the following, highlighting the effectiveness of each device in order to evaluate the adequateness of security measures to face the real threats.

4   System Dynamics Methodology

The data collected in our database, allows us to compare the damage of an attack to a railway infrastructure to the level and type of protection devices adopted in each station.

Starting from this point, we want to evaluate the level of protection of a site, typically a train station, considering some environmental factors among which the protection tools were adopted.

To do this, we refer to the Criminal Prevention Through Environmental Design (CPTED) theory, which first appeared in a 1971 book by the criminologist and sociologist C. Ray Jeffery [9] and was inspired by Jacobs' work [10] about the relationship between crime and the layout of streets and land use in American cities which was developed to promote public safety. CPTED is based on the hypothesis that "the proper design and effective use of the built environment can lead to a reduction in the fear and incidence of crime, and an Improvement in the quality of life" [11].

To apply the CPTED approach for analyzing the protection level in railway infrastructures, and help to take decision for improving the level of security, we used the open source software Vensim® to exploit the principles of System Dynamics, particularly useful and efficient in this case because of its qualitative approach that overcomes the impossibility to use quantitative approaches due to the nature of the problem.

Figure 6shows the elaborated model. Adopting the formalism of System Dynamics, the schema is composed of three different entities:

- **Stock:** is the term for any entity that accumulates or depletes over time, in the figure in boxes;
- **Flow:** is the rate of change in a stock, in the figure the bold arrow;
- **Auxiliary Variable:** can have a constant value, have an impact on flows and represents our sources of information, in the figure the thin arrow.

The auxiliary variables concur to compose the flows: for example, the sum of variables related to electronic security, barriers, guards and gates gives the "access control" flow. Similarly the other flows are composed by the sum (or the subtraction, if the arrow is outward) of auxiliary variables. Integrating the sum of ingoing or outgoing flows, we obtain the stocks. For example, the integration of "target hardening" and "access control" produce the "increasing of the effort". All the stocks in the left part of Figure 6 are strictly related to the considered asset and its characteristics rather than its security devices and systems. These stocks contribute to determine the "motivation to commit crime", which intuitively, decreases when the four stocks related to the asset increase, (i.e. "increase the effort", "increase the perceived risk associated with crime", "reduce anticipate rewards" and "induce shame of guilty"). At the same time the motivation to commit crime is increased by "personal factors" and the "vulnerability rating" of the asset. What we obtain from the model, from the motivation to commit the crime, is the "potential criminal attack", (i.e. the risk, the "real criminal attack" and the damage).

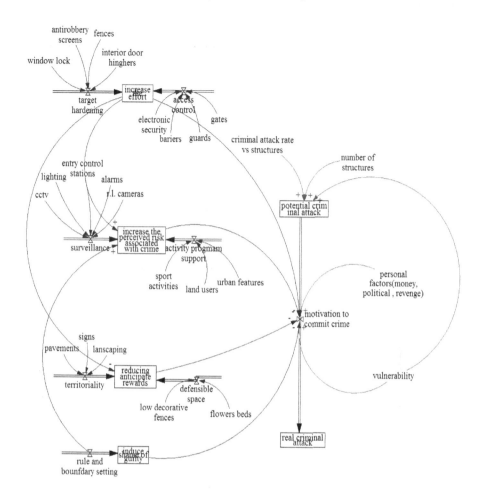

Fig. 6. System Dynamics model for the protection of a railway asset

As explained, we need to insert in this model the so-called auxiliary variables, which represent, in our case, a series of data regarding the security tools and protection devices of which the railway asset is provided.

We populated the model in part with the data arising from the attack database, in particular for variables related to the access control, the surveillance, (i.e. our data regarding equipment of security devices, barriers, guards, video-surveillance, etc.).

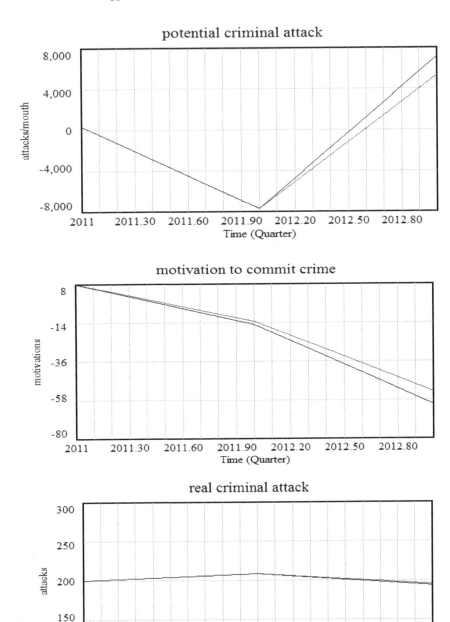

Fig. 7. (a) Potential Criminal Attacks, (b) Motivation to commit crime, (c) Real Criminal Attacks

Other source data came from the statics on the number and types of attacks and their relative damage to the asset.

Further values for variables have been obtained from statistics values found in literature [12].

In this way we obtain the "standard" value for the risk of an attack along a timeline. In particular, in Figure 8, the red line shows the estimation of "motivation to commit crime" (Figure 7b) which modified the trend of "potential criminal attack" (Figure 7a), which lead to an evaluation of the evolution of the risk of a "real criminal attack" (Figure 7c) along a timeline.

What is of our interest is to understand what is the influence of a different setting of security systems in an asset; by showing the impact to a "standard" asset if we increase the flow by 30% regarding "Target Hardening" and "Access Control". Thus, increasing the value of physical barriers and electronic and human ones can have an effect to the real risk (illustrated in Figure 8, blue line). We observe an increase of the "potential criminal attack" but a decrease in the "motivation to commit crime". Subsequently, this leads to an overall decrease of "real criminal attack".

5   Conclusions

In this paper we dealt with the issue of Railway Infrastructure Protection. The railway assets, in particular train and metro stations, are very attractive targets for terrorism because of the large amount of people circulating each day and the strategic importance that they hold in national mobility and logistics.

The analysis of data collected from open sources regarding attacks to railway assets, in coherence with other databases such as those reported by MTI [6], highlights how stations are the most appealing targets, and in the majority of cases the events are perpetrated through explosives, (i.e. bombs left in a station or in a train or via suicide bombs).

The added value of our database is highlighting the correlation between type and result of the attack and the security systems that the station are supplied with in order to understand their deterrence capability.

The integration of the CPTED approach and System Dynamics, using the statistical data arisen from the database, led us to the elaboration of a dynamic model that allows us to analyse the potential effect of integration of security systems within a defined asset or changes in other asset characteristics, ultimately aiding us in determining the overall effects to the risk level and the realistic probability and effect of an attack to the asset itself.

Acknowledgements. This work is partially supported by the European Commission, Directorate-General Home Affairs, within the Specific Programme on "Prevention, Preparedness and Consequence Management of Terrorism and other Security-related risks", under Grant HOME/2010/CIPS/AG/035 METRIP - MEthodological Tools for Railway Infrastructure Protection.

Moreover, we want to thank Letizia Di Giulio, Melania Basso and Francesca De Cillis for their contribution to the paper.

References

1. Uniting and Strengthening America by Providing Appropriate Tools Required to Intercept and Obstruct Terrorism Act (2001)
2. Department of Homeland Security, Physical Protection of Facilities and Real Properties (April 2003)
3. Proposal for a Directive of the Council on the identification and designation of European Critical Infrastructure and the assessment of the need to improve their protection, COM, 787 (2006)
4. Council Directive 2008/114/EC of 8 December 2008 on the identification and designation of European critical infrastructures and the assessment of the need to improve their protection.
5. Radzicki, M.J., Taylor, R.A.: Origin of System Dynamics: Jay W. Forrester and the History of System Dynamics. In: U.S. Department of Energy's Introduction to System Dynamics (2008)
6. Jenkins, B.M., Butterworth, B.R.: Explosives and Incendiaries Used in Terrorist Attacks on Public Surface Transportation: A Preliminary Empirical Analysis. Mineta Transportation Institute Report (March 2010)
7. De Cillis, F., De Maggio, M.C., Pragliola, C., Setola, R.: Analysis of criminal and terrorist related episodes in railway infrastructure scenarios. Publishing on Journal of Homeland Security and Emergency Management.
8. National CounterTerrorism Center, 2010 Report on Terrorism (April 30, 2011)
9. Ray Jeffery, C.: Crime prevention through environmental design. Sage Publications (1971)
10. Jacobs, J.: The Death and Life of Great American Cities. Random House (1961)
11. Crowe, T.D.: Crime Prevention through Environmental Design. National Crime Prevention Institute (2000)
12. Hedayati Marzbali, M., et al.: Validating crime prevention through environmental design construct through checklist using structural equation modelling. International Journal of Law, Crime and Justice 40(2), 82–99 (2012)

Contaminant Detection
in Urban Water Distribution Networks
Using Chlorine Measurements

Demetrios G. Eliades and Marios M. Polycarpou

KIOS Research Center for Intelligent Systems and Networks
Department of Electrical and Computer Engineering
University of Cyprus CY-1678 Nicosia, Cyprus
{eldemet,mpolycar}@ucy.ac.cy

Abstract. In this work we present a contamination detection methodology for water distribution networks. The proposed detection method is based on chlorine sensor measurements, which are compare to certain computed upper and lower periodic bounds. The bounds are computed using randomized simulations aimed at capturing the variations in chlorine concentration due to the significant uncertainty in the water demand patterns, average nodal consumptions, roughness parameters and reaction coefficients. The proposed method is applied to a set of high-impact contamination fault scenarios using a benchmark distribution network, for which on-line chlorine concentration sensors are assumed to have been installed at certain locations following an optimization procedure. The results indicate that by using the periodic bounds computed from the randomized simulations, for the proposed benchmark, contamination events are detected within reasonable time.

Keywords: Water Security, Contamination Detection, Water Quality, Drinking Water Distribution.

1 Introduction

Water utilities are responsible for distributing drinking water to consumers through a complex distributed network, which they must monitor and control so that its hydraulic and quality parameters are within certain desired limits. Maintaining water quality within the regulations specified by the European Commission (EC) [6] and the U.S. Environmental Protection Agency (EPA) [30], is an important challenge faced by water utilities. Water distribution networks are large-scale systems, which are comprised of pipe networks and dynamical elements such as water storage tanks, pumps and valves which control pressures and flows in the system, as well as sensors which measure various hydraulic and quality water characteristics, installed at various locations in the network. Communication of the actuators and sensors to the control center is through the Supervisory Control And Data Acquisition (SCADA) system.

B. Hämmerli, N. Kalstad Svendsen, and J. Lopez (Eds.): CRITIS 2012, LNCS 7722, pp. 203–214, 2013.
© Springer-Verlag Berlin Heidelberg 2013

According to the European Commission, critical infrastructures are those physical facilities and networks, which, if disrupted, would significantly affect the health, safety, security or economic well-being of citizens [7]. Due to their vital role, water systems are considered among the main critical infrastructures, along with power and telecommunications systems. From a security perspective, water distribution systems are vulnerable to malicious attacks seeking to cause economic losses and affect dramatically the population's health. A contamination injection attack could be initiated at the most critical locations of a drinking water distribution network, and at the most critical time instance, intending to cause the greatest "damage". A malicious contamination attack could be achieved through a back-flow attack, by using a pump at some node to inject some dangerous chemical agent or biotoxin [18]. In general, water contamination could be caused not only due to a malicious attack, but also by accidental faults in the source, treatment, distribution, monitoring and response process [12].

From a system's perspective, the inputs to the system are the pump/valve and disinfection regulation signals, and measurable outputs of the system are the flows, pressures and water quality parameters at different locations in the network. The goal is to control the system so that it delivers water to the consumers in the desired quantity and quality. The dynamics of water distribution systems are affected by consumer demands which correspond to uncontrollable inputs to the system. Fluctuations in water consumption can have significant effect on hydraulics and in contaminant propagation delays. An accidental or malicious contaminant injection can be considered as a water quality fault. In general, the contaminant type, the magnitude of the mass injected and the injection time are not known.

In the last decade the problem of water security has received significant interest both from the viewpoint of physical and cyber-physical security, as well as in terms of detecting and managing water contamination [2]. The use of early contamination warning systems have been proposed, whose specific goal is to utilize affordable sensors capable of detecting reliably and accurately any chemical, biological or radio-nuclear (CBRN) contamination [1]. These sensors can be strategically placed in the network, for example, by considering the TEVA-SPOT sensor placement methodology [21]. In general, a contamination warning system would be comprised of stations measuring various parameters such as chlorine concentrations, total organic carbon, oxidation-reduction potential, pH, conductivity, turbidity, temperature; these water quality sensors communicate through the SCADA system. The contamination warning system requires the development of algorithms to detect and characterize important contamination events, identify the contaminant or its type, estimate its concentration and determine the contamination extent; all these must be achieved as soon as possible to allow accommodation of the fault, and at the same time minimize false negatives and false positives [8].

In the present work, chlorine concentration measurements will be utilized for contamination detection. Chlorine concentration measurements are currently available in many water utilities and are used for water quality monitoring and control. A key challenge in utilizing water quality measurements for contamination detection is the fact that consumer demands are in general unknown and fluctuate in time, causing significant variations in the pipe flows, which in turn cause variability in water quality and specifically in the chlorine concentration measurements. The standard approach would be to consider constant upper and lower bounds of chlorine concentration at different parts of the network, and trigger alarms for possible contaminations when these bounds have been violated. This is a conservative detection approach, which may lead to longer detection times or even to failure in detecting the contamination fault. In general, most contamination detection methods do not sufficiently address the issue of water quality variability.

The contribution of this work is the development of a mathematical framework for contamination detection in water distribution systems using chlorine measurements, when the probability distributions of the various water distribution network parameters and the consumer demands are given. A finite set of different network conditions is constructed through randomized sampling with respect to the probability distributions, and based on these parameters the hydraulic and quality models are simulated using the EPANET and EPANET-MSX [27,28] to calculate periodic upper and lower bounds of the chlorine concentrations at nodes in the network where chlorine sensors have been installed. An alarm is triggered when the chlorine concentration violates a bound for a certain amount of time.

This paper is organized as follows: in Section 2, an overview of the contamination detection methodologies is provided. In Section 3 the mathematical formulation is presented and in Section 4 simulation results are demonstrated, based on a benchmark water distribution network. Finally, Section 5 presents the concluding remarks and future work.

2   Contamination Detection Methodologies

The use of chlorine sensors for contamination detection was proposed in [14], as chlorine concentration changes when reacting with some contaminants [9]. In general, the use of chlorine concentration sensors for contaminant detection provides a relatively inexpensive solution since sensors are often available and used for monitoring water quality.

Currently, a number of contamination detection methodologies focus on analyzing multiple-type measurements, such as chlorine concentrations, turbidity, total organic carbon, pH, etc, from a single location of the network. In [3], historical water quality data from one outflow point were taken into consideration for computing the standard deviation of four water quality parameters. Contamination detection was performed when these parameters were greater than 3 standard deviations from their average values. Other methodologies have also been proposed for the contamination detection problem: control charts, time series analysis, kriging analysis and Kalman filters [13]. An off-the-shelf solution is provided by Hach HST, in which various water quality parameters are considered to calculate a distance measure through a proprietary algorithm, which is used for contamination detection and isolation [18]. Field trials for contamination detection have been investigated in [4]. Data mining techniques used in computer networks have been applied to detect contaminations in water systems [26], using a set of normal-behaviour clusters.

In the CANARY event detection tool [10] provided by the US EPA, detection techniques based on linear filters [20] and multivariate distance metrics [15] have been implemented, as well as sensor fusion techniques to take into account the spatial distribution of water quality sensor measurements [16].

Fluctuations in water demands may cause significant variability in water quality measurements throughout the water distribution network, as demonstrated in [24] using Monte Carlo simulations. To accommodate uncertainty, a Bayesian Belief Network approach was presented in [22] as a method to infer the probability of contamination.

Multiple chemical reaction models have also been used for simulation and contamination detection. In [11], the EPANET-MSX software was used to simulate the chlorine response to the injection of certain biological agents, in a water distribution benchmark network. Furthermore, in [31], chlorine and contaminant reaction models have been considered in a real-time event adaptive detection, identification and warning methodology, to detect and classify the contaminant.

The present work demonstrates a contamination detection methodology which is based on simulating chlorine propagation considering the probability distributions of various system parameters, and calculating the estimated chlorine concentration at various locations in a water distribution network in order to construct the upper and lower periodic bounds which are used for contamination detection.

3 Design Methodology

Overall, the proposed contamination fault detection methodology is comprised of the following parts: 1) Construct the water distribution model and specify the system parameters and their possible bounds. 2) Construct a finite set of different system parameters selected at random or through grid sampling, and simulate the water distribution system in order to construct a set of disinfectant concentration time series for each node where a disinfectant concentration sensor has been installed. 3) Compute the upper and lower periodic bounds based on the simulated chlorine concentration time series. 4) Design the contamination fault detection logic.

Contaminants and disinfectants travel along the water flow within the pipe network, according to the advection and reaction dynamics. Advection is the transport mechanism of a substance in a fluid, which can be modelled as a hyperbolic partial differential equation and can be solved using numerical methods. Reaction dynamics describe the change in the substance concentration due to decay, growth [27] or multiple-species reactions [28], which may be solved using numerical methods. In general, multiple-species propagation and reactions in water distribution systems are modelled using sets of hyperbolic partial differential and algebraic equations. In the general case, the fundamental advection-reaction dynamics of reacting substances in a pipe, are described by

$$
\begin{aligned}
\frac{\partial}{\partial t} V(z,t) + \frac{Q(t)}{A} \frac{\partial}{\partial z} V(z,t) &= G_V(V(z,t), W(z,t)) \\
\frac{\partial}{\partial t} W(z,t) + \frac{Q(t)}{A} \frac{\partial}{\partial z} W(z,t) &= G_W(V(z,t), W(z,t))
\end{aligned}
\tag{1}
$$

where $V(z,t)$ and $W(z,t)$ are the disinfectant and contaminant concentration vectors, respectively, at continuous time t and distance z along the pipe, with water flow $Q(t)$ and a cross-sectional area of the pipe A, $G_V(\cdot)$ and $G_W(\cdot)$ are the concentration change rates due to reactions and decay for the disinfectant and contaminant respectively. Depending on the contaminant, an algebraic term may be required [28].

Except for simple cases, computing an analytic solution of the advection-reaction dynamics of water distribution systems is impossible. As a result, a numerical approximation method such as the *Finite Volumes* and *Forward Euler* approaches [19] are typically considered to formulate the advection and reaction dynamics into a discrete-time state-space representation [5]. Let k be the discrete time, with sampling time Δt, $v(k)$ the average disinfectant concentration state vector and $w(k)$ the average contaminant concentration state vector. Each state corresponds to the concentration in a finite volume. Furthermore, $u(k)$ corresponds to the controllable disinfectant concentration input and $d(k)$ the nodal water demands. The water distribution system model is described by

$$
\begin{aligned}
v(k+1) &= f_v(v(k), u(k), d(k); p_f) + g_v(v(k), w(k); p_g) \\
w(k+1) &= f_w(w(k), d(k); p_f) + g_w(v(k), w(k); p_g) + \phi(k; p_\phi).
\end{aligned}
\tag{2}
$$

Functions $f_v(\cdot)$ and $f_w(\cdot)$ are the advection functions for the disinfectant and contaminant substances respectively. The set p_f is comprised of the network parameters, such as pipe roughness coefficients. Functions $g_v(\cdot)$ and $g_w(\cdot)$ are the reaction functions for the disinfectant and contaminant substances respectively. The set p_g is comprised of the reaction parameters, such as the disinfectant decay rate. Function $\phi(\cdot)$ corresponds to the unknown non-negative contamination fault function. The set p_ϕ is comprised of the contamination fault parameters, such as starting time, duration and magnitude. In general, the parameters p_f, p_g and p_ϕ are unknown (or partially known).

In addition, the actual nodal water demands $d(k)$ which affect the contaminant and disinfectant propagation, are not known. In general, nodal water demands exhibit seasonality and periodicity, and as a consequence, disinfectant concentrations also exhibit periodic behaviour [25]. Let $d(k) = d_p(k; p_d)$, were $d_p(\cdot)$ is a known periodic function which describes the behaviour of the nominal nodal demands, and p_d is the set of unknown water demand parameters, such as average nodal demand and demand modelling uncertainty.

Let $p^* = \{p_f, p_g, p_d\}$ be the set of all the unknown system parameters, corresponding to the advection, reaction and demand dynamics. Since the actual system parameters in the set p^* are not known, certain assumptions can be made for each parameter, such as their upper and lower bounds or their probability distributions. Let $\mathcal{P}$ be the range set of all the possible parameter combinations, such that $p^* \in \mathcal{P}$.

In practice, it is not possible to consider all possible parameters in $\mathcal{P}$ (which may be infinite). The approach followed in this work is to construct a finite subset $\mathcal{P}_0$ of $\mathcal{P}$ with n elements using random or grid sampling, such that $\mathcal{P}_0 \subset \mathcal{P}$ and $\mathcal{P}_0 = \{p^1, ..., p^n\}$. The goal is to simulate the water distribution system using each system parameter in $\mathcal{P}_0$ under normal hydraulic and quality conditions, i.e. without contamination faults, and use the computed disinfectant concentration signals to calculate the upper and lower disinfectant concentration bounds, $\overline{y}(k)$ and $\underline{y}(k)$ respectively. For each set of system parameters, the system model is simulated using the EPANET [27] and the EPANET-MSX [28] tools to compute the disinfectant concentration variance in time.

Let T be the number of samples in one period, and let K be the set of simulated time steps for which water quality dynamics exhibit periodic behaviour. In addition, let $y(k; p^l) = Cv(k; p^l)$ correspond to the simulated disinfectant concentration at a sensing node, where C is the output matrix and $p^l \in \mathcal{P}_0$ is the l-th system parameter considered. The upper and lower periodic bounds are computed as:

$$\overline{y}_i(k) = \max\{y_i(\kappa; p^l) \mid \mathrm{mod}(\kappa, T) = \mathrm{mod}(k, T), \kappa \in K, \ p^l \in \mathcal{P}_0\}$$
$$\underline{y}_i(k) = \min\{y_i(\kappa; p^l) \mid \mathrm{mod}(\kappa, T) = \mathrm{mod}(k, T), \kappa \in K, \ p^l \in \mathcal{P}_0\}$$
(3)

where $\mathrm{mod}(\cdot)$ is the modulo operation.

A contamination alarm is triggered at time k_d, if one of the following inequalities holds for more that $h \geq 1$ consecutive time steps, i.e., $y_i(k) > \overline{y}_i(k)$ or $y_i(k) < \underline{y}_i(k)$, for $k \in \{k_d - h, ..., k_d\}$.

4   Case Study

In this section we consider a case study of the network shown in Figure 1, which depicts one of the benchmark networks in the "Battle of the Water Sensor Networks" design competition [23]. This network is composed of 178 pipes connected to 129 nodes (126 junctions, two tanks and one reservoir) with a set of realistic structural and hydraulic parameters defined. Each junction node is assigned a nominal daily average consumption volume as well as a nominal discrete signal describing the rate of water consumption with 48 hours periodicity and a 30-minute hydraulic time step. The network has been modified to add two chlorine disinfection actuators at the 'Reservoir' and 'Tank A', where the disinfectant substance, chlorine, is injected, and its concentration is regulated at 1.0 $\frac{mg}{L}$.

Chlorine sensors are considered to have been installed in the system after solving the optimization problem described in the "Battle of the Water Sensor Networks" competition [17,23]. In specific, we consider that water quality sensors are installed at nodes '17', '31', '45', '83' and '122', computed with respect to the 'N1A5' benchmark of the competition. The 4 benchmark objectives considered

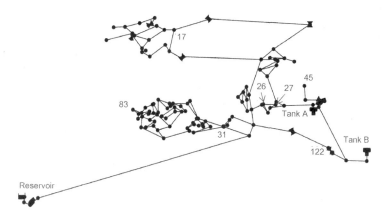

Fig. 1. A water distribution system with 129 nodes; five on-line chlorine concentration sensors are considered at nodes '17', '31', '45', '83' and '122'. Chlorine is regulated at the 'Reservoir' and the 'Tank A'.

in the competition were to maximize detection likelihood, minimize expected detection time, minimize expected population affected and minimize consumption of contaminated water prior to detection. A contamination can occur any time within a day, and at any node; considering a 5 minute sampling time, 37152 contamination scenarios were constructed for the 'N1A5' benchmark [23]. For the sensor placement scheme considered, the estimated detection likelihood was calculated as 75.6% with respect to the 37152 contamination scenarios, thus some contamination events cannot be detected with this scheme [23].

In practice, the actual system parameters $p^* \in \mathcal{P}$ are not known. As a result, there can be significant differences between the estimated and the actual flows and pressures, as well as the spatio-temporal distribution of chlorine concentrations, because of the uncertainties e.g., in the roughness coefficient of each pipe or the average demands of each node. We consider that for each unknown parameter, an upper and lower bound of the uncertainty with respect to the nominal values is known: a) chlorine decay rate has 10% maximum uncertainty, b) average daily nodal water consumption has 10% maximum uncertainty, c) nodal water consumption each time step has 10% maximum uncertainty, d) pipe roughness coefficients have 3% maximum uncertainty.

The parameter set $\mathcal{P}$ is comprised of all the parameter combinations. We construct a finite set $\mathcal{P}_0 \subset \mathcal{P}$ of $n = 50$ parameter sets, by simulating 20 'days' of the water distribution system operation when there are no faults, for each element in $\mathcal{P}_0$ and with a 5-minute water quality sampling time. The last 14 'days' of the simulation are considered, such that $K = \{1441, ..., 5472\}$, and for 2-day periodicity, $T = 576$ is the number of samples in one period. The outcome of the simulations is, for the l-th parameter set and for the i-th node with a chlorine concentration sensor, a time series corresponding to the estimated chlorine concentration $y_i(k; p^l)$ for the period $k \in K$. Thus, by using (3), we compute the periodic upper and lower bounds as the maximum and lower concentration values respectively of chlorine at a certain node and at a certain time. For the fault detection logic, an $h = 3$ discrete time delay, corresponding to 15 minutes, is considered.

To evaluate the effectiveness of the upper and lower periodic bounds in detecting contamination events with the minimum number of false positives, we consider the case of arsenite contamination (As(III)), which may cause arsenic poisoning. Its reaction dynamics with chlorine residual have been presented in [29]. For demonstrating purposes and by neglecting the advection dynamics in (1), the reaction terms are described by $G_V(V, W) = -6.9444 \times 10^{-4} V - 0.9263\, VW$ and $G_W(V, W) = -0.9789\, VW$, where $V(t)$ is the chlorine concentration and $W(t)$ the arsenite concentration. In general the coefficients of the bilinear reaction term may depend on other parameters, such as pH, which may not be monitored on-line.

We construct a set of possible contamination scenarios to examine the contamination fault detection algorithm. Each contamination scenario is a 2-tuple of an attack-location node and an injection time. Therefore, for 129 possible attack location nodes and 288 possible injection times within a day (considering a 5-minute time step), we construct 37152 scenarios. Through simulation we assign an impact damage metric for each contamination scenario, such as the volume of contaminated water consumed until the contamination was detected at one of the five monitored sensors. Based on the impact metrics computed, we construct a set of the 10% worst-case contamination fault scenarios, comprised of 3715 scenarios. These worst-case scenarios correspond to contaminations occurring in 27 different nodes in the network. To illustrate how well the proposed detection scheme detects extreme contamination events, we simulate a single constant contaminant injection at one of the 27 nodes, starting at 8 am of the 5-th simulated day. An alarm is triggered when the monitored chlorine concentration is outside the bounds for more than 15 minutes.

Figure 2 depicts the change of chlorine concentration at node '17' during normal circumstances and during an arsenite contamination attack at node '26' (see Figure 1). The upper figure demonstrates that the chlorine concentration in the within the upper and lower bounds computed. On the contrary, the lower figure demonstrates that the chlorine concentration is reduced below the bounds, due to the reaction of arsenite with chlorine. It is important to note that, if fixed detection thresholds had been considered, e.g., raising an alarm when chlorine penetration was below $0.2\ \frac{mg}{L}$, it would require more hours to detect the contamination occurrence by simply monitor node '17'.

Table 1 summarizes the results for contamination detection with respect to the 27 worst-case contamination scenarios and for various contaminant concentrations at the source location. The results provide the number of true detections, the number of missed detections and the average detection time. In general, detection time depends on the propagation path and the distance between the source location and the water quality sensors, as well as the contaminant concentration and the magnitude of the uncertainty bounds considered.

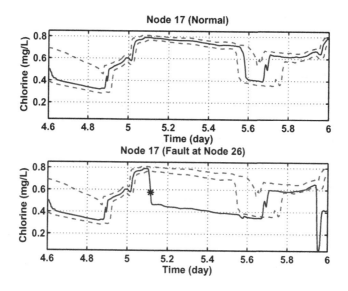

Fig. 2. Chlorine concentration at sensor node '17' during normal conditions and during a contamination attack with arsenic (0.5 $\frac{mg}{L}$ at node '26' at day 5). The star-shaped pointer indicates the instance when the fault alarm is triggered. The dashed lines correspond to the upper and lower periodic bounds.

Table 1. Detection results for the 27 worst-case contamination faults, for various contaminant concentrations

Contam. Conc. (mg/L)	True Detections	Missed Detections	Aver. Det. Time (hours)
0.1	16	11	2.1
0.2	18	9	3.1
0.5	22	5	4.2
0.7	23	4	2.3
1.0	24	3	2.3

In summary, as the contaminant concentration increases, the number of true detections is increased as well. In specific, for 0.1 $\frac{mg}{L}$ contaminant concentration injected, 16 out of the 27 contamination faults were detected, and 11 contamination faults were missed. For 0.5 $\frac{mg}{L}$, 22 out of the 27 contamination faults were detected and 5 contamination faults were missed. Finally, for 1.0 $\frac{mg}{L}$, contaminant concentration injected, 24 out of the 27 contamination faults were detected.

In general the larger the contaminant concentration, the faster the detection time. However, for the concentrations between 0.1 − 0.5 $\frac{mg}{L}$, the average detection time is increasing. This is because as the contaminant concentration increases, the effect on chlorine is increasing and the chlorine concentration will begin to approach the upper or lower bound and eventually, some contamination faults will be detected. However, if the contaminant concentration is larger, more contamination faults will cause chlorine concentrations to pass the upper and lower bounds at an earlier time.

5 Conclusions

In this work we have presented a contamination detection methodology in water distribution networks. The proposed detection method was based on chlorine sensor measurements in relation to certain upper and lower bounds. The bounds were computed using randomized simulations aimed at capturing the variations in chlorine concentration due to the significant variability in the water demand patterns, average nodal consumptions, roughness parameters and reaction coefficients. The proposed method was applied to a set of high-impact contamination fault scenarios using a benchmark distribution network with chlorine concentration sensors installed following an optimization procedure. The results indicated that by using the upper and lower periodic bounds computed from the randomized simulations, for the proposed benchmark, events were detected within reasonable time. In future work we will apply the proposed methodology on real water quality data. In addition, we will utilize adaptive bounds to capture changes in the water quality signal periodicity, enhance fault detection by using surrogate water quality measurements and apply sensor fusion to exploit the spatial-temporal water quality characteristics, as well as to implement algorithms for learning the unknown fault dynamics to isolate the contaminant type.

Acknowledgements. This research work has been funded by the Cyprus Research Promotion Foundation's Framework Programme for Research, Technological Development and Innovation, co-funded by the Republic of Cyprus and the European Regional Development Fund (New Infrastructure Project/Strategic/ 0308/26).

References

1. Critical infrastructure and key resources sector-specific plan as input to the national infrastructure protection plan. Tech. rep., US EPA & DHS (2007)
2. Guidelines for the Physical Security of Water Utilities (56-10) and Guidelines for the Physical Security of Wastewater/Stormwater Utilities (57-10). ASCE (2011)
3. Byer, D., Carlson, K.: Real time detection of intentional chemical contamination in the distribution system. Journal American Water Works Association 97(7), 12 (2005)
4. Cook, J.B., Byrne, J.F., Daamen, R.C., Edwin, A., Roehl, J.: Distribution system monitoring research at charleston water system. In: Proc. ASCE Water Distribution Systems Analysis, p. 20 (2006)
5. Eliades, D., Polycarpou, M.: A fault diagnosis and security framework for water systems. IEEE Transactions on Control Systems Technology 18(6), 1254–1265 (2010)

6. European Commission: Council Directive 98/83/EC of 3 November 1998 on the quality of water intended for human consumption. Official Journal of the European Communities (December 1998)
7. European Commission: Critical infrastructure protection in the fight against terrorism (October 2004), COM(2004) 702 final
8. Foran, J., Brosnan, T.: Early warning systems for hazardous biological agents in potable water. Environmental Health Perspectives 108(10), 993–995 (2000)
9. Hall, J., Zaffiro, A.D., Marx, R.B., Kefauver, P.C., Krishnan, E.R., Haught, R.C., Herrmann, J.G.: On-line water quality parameters as indicators of distribution system contamination. Journal American Water Works Association 99(1), 66–77 (2007)
10. Hart, D., McKenna, S.: User's Manual For CANARY. National Security Applications Dept., Sandia National Laboratories, Albuquerque, NM, USA, 4.3.1 edn. (September 2011), ePA 600/R-08/040B
11. Helbling, D.E., VanBriesen, J.M.: Modeling residual chlorine response to a microbial contamination event in drinking water distribution systems. ASCE Journal of Environmental Engineering 135(10), 918–927 (2009)
12. Hrudey, S., Huck, P., Payment, P., Gillham, R., Hrudey, E.: Walkerton: Lessons learned in comparison with waterborne outbreaks in the developed world. Journal of Environmental Engineering and Science 1(6), 397–407 (2002)
13. Jarrett, R., Robinson, G., O'Halloran, R.: On-line monitoring of water distribution systems: Data processing and anomaly detection. In: Proc. ASCE Water Distribution Systems Analysis, Cincinnati, Ohio, p. 14 (2006)
14. Jonkergouw, P.M.R., Khu, S.T., Savic, D.: Chlorine: A possible indicator of intentional chemical and biological contamination in a water distribution network? In: Proc. of IWA Conference on Automation in Water Quality Monitoring (AutMoNet), Vienna, Austria, p. 8 (2004)
15. Klise, K.A., McKenna, S.A.: Multivariate applications for detecting anomalous water quality. In: Proc. ASCE Water Distribution Systems Analysis, p. 11 (2006)
16. Koch, M.W., McKenna, S.A.: Distributed sensor fusion in water quality event detection. ASCE Journal of Water Resources Planning and Management 137(10), 10–19 (2011)
17. Krause, A., Leskovec, J., Guestrin, C., VanBriesen, J., Faloutsos, C.: Efficient sensor placement optimization for securing large water distribution networks. ASCE Journal of Water Resources Planning and Management 134(6), 516–526 (2008)
18. Kroll, D., King, K.: Laboratory and flow loop validation and testing of the operational effectiveness of an on-line security platform for the water distribution system. In: Proc. ASCE Water Distribution Systems Analysis, Cincinnati, Ohio, p. 16 (2006)
19. LeVeque, R.: Nonlinear conservation laws and finite volume methods. In: Steiner, O., Gautschy, A. (eds.) Computational Methods for Astrophysical Fluid Flow, pp. 1–160. Springer, Berlin (1998)
20. McKenna, S.A., Wilson, M., Klise, K.A.: Detecting changes in water quality data. Journal American Water Works Association 100(1), 74–85 (2008)
21. Murray, R., Haxton, T., Janke, R., Hart, W.E., Berry, J., Phillips, C.: Sensor Network Design for Drinking Water Contamination Warning Systems: A Compendium of Research Results and Case Studies Using the TEVA-SPOT Software. In: EPA (2010)
22. Murray, S., Ghazali, M., McBean, E.A.: Real-time water quality monitoring: Assessment of multisensor data using bayesian belief networks. ASCE Journal of Water Resources Planning and Management 138(1), 63–70 (2012)

23. Ostfeld, A., Uber, J.G., Salomons, E., Berry, J.W., Hart, W.E., Phillips, C.A., Watson, J.P., Dorini, G., Jonkergouw, P., Kapelan, Z., di Pierro, F., Khu, S.T., Savic, D., Eliades, D., Polycarpou, M., Ghimire, S.R., Barkdoll, B.D., Gueli, R., Huang, J.J., McBean, E.A., James, W., Krause, A., Leskovec, J., Isovitsch, S., Xu, J., Guestrin, C., VanBriesen, J., Small, M., Fischbeck, P., Preis, A., Propato, M., Piller, O., Trachtman, G.B., Wu, Z.Y., Walski, T.: The battle of the water sensor networks (BWSN): A design challenge for engineers and algorithms. ASCE Journal of Water Resources Planning and Management 134(6), 556–568 (2008)

24. Pasha, M.F.K., Lansey, K.: Effect of parameter uncertainty on water quality predictions in distribution systems-case study. IWA Journal of Hydroinformatics 12(1), 1–21 (2010)

25. Polycarpou, M., Uber, J., Wang, Z., Shang, F., Brdys, M.: Feedback control of water quality. IEEE Control Systems Magazine 22(3), 68–87 (2002)

26. Raciti, M., Cucurull, J., Nadjm-Tehrani, S.: Anomaly detection in water management systems. In: Lopez, J., Setola, R., Wolthusen, S.D. (eds.) Critical Infrastructure Protection. LNCS, vol. 7130, pp. 98–119. Springer, Heidelberg (2012)

27. Rossman, L.A.: EPANET 2 Users manual. National Risk Management Research Laboratory, Office of Research and Development, U.S. Environmental Protection Agency, Cincinnati, OH (September 2000)

28. Shang, F., Uber, J.G., Rossman, L.A.: EPANET Multi-Species Extension User's Manual. National Risk Management Research Laboratory, Office of Research and Development, U.S. Enviromental Protection Agency, Cincinnati, OH 45268 (January 2008), EPA/600/S-07/021

29. Umberg, K.A.: Performance Evaluation of Real-time Event Detection Algorithms. Master's thesis, University of Cincinnati (2006)

30. U.S. Government: National primary drinking water regulations - Title 40, Code of federal regulations, Part 141 - Enviromental Protection Agency (EPA) (2002)

31. Yang, Y.J., Haught, R.C., Goodrich, J.A.: Real-time contaminant detection and classification in a drinking water pipe using conventional water quality sensors: Techniques and experimental results. Journal of Environmental Management 90(8), 2494–2506 (2009)

Collaboration between Competing Mobile Network Operators to Improve CIIP

Peter Schoo[1], Manfred Schäfer[2], André Egners[3], Hans Hofinger[1],
Sascha Wessel[1], Marian Kuehnel[3], Sascha Todt[1], and Michael Montag[2]

[1] Fraunhofer AISEC, Garching near Munich, Germany
`firstname.lastname@aisec.fraunhofer.de`
[2] Nokia Siemens Networks Management International GmbH, Munich, Germany
`firstname.lastname@nsn.com`
[3] RWTH Aachen University, UMIC Research Centre, Aachen, Germany
`lastname@umic.rwth-aachen.de`

Abstract. Mobile Network Operators (MNOs) deploy a vital part of today's Critical Information Infrastructures (CII). Protection of these CIIs shall ensure operational continuity despite of the potential loss of system integrity and malware attacks. Sharing information about security related incidents allows MNOs to better react to attacks and anomalies, and to mitigate the impact of the observed phenomena. The fear to risk its reputation may hinder an MNO to share information that could help other MNOs to improve their protection and assure operational continuity. The contributions of this paper are technical solutions for collaboration between competing MNOs, which prevent loss of reputation and thus improve the acceptance to share information.

Keywords: CIIP, Collaboration, Information Sharing, Mobile Communications, Malware, Integrity Protection, User Equipment.

1 Introduction

Networks deployed by MNOs for mobile communications turned out to be a vital part of the CII of societies to date. These infrastructures are almost ubiquitous, highly reliable, increasingly usable at lower cost and allow interworking between MNOs. The networks allow handling a rich variety of heterogeneous technologies concerning the user device, the information media exchangeable, the Network Element (NE) products that can be deployed thanks to common standardization efforts in this industry. These properties make mobile communications technically and economically attractive as CII – although they have never been designed for it. Already to date, mobile communication has an essential role in supporting CI.

There are two trends observable [9], which make the protection of these networks an increasing challenge. First, mobile network devices needed to operate such infrastructures are getting cheaper; advanced and required technologies, like e.g. Home or Relay Nodes, are radio network devices closer to users than ever

B. Hämmerli, N. Kalstad Svendsen, and J. Lopez (Eds.): CRITIS 2012, LNCS 7722, pp. 215–227, 2013.
© Springer-Verlag Berlin Heidelberg 2013

before. Technically, this not only improves coverage, but also allows more than ever physical access to such infrastructure devices. Second, end user devices or User Equipments (UEs), especially attractive smartphones, are not sufficiently protected these days. This not only raise threats and risks to end users, but also to operators concerning the proper and integrity assured operation of their network infrastructures.

It is acknowledged that these CII are built according to a set of 3GPP standards. Similarities between these networks, made out of NEs, interworking interfaces and device portfolios, establish a common concern to exchange information between MNOs. Information exchange about situational risks and threats or actual attacks, is assumed to help MNOs to improve the protection of their networks. However, MNOs may be reluctant to share information as they compete and may fear to risk their reputation or risk a competitive disadvantage.

The ASMONIA project[1] addresses this situation and focuses on the detection of threats caused by the loss of integrity on UEs and NEs and the spreading of malware, which can create a negative effect on operations continuity of such CII. One of the key contributions of the project is the proposal of technical solutions for collaboration between competing MNOs, which prevent loss of reputation and thus improves the acceptance to share information.

Section 2 presents from a top perspective addressed use cases and the architecture of an ASMONIA Collaboration Network (ACN) that needs to conform with latest 3GPP standards. Integrity protection of NEs and UEs are discussed in Section 3 while malware related risks are presented and discussed in Section 4. Both serve as a kind of sensors for the shared information. The reputation loss preventing collaborative procedures for information sharing are presented in Section 5. Information sharing, to improve the CIIP, is basically not a new idea and hence in Section 6, related work concerning collaborative information sharing is discussed, before we take our conclusions.

This paper focuses on integrity protection, mobile malware and information sharing procedures. However, the ASMONIA project encompasses also further research and technology assessment, e.g. creation of and sharing input for situational awareness across different MNO organizations and the use of cloud computing technology to improve the operations of mobile communications in exceptional situations.

2   Use Cases and Architecture

The collaboration network solution of ASMONIA supports typical use cases of information sharing and collaboration between MNOs like:

Collaborative Attack Mitigation: A new autonomously spreading worm infects specific Smartphone across the administrative domains of different MNOs. Finally, the infected end devices form a botnet capable of taking

---

[1] http://www.asmonia.de, project term Sept 2010 – May 2013.

down the service of an operator by a Distributed Denial of Service (DDoS) attack [20].

The first operator detecting integrity protection events and analysing the new malware shares his insights with other operators. When the DDoS starts, all MNOs collaborate on mitigating the attack by sharing security status information and resources within the ACN.

Supporting a Global Early Warning System (EWS): An organization or authority operating an EWS (maintaining a global security status) is interested in collecting information about security incidents from MNOs, processing them, and making its conclusions available for participating MNOs.

Managing the ACN: Adding or removing ACN participants, setting up security associations between participants, and other management tasks.

The proposed ACN solution is a network of partners collaborating on network security concerns. Their objective is to improve their insights into the actual (local and global) security status and to increase the options to react. A partner can be a MNO or any service provider. The infrastructure of a partner's administrative domain is called the partners Operator Network (ON).

The collaboration is based on capabilities to share information (sensor data and analytical results) as well as storage and computing resources. The ACN framework defines concepts, procedures, protocols, data representations, interfaces, and functional components, which provide the technological foundation for the collaboration network.

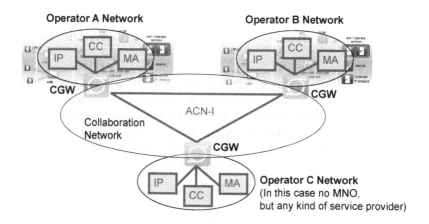

Fig. 1. Collaboration Network Components

Figure 1 provides an overview of an ACN, its main concepts, and the connections between the participating partners. Every partner runs a Collaboration Gateway (CGW) which provides all functionality needed to participate in the ACN. The CGW is the dedicated point of contact for other partners to the ON of the corresponding partner and the gateway between this ON and the ACN.

It is the border between the private ON, where the operator has full control, and the external ACN, where his control is limited. The external interface of the CGWs towards the ACN, resp. towards other CGWs is the ACN-Interface (ACN-I). CGW and ACN-I provide the functionality required for collaboration on the basis of sharing resources and information and for managing the ACN. The ACN comprises all participating CGWs and the ACN-I.

For enabling collaboration and integrating the infrastructure of a partner, each ON has to include Functional Cluster (FC) components. A FC implements a specific collaboration capability, which is a set of functionalities and interfaces related to a specific aspect of the collaboration. Following FCs are defined:

Integrity Protection (FC IP): Enables collaboration with respect to SW integrity. ACN emphasizes the importance of SW integrity protection by making related events and their processing a first class collaboration capability.

Collaborative Cloud (FC CC): Enables sharing of storage and computing resources, particularly by utilizing Cloud based technology. This is a very essential collaboration capability, however, it is not in the scope of this paper.

Monitoring and Analysis (FC MA): Enables to collect, provide, access and process (sensor) information and collaboration w.r.t. security analysis.

Not every ON has to support all FCs. Depending on the role and type of a partner in the ACN, not all collaboration capabilities may be needed. E.g., a partner only providing a Cloud resource for the collaboration network may only need to support FC CC. In specific cases it may even be sufficient to reduce the CGW to just an implementation of the ACN-I interface or even only parts of it.

3   Network Elements and End User Devices Integrity

Integrity protection is one approach to ensure the security of devices used within the Asmonia project. The main idea is to have a whitelist of trusted SW and data and to forbid access to untrusted content, especially the execution of untrusted executables. While the loss of integrity can be reported to a remote entity, the integrity measurement is typically enforced on the device itself, which requires local modifications. In this context, we have to distinguish between UEs and NEs. While NEs are usually owned and fully controlled by the MNO, this is usual not the case for UEs.

3.1   Integrity Protection of Network Elements

Regarding NE in 4G access, network security requirements exist from 3GPP SA3 ([1,2], for eNB, HeNB), implying SW integrity, authenticity, and involving trustworthy boot processes as a foundation for trusted execution environments. 3GPP focuses on co-operability and compatibility aspects, intending not to determine implementation details. Moreover, no security requirements exist for the run-time, assuring that a system withstands attacks against its integrity during long-lasting operation. In Asmonia related improvements and realization aspects have been examined, while extending 3GPP expectations accordingly and with a focused view on prevention of unauthorized system influences [9]. Applicable and harmonized methods have been important design objectives, as to provide extensible and adaptable solutions for a wider group of SW products and several use cases for integrity protection.

End-to-end integrity assurance based on signatures and vendor driven PKI governance is seen to have significant advantages over concepts relying on PGP-like key management or on pure hash values [10,17]. In particular the latter do not scale well and natively do not support self-defense capabilities or autonomous decisions (as particularly required for HeNBs). Both are much more difficult to manage, to validate, and require additional administrative security to impede man-in-the-middle attacks at system and network level. Another reason for preferring end-to-end integrity concepts lies in the operational model and the responsibility for dependability and security of NEs, which to a large extent behoves to vendors (manufacturers) that have to deliver trustworthy HW and in particular SW, including secure updates over an entire product life cycle. While such model advises vendor control and authenticity of SW (authorized during development and test processes) for specific target systems, the operator may also have obligations, for example maintenance control over installed SW versions or individual configurations. While not impeding this, protection concepts based on (vendor) PKIs reduce administrative security in the mobile network, and thus are well suited to minimize efforts and proprietary extensions in the highly standardized operator infrastructure, but allow integration of required components and methods into the product space.

The developed methods concentrate on realization aspects and on applicability to a variety of products and use cases, including SW delivery, SW storing, SW installation, run-time protection and secure boot concepts. Preferably they are based on same foundation of security (e.g., root CA certificates, signing certificates, and signed objects). While self-protection and autonomy have been important security objectives, generation and aggregation of messages in case of detected integrity violations is supported as well, so that expressive input can be given to relevant components of the ACN, in order to collect, assess, process, and share security information in a collaborative manner.

Although PKI based paradigms are preferred for NEs , there is no supporting HW available - which may raise specific efforts for proper implementation of validation concepts. However, also solutions based on TPMs [19] suffer from implementation weaknesses [13,22,10,11], and regarding attacks against trustworthy boot processes, the achievable security level depends on board-level implementation aspects. Moreover, functional limitations (addressing boot processes), temperature-range constraints, and CPU and chip set dependencies restrict applicability of PC security hardware for NEs, where selection criteria for security concepts and CPU families may not primarily depend on availability of COTS security components.

Integrity protection for NEs essentially rely on tailored mechanisms for secure boot, event triggered file-based SW integrity protection, and combined use of virtualization layers and hardening concepts for secure implementation of integrity checking during run-time [11]. To support secure boot principles a PKI controlled HW concept has been developed enabling self-validation and authorized updates of programmable memory content. It protects secrets, firmware, and validation data, and it serves as foundation of trust for integrity validation not only during the boot process, but also during installation and run-time. While such HW may be widely independent from an operating system, the elaborated run-time protection mechanisms are tailored for integration into Linux systems (as often used for NEs), and use the Network File System and KVM/QEMU as preferred virtualization solutions.

3.2   Integrity Protection of User Equipment

UEs are usually not the property of the MNO. For example, Machine-2-Machine (M2M) devices are the property of the operating company, and smartphones are the property of end users. However, smartphones are of increasing interest to MNOs because of their rapidly growing install base and because of the increasing risk of mobile malware (Section 4). While enforcing integrity protection on all UEs is not achievable for MNOs today, the integrity of selected mobile application can certainly be protected.

One key application for the integrity protection of separate applications on Smartphones (e.g. for payment) is the isolation of *normal* applications and *secure* applications. Depending on the expected security level, this can be achieved using an additional virtualization layer or directly in the operating system. We are using the L4 microkernel respectively Linux Containers for this purpose. The second key component is the integrity measurement itself beginning with the trust anchor up to the continuous measurement at runtime. While today's Smartphones usually offer a ROM-based Core Root of Trust for Measurement (CRTM), this is only utilizable by the manufacturer of the device. Therefore, we implemented a software-based trust anchor for ARM application processors. For runtime integrity protection we are using the mechanism proposed in [21]. In contrast to NEs, battery-constrained devices like Smartphones need special attention concerning power consumption and performance impact. This is especially true for runtime integrity protection mechanisms that provide better protection than boot-time mechanisms, but can introduce measurable overhead.

4   Detecting Mobile Malware

The growing trend of UEs becoming more powerful, more complex, and therefore more prone to flaws and security gaps is inevitable. As on desktop computers in the past, the most serious security threat for mobile devices are malwares. A malware defrauds users into installing a malicious application and thereby gains unauthorized privileges. These malicious applications are not necessarily downloaded from third party markets, but can also be found in official markets[2]. In particular, malware can turn UEs into instances awaiting attacker's commands called bots [3]. Although large networks of bots have not been detected yet, there have been indications of malware offering the necessary functionality. Mobile devices offer an always-on connection which is critical for steady availability. Once a mobile botnet is sufficiently large, it may endanger the mobile network itself. Therefore, the challenging task of countering the malware has become essential in all modern mobile network infrastructures [20].

Recent rise of malware targeting UEs has encouraged security researchers to invent novel approaches. In terms of the ASMONIA system architecture we follow a dual approach: UE centric anomaly detection and network centric malicious traffic detection caused by malware in the 4G infrastructure of the respective MNO. The anomaly detection relies on the logical coherence of system calls of processes or applications. Recorded system call sequences are transformed such that the individual system call numbers represent the input sequence for a Hidden Markov Model [18] training process. A benign system call sequence has to be recorded and used to train the model for the individual application. During runtime of the application, a sampled sequence can be compared to its known benign behavior. This enables to decide how likely the sequence has been generated by the model representing the benign behavior. Online detection of malicious behavior is also possible.

On the other hand, two types of sensors directly analyze 4G traffic in the MNO's infrastructure. Passive honeypots are well-known in non-mobile networks and represent independent security monitoring units designed to trap malware samples. A low interaction client honeypot runs a set of simulated services indistinguishable from real services. Since the low-interaction honeypots are passive and do not await incoming traffic, each new connection is assumed an attack vector and analyzed further. The honeypot records the attacker's steps, such that a security expert can reconstruct the attack vector. Consecutive identification, classification or clustering identify more specific properties of the sample w.r.t. known malware families. The more specific information the honeypot obtains from each sample, the higher the value for other defensive mechanisms and the collaborative information exchange.

In the mobile network, we not only observe malware related to the prior era of Internet, but also malware families threatening the mobile functionalities introduced in the 3GPP specifications. McAfee reports a significant increase of mobile malware up to 1200% in the first quarter of 2012 [6]. The main advantage of using 3GPP services in mobile malware is the fact that average users do not turn them off. Even if the mobile device is off for a period of time, all information are stored in the MNO's database and will be delivered as soon as the device establishes a connection to the MNO infrastructure. Therefore, our active sensors examine PDUs and parse content at the MNO's gateway. In case, the MNO does not learn any semantic information, strings of fixed length are hashed and compared with hashed strings of previously captured malicious strings.

---

[2] `play.google.com/store` or `www.apple.com/iphone/from-the-app-store`

While anomaly detection tries to model normal or benign behavior, it is rarely the case that the scope of meaningful models is known beforehand. It is required to train a model with a complete set of recorded trace files, i.e., with the behavior of all processes that were active during monitoring. Experiments indicated that these models have poor discrimination capabilities. Alternatively a bottom-up approach can be used, such that models for individual processes are created. In a next step, the models can be broadened to create models representing the behavior of a certain subset of the entire system behavior.

Passive and active sensors are more resilient and have lower false positive rates than anomaly detection. However, many new emerging mobile malware families complicate the classification and clustering process and the extraction of typical patterns reflecting its origin and purpose is very inefficient. Mechanism such as the anomaly detection approach can profit from the broad user base of mobile operators. Sharing information about the captured samples, as well as improving the modeling quality are important aspects considered for collaboration between operators. Besides the aforementioned quantities, active sensors are interesting for collaborative information exchange in context of ASMONIA providing type and frequency of attacks. Passive sensors obtain numbers and contents of phishing and scam messages and provide publicly available and readable lists of misused numbers for MNOs and their regular users.

5   Collaborative Procedures for Information Sharing

Collaboration, especially between competitors, comes along with a number of concerns regarding loss of privacy or reputation and thus competitive disadvantages. In Section 2, we depicted a general concept and architecture of an ACN, for collaboration in Mobile Communication Networks. Next we depict requirements that need to be fulfilled and which technical components are combined to build two major applications for an ACN.

Although some of the requirements listed in Table 1 seem to be conflicting (e.g. anonymity and non-repudiation) we have identified specific components to fulfill all mentioned requirements, even for ACNs with a very weak level of trust:

- Traceable Anonymous Certificates (TACs) [15]
- Anonymous Peer-to-Peer Overlay Networks, such as GNUnet incl. gap [4]
- Secure Multiparty Computation (MPC) frameworks, such as SEPIA [7]
- A standard for data exchange, such as IODEF [8]

Table 1 summarizes the requirements fulfilled by each component.

Brunner et al. [5] discuss the usage of TACs and P2P Overlay Networks to achieve anonymous and privacy-preserving information sharing for IT early warning systems. However, they focus on a high-level concept for information sharing, without going into details of the concrete procedures and the required protocols. They also mention the usage of MPC for IT early warning as a future research activity but do not discuss in detail its application in this area. ASMONIA examines the combination of the three proposed components TACs, GNUnet and

Table 1. Requirements for collaboration and components to fulfill them

	TAC	P2P	MPC	Data Format
Anonymity	x	x		
Privacy			x	
Non-repudiation	x			
Interoperability				x
Resilience		x		
Authentication (Data and Users)	x			
Integrity	x			
Confidentiality	x			
Fairness		x	x	

MPC extended by a common data exchange format and develops protocols for the two most important applications in an ACN, i.e., the sharing of warnings between participants as well as the sharing of data for collaborative detection and analysis of incidents.

Sharing of warnings can be done by distributing attack information either between single participants or by broadcasting them to an ACN. In the latter case the participants of the ACN receiving such warnings decide on their own if the information is relevant for them and how it is further processed. Prerequisite for an effective and efficient sharing of warnings is a common data format such as IODEF [8] allowing automated processing. For the distribution of warnings we create a closed user group as basis for the ACN using a full-meshed Virtual Private Network (VPN) between the participants based on X.509 certificates ensuring authentication, integrity, and confidentiality of the exchanged information. Building up a VPN based on authentication via certificates and signing the warnings assures the exclusiveness of the ACN as well as legitimacy and integrity of the warnings. However, participants may not want to be identified as the originator of a warning created and signed by them since they fear loss of reputation when revealing that their network is attacked. Here, TACs provide authenticity, non-repudiation and anonymity at the same time and furthermore allows to trace the real identity of a participant, e.g., in case of abusing the ACN. The TACs are issued by a CA trusted by all participants of an ACN and can therefore be used for signing warnings like regular X.509 certificates. To impede inference attacks all participants of the ACN shall be equipped with multiple TACs or the TACs of all participants shall be replaced with new ones on a regular basis. To avoid revealing the real identity of a participant based on the source IP address of a warning, the ACN should implement another layer of anonymization such as Onion Routing or anonymous P2P Overlay Networks. GNUnet and its gap provide such an anonymous P2P network by indirection of requests and responses over multiple nodes in the network. Thus, receiving a request or response from a specific node in the network does not imply that this node is the originator of this message.

A participant's real identity might be revealed by the content of a warning, too, which thus has to be sanitized carefully. Sanitizing a warning is a nontrivial task which is hard to be automated and should therefore be done manually by an expert. Due to the expected number of warnings this is assumed to be manageable. A warning should at least contain the following data: rather descriptive type and target of attack, e.g., OS, software version; impact and countermeasures, and references to related known vulnerabilities, e.g., CVE numbers.

Aggregating sensor data and attack information from multiple administrative domains using MPC techniques provides a larger data base for analysis than from one single source. The information required for this collaborative detection and analysis differs from that used for warnings distributed via the ACN: being unfiltered, information for MPC based processing must be converted into a MPC protocol specific format. For practical collaborative detection and analysis the participants providing their private input data furthermore need to agree on parameters to be shared.

Potential types of data for collaborative detection and analysis may include: malicious/suspicious IP addresses and URLs; entire netflows or scanned ports; (hashes of) malware binaries; or attack timestamps and properties or classes of attacked devices.

Although secret sharing based protocols, e.g., as used in SEPIA, provide privacy and fairness to the ACN participants, MPC normally does not fulfill other requirements as listed in Table 1. To cover these issues SEPIA provides an integrated P2P network based on SSL connections thereby fulfilling the requirements resilience, authentication, integrity and confidentiality.

6   Related Work for Collaborative Information Sharing

There are several approaches that address the challenges in collaborative information sharing, varying mostly in the privacy and infrastructure needs to be fulfilled within their anticipated application fields, i.e., operating environments, and among their participants. Examples for *collaborative security* are the implementation of collaborative, distributed intrusion detection systems across administrative domains by Locasto et al. [14] or DOMINO [23], which can provide a local and global view of intrusion and attack activity. Only the former addresses privacy issues but both do not take into account originator anonymity.

An approach for the sharing of information on IT-security relevant incidents is the ANL federated Model for Cyber Security [16] designed for multilateral privacy preserving information exchange among a closed user group. Nevertheless, originator anonymity is not addressed, too.

Within the centralized collaborative network CarmentiS [12] , the issue of originator anonymity is assured by pseudonymisation. However, results are accessible for the central instance only.

To control the distribution of sensitive information the NEISAS project, aiming at information sharing on CII within one and between different so called trust circles, makes extensive use of Information Rights Managements techniques; furthermore anonymous submission of content is possible. Within DEMONS, elements for network monitoring are not centralized but share their information with other elements in the own network and beyond; cross domain collaboration mechanisms, which respect customer's privacy rights, are to permit improved defense against global scale cooperative threats and operational failures.

ASMONIA follows a completely decentralized approach to improve resilience against attacks on the collaboration network by avoiding single points of failure. This approach also allows us to introduce mechanisms guaranteeing the originator anonymity of an attack report, thereby minimizing the risk of reputation loss for the participants. To the best of our knowledge only the DEMONS project plans to implement a completely decentralized architecture similar to the one proposed in ASMONIA.

7   Conclusions

The work presented here considers the communication infrastructures operated by MNOs as CII to be protected. The goal is operational continuity despite of the potential loss of integrity of NEs or UEs and despite of malware attacks. Integrity protection is more achievable in the mobile networks as MNOs and supporting vendors have a command on this CII, and less easily for the end user equipment. Risk avoidance has thus clear limitations.

Sharing information of security related incidents allows MNOs to better react to attacks and anomalies and to mitigate the impact of the observed phenomena. The fear to risk its reputation may hinder an MNO to frankly share information that could help other MNOs to improve their operational continuity. We present two significant ACN applications as a technical approach overcoming such a challenge.

The project proposes a technical solution for the collaboration between competing MNOs in one ACN. The demonstrations and prototypes that are prepared during the project will allow to validate the technical feasibility of some parts of the approach. This validation will be completed by additional simulations and advanced threat and risk investigations. The use of a set of different assessment instruments in the project and the involvement of associated partners concerned are planned to complete teh project results.

Certainly, there are also non-technical, company strategic, and legal barriers for deployment. However, economic profits and security improvements emerging from information sharing will motivate MNOs to collaborate. In addition, future regulations (as currently discussed at European level) even may *require* operators to closer work together.

The contribution of ongoing ASMONIA project presented here is not only to follow a decentralized approach, but also to apply it to scenarios in which competing parties are reluctant to share information. Although the technical approach addresses the scenario of competing operators, we think that these collaboration procedures can as well be applied to support collaboration between departments of one organization or enterprise.

Acknowledgement. This project has been partially funded by the German Federal Ministry of Education and Research under the references 01BY1010 - 01BY1015. The authors like to thank all their colleagues in the project that participated in work directly or indirectly for their collaborations and discussions. Our thank goes also to Sathyanarayanan Rangarajan for the textual improvements.

References

1. 3GPP: Security of Home Node B (HNB) / Home evolved Node B (HeNB)
2. 3GPP: System Architecture Evolution (SAE); Security architecture
3. Apvrille, A., Yang, K.: Defeating mTANs for Profit - part one. Technical report, Virus Bulletin (March 2011)
4. Bennett, K., Grothoff, C.: GAP – Practical Anonymous Networking. In: Dingledine, R. (ed.) PET 2003. LNCS, vol. 2760, pp. 141–160. Springer, Heidelberg (2003)
5. Brunner, M., Hofinger, H., Roblee, C., Schoo, P., Todt, S.: Anonymity and Privacy in Distributed Early Warning Systems. In: Xenakis, C., Wolthusen, S. (eds.) CRITIS 2010. LNCS, vol. 6712, pp. 81–92. Springer, Heidelberg (2011)
6. Bu, Z., Dirro, T., Greve, P., Lin, Y., Marcus, D., Paget, F., Schmugar, C., Shah, J., Sommer, D., Szor, P., Wostowsky, A.: McAfee Threats Report: First Quarter 2012. Technical report, McAfee Labs (2012)
7. Burkhart, M., Strasser, M., Many, D., Dimitropoulos, X.A.: SEPIA: Privacy-Preserving Aggregation of Multi-Domain Network Events and Statistics. In: USENIX Security Symposium, pp. 223–240 (2010)
8. Danyliw, R., Meijer, J., Demchenko, Y.: The Incident Object Description Exchange Format (IODEF). RFC 5070 (Proposed Standard) (December 2007)
9. Egners, A., Rey, E., Schmidt, H., Schneider, P., Wessel, S.: Threat and Risk Analysis for Mobile Communication Networks and Mobile Terminals. Deliverable D5.1 (II), ASMONIA Projekt (March 2012)
10. Egners, A., Schäfer, M., Wessel, S.: Evaluating Methods to assure System Integrity and Requirements for Future Protection Concepts. Deliverable D2.1, ASMONIA Projekt (April 2011)
11. Egners, A., Schäfer, M., Wessel, S.: Protection Methods for Target Systems - 4G Network Elements and Smart Phones. Deliverable D2.2, ASMONIA Projekt (July 2012)
12. Kossakowski, K., Sander, J., Grobauer, B., Mehlau, J.I.: A German Early Warning Information System - Challenges and Approaches. Presentation at 18th Annual FIRST Conference (June 2006)
13. Kursawe, K., Schellekens, D., Preneel, B.: Analyzing trusted platform communication. In: ECRYPT Workshop, CRASH - CRyptographic Advances in Secure Hardware (2005)
14. Locasto, M., Parekh, J., Misra, V., Stolfo, S.: Collaborative Distributed Intrusion Detection. Technical report, Columbia University (2004)
15. Park, S., Park, H., Won, Y., Lee, J., Kent, S.: Traceable Anonymous Certificate. RFC 5636 (Experimental) (August 2009)
16. Pinkerton, S.: A Federated Model For Cyber Security. In: Cyberspace Research Workshop, Shreveport, LA (November 2007)
17. Schäfer, M., Moeller, W.D.: Tailored Concepts for Software Integrity Protection in Mobile Networks. International Journal On Advances in Security (numbers 1 and 2), 54 – 66 (September 2011)

18. Stratonovich, R.: Conditional Markov Processes. Theory of Probability and its Applications 5(2), 156–178 (1960)
19. TCG: TPM Main Specifications, Parts 1-3, Specification Version 1.2, Level 2, Revisions 103. Technical report, TCG (July 2007)
20. Traynor, P., Lin, M., Ongtang, M., Rao, V., Jaeger, T., McDaniel, P., La Porta, T.: On Cellular Botnets: Measuring the Impact of Malicious Devices on a Cellular Network Core. In: Proceedings of the 16th ACM Conference on Computer and Communications Security, CCS 2009, pp. 223–234. ACM, New York (2009)
21. Wessel, S., Stumpf, F.: Page-based Runtime Integrity Protection of User and Kernel Code. In: Proceedings of 5th European Workshop on System Security, EuroSec 2012. ACM Press (April 2012)
22. Winter, J., Dietrich, K.: A Hijacker's Guide to the LPC Bus. In: Petkova-Nikova, S., Pashalidis, A., Pernul, G. (eds.) EuroPKI 2011. LNCS, vol. 7163, pp. 176–193. Springer, Heidelberg (2012)
23. Yegneswaran, V., Barford, P., Jha, S.: Global Intrusion Detection in the DOMINO Overlay System. In: NDSS (2004)

AMICI: An Assessment Platform for Multi-domain Security Experimentation on Critical Infrastructures

Béla Genge, Christos Siaterlis, and Marc Hohenadel

Joint Research Centre, European Commission
Institute for the Protection and Security of the Citizen
Via E. Fermi, 2749, Ispra (VA), 21027, Italy
{bela.genge,christos.siaterlis,marc.hohenadel}@jrc.ec.europa.eu

Abstract. This paper presents AMICI, a new Assessment/analysis platform for Multiple Interdependent Critical Infrastructures (CIs). Its architecture builds on our previous work and uses Emulab to recreate ICT software and hardware components and Simulink to run the physical process models. Our previous framework is extended with software components to provide a set of capabilities that would enable the analysis of complex interdependencies between multiple CIs: flexible integration of multiple physical process models; opened architecture to enable interaction with ad-hoc software; support experimentation with real software/malware; automated experiment management capabilities. The applicability of the approach is proven through a case study involving three CIs: ICT, power grid and railway.

Keywords: Critical Infrastructure, security, experimentation, testbed.

1 Introduction

As shown by recent studies [1], today's Critical Infrastructures (CIs) are highly dependent of each other. In fact, in many cases relationships are bidirectional and the successful operation of one CI might depend on an entire chain of interdependent CIs. On top of that, modern CIs, e.g. power plants, water plants and smart grids, rely on Information and Communications Technologies (ICT) for their operation since ICT can lead to cost reduction, flexibility and interoperability between components. In the past CIs were isolated environments and used proprietary hardware and protocols, limiting thus the threats that could affect them. Nowadays, CIs are exposed to significant cyber-threats, as shown by recent events such as Stuxnet [2] and Flame [3].

The complexity and the need to understand these interdependent systems lead to the development of a wide range of approaches for analyzing interdependencies between CIs [4–6]. Although these can effectively model and analyze bidirectional relationships at a conceptual level, in practice the propagation of disturbances and their magnitude might depend on parameters that are difficult to model.

B. Hämmerli, N. Kalstad Svendsen, and J. Lopez (Eds.): CRITIS 2012, LNCS 7722, pp. 228–239, 2013.

This aspect is especially true in ICT, where it is a well-known fact that models might recreate normal operations, but they fail to capture the complexity of real components, e.g. complex interactions between heterogeneous software/malware and hardware [7].

Existing approaches for cyber security experimentation with CIs either focus on a specific CI [8–10], or they do not enable experimentation with real software/malware [11, 12], that nowadays is a fundamental requirement for conducting experiments with ICT infrastructure [13]. Based on these facts in this paper we propose a new approach for conducting multi-domain security experiments on CIs. The approach builds on the framework developed in our previous work [14, 15] and extends it with software modules in order to enable experimentation with more than one CI. The final framework, called *AMICI* (*Assessment/analysis platform for Multiple Interdependent Critical Infrastructures*), uses simulation for the physical components and an emulation testbed based on Emulab [16, 17] in order to recreate the cyber part of CIs, e.g. BGP routing protocols, SCADA (Supervisory Control And Data Acquisition) servers, corporate network. The use of simulation for the physical layer is a very reasonable approach due to small costs, the existence of accurate models and the ability to conduct experiments in a safe environment. The argument for using emulation for the cyber components is that the study of the security and resilience of computer networks would require the simulation of all the failure related functions, most of which are unknown in principle. The novelty of the proposed approach is that it brings together a wide range of functionalities, most of which are missing in related approaches [8–12]. These include flexible experimentation with multiple CIs, support of real software and malware, and automated experiment management capabilities. The *flexibility* and *real* functionalities are ensured through the use of real hardware, e.g. PCs, switches, routers, and real Operating Systems that can run generic software/malware together with typical network protocols. Lastly, the *automated* functionality is inherited from Emulab and includes a wide range of sub-functionalities such as experiment configuration, event scheduling, and Operating System (OS) image management [14, 15]. The approach is validated through a case study showing the interdependencies between three CIs: the power grid, the railway system and the ICT infrastructure.

The rest of the paper is structured as follows. A discussion on the requirements for the design of AMICI, together with the proposed architecture and implementation are detailed in Section 2. The approach is validated in Section 3 through a case study that includes a cyber attack on the ICT infrastructure and a disturbance on the power grid, which propagates to the railway system, causing an immediate stop of several trains. The paper concludes in Section 4.

2 Design and Architecture of AMICI

2.1 Design Requirements

Ideally, an experimentation framework for multi-domain security research would support the execution of complex, large scale and disruptive experiments using

Table 1. Required functionalities for multi-domain security experimentation

ID	Functionality
F_1	Support a wide range of physical process models, e.g. power systems, railway
F_2	Support multiple models in parallel and enable data exchange between them
F_3	Support typical ICT components, e.g. SCADA servers, PLCs, Modbus protocols
F_4	Support real software and malware
F_5	Support interaction of models with ad-hoc software
F_6	Support automated and multi-user experiment management

rigorous scientific methods. The implemented functionalities should not only support a wide range of physical processes, e.g. industrial systems, transportation, healthcare, but should also take into account the presence of ICT and specifically of SCADA components commonly used in the monitoring and control of physical processes. Such components include SCADA servers (Masters), PLCs (Programmable Logic Controllers) and typical industrial protocols such as Modbus. Besides these, today's experimentation frameworks should not be closed and should facilitate their extension together with the addition of other custom or even proprietary software. On top of these, an experimentation framework would also need to include capabilities that facilitate the experimentation process and would support concurrent users at the same time. These capabilities are specific to Internet experimentation testbeds and include a wide range of aspects such as control of the experiment's environment, experiment automation, and secure remote access. For a more detailed presentation on the requirements of an Internet security testbed the reader should consult our previous work [14, 18]. A summary of these requirements is also given in Table 1.

2.2   Overview of Our Previous Work

The framework developed in our previous work [14, 15] was specifically designed to enable experimentation with SCADA systems. It includes one simulation unit to run a model of the physical process and software components to emulate real PLCs and SCADA servers. Communications between the simulation and PLC emulator units are implemented through .NET's binary implementation of RPC/TCP, while communications between PLC and SCADA server emulators are implemented through Modbus/TCP.

The framework currently supports the execution of control code, i.e. emulated PLCs, running sequentially and in parallel to the physical process model. In the sequential case, a *tightly coupled code* (TCC) is used, i.e. code that is running in the same memory space with the model. In the parallel case a *loosely coupled code* (LCC) is used, i.e. code that is running in another address space, possibly on another host. For the physical process simulator we used Matlab Simulink, since it is a general simulation environment for dynamic and embedded systems and

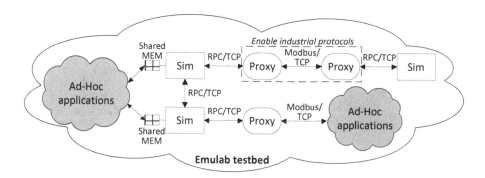

Fig. 1. Architecture of AMICI

covers a wide variety of physical processes, e.g. power plants, gas plants. From Simulink models the corresponding 'C' code is generated using Matlab Real Time Workshop and is integrated into the framework using an XML configuration file.

2.3 Extensions to Our Previous Work and Architecture of AMICI

The architecture of AMICI shown in Fig. 1 is an extension of the framework architecture proposed in our previous work [14, 15]. The main changes made in order to fulfill the previously stated requirements include: (i) addition of an RPC client module in the simulation unit (Sim) to enable communications with other Sim units; (ii) addition of a shared memory handler module in the Sim unit to enable exchange of data between the physical process model and ad-hoc software; and (iii) a new $Proxy$ unit that extends our previous PLC emulator with modules allowing it to translate Modbus to RPC and vice-versa. The architecture and its motivation for each unit are detailed in the remaining of this section.

Simulation Unit. The main role of the simulation unit (Sim) is to run the physical process model in real-time. This is done by coupling the model time to the system time in such a way to minimize the difference between the two. Models are constructed in Matlab Simulink from where the corresponding 'C' code is generated using Matlab Real Time Workshop. These are then integrated using an XML configuration file that is flexible enough so that researchers do not need to modify the code of AMICI. From the Sim unit's point of view each model is seen as a set of inputs and outputs. These are mapped to an internal memory region ($I/O MEM$) that is read/written by other software modules as well, e.g. TCCs, RPC. Compared to the previous version, the Sim unit allows an open access to its $I/O MEM$ by implementing OS level shared memory operations. This way, AMICI enables interaction with ad-hoc software that can write specific model inputs, i.e. OPEN/CLOSE a valve, and can read the status of the model, i.e. measured voltage. Interaction with other Sim units is enabled by implementing not only RPC server-side operations but client-side calls as well. By using only the XML configuration file, the Sim unit can be configured to

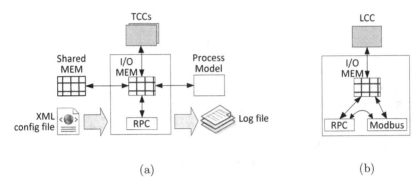

Fig. 2. Detailed architecture: (a) Simulation unit, and (b) Proxy unit

read/write inputs/outputs of models run by remote *Sim* units. These are mapped to the inputs/outputs of the model running locally, enabling this way complex interactions between models running in parallel on different hosts.

The *Sim* unit fulfills another important functionality that was previously handled by the SCADA master unit. In AMICI, SCADA server units are implemented as *Sim* units, where the global decision algorithm is the actual physical process model. As the *Sim* unit implements RPC and SCADA servers use industrial protocols, AMICI adopts the *Proxy* unit to map messages from RPC to Modbus and vice-versa. The architecture of the *Sim* unit is given in Fig. 2 (a).

Proxy Unit. The *Proxy* unit has several roles within AMICI. At the beginning, its main role was to enable running remote control code through the form of LCCs, enabling this way the integration of more complex PLC emulators. At the same time, it was used to handle Modbus calls coming from SCADA servers and transforming them to RPC calls that were finally sent to the *Sim* unit. AMICI keeps all these capabilities, but it enriches the protocol mapping capabilities of the *Proxy* unit in order to enable running industrial protocols between two *Sim* units. A more detailed architecture of the *Proxy* unit is given in Fig. 2 (b).

2.4   Real-Time Monitoring of Experiments

AMICI uses *Zabbix* [19], an open-source distributed network monitoring and visualization tool, to monitor experiments in real-time. It mainly consists of agents that are installed on the monitored nodes and servers that collect and store data from agents. Zabbix includes built-in monitoring of OS parameters, e.g. CPU, MEM, network traffic, but it also allows defining custom parameters. Such parameters are defined in the `zabbix_agentd.conf` file and have a unique ID that is used by the Zabbix server in the periodical pooling of agents. In AMICI the *Sim* unit writes the model input and output values for each execution step in a log file. From there, Zabbix agents extract specific parameters and send them to the Zabbix server.

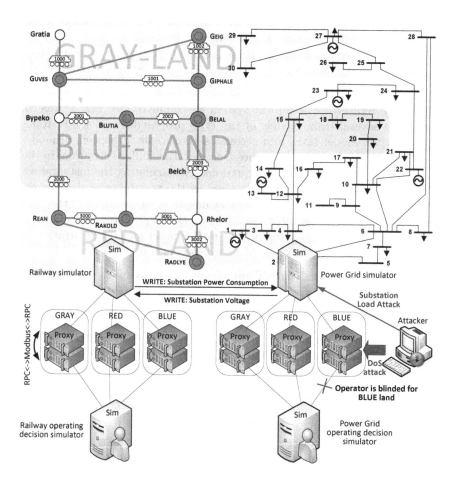

Fig. 3. Experiment setup

3   Case Study

In this section we use the AMICI framework to study the propagation of perturbations between three CIs: the power grid, the railway system and the ICT
infrastructure needed to monitor and control them. We show that the power grid
and railway system can be highly dependent of each other and in order to ensure
the stability of these two, the ICT infrastructure must be intact. We start with a
brief presentation of the experiment setup and scenario and then continue with
the analysis of the results.

3.1   Description of the Employed Critical Infrastructures

The Power Grid. The power grid employed in this experiment is the well-
known IEEE 30-bus model (see Fig. 3 for its graphical representation). It includes
6 generators and 30 substations that deliver power to connected loads through

transmission lines. For each substation there is a fixed load and a variable load. Fixed loads are needed to ensure the stability of the grid, while variable loads depend on the power consumed by trains running within the railway system. More specifically, we assume that each railway line, i.e. segment, is connected to one of the grid's substation.

The Railway System. The railway system we employed (see Fig. 3) was constructed from several train models of the type proposed by Ríos and Ramos in [20]. The train model takes into account several realistic aspects of modern transportation systems, e.g. weight, speed, acceleration and deceleration. In their paper, the authors also provide the equations for calculating the instantaneous power consumption of each train. This gives us the possibility to directly connect the output of the model, i.e. power consumption, to the input of the power grid model, i.e. load on each substation. Within this experiment we do not take into account traffic regulation algorithms, as our main focus is illustrating the applicability of AMICI in the study of interdependencies.

The ICT Infrastructure. The ICT infrastructure shown in Fig. 3 is responsible for the monitoring and control of the two infrastructures previously mentioned. For the power grid, the ICT infrastructure includes automated operational algorithms that can detect a change in substation voltage and can issue a command to start/stop backup generators. For the railway system operational algorithms can start/stop specific trains, but in reality there could also be traffic regulation algorithms running on the operator's side.

(Inter)Dependencies. As shown in Fig. 4, there can be several dependencies between the three CIs mentioned previously. First of all, it is clear that the railway system needs to be powered from the power grid. It is also clear that both the railway and the power grid need ICT control to ensure normal operation and that ICT infrastructures need to be powered from the power grid. What is particularly interesting, also depicted in Fig. 4, is that the railway system might have an undesirable effect on the normal operation of the power grid while the later one is subject to a heavy load. In such cases the power grid can be extremely sensitive to additional loads, i.e. starting trains, and if no additional measures are taken by operators, voltages can collapse, leading to other cascading failures. Another aspect highlighted in Fig. 4 is the ICT infrastructure that was split in two: the *Railway ICT* and the *Grid ICT*. Although separated, in reality physical links can be shared between the two, which means that there might be other dependencies that were not taken into account in this experiment.

3.2   Experiment Scenario

For the implemented scenario we defined three hypothetical regions that are common to the power grid and railway CIs (as shown in Fig. 3). These were named *GRAY-LAND*, *BLUE-LAND* and *RED-LAND*. Each substation included in each region powers one specific segment within the railway system. This means that in case voltages drop below an operating threshold, i.e. 0.95 p.u., trains will stop and operators will need to manually restart them. For each region we defined

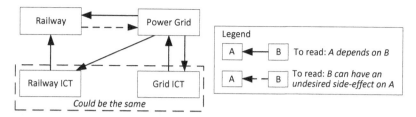

Fig. 4. Possible dependencies between three Critical Infrastructures

a set of ICT devices and one global operator for each of the two CIs, i.e. power grid and railway system.

The scenario involves an attacker that tries to stop trains running within the *BLUE-LAND* by issuing an attack in two phases. In the first phase the attacker runs a Denial of Service (DoS) against monitoring devices within the *BLUE-LAND* region, in order to inhibit any further data exchange between operators and the physical process. This completely blinds the operators that fail to receive any updates and to issue commands towards the *BLUE-LAND*. In the second phase the attacker breaks into the ICT infrastructure of substation 16 and issues remote commands to start all connected loads. This will lead to a sudden increase in the power demand that cannot be forecasted by automated algorithms. Because operators are completely blinded during the attack, they cannot intervene to start additional back-up generators. Consequently, the disturbance propagates to substations in *BLUE-LAND*, making voltages drop below their normal operating limit and cutting power from railway segments.

The scenario was implemented with the help of the AMICI framework and was tested within the Joint Research Centre's Experimental Platform for Internet Contingencies laboratory. The railway and power grid models were run by two separate *Sim* units and they exchanged data related to consumed power and voltage levels, as shown in Fig. 3. Operator decision units were also implemented as two separate *Sim* units. The experiment used the Modbus/TCP industrial protocol to transfer data between *Sim* units and a pair of *Proxy* units to map between RPC/TCP⟷Modbus/TCP messages for each region. The attacker code that increases the load at substation 16 was implemented as LCC code within a *Proxy* unit. The DoS attack was emulated by turning OFF network interfaces on the hosts running the *Proxy* units.

3.3 Experiment Execution and Analysis of Results

In a first step, the experiment architecture, including networks, PCs and OS, was described through an NS script. This was processed by Emulab that automatically allocated the required resources, it configured VLANs and IP addresses, and it loaded the OSs. Next, we configured the simulators and software components and launched the attack. The experiment employed real Modbus protocols, together with real OS software and real hardware to create a realistic ICT environment.

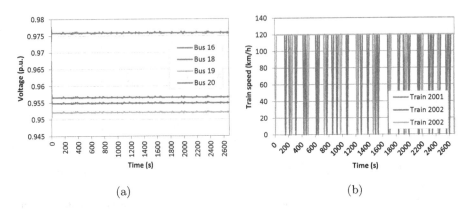

Fig. 5. Normal operation: (a) Power Grid, and (b) Railway System

Under normal operation the railway system is powered from the grid and operators can monitor and control in real time the two CIs. As shown in Fig. 5 (a), the level of voltages is directly influenced by the status of trains, i.e. running/stopped, that need to stop at each station and then start off again. Each time a train stops the power drawn from the grid drops to 0MW and increases back after it is started. A change in the load, i.e. in the status of trains shown in Fig. 5 (b), leads to small voltage fluctuations that do not affect the stability of the grid, but can be clearly seen in Fig. 5 (a).

Next, the attack is started on substation 16, where the attacker manages to start-up large consumers and to increase the load to 85MW. Due to interconnections and power flow properties of the power grid, the disturbance propagates to other three substations, i.e. 18, 19 and 20, that are responsible for powering trains in *BLUE-LAND* (see Fig. 6). Here, voltages drop below the operating limit of 0.95 p.u., causing a stop of trains powered by these substations. This clearly shows the side-effects behind strongly interconnected and interdependent systems such as the power grid together with the railway system. Furthermore, it also shows that the attacker does not need to take over substations directly powering train lines, but he can rely on physical properties and the propagation of disturbances to accomplish his goals.

This effect is also shown in Fig. 7, where the start of the attack is marked with *S1*. As power grid operators are completely blinded and unaware of the status of the grid in *BLUE-LAND*, they cannot take additional measures to power the stopped trains. As trains stop, the power consumption drops to 0MW, that is equivalent to the disconnection of several large consumers from the grid. Consequently, voltages increase above the normal operating limit (*S2*). At this point railway operators try to start-up trains again (*S3*), but this crashes voltages and trains stop again (*S4*).

Until this point we have seen the direct dependencies between the three CIs. We have seen that the railway depends on the power grid, but the power grid also depends on its ICT infrastructure to ensure normal operation. Without it,

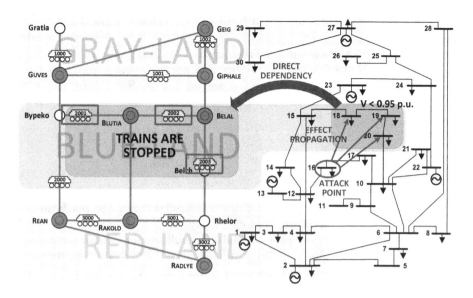

Fig. 6. Propagation of the effect of the cyber attack from the Power Grid to the Railway System

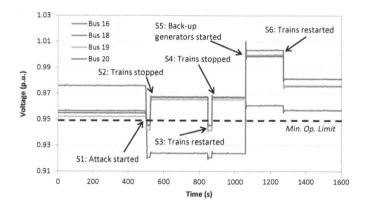

Fig. 7. Scenario execution and effects on power grid voltages

voltages drop below operating limits, leaving other critical infrastructures, i.e. railway, without power. However, if power grid operators would be able to realize that their physical infrastructure is under attack, they could take appropriate measures, such as turning ON back-up generators or isolating the substation that caused the perturbation. In our scenario we implemented this aspect by stopping the DoS attack, i.e. by re-enabling network interfaces, which has lead control algorithms to execute for the *BLUE-LAND* and inject an additional of 90 MVars into the grid. The effect can be seen in Fig. 7 at *S5*, where we notice an increase in the level of voltages. This is followed by a restart of trains at *S6*, that this time keeps voltages above their normal operating limit.

To conclude, the scenario presented in this section clearly showed the applicability of AMICI in security studies involving multiple CIs. The actual study performed on three CIs also confirmed the fact that the ICT infrastructure needs to be intact in order to ensure the stability and normal operation of CIs. Furthermore, as CIs get more interconnected and interdependent, there will be a special need of platforms as the one proposed in this paper to analyze these systems.

4   Conclusions

This paper presented AMICI, a novel experimentation platform for analyzing/assessing multiple interdependent Critical Infrastructures. The platform extends our previous work in the field of cyber-physical security experimentation with software components in order to enable a multi-domain experimentation that provides users with functionalities missing from other related approaches: (i) simple integration and inter-connection of multiple CI simulators; (ii) support experimentation with real software and malware in a safe environment; (iii) provides software units that recreate ICT software typically used in monitoring/control of CIs, e.g. SCADA servers, Modbus protocol; and (iv) include automated experiment management capabilities together with a multi-user support. The applicability of AMICI was demonstrated by studying the propagation of perturbations from the ICT infrastructure to a power grid and then to a railway system. The scenario showed that today's CIs are highly interconnected and their normal operation depends on the ICT infrastructure as well as on operator's reactions to contingencies. As future work we intend to apply AMICI to study even more complex systems and interdependencies, with a special focus on ICT infrastructures that can play a crutial role in the outcome of cyber attacks.

Acknowledgments. The authors would like to thank Dr. Roberto Filippini for the very helpful discussions on (inter)dependencies between CIs.

References

1. Bobbio, A., Bonanni, G., Ciancamerla, E., Clemente, R., Iacomini, A., Minichino, M., Scarlatti, A., Terruggia, R., Zendri, E.: Unavailability of critical scada communication links interconnecting a power grid and a telco network. Reliability Engineering & System Safety 95(12), 1345–1357 (2010)
2. Chen, T., Abu-Nimeh, S.: Lessons from Stuxnet. Computer 44(4), 91–93 (2011)
3. McElroy, D., Williams, C.: Flame: world's most complex computer virus exposed (2012), http://www.telegraph.co.uk/news/worldnews/middleeast/iran/9295938/Flame-worlds-most-complex-computer-virus-exposed.html# (accessed June 2012)
4. Rinaldi, S., Peerenboom, J., Kelly, T.: Identifying, understanding, and analyzing critical infrastructure interdependencies. IEEE Control Systems 21(6), 11–25 (2001)

5. Svendsen, N.K., Wolthusen, S.D.: An analysis of cyclical interdependencies in critical infrastructures. In: Lopez, J., Hämmerli, B.M. (eds.) CRITIS 2007. LNCS, vol. 5141, pp. 25–36. Springer, Heidelberg (2008)

6. Di Giorgio, A., Liberati, F.: Interdependency modeling and analysis of critical infrastructures based on dynamic bayesian networks. In: 2011 19th Mediterranean Conference on Control Automation (MED), pp. 791–797 (June 2011)

7. Chertov, R., Fahmy, S., Shroff, N.B.: Fidelity of network simulation and emulation: A case study of tcp-targeted denial of service attacks. ACM Trans. Model. Comput. Simul. 19(1), 4:1–4:29 (2009)

8. Davis, C., Tate, J., Okhravi, H., Grier, C., Overbye, T., Nicol, D.: SCADA cyber security testbed development. In: 38th North American Power Symposium, NAPS 2006, pp. 483–488 (2006)

9. Hopkinson, K., Wang, X., Giovanini, R., Thorp, J., Birman, K., Coury, D.: Epochs: a platform for agent-based electric power and communication simulation built from commercial off-the-shelf components. IEEE Transactions on Power Systems 21(2), 548–558 (2006)

10. McDonald, M., Conrad, G., Service, T., Cassidy, R.: Cyber effects analysis using VCSE. Technical Report, SAND2008-5954, Sandia National Laboratories (2008)

11. Queiroz, C., Mahmood, A., Hu, J., Tari, Z., Yu, X.: Building a SCADA security testbed. In: Proc. of the 2009 Third International Conference on Network and System Security, pp. 357–364 (2009)

12. Chabukswar, R., Sinopoli, B., Karsai, B., Giani, A., Neema, H., Davis, A.: Simulation of network attacks on SCADA systems. In: 1st Workshop on Secure Control Systems, Cyber Physical Systems Week (2010)

13. Mirkovic, J., Benzel, T., Faber, T., Braden, R., Wroclawski, J., Schwab, S.: The DETER project: Advancing the science of cyber security experimentation and test. In: Proc. of the IEEE International Conference on Technologies for Homeland Security (HST), pp. 1–7 (2010)

14. Genge, B., Siaterlis, C., Fovino, I.N., Masera, M.: A cyber-physical experimentation environment for the security analysis of networked industrial control systems. Computers & Electrical Engineering 38(5), 1146–1161 (2012)

15. Genge, B., Siaterlis, C., Hohenadel, M.: Impact of network infrastructure parameters to the effectiveness of cyber attacks against industrial control systems. International Journal of Computers, Communications & Control 7(4), 673–686 (2012)

16. White, B., Lepreau, J., Stoller, L., Ricci, R., Guruprasad, S., Newbold, M., Hibler, M., Barb, C., Joglekar, A.: An integrated experimental environment for distributed systems and networks. In: Proc. of the 5th Symposium on Operating Systems Design and Implementation, pp. 255–270 (2002)

17. Siaterlis, C., Garcia, A., Genge, B.: On the use of Emulab testbeds for scientifically rigorous experiments. IEEE Communications Surveys and Tutorials PP(99), 1–14 (2012)

18. Siaterlis, C., Masera, M.: A survey of software tools for the creation of networked testbeds. International Journal On Advances in Security 3(2), 1–12 (2010)

19. Zabbix (2012), http://www.zabbix.com/ (accessed June 2012)

20. Ríos, M.A., Ramos, G.: Power system modelling for urban massive transportation systems. In: Infrastructure Design, Signalling and Security in Railway, pp. 179–202 (2012)

Assessment of Social Impact Costs and Social Impact Magnitude from Breakdowns in Critical Infrastructures

Mats B-O Larsson[1], Gunnar Björkman[2], and Mathias Ekstedt[3]

[1] MML Analys & Strategi AB, Åhus, Sweden
mats@mml.se
[2] ABB AG, Mannheim, Germany
gunnar.bjoerkman@de.abb.com
[3] Industrial Information and Control Systems,
KTH - Royal Institute of Technology, Stockholm, Sweden
mathias.ekstedt@ics.kth.se

Abstract. The purpose of this paper is to describe a new and innovative method for the calculation of societal consequences from breakdowns in critical infrastructures. Both a Social Impact Cost is calculated as lost Gross Domestic Product and non-economic consequences are quantified. For the non-economic consequences a new measure is introduced called Social Impact Magnitude that resembles the Richter scale. The paper describes the methods used and the design of the software tool developed for this purpose. The second part of the paper includes some practical examples how the societal consequences have been calculated for a number of power outage scenarios. Future potential development to cover other types of critical infrastructures and dependencies between infrastructures are indicated at the end.

Keywords: Critical infrastructures, Impact analysis, Impact Costs, Impact Magnitude, Societal consequences, Virtual society, Blackout scenarios, Restoration, Load profiles, Outage assessment, SCADA security, Infrastructure dependence.

1   Introduction

Society is increasingly dependent on the proper functioning of the electric power system, which in turn supports most other critical infrastructures: water and sewage systems; telecommunications, internet and computing services; air traffic, railroads and other transportation. Many of these other infrastructures are able to operate without power for shorter periods of time, but larger power outages may be difficult and time consuming to restore. Such outages might thus lead to situations of non-functioning societies with devastating economical and humanitarian consequences.

The scope of this paper can be summarized in the following made-up telegram from a news agency describing a blackout in a major European city:

"A local power blackout with the Social Impact Magnitude of 6,8 occurred last evening in Folkvang, Germany. About 380.000 inhabitants in Folkvang and surrounding villages lost their power at a quarter past 10 o'clock in the evening. The central

B. Hämmerli, N. Kalstad Svendsen, and J. Lopez (Eds.): CRITIS 2012, LNCS 7722, pp. 240–251, 2013.

parts of the city were restored after half an hour but the complete restoration lasted until a quarter past one in the night. The blackout societal cost for Folkvang is estimated to 8.2 million Euros."

This telegram does not describe a real event but an invented blackout scenario. An essential question in connection to such a scenario, or in a real-life event, is how the costs and other non-economic consequences from a blackout can be estimated, i.e. how the numbers in the telegram above have been calculated. In this paper a comprehensive method for the assessment of these costs and other consequences caused by breakdowns in critical infrastructures is presented. Costs are measured as lost Gross Domestic Product and a new measure for non-economic consequence is introduced, the Social Impact Magnitude (SIM), which closely resembles the Richter scale used at earthquakes. The assessment is based on a comprehensive and versatile model of the society which can be parameterized to the different countries in the European Union plus Norway and Switzerland.

2   Design of the Virtual Society

The methods described in this paper are concerned with models of societies and are proposed to be used to assess impacts on real societies experiencing disturbances in critical infrastructures. However, there are many problems in making detailed society models. One is that it is hard to translate a society model from one country to another. Another problem is the concerns of homeland security. There are many restrictions related to detailed models of the society, especially when they include descriptions of the electrical transmission and distribution grid. The decision was therefore to develop methods and tools for a virtual society that can be parameterized to represent many real countries.

Overview of the Virtual Society. The virtual society is a simplified society with many of the essential characteristics of a real society. It has static as well as dynamic properties and includes infrastructures with blocks, apartments, streets, electricity grids. In the society there are big and small companies, public and private service organizations producing welfare and there are people living in residential areas, having a comfortable life and consuming welfare. The virtual society is a dynamic society modeling business activities and has the critical infrastructure to support the population. The virtual society relates electrical power demand to the economic life; to business activities and to consumption of welfare, i.e. it relates power demand to the production and consumption of Gross Domestic Product (GDP). The virtual society has dynamics; the life in the city is managed by setting and incrementing the system time and by the activity profiles. It creates individual Power Load Profiles and Business Activity Profiles for each individual and relevant object in the city. Thus, the virtual society "lives" with its own system time, electrical loads and business activities. The society responds to commands from outside and sends back information about its activities as a function of the system time.

The virtual society can be more or less severely disturbed by the introduction of power outages. After an outage, the lost production and lost consumption of welfare are assessed as the difference in GDP between a disturbed and undisturbed society. The virtual society is created and assessed by a software package called ViCiSi, the

Virtual Cities Simulator.. ViCiSi has been developed in the VIKING project *[16]*, an ICT and Security project under the EU Framework 7 Programme. In the first version of ViCiSi only the electrical grid is modeled but ViCiSi is prepared for the modeling of other critical infrastructures. ViCiSi can model the virtual society to resemble all European countries plus Norway and Switzerland by importing individual demography and economic information. Statistical data is imported from different sources and ViCiSi automatically configures the virtual society to the characteristics of the targeted country. During execution ViCiSi provide the active and reactive loads, and the value of the business activities, in all requested load points with 10 ms resolution. If an outage occurs in one or more feeding points, or on medium and low voltage levels, the outage costs and impact magnitude will be calculated.

Input Sources. The following sources have been used to create the virtual society:

ENTSO-E [1], The European Network of Transmission System Operators for electricity, provides electrical load values on a national level for each hour during a year.

Eurostat [2] is the statistical office of the European Union. Its task is to provide the European Union with statistics on the European level such as Gross Domestic Product (GDP), energy consumption, branch statistics and country area.

Set of Parameters. In addition, a set of parameters, controlling the creation of the virtual society, is used by ViCiSi. Many of these parameters are related to the creation of the distribution electrical grid in the virtual society.

Power Load Profiles. When the virtual society is created from the input files, Power Load Profiles ($p_i(t)$) are associated to all individual power consumers (i) in the society, such as companies, public services and residential houses. Thus all power consumers have their own Power Load Profile (Fig 1) depending on their type with their own load factor (P_{max}/P_{mean}). A household has a high load factor, an industry has a lower load factor and a public service (for example telecommunications) has a quite flat load factor.

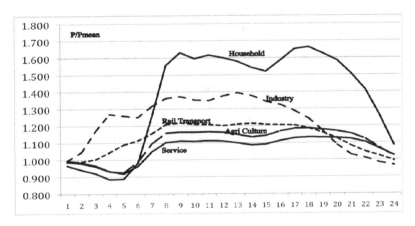

Fig. 1. The 24 h curve of the created Power Load Profiles (winter time) for different sectors with different load factor (P_{max}/P_{mean})

It is necessary to make the individual Power Load Profiles consistent with the national Power Load Profile from ENTSO-E for each moment in time and summed up for a whole year. Thus, the following is valid for the individual Power Load Profiles $p_i(t)$

$$\sum\nolimits_{\text{All consumers}} \left(\int_{\text{one year}} p_i(t)\, dt \right) = E \qquad (1)$$

where E is the total power consumption for a specific country over one year from the ENTSO-E database.

3   Assessment of Social Impact Costs

Related Work. Basically there are three ways to assess social costs [4,5] from a power outage (1) Blackout case studies, (2) Customer surveys and (3) Analytical methods. *Blackout case studies* imply a case study of a specific disturbance, often a major blackout. The *Customer survey methods* focus on the customer evaluation of the outage, normally in monetary terms [6-8]. In *Analytical methods* a common approach is to assess the value of lost production in the society by taking the ratio of the annual gross domestic product (GDP) to the total electrical consumption to estimate the value of each kWh of electrical power. None of the approaches are perfect and they all have their pros and cons. The survey method is the most commonly used method. However, for several reasons, the analytical method is chosen for ViCiSi. A discussion on why the analytical approach has been decided can be found in [9]. The most important reasons are the possibility to base the virtual society on different template countries, the properties for marginal cost assessment and the problem with the dependency on question formulation in the survey methods. The answer to *"what is your cost of an outage?"* differs significantly to *"how much are you willing to pay to avoid an outage?"*.

Gross Domestic Product (GDP) Approach. The Gross Domestic Product is one of the cornerstones in EU statistics and a basis for the politicians in planning the European future [10]: GDP is a summary measure for economic production of a country and it is generally considered to be an overall indicator of the development of the economy. It is the value of all goods and services created during the accounting period, less the value of the goods and services imported in the production processes. This difference between the output value and the input value is also called gross value added. However, it is not without problem to use the GDP as a base for the cost assessment. A number of problems have to be solved. One problem is to get a temporal distribution of the GDP. GDP is a monthly, quarterly or annual sum of economic activities. But the production varies throughout the day, week and year. The GDP figure in the Eurostat database is aggregated for one year. To be used in a simulation model a value of the momentarily economic activity at an arbitrarily time is required. The value of the economic activity must be consistent, i.e. when all economic values throughout a year are summed up it must equal the GDP in the Eurostat database.

There is a close, but complex, relationship between GDP and electricity demand [11] in the society. A high GDP requires high electricity consumption. But this does not necessarily mean that the GDP will increase if the electricity consumption is increased. A more effective use of energy normally only influences the GDP marginally. Energy saving requires smarter production technology and this might even increase the GDP. There are also demographic and geographic issues which influence the electricity demand, such as the high amount of electricity for heating houses in the northern countries of Europe. Electricity demand and economic growth are tied together in the long term but there is no evidence for a short term causal relationship [12,13]. Thus, one has to be careful when the electric energy is used for predicting GDP in the short term. However, in the creation of the virtual society presented in this paper, the electricity consumption is not used as a direct indicator of GDP production or the growth in GDP. The electricity consumption is rather used as an indicator of the activity in the society. The GDP is defined by statistical data and is not predicted.

Business Activity Profiles. ViCiSi takes the Power Load Profiles as input and by a series of calculations so called Business Activity Profiles, $b_j(t)$, are created. These activities give a momentarily value of the economic activity of each relevant (j) object and describe the dynamic features in the society. Each object in ViCiSi will have an individual Business Activity Profile and each profile is related to a specific branch (Industry, Service, Public utility etc.). These profiles define the momentarily value (EUR/h) of the economic activity. The created Business Profiles are consistent with branch-statistics as well as at an aggregated national level, such as:

$$\sum_{\text{Economic entities}} \left(\int_{\text{One year}} b_j(t)\, dt \right) = \text{GDP} \tag{2}$$

where GDP is the annual value from the national accounts at Eurostat. If all activities are summed up for one year and for all objects the GDP of the template country is reached.

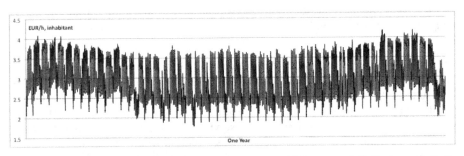

Fig. 2. GDP presented as a hour-by-hour one year curve of the sum of all Business Activity Profiles for Germany (EUR/h, inhabitant). The peaks represent typical rush hours.

Outage and Restoration. The occurrence of an outage is simple to model both for the power demand as well as for the business activity. At the outage time everything gets black and all economic activity will stop as long as the outage lasts, i.e. no production or consumption of welfare occurs. In reality the situation is a bit more complex but this is a reasonable simplification.

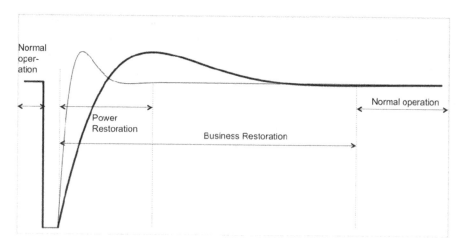

Fig. 3. Restoration functions for power activity ($p_i(t)$) and business activity ($b_i(t)$)

When the power returns the further development is considerably more complex. It is not possible to directly connect all electrical loads and the society gradually starts to consume electrical energy. Some of the not delivered energy will now be restored. For example a refrigerator will run intensively for a while and restore some of the not delivered energy. But a lamp will not restore any of the lost energy. Thus, the recovery of the society has open loop as well as closed loop characteristics [14].

The *economic restoration of the society* is even more complex due to dynamics in the business processes. After an outage a department store, for example, has to turn on the light, check the refrigerators, start the computer system etc. And moreover the business will not start before the payment system is working. Only after this the department store can open their doors and continue the business. The same scenario is more or less valid for many other business activities in the society. It takes time to start the business after a blackout. The virtual society has its own model of restoration (Fig 3), including open loop as well as closed loop properties for restoration. Thus it is possible to model long as well as short outages. This function is used to model the restoration of the power as well as the business, but with different set of parameters.

The function used to model the restoration is the step-function response of a second order closed loop system[17]:

$$S(t) = 1 - k*e^{-\delta t} * \sin(\mu t + \varphi) \tag{3}$$

Where δ is the damping, μ gives the oscillation frequency ($\mu = 0$ gives an open loop). The parameter φ and k are related to the overshoot (the energy recovery) of the step response. This function has been refined to model the energy and business recovery and the dependency of the outage length.

Social Impact Costs Assessment. The social cost in a society after a power outage is calculated as the difference in GDP with and without the outage, reflecting the open and close loop properties in equation (3). In this paper these costs are called Social

Impact Costs (SIC). The societal cost assessment is a comparison of the economic activity in a non disturbed society (b_{Normal}) with a disturbed society (b_{Outage}). The social impact activity, $b_{SocialImpactActivity}$, is the difference between those measures. The Social Impact Cost (SIC), $B_{SocialImpactCost}$, is the accumulated value of the social business activity and is calculated by integration over time. The Social Impact Cost (Fig 4) is thus the value of the lost GDP production:

$$b_{SocialImpactActivity}(t) = b_{Normal}(t) - b_{Outage}(t) \tag{4}$$

$$SIC = B_{SocialImpactCost} = \int b_{SocialImpactActivity}(t)\, dt = \int (b_{Normal}(t) - b_{Outage}(t))dt \tag{5}$$

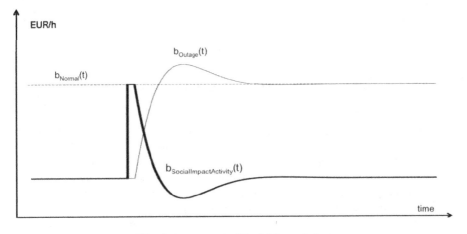

Fig. 4. Assessment of Social Impact Cost

4   Assessment of Social Impact Magnitude

Cost assessment is a very important way of describing the consequences from a power outage. However, there are other ways to evaluate the consequences of a blackout that will give additional information and is simpler to calculate. In this paper a new non-economic approach to measure the consequences is defined – the Social Impact Magnitude (SIM) - as a complement to the Social Impact Cost assessment (SIC). In this new approach the society impacts are viewed and assessed from both a micro and a macro perspective. From the micro perspective, i.e. from the individual standpoint, the length of an outage is the most interesting dimension. In the micro perspective an outage means the loss of welfare, inconvenience, problems with transportation, no fuel at the gas station, problems with emergency calls etc. The number of affected people is not assessed in the micro perspective. From a society standpoint - or the macro perspective - the consequences are related to the number of affected people. In the macro perspective society risks are assessed, for example disease proliferation, riot and other crimes, antagonist attacks etc. The magnitude of the aggregated risks is related to both the number of affected persons and the length of the outage. The composite Social Impact Magnitude is built from both the micro and macro assessment. The micro dimension is covered by the so called *Disturbance Length Order* where the length of the outage is the essential information. The macro dimension is calculated from the number of impacted people and named the *Impact Incidence*.

The definitions of Social Impact Magnitude, Disturbance Length Order and Impact Incidence have similarities with the Richter Magnitude Scale for earth quakes [19]:

$$\text{Social Impact Magnitude} = {}^{10}\text{Log}(A_{people} * A_{length}) = {}^{10}\text{Log}(A_{people}) + {}^{10}\text{Log}(A_{length}) \quad (6)$$

$$\text{Impact Incidence} = {}^{10}\text{Log}(A_{people}) \quad (7)$$
$$\text{Disturbance Length Order} = {}^{10}\text{Log}(A_{length}) \quad (8)$$

where

A_{length} = Average Disturbance Length (in seconds)
A_{people} = Number of affected people / 1000

$$\text{Social Impact Magnitude} = \text{Impact Incidence} + \text{Disturbance Length Order} \quad (9)$$

$$\text{Impact Magnitude} \in [0, \approx 10+[$$

$$\text{Disturbance Length Order} \in [0, \approx 5+[$$

$$\text{Impact Incidence} \in [0, \approx 5+[$$

The definition of A_{people} is the number of affected people / 1000. The reason for the division by 1000 is to calibrate it to the Richter Magnitude Scale. It should be noted that SIM has a logarithmic/exponential behavior, which implies that an increase in SIM gives greater consequences in absolute values for large SIM-values than for small SIM-values.

An outage can – as well as an earthquake – range from minor to disaster. One obvious advantage with the SIM is that it is very easy to calculate. The only information that is required is the outage length and the number of people affected by the outage.

The Social Impact Magnitude, Disturbance Length Order and Impact Incidence can be unified into a single diagram and well-known historic blackouts can be plotted in the diagram to illustrate the use of SIM (Fig 6) and its resemblance with the Richter scale (Fig 5). The numeric values of Fig 6 are shown in Table 1. The similarities with the Richter Magnitude Scale are obvious. If the magnitudes in Table 1 are compared to the Richter scale they are of the same order. The largest electrical outage is the Northeast USA blackout, 2003 with the SIM magnitude 9.7. The largest earthquake recorded is the Valdivia earthquake (Chile), 1960, with a Richter magnitude of 9.5.

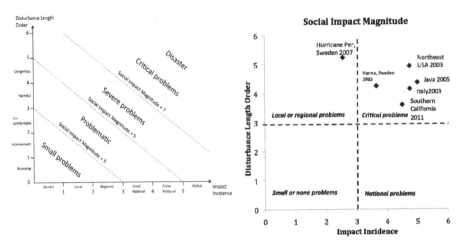

Fig. 5. Social *Impact Magnitude*, Disturbance Length Order and Impact Incidence

Fig. 6. Historic blackouts plotted as *Social Impact Magnitude*, Disturbance Length Order and Impact Incidence

Table 1. Historic blackouts assessed as SIM

	Social Impact Magnitude	Disturbance Length Order	Impact Incidence
Java blackout 2005	9.4	4.37	5
Northeast USA blackout 2003	9.7	4.93	4.74
Sweden Hamra 1983	7.9	4.25	3.65
Southern California blackout 2011	8.1	3.6	4.5
Italy 2003	8.9	4.15	4.75
Hurricane Per, Sweden 2007	7.8	5.23	2.56

5   Use of ViCiSi in Blackout Scenarios

In the VIKING project *[16]* 13 different cyber attack scenarios, called Story Boards, have been defined and described. All 13 attacks describe disturbances or blackouts, ranging from small to very big, in the electrical power supply. For each Story Board the background, assumptions for the attack and the attack path have been defined. The likelihood of attack success has been calculated considering the control system configuration and protection mechanisms using the Cyber Security Modeling Language *[18]*. The societal consequences have been calculated the using methods and tools described in this paper. Each Story Board also includes proposals for mitigation against the described attack.

This chapter very briefly describes three of these Story Boards and lists, in Table 2, the results calculated by ViCiSi for each of these Story Boards. This has been done to illustrate how ViCiSi can be used in real life situations to calculate societal consequences from blackouts in the electrical grid ranging from very big disturbances to very small.

Story Board A. This Story Boards corresponds to the news telegram in the Introduction. A criminal organization has managed to get access to the inter-center communication link between the national control center and the local utility control center for a major city and its surroundings. They succeed to introduce a false command using a commercially available listening device on the communication link. This command opens the breakers between the national high voltage grid and the local sub-transmission grid and creates a blackout in the city and the surroundings that take one to three hours to restore. All the loads can not be connected at the same time since this would overload the grid. Therefore a step-by-step, predefined restoration scheme has to be followed that takes a certain time to execute. In this scenario no power plants have to be restarted which reduces the restoration time substantially.

Story Board B. This Story Board is modeled from the infamous Stuxnet attack. Using a USB stick an attacker manage to compromise the national control system supervising and controlling the high voltage grid of a nation. Such control systems includes predefined, automatic control sequences that can automatically operate high voltage breakers without operator intervention similar to PLC sequences. The malicious payload of the USB virus implements false command sequences into the control system. These manipulated sequences opens several high voltage breakers at a predefined times. This leads to a nationwide blackout that takes up to three days to restore because of the time required to restart power generation including nuclear power plants.

Story Board C: This Story Board describes a much smaller attack where a nighttime unmanned, small regional utility office is compromised by single individual that wants to make a "practical joke" on the neighboring village. By using a remote workstation connected to the control center and a note with usernames and passwords glued to the screen he manage to open the medium voltage breaker that feeds the neighboring small city which causes a two hours blackout.

Table 2. Story Boards evaluation with SIC and SIM

Story Board	Social Impact Cost MEUR	Created GDP with outage MEUR	Without outage MEUR	Social Impact Magnitude	Impact Incidence	Disturbance Length Order
A	**4.0**	251	255	**6.4**	2.5	3.9
B	**550**	3094	3645	**8.8**	3.6	5.2
C	**0.1**	573	573	**5.1**	1.2	3.9

It should be noted that the Social Impact Costs in these examples are calculated on a virtual society with the same demographic, economic and industrial structure as Germany (with data imported from Eurostat). The virtual country is, however, a much smaller country than Germany from an economic and population point of view and represents only about 5% of the real Germany. If the Story Board B, with the national blackout, would happen in the Germany it would have approximately 20 times higher impact than described in Table 2.

6   Discussion and Conclusions

In this paper an innovative and versatile method is described for the calculation of societal consequences from disturbances in the electrical supply. The electricity supply has been selected for study because it is the critical infrastructure which is the base for many other critical infrastructures. Two complementing measures have been introduced to describe these consequences; one is the loss in Gross Domestic Product (GDP) from an outage and the other assesses non-economic, but equally important, consequences for the individuals and the society. The non-economic value, SIM (Social Impact Magnitude), has been designed to closely resemble the well-known Richter scale used for defining earth quakes.

The described method has been calibrated to the power demand in EU countries taken from ENTSO-E [1] data and to the Gross Domestic Product (GDP) from Eurostat [2] for the same countries. The method has been tested against real and made-up blackouts and has been found to give realistic values both for very big disturbances, like national blackouts, and down to small and very limited outages, e.g. in a minor village. The resemblance to the Richter scale is striking in these examples.

However, the design of ViCiSi and the assessment of Social Impact Cost (SIC) and Social Impact Magnitude (SIM) is not restricted to outages in the electricity supply. It is a generic method that can be applied to many areas and for different kinds of critical infrastructure, such as telecommunication, water and waste water, transportation, garbage removal, etc. In the current version of ViCiSi mutual dependencies between different infrastructures are not modeled in the assessment of Social Impact Cost (SIC), e.g. an outage in the electrical supply would impact on telecommunication and water supply. This will be a topic for further development. On the other hand Social Impact Magnitude (SIM) is covering mutual dependencies, since it gives an overall assessment of all activities. It would also be possible to extend the ViCiSi with information of human behavior using the Time use statistics from the European statistical databases [3]. This will give a more detailed assessment of the cost consequences on the micro level.

The above described method could be used to give decision makers and society planners reliable numbers to base their decisions on for investments in improved resilience of infrastructures and the corresponding control systems. It can also be used to set a measure on the severity of societal disturbances and to use this measure to implement different levels of response, safety and restoration procedures.

References

1. https://www.entsoe.eu/
2. http://epp.eurostat.ec.europa.eu
3. https://www.h2.scb.se/tus/tus
4. Kjolle, G.H., Samdahl, K., Kvitastein, O.A.: Customer Costs Related to Interruptions and Voltage Problems: Methodology and Results. IEEE Transactions on Power Systems 23 (2008)
5. Alvehag, K.: Impact of Dependencies in Risk Assessments of Power Distribution Systems. KTH, Royal Institute of Technology, Stockholm (2008)

6. Larsson, M.B.-O.: he Network Performance Assessment Model A new framework of regulating the Electricity Network Companies. KTH, Royal Institute of Technology, Stockholm (2005)
7. Carlsson, F., Martinsson, P.: Kostnader av elavbrott, en studie av svenska elkunder (Social Impact Costs, a study of Swedish electricity customers, In Swedish) (Vol. Rapport 06:15). Elforsk (2006)
8. Svenska Kraftnät (Swedish Transmission System operator). Stamnätets tekniskt-ekonomiska dimensionering (In Swedish, The technical/economical design of the transmission power grid) (vol. 113). Svenska kraftnät, Stockholm (2009)
9. Larsson, M. B.-O. Consequence and cost analysis of SCADA systems vulnerabilities, vol. 3.3. The Viking Project, Åhus (2012), http://www.vikingproject.eu
10. Eurostat Statistical Books, Principal European Economic Indicators A statistical guide. Eurostat, European Commission (2009)
11. The Outlook for Energy A View to 2030. Exxon Mobil (2030)
12. Ciarreta, A., Zarraga, A.: Economic Growth and Electricity Consumption in 12 European Countries: A Causality Analysis Using Panel Data. In: 6th International Conference on the European Energy Market, EEM 2009. IEEE, Spain (2009)
13. Böhm, D.C.: Electricity Consumption and Economic Growth in the European Union: A Causality Study using Panel Unit Root and Cointegration Analysis. In: 5th International Conference on European Electricity Market, EEM 2008. IEEE, Germany (2008)
14. Agneholm, E.: Cold Load Pick-up, PhD thesis. Gothenburg: Chalmers University of Technology, School of Electrical and Computer Engineering (1999) ISBN 91-7197-756-2 ISSN 0346-718X
15. Frost, C., Barck-Holst, S., Ånäs, P.: Acceptabla elavbrott? Fyra strategier för säker elförsörjning (Unacceptable outages? Four stratgies for resilant power supply. In: Swedish) (vols. FOI-R–1163–SE). Totalförsvarets Forskningsinstitut (2004)
16. http://www.vikingproject.eu
17. Melsa, J., Schultz, D.: Linear Control Systems. McGraw-Hill Book Company (1969)
18. VIKING Consortium, Delivery 3.1: Vulnerability assessment of SCADA systems (2011)
19. Richter, C.F.: An instrumental earthquake magnitude scale. Bulletin of the Seismological Society of America 25(1-32) (1936)

Hidden Vulnerabilities
Due to Interdependencies between Two Systems

Cen Nan[1], Irene Eusgeld[2], and Wolfgang Kröger[1]

[1] ETH Zürich, Zürich, Switzerland
`cen.nan@usys.ethz.ch, wkroeger@ethz.ch`
[2] University of Duisburg-Essen, Essen, Germany
`eusgeld@cs.uni-due.de`

Abstract. Critical infrastructures (CIs) deserve increased attention as our socie-ties simply rely on most of the goods and services they are expected to conti-nuously supply. Interdependencies within and among CIs have dramatically increased the overall complexity of related infrastructure systems, making them more vulnerable to cascading failures with widespread unpredicted conse-quences. It is vital to get a clear understanding of these often hidden interde-pendency issues and tackle them through advanced techniques. In this paper, the interdependencies between Industrial Control Systems (ICS), in particular the SCADA (Supervisory Control and Data Acquisition) system, and the under-lying System Under Control (SUC) are identified and assessed using model-ing/simulation methods by following a modified 4-step methodical framework. This paper mainly focuses on those techniques and analytical experiments de-veloped for the essential step of this methodical framework, the in-depth analy-sis, i.e., applying a hybrid modeling/simulation approach and three in-depth ex-periments.

Keywords: Critical Infrastructure (CI), Interdependency study, SCADA, Simu-lation and Modeling.

1   Motivations

From a technical perspective, the term *dependency* depicts a linkage between two sys-tems (CIs) through which the state of one system influences the state of the other, whe-reas *interdependency* is a bidirectional relationship through which the state of each sys-tem is correlated to the state of the other [1]. It should be noted that two systems, as mentioned above, can correspond to one CI (internal interdependency) or more CIs (external interdependency). Interdependencies[1]can also be of different types, e.g., physi-cal, cyber, geographic, and logic [1]. Interdependencies within and among infrastructure systems have dramatically increased the overall complexity of the related systems, caus-ing the emergence of unpredictable negative impacts and making them more vulnerable to cascading failures with widespread disasters [2]. Modern CIs, such as power supply,

---

[1] This paper will use the general term interdependency to describe the interactions within and between CIs including both interdependency and dependency.

B. Hämmerli, N. Kalstad Svendsen, and J. Lopez (Eds.): CRITIS 2012, LNCS 7722, pp. 252–263, 2013.

telecommunication, and rail transport are all large-scale, complex, highly integrated and particularly interconnected. The operators of these systems must continuously monitor and control them to ensure their proper operation [3]. These industrial monitor and control functions are generally implemented using a SCADA system, which can also be regarded as the ICS. The fundamental purpose of SCADA[2] system is to allow a user (operator) to collect data from one or more remote facilities and send control instructions back to those facilities. For instance, voltage, frequency and phase angle are all important parameters in the power supply CI sector, which are continuously monitored for maintaining a normal working environment. An important characteristic of SCADA system is its inherent structural complexity. It generally comprises remotely located field level devices, which are connected to a centrally located control room through a variety of communication devices. Ensuring and securing functionalities of a SCADA system and its controlled/monitored SUC generally face three challenges: (1) access control restriction, (2) improvement of protocol security, and (3) investigation of failures of devices installed at substations. While first two challenges are related to security and the last one is related to reliability. The interdependency-related vulnerabilities between a SCADA system and associated SUC have been addressed by a number of researchers for many years [4, 5]. Most publications are related to the investigation regarding pervasive use of ICT. For example, the communication protocol Modbus has become one of the most widely discussed topics for securing the data transmission between the control centre and remote substation sites. However, the importance of devices (components) installed at substations should not be underestimated due to the fact that their failures can also pose serious threats to a SCADA system and even other systems it connects to.

The objective of this paper is to identify and assess hidden vulnerabilities due to (internal) interdependencies between SCADA and its interconnected SUC. It mainly focuses on the third challenge and disclaims the security aspect. Devices installed at the substation level of the SCADA system are systematically analyzed due to the fact that the vulnerable field level devices installed in the substation could impact the vulnerability of the whole system. The Electricity Power Supply System (EPSS) is used as an example of CI in this paper. The identification and assessment of hidden vulnerabilities follows a methodical framework for analyzing vulnerabilities due to CI interdependencies, which is based on the framework proposed in [6], including 4 steps: *preparatory phase*, *screening analysis*, *in-depth analysis*, and *results assessment*. It should be noted that the focus of this paper is mainly related to the step of in-depth analysis.

2   Step 1: Preparatory Phase

The main purpose of this step is to reach a clear understanding regarding the objectives of the task, as well as of the CIs and/or subsystems within a CI to be analyzed. Obvious vulnerabilities can be recognized by the screening analysis, while hidden vulnerabilities need the in-depth analysis using more comprehensive and advanced

---

[2] In this paper, SCADA will be referenced as a system if it is individually introduced and discussed. Nevertheless, if the discussions are related to interdependency study within one infrastructure system, SCADA will be referenced as a subsystem.

techniques such as the system modeling and simulation. Furthermore, it is necessary to identify characteristics of interdependencies, e.g., types of interdependencies. According to [1] and [7], the interdependencies can be described by six dimensions, e.g., type of failure, type of interdependencies, coupling/response behavior, etc. It is very important to decide which CIs (analysis among CIs) or subsystems (analysis within a CI) should be analyzed. Then, the general term "to find system(s) vulnerabilities due to interdependencies" can be stated precisely. In this paper, two subsystems, SCADA and SUC, within the EPSS are selected. The Swiss 220kV/380kV electricity transmission network is used as an exemplary SUC. It is assumed that this transmission network is a stand-alone system and the energy exchange with the neighboring countries is regarded as independent positive or negative power injections at the respective boundary substations. According to the general understanding of a SCADA system and its associated SUC, their interdependencies can be characterized as physical, cyber, geographic interdependencies. Based on the definition of the degree of coupling, introduced in [7], the SCADA system and its associated SUC are *tightly coupled*. After framing the task and gaining general understanding of studied interdependencies, methods and approaches available for performing the task need to be checked.

The challenges regarding understanding, characterizing, and investigating interdependencies within and among CIs are immense and research in this area is still at an early stage [2, 4, 8, 9]. In general, the interdependency-related study can be divided into *knowledge-based* and *model-based approaches*. Knowledge-based approaches, e.g., empirical investigations and brainstorming, intend to use data collected by interviewing experts and/or analyzing past events to acquire information and improve the understanding of dimensions and types of interdependencies. Model-based approaches intend to represent interdependencies comprehensively using advanced modeling techniques, with capabilities of providing both quantitative and qualitative assessment. Currently, a variety of models have been applied, e.g., Complex Network Theory (CNT), Input-output Inoperability Modeling (IIM), Agent-based Modeling (ABM), PetriNet(PN)-based modeling, etc. It is difficult to compare these approaches since all of them have their own advantages and disadvantages: the knowledge-based approaches are straightforward and easy to understand, while the model-based approaches promise to gain a deeper understanding of behaviors of studied system(s). Among these approaches, the ABM approach seems to be most promising, not just due to its capability for representing the complexity of any infrastructure systems, but also its modeling flexibility and adaptability. For example, the ABM approach can be integrated with many other modeling/simulation techniques and even be used to implement other models, e.g., CNT, PN-based modeling, IIM, etc. Some non-technical components, such as human behavior can also be modeled and simulated by using the ABM (see [10] for more information).

3   Step 2: Screening Analysis

The purpose of this step is to reach a further understanding of the previously framed task by acquiring sufficient information/knowledge of main functionalities, interfaces, and components of each studied system, as well as interdependencies among previously determined systems, in order to decide which to evaluate in more detail. In this step, obvious vulnerabilities should be identified using the methods such as empirical investigations and topological analysis. Although the studied system(s) has (have) been described and its (their) boundaries have been defined at the Step 1, it is still important to further develop an adequate understanding of system, which aims to improve accuracy of results obtained from the screening analysis and collect more detailed information for the following in-depth analysis. To achieve these goals, components of the studied system(s) need to be analyzed at first and then corresponding failure modes for each system component need to be defined. In general, a standard SCADA system consists of following essential components: Field Level Control and Instrumentation Device (FID and FCD), Remote Terminal Unit (RTU), Communication Unit (CU), and Master Terminal Unit (MTU). More information regarding adequate understanding of the SUC and SCADA system can be found in [11] and [12]. In this paper, only components installed at the substation of a standard SCADA system, i.e., FID, FCD and RTU, will be analyzed due to the their importance for the interdependency-related vulnerability analysis between SCADA system and SUC. In total, 8 functional failure modes are defined: FCD FO (Failure to Open), FCD FC (Failure to Close), FID FRH (Failure to Run (too high)), FID FRL (Failure to Run (too low)), RTU FRW (Failure to Run due to hardware failure), RTU FRF (Failure to Run with Field Device), and RTU FRC (Failure to Run due to communication error).

One of the established methods to identify obvious vulnerabilities is the topological analysis. For example, the SCADA system in general can be represented as a network: the SCADA system for the 220kV/380kV Swiss electric power transmission network consists of 149 substations, connecting 219 transmission lines in total. Some substations connect only one transmission line and some up to 11 transmission lines. Generally, the failures of substations connecting more transmission lines could have more negative effects on the reliability of whole system, compared to substations connecting less transmission lines. Therefore, it is important to identify these highly interconnected substations. If considering the SCADA system as an undirected and unweighted graph, it contains 149 nodes and 219 links. Based on the results of the analysis, the degree distribution[3] of the SCADA system peaks at k=2 and also has large values when k=1 and 3, which means most substations connect less than 3 transmission lines. It should be noted that substations with k=1 are boundary substations. The number of substations with k≥6 is very small. This graph can be regarded as a scale-free network, as defined in [13] and [14]. The characteristic of such type of networks is that most nodes have small degrees but there is a finite possibility of identifying nodes with intermediate and large degrees. The nodes with a higher value of degree play a specific role in the structure of the network [13]. It has been demonstrated in [15] that the removal of these nodes usually causes a quite rapid destruction of the structure of the network. Due to the importance of these nodes (substations), it is assumed that substations with k≥6 can be considered as key substations.

4   Step 3: In-Depth Analysis

After the preparatory phase and screening analysis have demonstrated the necessity, a more sophisticated analysis has to be performed, calling for advanced modeling and

---

[3] The degree distribution P(k) represents the probability that a generic node in the network is connected to k other nodes.

simulation techniques to represent interdependencies within and among CIs. A number of model-based approaches have been briefly introduced in Section 2. In order to fully understand and be capable to represent behaviors of these interdependent CIs sufficiently, a novel approach needs to be developed for an in-depth analysis, which faces two major methodical challenges. The first challenge is to a model a single CI with its inherent characteristics such as dynamic/nonlinear behavior, and intricate rules of interaction including with the environment due to their openness and high degree of interconnectedness. Classical approaches and methods, based on decoupling and decomposition like fault and event trees, reach the limit of their capacity [16, 17]. The second challenge appears when more than one CI or subsystem within a CI must be considered and interdependencies among them need to be tackled. It has proven necessary to integrate different types of modeling approaches into one simulation tool in order to fully utilize benefits/advantages of each approach and optimize the efficiency of the overall simulation. One of the key challenges for developing such type of simulation tool is the required ability to create multiple-domain models, e.g., discrete and continuous time models, time-based and frequency-based models, etc, and effectively exchange data among them [18]. In practice, there is still no "silver bullet" approach. To find a more promising solution for solving these challenges and handling these technical difficulties, a hybrid modeling/simulation approach is proposed and discussed in [10] and [19], which combines various simulation/modeling techniques by adopting the technology of distributed simulation and the concept of modular design. Based on this approach, a real-time simulation platform has been created, which is currently used to explore and identify interdependency-related vulnerabilities between two interdependent subsystems, i.e., SUC and its SCADA system. It consists of four major simulation components: SUC model, SCADA model, RTI (Run Time Infrastructure) server, and simulation monitor system. The High Level Architecture (HLA) simulation standard [4] is adapted to handle data transmission among different simulation components. The SUC model is a continuous-time model, while the SCADA model is a discrete-event model. The RTI server is responsible for simulation synchronization and communication routing among all components through a local RTI interface of each model (see [10] and [19] for more details). In order to investigate hidden vulnerabilities due to interdependencies between two systems under study, three in-depth experiments have been developed: substation level single failure mode experiment (1), small network level single failure mode experiment (2), and whole network worse-case failure modes experiment (3).

In the first experiment, different failure modes of each substation level component are evaluated by performing a number of tests related to each failure mode. During each test, the scenarios that will trigger power line overload alarm are generated at the beginning of the simulation. Each test starts in the operation mode (a device mode) and one of the agent states. Within a given time period, the device mode of a respective component will change to one failure mode. The transition time from the operation mode to this failure mode is assumed to be exponentially distributed with constant failure rates λ. After a given time period, the device mode will go back to operation mode. The transition time from this failure mode to operation mode is assumed to be exponentially distributed with repair rate μ. The transitions between different device modes will have influences on corresponding agent states resulting in the change of behaviors of the SCADA system

---

[4] It should be noted that the RTI is part of HLA simulation standard.

and SUC. According to the conclusion of this experiment, among all the simulated SCADA-related devices, negative effects caused by failures of the RTU device seem more significant on its interconnected SUC (see [10] for more information).

4.1   Experiment 2: Small Network Level Single Failure Mode Experiment

This experiment extends the scope of the first experiment to a small network including more components of SCADA system and SUC (40 substations and 50 transmission lines). The aim of this experiment is to identify the failure modes that can cause more negative effects due to interdependencies between two studied systems. In this experiment, one key substation from the SUC model is selected for triggering the failure modes of substation level components during the simulation. For each single failure mode, two types of tests are implemented: normal and worse-case. The modeling scenarios of these two tests are summarized below:

Normal Test: The modeling scenarios are similar to of the tests in the substation level single failure mode experiment. In contrast to first experiment, the transition from the operation mode to the respective failure mode at the beginning of each test is triggered manually instead of within given time based on the failure rate[5]. This adjustment ensures that the transition time from the operation mode to each failure mode is the same.

Worse-Case Test: This test represents the worse-case situation when the operator is unable to handle any alarm received by the control centre due to natural hazards or technical failures, e.g., the failure of the control panel, flooding/fire in the control centre, etc. The purpose of performing experimental tests under this situation is to observe corresponding consequences if the SCADA system fails to monitor and control the SUC through the MTU.

The following parameters are proposed to analyze test results:

- **ASSAI** (Average Substation Service Availability Index): This parameter represents the ratio of the total number service hours provided by all available substations during a given time period to the total hours demanded (Equation 1).

$$\text{ASSAI} = \frac{N_S \times (\text{number of hours}) - \sum_{i=1}^{N} R_i}{N_S \times (\text{number of hours})} \tag{1}$$

where R_i = Restoration time for ith substation (if service interruption exists)
N_S = Total number of substations

- **DI** (Degree of Impact): The purpose of developing this parameter is to qualify negative effects caused by each failure mode using three other parameters as indicators obtained during each test: ASSAI (indicator 1), the number of SCADA components (interdependency failures) (indicator 2), and the number of affected SUC components (dependent failures) (indicator 3). All of these three indicators receive value between 1-5 according to their real value. In addition, a weighting factor (W_i) is defined for each indicator showing its importance for calculating the degree of impact. The degree of impact caused by each failure mode can be obtained according to the Equation 2 (see [20] for more information).

$$DI = \sum_{i=1}^{N} W_i I_i \tag{2}$$

Where N=the number of indicators

---

[5] This experiment is considered as a semi-quantitative experiment due to this adjustment.

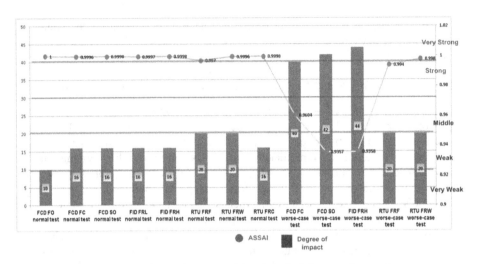

Fig. 1. Summary of the small network level single failure mode experiment

The test results from this ion-depth experiments are summarized in Fig 1. During normal tests, the consequences caused by the FCD FC mode and SO mode are similar, although the causes of these two failure modes are different. The results collected from FID FRL tests are close to the results from FID FRH tests according to DI value and ASSAI, although the FRL mode extends the period the appearing of first overload alarm and FRH shortens this period. During RTU FRF and FRW tests, the RTU device loses its connection to field level devices and then becomes blind, which are the causes of further negative events, i.e., loss of alarms, extended period of the line disconnection. During worse-case tests, the cause of continuous transmission line disconnections is the combination of the lack of responses from operators in the control centre and the failure of the hardware located in the substation meaning that the hardware failure is not sufficient enough to affect the system service availability significantly. Compared to the results from FCD FC tests, FCD SO tests have more negative effects according to the calculated parameters (average number of alarms and average ASSAI) since the FCD FC mode is not capable to cause the overload of the studied transmission line. However, the FCD SO failure mode is capable to trigger the spurious overload alarm although it should not. Results collected from FID FRH tests are similar to the results of FCD SO tests. During these two tests, the threshold of overload alarms is affected (modified). This is the reason why the ASSAIs calculated in both tests are very close. Results from all RTU tests indicate that ASSAIs from these tests are larger compared to tests of other two devices (FID and FCD). However, this does not mean that negative effects caused by failures of the RTU device on the system service availability become much less significant. As shown in Fig 1, in average, negative effects due to interdependencies are aggravated during worse-case tests showing very strong DIs are observed. The average DI from FID FRH tests is 44 meaning its impact is very strong. The DIs from all RTU failure mode tests are between middle and weak, which seems not as serious as for the FID and FCD. As the failure of this device means interruption of service provided by the SCADA substation level components, it is still worthy to develop further tests on this device, as well as the FID device, in the next experiment.

4.2   Experiment 3: Whole Network Worse-Case Failure Modes Experiment

This experiment extends the scope of the previous experiment to the whole network including all simulated components of the SCADA system and the SUC, by which negative consequences caused by interdependencies can be observed and analyzed. In this experiment, instead of just considering single failures, double failures occurring simultaneously at different substations are also included. The same modeling scenarios as in the worse-case tests of the previous experiment are applied, but in addition, two key substations and non-key substations are selected as exemplary substations. The experiment mainly focuses on two failure modes, i.e., FID FRH and RTU FRW, based on the results of the experiment 2.

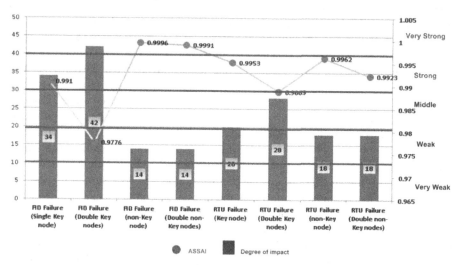

Fig. 2. Summary of whole network failure modes experiment

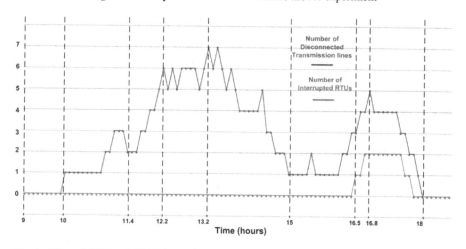

Fig. 3. Affected SUC and SCADA components in one of FID single failure tests (key substation)

The test results of this experiment are depicted in Fig 2. In the first four tests (single failure tests), the average DI from FID single failure tests (key substation) shows the highest value, as both SUC and SCADA components are affected by this technical failure. As shown in this Fig 3, at time 10 hours, one transmission line (a component of the SUC) was disconnected due to the wrong overload alarm caused by the technical failure of its FID and the absence of operator action. At time 13.2 hours, the number of failed SUC components (disconnected lines) reached to the maximum value. Then this number started to drop and only one line was disconnected. Observed at time 16.5 hours, SCADA components (RTUs) were also affected and the number of affected components (interrupted RTU devices) was 1. The maximum number of affected SCADA components was 2 at time 16.8 hours. After that, the numbers of both affected SCADA and SUC components started to drop and returned to zero at time 18 hours. In this test, the number of affected SUC components is 18, meaning 18 transmission lines became overloaded. As observed from this test, failures of SUC components seem not to affect its interconnected SCADA system instantly. It took about 6 hours before failures started to propagate from one system to another, which can be considered as the *delay of dependency failures*. Results from the RTU single failure tests (both key substation and non-key substation) show that the failure of RTU device does not cause significant cascading effects in the SUC and not able to propagate back into the SCADA system affecting more components. The results from double failure tests are similar to the results from previous single failure tests. The DI from the test of double FID failures (in key substations) is very strong, highest one compared to same parameter from other three tests. According to the result of this test, more SUC and SCADA components are affected if FID technical failures are triggered in two key substations. The maximum number of simultaneously affected SUC components (transmission lines) is 8, one more than the maximum number of total affected SUC components of single FID technical failure test. Compared to the single failure test, delay of dependency failures in this case is about 5 hours, meaning that it took less time before failures start to propagate from one system to another. Furthermore, both SUC and SCADA system became less resilient indicated by the increase of "back to normal time" (8 hours in single failure tests and 12 hours in double failure tests). More SUC and SCADA components are affected if FID technical failures are triggered in two key substations. Both double FID and RTU failure tests on the non-key substations show much less negative consequence. The DIs of these two tests are weak and none of SUC or SCADA components are affected.

5   Step 4: Results Assessments

Based on these three in-depth experiments, hidden vulnerabilities caused by interdependencies between the two systems under study are summarized as follows:

1. **Importance of Field Level Devices Should Not Be Underestimated:** According to [12], the field level device such as FID and FCD can be regarded as interface device connecting a SCADA system to related controlled/monitored physical

processes (SUC). In general, most past modeling efforts related to SCADA systems focus on RTU devices, which belong to the substation level in a standard SCADA system, and underestimate the existence of field level devices [21-23]. However, as shown by worse-case tests of in-depth experiments, negative consequences caused by failures of field level devices can also be significant. As observed in the small network level single failure mode experiment, results from normal case tests show that negative consequences caused by failures of the RTU device seem significant (highest degree of impacts and lowest ASSAI). However, if assuming the operator is unable to handle any alarm (worse-case scenarios), consequences caused by failures of field level devices become worse compared to failures of RTU devices. The simulation results from three worse-case single failure mode tests related to field level devices (FCD FC, FCD SO, and FID FRH) in this experiment demonstrate very strong degree of impact and smaller ASSAI. This phenomenon is also observed in the whole network worse-case failure modes experiment. In this experiment, the ASSAI obtained from key substation single FID failure test is 0.991, while it is 0.9996 in key substation single RTU failure test. In the same experiment, the degree of impact caused by single FID failure is strong, while it is middle in RTU failure test.

2. **A Predictable Delay of Dependency Failures Is Important:** As observed in FID single key substation failure tests and FID double key substation failure tests, the propagation of failures crossing interlinked systems needs certain time, and does not start instantly (delay of dependency failures). For example, this delay is about 6 hours in FID single key substation tests and about 5 hours in FID double key substation tests. It seems that the delay of dependency failures is proportional to the degree of impact and inversely proportional to ASSAI meaning worsen consequences shorter delay period. This period is very important for minimizing negative effects caused by interdependencies. If failures were able to stop cascading within this period, it is possible to avoid propagation of failures into another system.

3. **Negative Consequences Caused by Failures of Devices in Key Substations Are Significant:** The whole network worse-case experiment also demonstrates the importance of key substations of the SCADA system since increasing the number of failed key substations and non-key substations show very different results. In this experiment, negative consequences caused by failures of devices become more significant if the number of failed key substations increases. For example, the ASSAI value calculated in FID single key substation failure tests is 0.991, while the value drops to 0.9776 when failures of two key substations are triggered (degree of impact increases after increasing the number of failures of key substations in this case). This phenomenon is observed during RTU failure tests as well. However, increasing the number of failures of non-key substations seems to cause no significant negative effects. The degree of impact remains the same after triggering failures of two non-key substations during both FID and RTU non-key substation tests. Therefore, the reliability of key substations of the SCADA system is important for the whole system.

6   Conclusion

In this paper, the hidden vulnerabilities between the SCADA system and its associated SUC due to their interdependencies are identified and assessed by using
advanced modeling and simulation techniques. The investigation follows a 4-step
methodical framework and focuses on the third step, in-depth analysis, for which a
hybrid modeling and simulation approach is developed and applied. Three in-depth
experiments are designed and performed. These experiments show the importance of
mapping complex physical systems from the real world to the simulation world and
then project data from simulation world back into real world. Furthermore, the simulation results from these experiments demonstrate the capability of the methodical
framework as well as the hybrid approach to analyze CIs in a complex way, which
allows us to identify and assess both obvious and hidden vulnerabilities. For instance,
several hidden vulnerabilities due to interdependencies between the SCADA system
and the SUC have been identified and presented in this paper, such as the importance
of field level devices, the discovery of the delay of dependency failures, etc. The hybrid modeling/simulation approach changes the way to develop simulation tools by
allowing the integration of different types of modeling/simulation methods into one
simulation platform to optimize the efficiency of the overall simulation and therefore,
clears the technical difficulties for future research efforts that are required to handle
complexities of CIs. More implementations of this approach to investigate and identify interdependency-related vulnerabilities among various CIs are currently under
development.

References

[1] Rinaldi, S.M., Peerenboom, J.P., Kelly, T.: Identifying, Understanding, and Analyzing
    Critical Infrastructure Interdependencies. IEEE Control Systems Magazine 21, 11–25
    (2001)
[2] Griot, C.: Modelling and simulation for critical infrastructure interdependency assess-
    ment: A meta-review for model characterisation. International Journal of Critical Infra-
    structure 6, 363–379 (2010)
[3] Igure, V.M., Laughter, S.A., Williams, R.: Security Issues in SCADA Networks. Journal
    of Computers and Security 25, 498–506 (2006)
[4] Christansson, H., Luiijf, E.: Creating a European SCADA Security Testbed. In: Goetz, E.,
    Shenoi, S. (eds.) Critical Infrastructure Protection. IFIP, vol. 253, pp. 237–247. Springer,
    Boston (2007)
[5] Johnson, R.E.: Survey of SCADA security challenges and potential attack vectors. In: In-
    ternet Technology and Secured Transactions (ICITST) 2010, p. 5 (2010)
[6] Eusgeld, I., Kröger, W.: Towards a Framework for Vulnerability Analysis of Intercon-
    nected Infrastructures. In: 9th International Probabilistic Safety Assessment & Manage-
    ment Conference (2008)
[7] Kröger, W., Zio, E.: Vulnerable Systems. Springer (2011)
[8] Pederson, P., Dudenhoeffer, D., Hartly, S., Permann, M.: Critical Infrastructure Interde-
    pendency Modeling: A Survey of U.S and International Research. Idaho National Labora-
    tory (2006)

[9] Johansson, J., Hassel, H.: An approach for modelling interdependent infrastructures in the context of vulnerability analysis. Reliability Engineering and System Safety 95, 1335–1344 (2010)

[10] Nan, C., Kröger, W., Probst, P.: Exploring critical infrastructure interdependnecy by hybrid simulation approach. In: ESREL 2011, pp. 2483–2491 (2011)

[11] Schläpfer, M., Kessler, T., Kröger, W.: Reliability Analysis of Electric Power Systems Using an Object-oriented Hybrid Modeling Approach. In: 16th Power Systems Computation Conference (2008)

[12] Nan, C., Eusgeld, I.: Exploring impacts of single failure propagation between SCADA and SUC. In: IEEE International Conference on Industrial Engineering and Engineering Management (IEEM) 2011, pp. 1564–1568 (2011)

[13] van Steen, M.: Graph Theory and Complex Networks: An Introduction, 1st edn (2010)

[14] Caretta Cartozo, C.: Complex networks: from biological applications to exact theoretical solutions. In: EPFL (2009)

[15] Gallos, L.K., Cohen, R., Argyrakis, P., Bunde, A., Havlin, S.: Stability and Topology of Scale-Free Networks under Attack and Defense Strategies. Physical Review Letters 94, 188701 (2005)

[16] Kröger, W.: Critical infrastructure at risk: A Need For A New Conceptual Approach and Extended Analytical Tools. Reliability Engineering and System Safety 93, 1781–1787 (2008)

[17] Eusgeld, I., Nan, C., Dietz, S.: System-of-systems. Approach for Interdependent Critical Infrastructures. Reliability Engineering and System Safety 96, 679–686 (2011)

[18] Bloomfield, R., Chozos, N., Nobles, P.: Infrastructure interdependency analysis: Introductory research review (2009)

[19] Nan, C., Eusgeld, I.: Adopting HLA standard for interdependency study. Reliability Engineering and System Safety 96, 149–159 (2010)

[20] Nan, C., Eusgeld, I., Kroeger, W.: Assessing CI Interdependency Issues using an HLA-compliant Simulation Platform. In: The 2012 Annual European Safety and Reliability Conference, ESREL (2012)

[21] Balducelli, C., Bologna, S., Lavalle, L., Vicoli, G.: Safeguarding information intensive critical infrastructures against novel types of emerging failures. Reliability Engineering and System Safety 92, 1218–1229 (2007)

[22] Nai Fovino, I., Masera, M., Guidi, L., Carpi, G.: An experimental platform for assessing SCADA vulnerabilities and countermeasures in power plants. In: 3rd Conference on Human System Interactions (HSI), pp. 679–686 (2010)

[23] Queiroz, C., Mahmood, A., Jiankun, H., Tari, Z., Xinghuo, Y.: Building a SCADA Security Testbed. In: 3rd International Conference on Network and System Security, pp. 357–364 (2009)

Threat Modeling of AMI

Inger Anne Tøndel, Martin Gilje Jaatun, and Maria Bartnes Line

SINTEF ICT, Trondheim, Norway
inger.a.tondel@sintef.no

Abstract. The introduction of an advanced metering infrastructure (AMI) into the power grid forces the power industry to address information security threats and consumer privacy more extensively than before. The industry needs practical advice on methods and tools to use in this context. Threat modeling is well-known among information security professionals as a method for investigating a system's vulnerabilities. This paper documents the threat modeling of one actual AMI configuration. The results are both a demonstration of how these techniques can be applied to AMI, and a documentation of risks associated with this specific AMI configuration.

Keywords: Smart Grid, Advanced Metering Infrastructure, Information Security, Privacy, Threat Modeling, STRIDE.

1 Introduction

An Advanced Metering Infrastructure (AMI) is the most visible component of the smart grid. The new technologies in AMI and smart grid, with increased connectivity and new trust models, lead to new threats and a pressing need to deal with information security and consumer privacy [1,2].

Information security for smart grid and AMI have been addressed by several actors. Important resources include the NISTIR 7628 report [3] that deals with security of smart grids at large and the AMI-SEC task force security profile for AMI [4]. These documents identify central components as well as security requirements. However, despite the available resources, industry is still in need of support in understanding the information security challenges they are facing. In our interactions with the Norwegian power industry, we sense a need for practical advice and easy-to-use information security methods.

Threat modeling increases awareness of threats, and is invaluable as preparation for risk assessments. In this paper, a well established threat modeling approach (Section 2) is applied to a specific type of AMI configuration (see Figure 1). The approach is lightweight and easy to apply, and results in a graphical overview of the system, threats, and the potential attacker goals. The paper i) demonstrates that general threat modeling techniques are applicable for AMI infrastructure (Sections 3-5), ii) provides an overview of threats that can be reused by industry (Sections 4-5), and iii) provides a method for working with and using threat models as input to risk assessments of AMI infrastructure (Section 6). We discuss our contribution in Section 7, and offer conlcusions in Section 8.

B. Hämmerli, N. Kalstad Svendsen, and J. Lopez (Eds.): CRITIS 2012, LNCS 7722, pp. 264–275, 2013.
© Springer-Verlag Berlin Heidelberg 2013

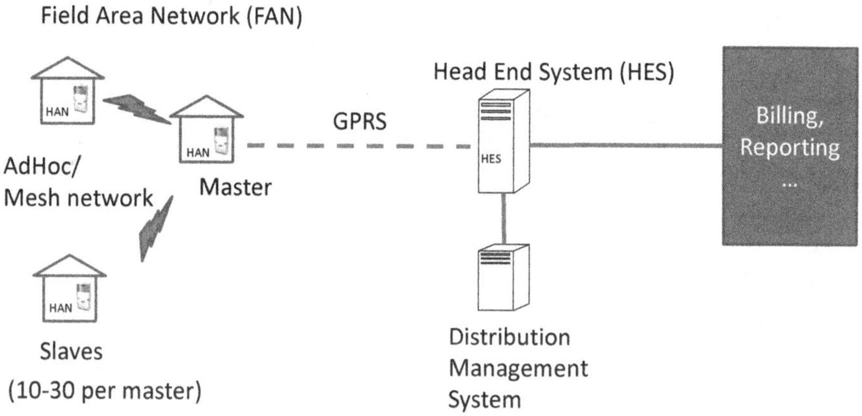

Field Area Network (FAN)

Fig. 1. An overview of the AMI system considered in this study

2   The Threat Modeling Method

In the field of secure software engineering, threat modeling is a common activity and several techniques exist. Some are formal and require special skills, while others are more lightweight. Of the informal ones, Microsoft's technique [5] is popular and has been described as *"a practical approach, usable by non-experts"* [6]. Their technique mainly works as follows. First, the system is modeled with an emphasis on the system's entry points (using e.g. Data Flow Diagrams (DFDs)), and then the threats towards the system are identified. In order to ensure coverage, the STRIDE classification of threats (Spoofing, Tampering, Repudiation, Information disclosure, Denial of service, Elevation of privileges) can be used as a resource. Then threats are analysed to evaluate the system's vulnerability.

Attack trees [7] are also widely adopted in the information security community. Such trees model how attackers may go about achieving their attack goals. Experiments show that attack trees are easy to grasp [8], which makes them particularly useful for communicating threats among stakeholders. They are also to a large extent reusable [7,9].

In this paper the threats towards AMI are addressed from two viewpoints:

- *Threat Overview:* The AMI system is modeled using DFD and the interfaces are identified. For all interfaces, threats are identified using STRIDE. (Section 4)
- *Attacker Strategies:* The most important assets of the system are identified in a brainstorming session [10] and by investigating the system. Then attack goals are associated with these assets, and the possible ways to achieve the goals are detailed in attack trees. (Section 5)

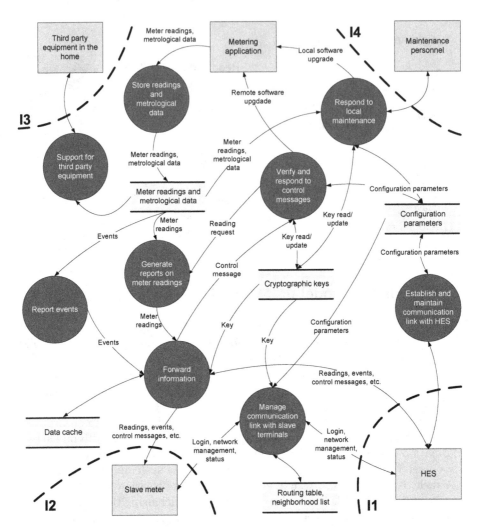

Fig. 2. A Data Flow Diagram (DFD) showing the data flow related to a master meter

3   Scope: The AMI System

As was shown in Fig. 1, we consider AMIs where meters are organised in mesh networks and communicate with the Head End System (HES) of the Distribution Service Operator (DSO) via GPRS. In each mesh network, one node (the master) is responsible for the communication channel towards the HES, and the other nodes (the slaves) communicate with HES via that node. At the DSO, the HES is connected to other systems, such as the distribution management system and systems for billing.

Fig. 2 gives an overview of the main data flow related to a master meter. Slave meters would have similar data flows, except from the communication link with

Table 1. Interfaces

ID	Where	Communication
I1	Meter - HES	Establishment and maintenance of communication link; Readings and events; Control messages (including software updates, configuration changes, meter reading requests and updated keys); Login management; Status
I2	Meter - Meter	Network management; Readings and events; Control messages; Login management; Status
I3	Meter - Third Party Equipment	Meter readings; Reading requests
I4	Meter - Local Maintenance	Requests; Credentials; Configuration data; Stored meter data and logs; Test results

the HES. In the DFD, interactors are represented as rectangles, processes are represented as circles, data stores are represented as horizontal lines and data flows are represented as arrows. The model shows four main interfaces: An interface with the HES (I1), an interface with other meters (slaves) (I2), an interface towards third party equipment such as displays (I3) and an interface towards maintenance personnel with physical access to the meter (I4). The meter itself can be considered to consist of two parts: A metering application that measures power consumption as well as metrological data, and a terminal responsible for all communication. The terminal's main tasks include reporting of meter values, generation of events, and responding to control messages and local maintenance. Master terminals are also responsible for establishing and maintaining communication with the HES and with slave terminals in its mesh network. All terminals are expected to forward messages from/towards slave nodes. A description of the main communication on the interfaces is given in Table 1.

4   Threat Overview

In this section we go through the STRIDE threat effect classification for each interface of a master terminal. The identified threats are listed in Table 2.

4.1   Spoofing

Spoofing is defined by Swiderski and Snyder [5] as something that *"[a]llows an adversary to pose as another user, component, or other system that has an identity in the system being modeled."* On I1 and I2, spoofing of meter identities and HES identities are potential threats (T1-T3 in Table 2). With HES spoofing, attackers will get access to messages and will be able to send fake commands to the system. Meter spoofing can result in increased access to information (e.g. in the case of master spoofing) and false meter reports. On I3, spoofing is not considered relevant as communication is not dependent on any identities. On I4, spoofing of meter identity is not an issue as the physical location of the meter,

Table 2. Threats

ID	Name	Interface
Spoofing		
T1	Fake HES	I1
T2	Fake meter ID	I1, I2
T3	Fake master meter	I2
T4	Attacker is authenticated as maintenance personnel	I4
Tampering		
T5	Tamper with communication between HES and master meter	I1
T6	Tamper with communication in mesh network	I2
T7	Tampering before forwarding message	I1, I2
T8	Local maintenance alters meter data or software	I4
T9	Meter reports wrong data to local maintenance	I4
Repudiation		
T10	Meter denies having received a message	I1, I2
T11	Meter denies sending of message	I1, I2
T12	Maintenance dispute	I4
Information disclosure		
T13	Eavesdrop on communication between master and HES	I1
T14	Meter leaks configuration information	I1, I2
T15	Eavesdrop communication in the mesh network	I2
T16	Leaking of forwarded messages	I2
T17	Meter leaks information about third party equipment	I3
Denial of service		
T18	Denial of service attack on HES	I1
T19	Meter errors/attacks make meter unable to communicate with HES	I1
T20	Communication failure on the link between HES and master meter	I1
T21	Meter refuses to communicate with HES	I1
T22	Denial of service attack on meter	I2
T23	Disrupt communication in mesh network	I2
T24	Node lockout	I2
T25	Meter unavailability caused by third party equipment	I3
T26	Meter unavailability due to local maintenance	I4
T27	Physical disabling of meter communication	I4
Elevation of privileges		
T28	Remote access to HES	I1
T29	Remote access to meter	I1, I2, I3
T30	Local meter compromise	I3, I4

and thus the real identity, is known by the maintenance personnel. The ability to spoof as maintenance personnel (T4) should however be considered.

A system's vulnerability towards these threats depends on the authentication mechanisms in place as well as procedures for contact establishment and the presence of spoofing detection mechanisms.

4.2   Tampering

Tampering refers to *"[t]he modification of data within the system to achieve a malicious goal"* [5]. Tampering attacks the data integrity, a quality that is essential for AMI, e.g. for the purpose of billing [3].

In this study we only consider the security of the meter node and its communication link towards the HES and other meters. Tampering that occurs at, e.g., the HES is out of scope. For interface I1 and I2 we are thus left with threats related to tampering on the GPRS link, the RF/mesh network and at the intermediate nodes on route to HES (T5 - T7 in Table 2). Such tampering may lead to errors in meter reading reports, wrong configuration settings, unauthorized changes of software, or erroneous or missing alarms. It can also open up for attacks on the HES or on the meter nodes (exploits). Tampering of data from third party equipment (I3) is not considered a threat, as no such data is stored in the meter. On interface I4, tampering can happen at both sides, either by local maintenance personnel altering meter data or software[1], or by meters that report wrong data to local maintenance (T8 - T9 in Table 2).

A system's vulnerability towards threats T5 - T7 depends on the security of the communication infrastructure and protocols, and the strength of any integrity protection. For threat T8, the vulnerability towards threat T4 (Attacker is authenticated as maintenance personnel) and also the ability to detect unauthorised changes are essential. Threat T9, and also T7, depend on the extent to which meters can be compromised (see Subsection 4.6 on elevation of privileges).

4.3   Repudiation

Repudiation threats allow adversaries *"to deny performing some malicious activity because the system does not have sufficient evidence to prove otherwise"* [5]. Cleveland [1] points at accountability or non-repudiation as critical for AMI and its financial transaction, metrology information and responses to control commands. On I1 and I2, meters may deny the reception of messages or the sending of messages (T10 and T11 in Table 2). On I3, it is possible to imagine scenarios where an erroneous message from a meter causes harm to third party equipment, and that the meter denies sending the message. This threat is however considered out of scope. On I4, there is the threat that maintenance is denied, either from the meter side or the maintenance personnel side (T12). This may reduce the abilities to identify the source of problems with meters.

A system's vulnerability towards threats T10 and T11 depends on the ability to prove the origin of messages, as well as on the integrity protection of messages and the extent to which responses are required. For threat T12 it is relevant to consider any logging functionality in the meter or in the maintenance equipment, and the protection of the audit logs.

---

[1] Note that in this study we do not consider physical tampering of meters in order to change the way power consumption is measured.

4.4   Information Disclosure

Information disclosure results in *"[t]he exposure of protected data to a user that is not otherwise allowed access to that data"* [5]. As shown in Fig. 2, data stored and communicated in an AMI includes private consumption data, encryption keys, alarms, control messages and software upgrades. Information disclosure can happen at the meter; by meters leaking configuration settings, keys or software received from HES (T14), by meters leaking messages that are forwarded through the meter (T16), or by meters leaking information about the third party equipment connected to the meter (T17). Information disclosure can also happen at the communication links (T13 and T15).

A system's vulnerability towards these threats depends on similar factors as those of tampering. One should consider the security of the communication infrastructure and protocols, the strength of the encryption and how easy meters can be compromised.

4.5   Denial of Service

A *Denial of service* (DoS) attack *"[o]ccurs when an adversary can prevent legitimate users from using the normal functionality of the system"* [5]. NISTIR 7628 states that *"[a]vailability of meter data is not critical, since alternate means for retrieving metering data can still be used."* AMIs, however, process a variety of data, and the dependence on e.g. timely alarms and control messages should be assessed. Below we mainly consider the unavailability of individual components. When assessing consequences, the effects of having several components unavailable simultaneously in critical situations need to be taken into account [1].

On I1, attackers could reduce availability of the HES[2], the meter or the GPRS link (T18 - T21 in Table 2). On I2, DoS attacks may affect meters or the mesh network (T22 - T24). In general, DoS attacks may be of two types: i) A distributed denial of service (DDoS) attack where a large number of requests from a multitude of sources render a node unavailable for legitimate requests, and ii) malware or specifically crafted messages that exploit vulnerabilities in such a way that the node is made unavailable. DoS may also be caused by errors, e.g. in software or configurations (T19). Attacks may affect a large number of nodes (e.g. by jamming the mesh network (T23)) or individual nodes (e.g. by refusing to forward messages to/from a given node in the mesh network (T24)). In addition to the above, the sending of a fake circuit break command could be considered a special case of DoS (denial of power), but this is covered by other threats[3].

On I3, third party equipment can pose a threat to the availability of the meter (T25), though the likelihood of this is low due to the limited communication on

---

[2] As the security of the HES is out of scope, we only consider threats to the availability of the HES that originate from the meter side.

[3] On I1, this threat is covered by threats T1, T5 and T28. On I2 this threat is covered by threats T6 and T7.

this interface. On I4, there is the risk that local maintenance causes unavailability of the meter (T26). It should also be noted that attackers with physical access to the meter may disable communication (T27).

For some of the DoS threats, the vulnerability of the system is related to the capacity of the communication lines used and the capacity of the nodes. Software quality is also essential, and the ability to withstand intrusion attacks (see Subsection 4.6 on elevation of privileges, below).

4.6   Elevation of Privileges

Elevation of privileges occurs *"when an adversary uses illegitimate means to assume a trust level with different privileges than he currently has"* [5]. On I1, there are two systems that could be compromised, the HES and the meter (T28 and T29 in Table 2). Meters can also be attacked remotely via I2 or I3[4]. Local attacks are also possible, where attackers with physical access to the meter physically compromise the meter (T30).

For remote access threats the vulnerability of a system depends on the software quality and the general protection of the system, including the patching regime, the presence of malware protection and detection software and the security mechanisms controlling remote software updates. For local meter compromise it is important to consider the presence of any physical anti-tampering mechanism and also the abilities to detect unauthorised changes.

5   Attacker Strategies

An asset is anything of value "that needs protection" [10]; assets can comprise information, processes, physical devices, and even intangible concepts such as reputation.

The main assets of the AMI system were identified in a brainstorming session [10] involving stakeholders from industry, as well as information security experts. All participants were to write down potential assets on Post-it® notes, and the resulting assets and the potential threats towards these assets were discussed in the group. After the brainstorming session, the security experts were responsible for documenting the assets and evaluating the set of assets for completeness. The resulting asset groups are listed in Table 3, together with their associated attack goals.

Attack trees have been created for all the (important) attack goals, but due to space limitation, we here only provide a partial tree for the attack goals associated with asset A7 - the meter. As the attack tree in Fig. 3 illustrates, remote access can be achieved through installing a rogue SW upgrade (containing a back door), misusing the remote control mechanism (if it exists), or employing some sort of meter-specific exploit. A rogue SW upgrade can be installed either

---

[4] Third party equipment is online and is compromised remotely. Attacker then attacks the meter via the third party equipment.

Table 3. Assets and associated attack goals

ID	Asset	Attack goal
A1	The configuration/topology of the power grid	- Get knowledge of the topology of the power grid in order to perform physical or online attacks
A2	The identities of meters (including the ability to authenticate meters)	- Manipulate energy bills by reporting consumption as another meter - Insert a rogue meter as part of an attack
A3	Control messages, including messages such as alarms, configuration and software updates and status messages	- Injection of false control messages, in order to manipulate meters (configuration settings, software, keys) - Have meters turn off power
A4	Meter values that can reveal consumption patterns	- Get access to consumption data in order to use this for marketing, or for criminal activities, or other unintended uses - Modify consumption data in order to manipulate bills
A5	The HES	- Break into HES, and the systems beyond HES
A6	The tariffs in meters	- Cause instability of the power grid
A7	The actual meter	- Manipulation of power measurements (stored, reported) in order to reduce bill - Use meter to attack other meters or the HES - Limit the availability to access/control meters

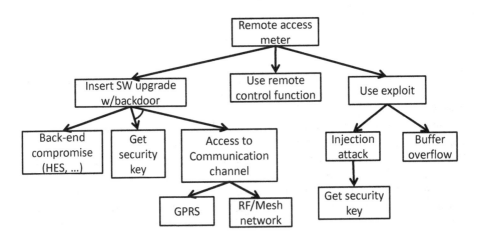

Fig. 3. An example attack tree for "remote access to meter" attack

through compromising the back-end system[5], or through the regular communication channel of the meter; in the latter case the attacker also needs to get access to the encryption key used to encrypt data sent to the meter.

---

[5] The back-end system could for instance be compromised by malware introduced through USB memory sticks, as in the case of Stuxnet.

When modeling the attack trees, the DFDs and the threats identified have been used as inspiration. As an example, the top node of the attack tree included in this paper is the threat T29, and the node "Communication channel" and its child nodes "GPRS" and "RF/Mesh network' correspond to threats T5-T7.

6   Method for Risk Assessment Based on the Threat Models

The threat modeling activities described in this paper help identify and understand the relevant threats and attack goals. However, in order to choose how to deal with the threats identified, it is essential to evaluate the consequences of the attacks, as well as their likelihood of success. Such an evaluation is not presented in this paper, as it is highly dependent on the individual systems. Still, we sketch how the threat models can be used as valuable input to a risk assessment process below.

This paper has provided a DFD of one type of AMI configuration and identified several threats that should be considered. For systems that are similar to that described in the DFD, all threats listed in Table 2 should be evaluated to assess the degree to which the system is vulnerable to these threats. The assessment should be documented. If the system is different from the one described in the DFD, it should be assessed whether these differences change the relevance of the threats, and whether new threats should be considered. This can be done by using the STRIDE approach on the functionality that is different.

The list of assets provided in this paper can be used as input to an asset identification process for other systems. The asset identification method [10] used in this paper also recommends assigning values to the assets in order to be able to prioritise which assets are the most important. A coarse scale is sufficient (e.g. high, medium, low). If appropriate, one can also consider the value of the asset for different stakeholders (e.g. for the DSO, the energy customer or the attacker) and also which aspect of the asset is the most important (i.e. confidentiality, integrity, or availability). The value assignment is important in order to prioritise the potential countermeasures later on.

For the prioritised assets, it should be determined how attackers may go about attacking the asset. This is modeled in attack trees. When an attack tree has been created, it should be determined for each attack path whether this path is sufficiently difficult to follow for an attacker, or if additional measures are needed. In this process the assessment of the system's vulnerability towards the threats already identified (see Table 2) is essential input. These measures should then be prioritised based on the importance of the asset(s) at stake. Note that the DREAD (Damage, Reliability, Exploitability, Affected users, Discoverability) approach can be seen as a refinement when evaluating each identified threat [5].

If the system changes, the changes should be reflected in the DFD, and STRIDE should be used to assess whether the changes affect some of the already identified threats or result in new ones. Any change in threats may also affect the attack trees, thus the attack trees should be revisited with the modified threats in mind, and the necessary updates should be made. The same way, it should be considered whether the changes add or remove assets to the system. Any change in assets may result in the need to add, delete or modify attack trees.

7   Discussion

The method we have described in this paper is easy to learn and easy to use, and has been well received in the industry. The graphical representation is an advantage in itself, resulting in models that are easy to understand both by security professionals and other stakeholders, and works particularly well for communication of security issues with the latter.

The method can assist the stakeholders in assessing how the threats change as a function of system changes that occur after the initial assessment has been carried out. Performing a STRIDE process from scratch requires not insignificant effort, but once the foundation is laid, it requires relatively little effort to update when minor system changes occur. The result is a living security model that can conveniently be kept up to date.

The brainstorming process when identifying assets and threats may be seen as possible weak spot, where the results may depend heavily upon the personal characteristics of the participating stakeholders. However, much of the uncertainty can be compensated by having security professionals participate in the process, e.g. by getting the discussion back on track in cases where it veers off course. Use of the STRIDE method also helps ensure broad coverage of security issues, even if it does not directly help with prioritizing threats.

It has been claimed that the strict real-time requirements in the smart grid represent a limitation on the kind of security solutions that are applicable [11], but our experience in the smart metering segment is that the same security considerations and solutions as for generic computer networking apply. Admittedly, the performance aspect is not given foremost attention in the threat modeling process, but any implemented controls and countermeasures clearly have to take performance into account. Even though customer privacy has not been a main focus for our efforts, we argue that there should be no inherent barrier to using STRIDE to model privacy threats, under the "information disclosure" heading.

Even a lightweight threat modeling approach requires a minimum of security expertise to ensure proper maintenance, but our experience shows that if the foundational security modeling work has been performed with the support of security experts, a domain professional with a basic working knowledge of security concepts can adequately handle the maintenance phase and smaller updates.

8   Conclusion

AMI has received a lot of attention from European data protection authorities and consumer groups, and a credible process for ensuring security and privacy is vital for an AMI deployment process to succeed. Since the DSOs are responsible for the deployment, it falls to them to ensure that suppliers of meters and infrastructure satisfy privacy regulations of the relevant jurisdictions. Furthermore, the DSOs must satisfy the requirements from the end-users' perspective as well, and they can not expect the end-users to specify these requirements themselves. Thorough analyses of relevant threats, attackers, vulnerabilities and risks need to be performed, and in this respect the industry needs guidance regarding methods and tools.

This paper has described a threat modeling method that is simple enough to be used by all stakeholders with minimal support from security experts. We have applied this method to a specific type of AMI configuration, and our high-level results, such as threat overview and examples of attack trees and Data Flow Diagrams, can be reused by the industry.

Acknowledgments. The research reported in this paper has been supported by the Telenor-SINTEF research agreement, Smart Grid initiative. The authors thank the participating vendors and DSOs for their cooperation.

References

1. Cleveland, F.: Cyber security issues for Advanced Metering Infrastructure (AMI). In: 2008 IEEE Power and Energy Society General Meeting - Conversion and Delivery of Electrical Energy in the 21st Century, pp. 1–5 (July 2008)
2. Line, M.B., Tøndel, I.A., Jaatun, M.G.: Cyber security challenges in Smart Grids. In: 2nd IEEE PES International Conference and Exhibition on Innovative Smart Grid Technologies (ISGT Europe), pp. 1–8 (December 2011)
3. The Smart Grid Interoperability Panel - Cyber Security Working Group: NISTIR 7628: Guidelines for smart grid cyber security (2010)
4. The Advanced Security Acceleration Project (ASAP-SG): Security Profile for Advanced Metering Infrastructure (2010)
5. Swiderski, F., Snyder, W.: Threat Modeling. Microsoft Press (2004)
6. Shostack, A.: Experiences threat modeling at microsoft. In: Modeling Security Workshop (2008), http://www.comp.lancs.ac.uk/modsec/program.php
7. Schneier, B.: Attack Trees – Modeling security threats. Dr. Dobb's Journal (July 2001)
8. Opdahl, A.L., Sindre, G.: Experimental comparison of attack trees and misuse cases for security threat identification. Information and Software Technology 51(5), 916–932 (2009)
9. Meland, P.H., Tøndel, I.A., Jensen, J.: Idea: Reusability of threat models – two approaches with an experimental evaluation. In: Massacci, F., Wallach, D., Zannone, N. (eds.) ESSoS 2010. LNCS, vol. 5965, pp. 114–122. Springer, Heidelberg (2010)
10. Jaatun, M.G., Tøndel, I.A.: Covering your assets in software engineering. In: The Third International Conference on Availability, Reliability and Security (ARES 2008), Barcelona, Spain, pp. 1172–1179 (2008)
11. Qi, H., Wang, X., Tolbert, L.M., Li, F., Peng, F.Q., Ning, P., Amin, M.: A Resilient Real-Time System Design for a Secure and Reconfigurable Power Grid. IEEE Transactions on Smart Grid 2(4) (December 2011)

Author Index